First World War
and Army of Occupation
War Diary
France, Belgium and Germany

51 DIVISION
154 Infantry Brigade
Princess Louise's (Argyll & Sutherland Highlanders)
1/7th Battalion
1 March 1916 - 31 March 1919

WO95/2886/1

The Naval & Military Press Ltd
www.nmarchive.com
Published in association with The National Archives

Published by

The Naval & Military Press Ltd

Unit 10 Ridgewood Industrial Park,

Uckfield, East Sussex,

TN22 5QE England

Tel: +44 (0) 1825 749494

www.naval-military-press.com

www.nmarchive.com

This diary has been reprinted in facsimile from the original. Any imperfections are inevitably reproduced and the quality may fall short of modern type and cartographic standards.

© Crown Copyright
Images reproduced by permission of The National Archives, London, England, 2015.

Contents

Document type	Place/Title	Date From	Date To
Heading	WO95/2886-1 7 Battalion Argyll and Sutherland Highlanders		
Heading	51st Division 154th Infy Bde 7th Bn A. & S. Hdrs Mar 1916-Mar 1919		
Heading	7th Argyll & Sutherland Highdrs War Diary March 1916 Vol XV		
War Diary		01/03/1916	23/03/1916
Heading	War Diary 7th Argyll & Sutherland Highlanders April 1916 Vol XVI		
War Diary		01/04/1916	30/04/1916
Heading	7th Argyll & Sutherland Highlanders War Diary May 1916 Vol 18		
War Diary		01/05/1916	31/05/1916
Heading	War Diary 1/7th Argyll & Sutherland Highlanders June 1916 Vol 19		
War Diary		01/06/1916	30/06/1916
Heading	154th Brigade 51st Division 1/7th Battalion Argyle & Sutherland Highlanders July 1916		
Heading	War Diary July 1916 7 Arg & Suth. Hrs. Vol 20		
War Diary		01/07/1916	31/07/1916
Heading	154th Brigade 51st Division 1/7th Battalion Argyle & Sutherland Highlanders August 1916		
War Diary		01/08/1916	13/08/1916
War Diary	Wallon Cappell	14/08/1916	14/08/1916
War Diary	Armentieres	15/08/1916	24/08/1916
War Diary	Trenches	25/08/1916	26/08/1916
War Diary	Near Bailleul	27/08/1916	31/08/1916
Heading	7th Arg. & Suth Highdrs War Diary September 1916 Vol 22		
War Diary	Bailleul	01/09/1916	02/09/1916
War Diary	Papot	02/09/1916	03/09/1916
War Diary	Chapelle	03/09/1916	03/09/1916
War Diary	Rompue	04/09/1916	08/09/1916
War Diary	Trenches	09/09/1916	11/09/1916
War Diary	Trenches In Right Sub Sector	12/09/1916	14/09/1916
War Diary	Subsidiary Line	15/09/1916	19/09/1916
War Diary	Trenches Subsidiary Line	20/09/1916	22/09/1916
War Diary	Billets	23/09/1916	24/09/1916
War Diary	Hutments	23/09/1916	24/09/1916
War Diary	Estaires	25/09/1916	30/09/1916
Heading	7th Arg. & Suth. Highdrs. War Diary October 1916 Vol 23		
War Diary	Fienvillers	01/10/1916	03/10/1916
War Diary	Thievres	03/10/1916	03/10/1916
War Diary	Bus-Les-Artois	04/10/1916	07/10/1916
War Diary	Support	08/10/1916	12/10/1916
War Diary	Louvencourt	13/10/1916	17/10/1916
War Diary	Raincheval	18/10/1916	18/10/1916
War Diary	Lealvillers	19/10/1916	20/10/1916
War Diary	Forceville	20/10/1916	22/10/1916

War Diary	Trenches	23/10/1916	26/10/1916
War Diary	Mailly Wood	27/10/1916	30/10/1916
War Diary	Raincheval	31/10/1916	31/10/1916
Heading	7th Argyll & Sutherland Highlanders War Diary November 1916 Vol 24		
War Diary	Raincheval	01/11/1916	04/11/1916
War Diary	Trenches	05/11/1916	08/11/1916
War Diary	Mailly Wood	08/11/1916	13/11/1916
War Diary	Trenches	13/11/1916	24/11/1916
War Diary	Puchevillers	25/11/1916	30/11/1916
Heading	7th Arg. & Suth. Highdrs War Diary Decr-1916 Vol 25		
War Diary		01/12/1916	06/12/1916
War Diary	X 8 D.	07/12/1916	08/12/1916
War Diary	Bouzincourt	09/12/1916	15/12/1916
War Diary	Ovillers	16/12/1916	24/12/1916
War Diary	Trenches	25/12/1916	26/12/1916
War Diary	Bruce Huts Aveluy	27/12/1916	27/12/1916
War Diary	Senlis	28/12/1916	31/12/1916
Heading	7th Arg. & Suth. Highdrs War Diary 2January 1917 Vol 6		
War Diary	Senlis	01/01/1917	03/01/1917
War Diary	Aveluy-Ovillers	03/01/1917	11/01/1917
War Diary	Trenches	12/01/1917	12/01/1917
War Diary	Rubempre	13/01/1917	13/01/1917
War Diary	Candas	14/01/1917	14/01/1917
War Diary	Coulonvillers	15/01/1917	15/01/1917
War Diary	Bonnelle	16/01/1917	16/01/1917
War Diary	Le Crotoy	17/01/1917	31/01/1917
Operation(al) Order(s)	154th Infantry Brigade Operation Order No. 89	01/01/1917	01/01/1917
Miscellaneous	March Table	02/01/1917	02/01/1917
Operation(al) Order(s)	154th Infantry Brigade Operation Order No. 90	06/01/1917	06/01/1917
Miscellaneous	Relief Table (Part 2)	08/01/1917	08/01/1917
Miscellaneous	Relief Table	08/01/1917	08/01/1917
Operation(al) Order(s)	154th Infantry Brigade Operation Order No. 91	07/01/1917	07/01/1917
Operation(al) Order(s)	154th Infantry Brigade Operation Order No. 92	10/01/1917	10/01/1917
Miscellaneous	Table Of Relief	12/01/1917	12/01/1917
Miscellaneous	O.C. 9th Royal Scots	11/01/1917	11/01/1917
Heading	7th Arg. & Suth. Highdrs War Diary February 1917 Vol 27		
War Diary	Le Crotoy	01/02/1917	04/02/1917
War Diary	Bonelle	05/02/1917	05/02/1917
War Diary	Noyelle	06/01/1917	06/01/1917
War Diary	Vacquerie	07/02/1917	07/02/1917
War Diary	Qe U F	08/02/1917	08/02/1917
War Diary	Monchy Breton	09/02/1917	10/02/1917
War Diary	Ecoivres	11/02/1917	20/02/1917
War Diary	ACQ	21/02/1917	27/02/1917
War Diary	Ecurie	28/02/1917	28/02/1917
Operation(al) Order(s)	154th Infantry Brigade Operation Order No. 108	25/02/1917	25/02/1917
Miscellaneous	Relief Table	25/02/1917	25/02/1917
Miscellaneous	Working Party Table Issued With Operation Order No. 106		
Miscellaneous	Addendum To Operation Order No. 106	26/02/1917	26/02/1917
Heading	7th Arg. & Suth. Highdrs War Diary March 1917 Vol 28		
War Diary	Ecurie	01/03/1917	16/03/1917

War Diary	Maroeuil	17/03/1917	17/03/1917
War Diary	La Comte	18/03/1917	25/03/1917
War Diary	Frevillers	26/03/1917	31/03/1917
Miscellaneous	Amendment No. 2 To 154th Infantry Brigade Operation Order No. 109	16/03/1917	16/03/1917
Miscellaneous	Amendment No. 1 To 154th Infantry Brigade Operation Order No. 109	15/03/1917	15/03/1917
Operation(al) Order(s)	154th Infantry Brigade Operation Order No. 109	13/03/1917	13/03/1917
Miscellaneous	Relief Table	14/03/1917	14/03/1917
Miscellaneous	O.C. 9th Royal Scots.	13/03/1917	13/03/1917
Heading	War Diary 7th Argyll & Sutherland Highrs. April 1917 Vol. 29		
Heading	7th Argyll & Sutherland Highlanders War Diary April 1917 Vol 29		
War Diary	Frevillers	01/04/1917	04/04/1917
War Diary	Camp Maroevil	05/04/1917	08/04/1917
War Diary	Line	09/04/1917	09/04/1917
War Diary	Vimy Ridge	10/04/1917	11/04/1917
War Diary	Laresset Huts	12/04/1917	15/04/1917
War Diary	Support Pos.	16/04/1917	17/04/1917
War Diary	Front Line & Bde. Support	18/04/1917	18/04/1917
War Diary	Athies	20/04/1917	22/04/1917
War Diary	Front Line	22/04/1917	23/04/1917
War Diary	Sunken Rd.	24/04/1917	24/04/1917
War Diary	Arras	25/04/1917	25/04/1917
War Diary	Penin	26/04/1917	30/04/1917
Miscellaneous	154th Brigade Instructions With Regard To Forthcoming Offensive Operations		
Miscellaneous	O/C 1/7 Argyll & Sutherland Highlanders	03/04/1917	03/04/1917
Miscellaneous	D.D. Messages to be sent and each Message sent at least three times.	01/04/1917	01/04/1917
Miscellaneous	Old Observation Line		
Operation(al) Order(s)	154th Infantry Brigade Operation Order No. 112	04/04/1917	04/04/1917
Miscellaneous	Reference Operation Order No. 112	05/04/1917	05/04/1917
Miscellaneous	Amendments And Addenda To ZZ.1/2 Are Issued	04/04/1917	04/04/1917
Diagram etc	Diagram Showing Units On Either Flank Of 154th Inf Bde. At The Different Objectives		
Map	Map		
Miscellaneous	O.C. 9th Royal Scots	14/04/1917	14/04/1917
Miscellaneous	154th Infantry Brigade Warning Orders	14/04/1917	14/04/1917
Miscellaneous	154th Infantry Brigade Instructions No. 1		
Miscellaneous	A Form Messages And Signals		
Miscellaneous	154th Infantry Brigade Instructions No. 2	20/04/1917	20/04/1917
Operation(al) Order(s)	154th Bde. O.O. No. 114	22/04/1917	22/04/1917
Miscellaneous	Operation Orders by Lt Col H.G. Hyslop D.S.O.	22/04/1917	22/04/1917
Miscellaneous	A Form Messages And Signals		
Miscellaneous		29/04/1918	29/04/1918
Miscellaneous	All Coys.	28/04/1918	28/04/1918
Operation(al) Order(s)	45th Infantry Brigade Operation Order No. 91	29/04/1918	29/04/1918
Miscellaneous	45th Infantry Brigade No. A/1/153	29/04/1918	29/04/1918
Miscellaneous	45th Infantry Brigade Defence Scheme	05/05/1918	05/05/1918
Map	Trench Map 51 N.W. 2		
Map	Trench Map 51 B N. W. 2 (Part Of)		
Diagram etc	Map No. 1		
Map	Roclincourt E		
Miscellaneous	Roclincourt Edition 5 A		

Miscellaneous	Glossary			
Heading	War Diary 7th Arg. & Suth. Highrs. May 1917 Vol 30			
War Diary	Penin		01/05/1917	13/05/1917
War Diary	Arras		14/05/1917	16/05/1917
War Diary	Embankment H. 13.d.		17/05/1917	24/05/1917
War Diary	Support Battn.		25/05/1917	25/05/1917
War Diary	Support Position		26/05/1917	26/05/1917
War Diary	H.23.C & H.24.b		27/05/1917	31/05/1917
Operation(al) Order(s)	154th Infantry Brigade Operation Order No. 117		13/05/1917	13/05/1917
Miscellaneous	March Table			
Map	Detail And Trenches Revised To 13-5-17			
Operation(al) Order(s)	154th Infantry Brigade Operation Order No. 118		27/05/1917	27/05/1917
Miscellaneous	Relief Table		30/05/1917	30/05/1917
Heading	7th Arg. & Suth. Highdrs War Diary June 1917 Vol 31			
War Diary	Arras		01/06/1917	01/06/1917
War Diary	Chelers		02/06/1917	04/06/1917
War Diary	Bours		05/06/1917	05/06/1917
War Diary	Verchin		06/06/1917	07/06/1917
War Diary	Zouafques		08/06/1917	22/06/1917
War Diary	Crome Straete		23/06/1917	30/06/1917
Heading	7th Argyll & Suth. Highrs. War Diary July 1917 Vol 32			
War Diary	Crome-Straete		01/07/1917	09/07/1917
War Diary	A.30 Central		10/07/1917	12/07/1917
War Diary	Trenches		13/07/1917	13/07/1917
War Diary	A.30 Central & Trenches		13/07/1917	15/07/1917
War Diary	A.30 Central		16/07/1917	27/07/1917
War Diary	Camp. A. 30 Central		28/07/1917	31/07/1917
Operation(al) Order(s)	154 Inf. Bde. Operation Order No. 123		11/07/1917	11/07/1917
Miscellaneous	Operation Orders By Lieut. Col. H. G. Hyslop D.S.O. Commanding 7th Arg. & Sutherland Highrs.		12/07/1917	12/07/1917
Miscellaneous	Operation Orders By Lieut. Col. H. G. Hyslop D.S.O. Commanding 7th Arg. & Sutherland Highrs.		15/07/1917	15/07/1917
Operation(al) Order(s)	154 Inf. Bde. Operation Order No. 124		12/07/1917	12/07/1917
Miscellaneous	Amendment No. 1 To 154 Inf Bde Operation Order No. 124		14/07/1917	14/07/1917
Operation(al) Order(s)	154 Inf Bde Operation Order No. 125		13/07/1917	13/07/1917
Map	Map			
Operation(al) Order(s)	Operation Order No. 2 By Lieut. Col. H. G. Hyslop D.S.O.		22/07/1917	22/07/1917
Map	Trenches Corrected From Information			
Miscellaneous	War Diary			
Miscellaneous	Report On Daylight Raid Carried Out By 7th Argyll & Sutherland Highlanders		24/07/1917	24/07/1917
Miscellaneous	Instructions For Offensive Operations			
Heading	7th Arg. & Suth. Highdrs War Diary August 1917 Vol 33			
War Diary	Trenches		01/08/1917	04/08/1917
War Diary	Front Line		04/08/1917	07/08/1917
War Diary	Canal Bank		08/08/1917	08/08/1917
War Diary	St. Janster Biezen		09/08/1917	09/08/1917
War Diary	Ganspette-Hellebroucq		10/08/1917	23/08/1917
War Diary	St. Janster Biezen		24/08/1917	29/08/1917
War Diary	Murat Camp Brielen		29/08/1917	31/08/1917
Operation(al) Order(s)	154 Inf. Bde. Operation Order No. 131			
Miscellaneous	Warning Order		05/08/1917	05/08/1917
Operation(al) Order(s)	154 Infantry Bde. Operation Order No. 132		05/08/1917	05/08/1917

Miscellaneous	Relief Table		
Miscellaneous	March Table	08/08/1917	08/08/1917
Miscellaneous	Administrative Instructions To 154th Inf. Bde. O. O. 132	06/08/1917	06/08/1917
Operation(al) Order(s)	154th Infantry Brigade Operation Order No. 134		
Miscellaneous	March Table		
Miscellaneous	154th Infantry Brigade Administrative Instructions No. S.S. 58	27/08/1917	27/08/1917
Miscellaneous	154th Infantry Brigade Amendment To O.O. No. 134	28/08/1917	28/08/1917
Heading	7th Argyll & Sutherland Highlanders War Diary September 1917		
War Diary	Murat Camp B.30.a	01/09/1917	03/09/1917
War Diary	Dirty Bucket Camp	04/09/1917	04/09/1917
War Diary	A.30. Central	05/09/1917	06/09/1917
War Diary	Canal Bank	07/09/1917	09/09/1917
War Diary	Front Line	09/09/1917	12/09/1917
War Diary	Siege Camp	13/09/1917	19/09/1917
War Diary	Line	20/09/1917	21/09/1917
War Diary	Siege Camp	21/09/1917	23/09/1917
War Diary	Poperinghe	24/09/1917	29/09/1917
War Diary	Courcelles & Comte	29/09/1917	30/09/1917
Operation(al) Order(s)	Operation Order No. 3 by Lieut Col E.C. Hill-Whitson Commanding 7th Arg & Suth Highrs		
Map	Map		
Map	Map "A"		
Miscellaneous	7th Argyll & Sutherland Highlanders	18/09/1917	18/09/1917
Miscellaneous	Administrative Instructions For Offensive Operations Issued With Operation Orders No. 3		
Miscellaneous	Administrative Instructions Addenda No. 1		
Miscellaneous	7th Argyll & Sutherland Highlanders	15/09/1917	15/09/1917
Map	Map		
Miscellaneous	Visual Scheme For Communication Trenches Blue Line And Bulow Farm		
Map	Map		
Heading	7th Argyll & Sutherland Highlanders War Diary October 1917 Vol 35		
War Diary	Courcelles Le Comte	01/10/1917	05/10/1917
War Diary	M.22.b.8.3.	06/10/1917	12/10/1917
War Diary	Line	13/10/1917	21/10/1917
War Diary	Carlisle Lines M. 17a	22/10/1917	28/10/1917
War Diary	Lattre-St-Quentin	29/10/1917	31/10/1917
Operation(al) Order(s)	154th Infantry Brigade Order No. 143	11/10/1917	11/10/1917
Heading	154th Brigade 51st Division 7th Battalion Argyle & Sutherland Highlanders November 1917		
War Diary	Lattre-St-Quentin	01/11/1917	17/11/1917
War Diary	Beaulencourt	18/11/1917	19/11/1917
War Diary	Metz	20/11/1917	20/11/1917
War Diary	Trescault	20/11/1917	21/11/1917
War Diary	Fontaine Notre Dame	21/11/1917	21/11/1917
War Diary	Line Near Fontaine Notre Dame	22/11/1917	24/11/1917
War Diary	Ribemont	25/11/1917	30/11/1917
Miscellaneous	Count Of Active Operations Carried Out By 7th A. & S. H.	27/11/1917	27/11/1917
Miscellaneous	Remarks	27/11/1917	27/11/1917
Miscellaneous	A Form Messages And Signals		
Map	Map		

Type	Description	Start	End
Miscellaneous	Message Form	00/00/1917	00/00/1917
Map	Map		
Miscellaneous	App II	00/00/1917	00/00/1917
Heading	7th Argyll & Sutherland Highlanders War Diary December 1917 Vol 37		
War Diary	Rocquigny	01/12/1917	01/12/1917
War Diary	Bertincourt	01/12/1917	01/12/1917
War Diary	Support Line	02/12/1917	04/12/1917
War Diary	Beugny	05/12/1917	16/12/1917
War Diary	J.17.a.5.7	17/12/1917	27/12/1917
War Diary	Fremicourt	27/12/1917	31/12/1917
Operation(al) Order(s)	154th Infantry Brigade Operation Order No. 152	01/12/1917	01/12/1917
Operation(al) Order(s)	154th Infantry Brigade Operation Order No. 153	03/12/1917	03/12/1917
Miscellaneous	O.C. 7th A. & S. Highrs.	03/12/1917	03/12/1917
Operation(al) Order(s)	154th Infantry Brigade Operation Order No. 154	04/12/1917	04/12/1917
Operation(al) Order(s)	154th Infantry Brigade Operation Order No. 155	15/12/1917	15/12/1917
Operation(al) Order(s)	154th Infantry Brigade Operation Order No. 156	21/12/1917	21/12/1917
Miscellaneous	O.C. 7th A. & S. Highrs.	22/12/1917	22/12/1917
Heading	7th Argyll & Sutherland Highlanders War Diary January 1918 Vol 38		
War Diary	J.17.a.5.7.	01/01/1918	07/01/1918
War Diary	Fremicourt	08/01/1918	10/01/1918
War Diary	Bailleulmont	22/01/1918	31/01/1918
Operation(al) Order(s)	154th Infantry Brigade Operation Order No. 1	06/01/1918	06/01/1918
Miscellaneous	Relief Table To Accompany 154th Infantry Brigade O.O. No. 1		
Operation(al) Order(s)	154th Infantry Brigade Operation Order No. 2	13/01/1918	13/01/1918
Miscellaneous	Table "A" To Accompany 154th Inf. Brigade O.O. No. 2		
Miscellaneous	Table "B" To Accompany 154th Inf. Brigade O.O. No. 2		
Operation(al) Order(s)	154th Infantry Brigade Operation Order No. 3	16/01/1918	16/01/1918
Miscellaneous	Relief Table To Accompany 154th Inf. Brigade O.O. No. 3		
Heading	War Diary February 1918 7th Argyll & Sutherland Highlanders Vol 39		
War Diary	Bailleulmont	01/02/1918	02/02/1918
War Diary	Logeast Camp	03/02/1918	13/02/1918
War Diary	Lebucquiere	14/02/1918	19/02/1918
War Diary	J.17.a.6.7.	20/02/1918	28/02/1918
Miscellaneous	154th Infantry Brigade Operation Order No. 8	19/02/1918	19/02/1918
Miscellaneous	Table "A" To Accompany 154th Infantry Brigade Operation Order No. 8		
Miscellaneous	Table "B" To Accompany 154th Infantry Brigade Operation Order No. 8		
Heading	51st Division 154th Infantry Brigade War Diary 1/7th Battalion Argyle & Sutherland Highlanders March 1918		
War Diary	J.17.a.6.7	01/03/1918	02/03/1918
War Diary	Ambulance Camp.	03/03/1918	04/03/1918
War Diary	J.16.c.4.1 (Sheet 57C.N.E)	05/03/1918	08/03/1918
War Diary	J.16.c.4.0	09/03/1918	09/03/1918
War Diary	J.18.a.9.9 Sunken Road	10/03/1918	29/03/1918
War Diary	P.7.a Cantrainne	30/03/1918	31/03/1918
Miscellaneous	Account Of The Part Played By The 7th Argyll & Sutherland Highlanders In The German Offensive	30/03/1918	30/03/1918

Operation(al) Order(s)	7th Argyll And Sutherland Highlanders Operation Order No. 27	08/03/1918	08/03/1918
War Diary	O.C. 7th A. & S. Highrs.	28/02/1918	28/02/1918
Operation(al) Order(s)	154th Infantry Brigade Operation Order No. 9	27/02/1918	27/02/1918
Miscellaneous	Table "A" To Accompany 154th Infantry Brigade O.O. No. 9		
Miscellaneous	Table "B" To Accompany 154th Infantry Brigade Operation Order No. 9		
Map	Sketch Map Or 154th Inf Bde Dispositions		
Operation(al) Order(s)	154th Infantry Brigade Operation Order No. 10	04/03/1918	04/03/1918
Operation(al) Order(s)	154th Infantry Brigade Operation Order No. 12	09/03/1918	09/03/1918
Miscellaneous	Amendment No. 1 To 154th Infantry Brigade Operation Order No. 12	09/03/1918	09/03/1918
Map	Map		
Heading	51st Division 154th Infantry Brigade War Diary 7th Battalion The Argyll & Sutherland Highlanders April 1918		
Heading	7th Argyll & Sutherland Highlanders War Diary April 1918 Vol 41		
War Diary	Cantrainne	01/04/1918	03/04/1918
War Diary	Lozinghem	04/04/1918	08/04/1918
War Diary	Mount Bernenchon	09/04/1918	24/04/1918
War Diary	St Hilaire	25/04/1918	30/04/1918
Miscellaneous	7th Arg. & Suth. Hrs.	20/04/1918	20/04/1918
Miscellaneous	Headquarters 154th Infantry Brigade	20/04/1918	20/04/1918
Heading	7th Argyll & Sutherland Highlanders War Diary May 1918 Vol 42		
War Diary	St Hilaire	01/05/1918	05/05/1918
War Diary	Ecoivres	06/05/1918	07/05/1918
War Diary	Ecurie	08/05/1918	10/05/1918
War Diary	Line	11/05/1918	31/05/1918
Operation(al) Order(s)	154th Infantry Brigade Operation Order No. 21	10/05/1918	10/05/1918
Operation(al) Order(s)	154th Infantry Brigade Operation Order No. 22	16/05/1918	16/05/1918
Operation(al) Order(s)	154th Infantry Brigade Operation Order No. 24	22/05/1918	22/05/1918
Miscellaneous	March Table		
Operation(al) Order(s)	154th Infantry Brigade Operation Order No. 25	28/05/1918	28/05/1918
Miscellaneous	Table "A" To Accompany 154th Infantry Brigade O.O. No. 25		
Miscellaneous	45th Infantry Brigade No. 227/G.	08/05/1918	08/05/1918
Miscellaneous	45th Infantry Brigade No. 227/I.G.	05/05/1918	05/05/1918
Miscellaneous	45th Infantry Brigade No. 201/2 G.	08/05/1918	08/05/1918
Diagram etc	Trace "A"		
Diagram etc	S.O.S. Dispositions		
Diagram etc	Trace "C"		
Diagram etc	Trace "B"		
Diagram etc	To Superimpose On Sheet 51 N. W. 1/20,000		
Heading	War Diary For June 1918 Of 7th Arg. & Suth. Hrs Vol 43		
War Diary	Line	01/06/1918	10/06/1918
War Diary	Roclincourt	10/06/1918	15/06/1918
War Diary	Roclincourt Line	16/06/1918	16/06/1918
War Diary	Line	16/06/1918	27/06/1918
War Diary	Line Roclincourt	28/06/1918	28/06/1918
War Diary	Roclincourt	29/06/1918	30/06/1918
Heading	154th Brigade 51st (Highland) Division 7th Battn. Argyll & Sutherland Highlanders July 1918		

War Diary	Roclincourt	01/07/1918	04/07/1918
War Diary	Line	04/07/1918	11/07/1918
War Diary	Anzin	11/07/1918	12/07/1918
War Diary	Magnicourt	12/07/1918	13/07/1918
War Diary	Frevillers	13/07/1918	14/07/1918
War Diary	Frevillers In Train	15/07/1918	15/07/1918
War Diary	Train Nogent	16/07/1918	16/07/1918
War Diary	Wood Near Chouilly	17/07/1918	18/07/1918
War Diary	Wood Near Chouilly & Bellevue	19/07/1918	19/07/1918
War Diary	Wood Near Nanteuil	20/07/1918	20/07/1918
War Diary	Line	21/07/1918	26/07/1918
War Diary	Bellevue Wood	26/07/1918	26/07/1918
War Diary	Wood Near Bellevue & St Denis	27/07/1918	27/07/1918
War Diary	St Denis & Bois D'Aulnay & Line	28/07/1918	28/07/1918
War Diary	Line	28/07/1918	31/07/1918
Heading	War Diary Of 7th Battalion Arg. & Suth. Hrs For August 1918 Vol 45		
War Diary	Nanteuil Belle Vue	01/08/1918	01/08/1918
War Diary	Champillon	02/08/1918	02/08/1918
War Diary	Champillon Epernay Train	03/08/1918	03/08/1918
War Diary	Brias	04/08/1918	04/08/1918
War Diary	Savy-Berlette	04/08/1918	04/08/1918
War Diary	Savy	05/08/1918	15/08/1918
War Diary	Line	15/08/1918	28/08/1918
War Diary	Athies	29/08/1918	29/08/1918
War Diary	Line At Greenland Hill	29/08/1918	29/08/1918
War Diary	Line	30/08/1918	31/08/1918
Heading	7th A. & S. H. War Diary September 1918 Vol 46		
Miscellaneous	Headquarters 154th Infantry Brigade	01/10/1918	01/10/1918
War Diary	Line	01/09/1918	04/09/1918
War Diary	Railway Embankment	04/09/1918	04/09/1918
War Diary	Athies	04/09/1918	11/09/1918
War Diary	Fraser Camp Mont St Eloi	11/09/1918	11/09/1918
War Diary	Mont St. Eloi	11/09/1918	23/09/1918
War Diary	Mont St. Eloi & Support trenches Greenland Hill	24/09/1918	24/09/1918
War Diary	Support Line	25/09/1918	29/09/1918
War Diary	Support Line & Front Line	30/09/1918	30/09/1918
War Diary	Greenland Hill Sector (Showers)	30/09/1918	30/09/1918
Heading	7th Arg. & Suth. Highrs. War Diary October 1918 Vol 47		
War Diary	Front Line	01/10/1918	01/10/1918
War Diary	Greenland Hill Sector	01/10/1918	01/10/1918
War Diary	Mont St Eloi	02/10/1918	06/10/1918
War Diary	Mont St Eloi & Inchy	07/10/1918	07/10/1918
War Diary	Inchy	08/10/1918	09/10/1918
War Diary	Inchy and St. Olie (Cambrai)	10/10/1918	10/10/1918
War Diary	St. Olie	10/10/1918	11/10/1918
War Diary	Escaudoeuvres	11/10/1918	11/10/1918
War Diary	Line	11/10/1918	11/10/1918
War Diary	Line At Iwuy	12/10/1918	12/10/1918
War Diary	Open Ground between Iwuy	13/10/1918	13/10/1918
War Diary	Lieu St Amand	13/10/1918	13/10/1918
War Diary	Iwuy	13/10/1918	13/10/1918
War Diary	Thun St. Martin	15/10/1918	17/10/1918
War Diary	Avesnes Le Sec	18/10/1918	19/10/1918
War Diary	Noyelles	20/10/1918	21/10/1918

War Diary	Thiant	22/10/1918	23/10/1918
War Diary	Haulchin	24/10/1918	26/10/1918
War Diary	Maing	27/10/1918	29/10/1918
War Diary	Thunville	30/10/1918	30/10/1918
War Diary	St Roch	31/10/1918	31/10/1918
Miscellaneous	Narrative Of Operations By 1/7th Battalion Argyll & Sutherland Highlanders	16/10/1918	16/10/1918
Miscellaneous	Operation Of The 7th Battn. Argyll And Sutherland Highrs. Leading to the occupation of Noyelles and Thiant between October 17th and 22nd 1918.	17/10/1918	17/10/1918
Miscellaneous	Narrative Of Operations Of 7th Bn. Argyll And Sutherland Highlanders	23/10/1918	23/10/1918
Heading	War Diary November 1918 Vol 48		
War Diary	St. Roch.	01/11/1918	30/11/1918
Heading	7th Arg. & Suth. Hrs. War Diary December 1918 Vol 49		
War Diary	St. Roch (Cambrai)	01/12/1918	01/01/1919
War Diary	St. Roch	02/01/1919	10/01/1919
War Diary	St. Roch & La Louviere	11/01/1919	11/01/1919
War Diary	La Louviere	12/01/1919	16/03/1919
War Diary	Seneffe	17/03/1919	31/03/1919
Miscellaneous	Daily Strength Return 1/3/19-31/3/19		

WO/95/2886/1

1 Battalion Argyll and
Sutherland Highlanders

51ST DIVISION
154TH INFY BDE

7TH BN A. & S. HDRS

MAR 1916 – MAR 1919

FROM 4 DIV
10 BDE

51ST DIVISION
154TH INFY BDE

154/51

Joined Bgn 1-3-16

1/7

7th ARGYLL & SUTHERLAND HIGHDRS.

WAR DIARY

MARCH 1916.

Vol XVB

Army Form C. 2118.

WAR DIARY
INTELLIGENCE SUMMARY
(Erase heading not required.)

Instructions regarding War Diaries and Intelligence Summaries are contained in F.S. Regs., Part II. and the Staff Manual respectively. Title pages will be prepared in manuscript.

Map. France – Sheet LENS. 11

1916 Hour, Date, Place		Summary of Events and Information	Remarks and references to Appendices
March 1	12.30 PM	Battn moved from MONDICOURT to PIERREGOT, and joined	154th Inf Bde – 51st Div.
2		Reinforcements 43 O.R. arrived	
3		In billets, cleaning arms and equipment.	
4/5		Inspection by G.O.C. 154th Inf Bde – Training	
6	9 am	Battn moved along with Remainder of Bde to DOULLENS.	
7		In billets	
8	9 am	Battn moved with Bde. 3 Coys to IVERGNY. 1 Coy to BEAUDRICOURT.	
9			
10	8 PM	Moved to ETRUN.	
11		Relieved left Battn of 138th French Regt in trenches astride the Route de LILLE 3¼ miles N.E. of ARRAS. (Sheet 51.B. A.27.B.C.) 4th Seaforth Highrs 5th Seaforths on our right; French on our left till night of 11/12th – when locally about 20 Trenchs Minenwerfer, or locally Enemy quiet except for about 20 Trenches ? Mining reported by French near our Saps rather damaged. Minenwerfer especially at A.22.a.8.7. when the French exploded a camouflet torpedo. 1 aerial A.22.a.8.6. successful for 7 minutes? Enemy artillery very quiet. Rifle grenades only 2 out of 7 exploded. were also thrown into our Coys of hostile mining were heard.	
12		Enemy very active with trenches and small Trench Mortar bombs. about 10 field-gun shells burst near communication trench at 11 am. Hand Grenades were also thrown in the afternoon and our Grenadiers retaliated. Normal mining again heard – Enemy transport heard on Route de LILLE between 7.10 and 7.45 P.M.	

J.E. Hyslop Lt. Col.
Comdg 7 Seaforth Highrs

WAR DIARY or INTELLIGENCE SUMMARY

Army Form C. 2118.

Hour, Date, Place	Summary of Events and Information	Remarks and references to Appendices
March 13 1916	At 10.45 am ten 77 mm shells were fired on communication trench. Our [?] damage done between 3 + 4 pm. Other 10 were fired on front line but 9 of these did not explode — Enemy small trench mortars less active at 4.35 pm an aeroplane of unknown nationality was seen amongst trenches two miles [?] after being shelled by enemy anti-aircraft fire. Enemy still heard mining except between 8 pm and 12 midnight.	
14	Enemy snipers and artillery fairly active. At 10.30 am ten 77 mm were fired into ECURIE. A very fair hostile aeroplane (probably a Fokker) was seen to our north about 11 [?]. Hostile aeroplane was also seen 12.30 pm. At 1.15 pm a French aeroplane was seen to fight & shell and it fell in the enemy's lines behind THELUS. Inwards party carrying trench boards and wires was seen at 5 pm in area B.1. A 8.9	
15	Artillery and snipers fairly active throughout the day; to hammer chiefly on our support lines, on ECURIE and on the LILLE RD and ECURIE crossroads. Hostile aeroplanes very active. Enemy were [?] [?] on front line and were stopped by our trench mortars at 6 A.M. Bombard[?] east of Route de LILLE on our patrols found enemy [?] Several [?] of knife rests. Mining continues intermittently. (5 Canadier [?] from a sniping post work parties at 14.18.12.10 + 30 was seen by [?] 5.10 and 5.30 pm in area B.7. d. 8.9. Single enemy infantry also seen [?] were also seen frequently in this area.	
16	Artillery quiet snipers fairly active. Enemy [?] lane [?] bombs some [?] did no damage — [?] [?]	

page 3
7th Cav + Suff Regt

WAR DIARY
or
INTELLIGENCE SUMMARY

Army Form C. 2118.

Hour, Date, Place	Summary of Events and Information	Remarks and references to Appendices
1916 March 16 (Cont)	Made of old craval two three men were seen working in enemy's wire and were dispersed by rifle fire at 7 pm. Half an hour later a working party was seen on parapet and was also dispersed. Rifle and immediately short. LILLE Rd. One man was seen on parapet at 7 pm and immediately shot. An enemy rifle battery of about 4 rifles was heard firing on LILLE Rd about 6 pm from 2 positions at enemy's support line — Mining — sounds heard in afternoon from a new point.	
10.30 p.m.	Relief by 9th Royal Scots complete; Battns marched independently to billets at ETRUN.	
17 do	In billets. Reinforcements 1 Officer (2/Lt T.E. CAIRNS) and 63 O.R. arrived	
18/21st	In billets. 2 Coys inoculated with new mixed typhoid vaccine.	
22nd 9.45 p.m.	Relieved 9th Royal Scots in Trenches. Very dark night. At 10.45 p.m. our Trench mortary made direct hit on enemy's trench, cries were heard. At 9.50 p.m. enemy sent over 6 trench mortars. One made direct hit - killing one man. Enemy's M.G. fired on route de LILLE at intervals during night. Artillery inactive	
23rd	Enemy snipers who has been busy during forenoon were silenced by 1.30. Early in afternoon, Boche enemy started to fire 10" (?) enemy trench mortars intermittently doing no damage. At 9.30 p.m. they fired an aerial torpedo at Cardes Shaft and did not explode.	

J.G. Hopper Lt. Col
Comdg 7th Cav 7th R Hopp[?]

WAR DIARY.

7TH ARGYLL & SUTHERLAND HIGHLANDERS'.

APRIL 1916.

Vol XXII

7th Aug - Lieut. Highgate

Army Form C. 2118.

WAR DIARY
or
INTELLIGENCE SUMMARY
(Erase heading not required.)

Ref map France 40,000. 51.B

Instructions regarding War Diaries and Intelligence Summaries are contained in F. S. Regs., Part II. and the Staff Manual respectively. Title pages will be prepared in manuscript.

1916 Hour, Date, Place	Summary of Events and Information	Remarks and references to Appendices
April 1.	Enemy was seen working behind his TRENCHES at 11 A.M. and our artillery. Aeroplanes very active on both sides. Enemy put a few light shells near abri Central (A.28.B.5.9)	was dispersed by enemy afternoon
2.	Enemy again shelled abri Central at 8.30 A.M. opposite our line. They were immediately attacked by one of our guns and driven off. At 3 P.M. Germans commenced shelling support trenches E of LILLE Rd. but retaliation from our guns silenced them by 3-30 P.M. At 6.45 P.M. our artillery bombarded enemy trenches E of Lille Rd.	At 10 A.M. 3 hostile aeroplanes
3.	At 7.15 P.M. enemy exploded a mine on our left; heavy bombardment on both sides followed; remainder of night quiet. At 12.20 P.M. Germans put up a single rocket - followed at half a minute between each. Another rocket went up at 12-50. Hostile aircraft had a very bright flare. Hostile aircraft were about but no action followed.	
4.	At 7.15 P.M. enemy fired 3 rifle grenades, and at 11 P.M. heavy trench mortar. No damage done; day too dull for observation.	
5.	At 9.20 A.M. enemy aeroplane flew along our line at low altitude. Rifle and Machine Gun fire was opened without result. Artillery quiet. Our Snipers claim to have shot one of the enemy at 1 P.M. a few grenades and a Lanset canister bombs at A.21.b.2.3. followed by one at this left. At 6.30 P.M. enemy were active with rifle grenades, light trench mortars and canister bombs.	At 12.45 P.M. on A.21.b.2.8 came into action and aerial torpedoes & shrapnel.

H.J. Highgate Lieut
Commdg 7th Bn Suff Highlrs |

WAR DIARY / INTELLIGENCE SUMMARY

2nd Argyll & Sutherland Highlanders
page 2

Army Form C. 2118.

1916 Hour, Date, Place	Summary of Events and Information	Remarks and references to Appendices
April 5 (Cont.)	Movement was observed on Roads to ROTIMEULS and THELUS. Red Cross Car came from direction of FARBUS, and another behind BOIS CARRÉ, returning at 12.35.	At 12.15 P.M. behind BOIS CARRÉ.
6	Reinforcements 36 O.R. arrived. At 12.45 P.M. one of our Snipers broke a large mirror at A.22.B.6.4. that the enemy had been using as a periscope. Between 9 p.m. and midnight enemy bombers showed recoil on left of LILLE Rd. Heavy transport was heard near THELUS between 11 P.M. and 3 P.M. Enemy very quiet during the day.	
7	New earth thrown up during night by enemy at A.22.B.4.4. Our Stokes guns, Bombers and artillery were active about 6 P.M. and completely silenced enemy, who fired some of the little fellows to explode. Company came in at 5-30 P.M.	our trench mostly failed to explode.
8	At A.22.B.76. A white safe was noticed and thought to be marking enemy mines and workings. About 2.30 P.M. work was heard being done near this point. A patrol reported enemy working on left of LILLE Rd. At 11.15 P.M. a party of our bombing threw 25 bombs and 15 rifle grenades from Sap road into German trenches opposite L.28. German Snipers have for much quieter.	
9	Enemy unusually quiet. Batt: was relieved during evening by C.Y.S.C. and moved to Gillets at ETRUN.	
10/14	At Gillets – overhauling clothing and equipment. Training Specialists and providing working parties.	

H.G. Hyslop Lt. Col.
Commdg. 7th Arg. & Suth. Highlanders

7th Argyll + Sutherland Highlanders

Apl - page 3.

Army Form C. 2118.

WAR DIARY
or
INTELLIGENCE SUMMARY

(Erase heading not required.)

1916 Hour, Date, Place	Summary of Events and Information	Remarks and references to Appendices
Apl 15.	Relieved 9th Royal Scots in trenches during afternoon and evening about 10.15 P.M. An aeroplane was heard overhead in direction of THEUS. Artillery quiet, except for a few heavy shells fired before 10 P.M. and midnight near Batt. H.Q.	
16.	A train was heard behind THEUS at 1.40 A.M. At 10.30 A.M. 3 Germans were seen in shallow communication trench A.22.6.36. One was shot. In reply 6 guns fired light shells on our communication trenches, but did no damage. Desultory shelling by both sides during afternoon. Reinforcements 3 officers (2/Lts. Walker, Silbert and Jones) and 27 O.R. arrived.	
17.	At 6.30 P.M. enemy fired 6 heavy Konisberg shells near Batty H.Q. about 3.30 P.M. we fired 10 rifle grenades into enemy trenches from a s/p. Enemy reply did no damage; more being directed on s/p we occupied. At 11.55 P.M. bombing group from right Coy threw about 50 bombs into enemy's front line. Between 1.45 + 2.10 A.M. enemy threw light shells at our support line and Battery. 10 to 11 P.M. heavies near Batty H.Q.	
18.	At 12.10 A.M. enemy rifles will be bursts and our artillery retaliated on their trenches. Sudden by rifle fire on east occasion enemy line is fairly strongly held. Thoroughly shell held being near BOIS CARRÉ but in smaller burst was continued during afternoon we fired a few rifle grenades and Stokes fired that enemy did not reply. A fixed rifle was laid on a point A.22.6.3.6 from which enemy had been sniping at night. We fired occasional shots as enemy had ceased a patrol looked into crater on right of Route de LILLE and found it unoccupied and not wired. New camp is being thrown up at A.22.6.6.3. Batty H.Q.: shelled with 6 heavy shells at 12.30 P.M. and again at 10 P.M. No damage done.	
19	Other 6 shells fell near Batt H.Q. at 9.15 A.M. Enemy working party seen on skyline on night of THEUS were dispersed by our artillery.	Hy Hewitt Lt Colonel Comdg 7/Argyll + Suth'd Highlanders

7th Argyll + Sutherland Highlanders
Apl - page 4

WAR DIARY or **INTELLIGENCE SUMMARY**

Army Form C. 2118.

1916 Hour, Date, Place	Summary of Events and Information	Remarks and references to Appendices
Apr. 19. (cont?)	Listening patrol reported hearing pumping in enemy trenches. Artillery on both sides fairly active but beyond damping several places, we suffered no damage.	(5 Trenches in German trenches,
20	Sentries report that from time to time a low whistle is heard and this is generally followed by rifle grenades or trench mortar bombs. About 3 P.M. enemy fired 40 aerial torpedoes, and T.M's on our front line on left of Route de LILLE. No damage done except to 10 yds of parados + parapet of our front. At 6 P.M. trench mortars made direct hit on our observation trench (A. 22. b.) wounding 4 men. Artillery much more active, especially during afternoon on firing line and support trench.	
21	At 6 A.M. German light shell (fire) made direct hit on fire trench close to Route à LILLE killing 1 man and wounding 2 seriously. Enemy appears to be working on forward observation line (A. 22. b. 3. 6). A large mirror is in use as a periscope, and in this men can be seen having their toilets, they wear sunk blue uniforms and forage caps. Our stokes gun caused much (to cease?). Batt. H.Q. shelled with 7½ cm. accurately at 3.30 P.M. 25/7D 1/Rifle, were relieved Batn. was relieved during evening by 9th Royal Scots, and moved to ECURIE, has 1 Coy is ABRI CENTRAL (A. 28. 2. 5. 9) and 1 Coy is ÉCURIE, ÉTRUN.	
22	Aeroplanes very active, artillery on both sides fairly active.	
23	Four enemy observation balloons up all day, and aircraft action. About 9.30 P.M. our left H.E's fired rapid. Struck road between ÉCURIE and MADAGASCAR (A. 27. C) only 4 or 5 burst, and change am. M.K. H/Highlds 21 Island handy 7th North Highlanders

1st Argt + Suth. High[rs]
Apl - page 5.

WAR DIARY
or
INTELLIGENCE SUMMARY
(Erase heading not required.)

Army Form 'C. 2118.

Instructions regarding War Diaries and Intelligence Summaries are contained in F. S. Regs., Part II. and the Staff Manual respectively. Title pages will be prepared in manuscript.

1916 Hour, Date, Place	Summary of Events and Information	Remarks and references to Appendices
Apl. 24/27	Aircraft and artillery active. Battnn. on Rouets Aleuré (A.28.a) being shelled daily. 1 casualty during afternoon and evening relieved by R.S. in Trenches.	
27th		
28.	At 2.7 A.M. enemy exploded two mines in front of our Trenches, and 10 others one at A.D.B.O.4., the other at A.D.a.E.G. Heavy bombardment followed till 3.30 am. Our casualties, Officers (4) O.C.B.Jones - slightly) and 7 O.R. wounded, cut telephone wires in front. Enemy Coy there cut almost immediately after explosion, but telephone was cleared and mended before dawn — The remainder of 24 hours very quiet.	on left of our sector,
29.	At 9.15 A.M. enemy aeroplane was brought down behind our lines, at 9.30 am another was seen descending hurriedly behind German lines. A few fires every ten minutes from midnight to 2 AM., from direction of Bois Carré (B.7.b). Trench mortars, on both sides active about 3 P.M. Snipers active in early morning. During night enemy fired during Stoke, and (putting up wire. A failure with bombs, failed to find the enemy, but work was Started by Thirty rifles Lambé, and Stokes grin. At 7.55 P.M. enemy fired about 6 calibre of 77 My. Shells, on our firing line, No damage - otherwise artillery was quiet.	
30.	Enemy very quiet. Between 6 + 7 P.M. our artillery bombarded enemy Trench, on our immediate left with good effect. at 12.30 P.M. Smoke + gas shells from Bois Carré towards TITHEWS, our opinion were seen moving 3 rounds at it. Enemy Snipers rather active in night of TITHEWS. Our guns fired during afternoon. —	

H.J. Hyslop Lt. Col.
Comdg 7th Argt. & Suth. Highlanders

7TH ARGYLL & SUTHERLAND HIGHLANDERS.

WAR DIARY.

MAY 1916.

Argyll + Sutherland High[landers]

Army Form C. 2118.

WAR DIARY
or
INTELLIGENCE SUMMARY
(Erase heading not required.)

Ref. Maps FRANCE 51· B + C

Instructions regarding War Diaries and Intelligence Summaries are contained in F. S. Regs., Part II. and the Staff Manual respectively. Title pages will be prepared in manuscript.

1916 Hour, Date, Place	Summary of Events and Information	Remarks and references to Appendices
May 1st	About 9.30 P.M. a patrol went out on left of LILLE RS. and bombed an enemy listening post. It was intended to draw enemy's bombs and rifle fire, but they retaliated with trench mortars. We replied with Lewis guns and from Stokes gun. Enemy snipers were active during the day, and M.G.s and mortars at night. Between 6 and 7.30 P.M. there were two false alarms for gas.	
2nd	At 1.5 P.M. enemy fired 12 trench mortars which landed near fire trench on left of LILLE RS – which is much further than their usual range of TM's. Shells were fired at our firing line near LILLE Rs during afternoon – otherwise artillery was quiet.	
3rd	In retaliation for our Stokes gun fire on their trenches, enemy shelled our firing line with 77 mm. during afternoon – casualty killed 1 O.R.	
9 P.m.	Batt[alio]n was relieved in trenches by 9th R.S. and marched to billets at ETRUN.	
4/5th	In billets. Paraded working parties, and trained specialists.	
9th	Reinforcements. 31 O.R. arrived. Relieved 9th R.S. in trenches during evening.	
10.	A patrol went out on left of LILLERS to examine new craters. This was found to be about 40 ft. deep, 60 ft. in diameter and unoccupied. German line is 25/30 yds. away and strongly wired in front. It appears to be held in considerable strength. At 3 P.m. enemy shelled it at 10 yd intervals. Light shells were fired into our front line at 11.45 A.M. and between 1.30 P.m. + 3 P.m. also heavies on support line at 12.30 P.m. No damage.	

J. Munro Major
Comm[andin]g 7th A+s'r Suth Highrs

1247 W 3290 200,000 (E) 8/14 J.B.C. & A. Forms/C. 2118/11.

7th Argyll & Sutherland Highdrs.

Army Form C. 2118.

WAR DIARY or INTELLIGENCE SUMMARY

(Erase heading not required.)

Ref maps FRANCE 51. B & C.

1916 Hour, Date, Place		Summary of Events and Information	Remarks and references to Appendices
May	11	At 3.15 P.M. our Stokes gun made direct hit on M.G. at Suther's enfilade Two men were seen to enter immediately before it was blown up. Considerable movement in Spell being seen around THELUS. Artillery again fairly active during afternoon on our firing line with 77-mm shells.	
	12	At 12.30 P.M. Stokes gun destroyed Snipers' post at A.22.c.3.7. and damaged another 15 yds to right. A patrol on right of Route de Lille reports great deal of movement in German front line. Aircraft appeared to be taking place about midnight G.R. 1 P.M. Artillery fairly active – a few rounds being fired between G.R. 1 P.M.	
	13	Reinforcements 2 officers arrived (2/Lts T. HEASK and J. ROBB attached from 9th A. & S.H) artillery fairly active with rifle shells during afternoon. Otherwise a quiet day.	
	14	Our Stokes gun fired at intervals during day and tonnes a snipers plate at A.22.c.8.3.5 some Shelling of our front line including on direct hit. Casualty 1. O.R. wounded. I.O.R.	
	15	Two T.M. Battery fired on enemy front line on left of LILLE Rd about 4 P.M. Enemy artillery fire was directed towards ECURIE our guns replies on German support trench at 1.15 P.M. and 1.15 P.M. Battn. was relieved by 9th R.S. during afternoon and moved H.Q. and 2 Coys to ECURIE, 1 Coy (6 abri centrale, (A.18.6) and 1 Coy (6 ETRUN. in local reserve	
	16	" Reinforcements. 21 O.R. arrivines.	
	17	"	
	18	"	
	19	"	
	20	"	
	21	" Lachrymatory shells fired into Ecurie about 7 P.M.	

1st Argyll & Sutherland Highlanders

Army Form C. 2118.

WAR DIARY
or
INTELLIGENCE SUMMARY

May Page 3

1915

Hour, Date, Place	Summary of Events and Information	Remarks and references to Appendices
May 22	Moved to former positions in front line. Heavy bombardment during evening but no casualties.	
23	Went to hadjustment sectors. Batn. left was an extended front line from A22c83.40 to A16c32.62 during afternoon - relieving 5th Seaforths. Enemy fired a large number of canister bombs into our front trenches, and also some rifle grenades. Our two fine snipers, enemy working parties, artillery retaliated.	
24	Enemy very active with small trench mortars which were accurate we retaliated with Howitzers. Otherwise fairly quiet. Casualties: Killed 1 O.R. Wounded 3 O.R.	
25	Trench mortars again active during day, but quiet at night. 4 or so bombs burst in craters behind our front line about 9 p.m. Enemy field guns very active but our retaliation was effective.	
26	Trench mortars very active from morning. Enemy appeared to be firing simultaneously. Our heavy and our light. Another enemy mortar had a long range; nothing but support line. 2/Lt. LEASK (9th Batt: attached) left 15.30 in M.G. training centre. Casualties: Wounded 1 Officer. 1 O.R. 2/Lt T.D.C.B. Jones.	
27	Trench mortars very quiet all day. At 10.50 a.m. enemy exploded a small mine 20 yds in front of our line. No artillery following. Reinforcement Officer 4/Lt D.S. Cantrell arrived (attached from 9th A.+S.H.).	
28	At 4.A.M. enemy exploded a mine in front of batt position on our left. Heavy bombardment followed till 2.30 a.m. Casualties, Killed 5 O.R. Wounded 6 O.R. (including 2 by G.R.S. and bruised) 1½ buried in debris.	Flew a camouflet.
29/31	During afternoon trench was relieved by Q=K.R.S. arriving.	
31	Reinforcements. 31 O.R. arrived.	

J.J.Jones Major
Comdg. 1st A+S Suth Highrs.

WAR DIARY

1/7th ARGYLL & SUTHERLAND HIGHLANDERS.

JUNE 1916.

7th Argyll & Sutherland Highrs.

WAR DIARY or INTELLIGENCE SUMMARY

Army Form C. 2118.

(Erase heading not required.)

Ref maps. FRANCE, 51. B., & C.

1916	Hour, Date, Place	Summary of Events and Information	Remarks and references to Appendices
June	1st/2nd	In billets at ETRUN.	
	3rd	Relieved 9th Royal Scots in trenches. An arranged bombardment of German lines by our guns commenced about 8.40 P.m. Practically no reply was made. Casualty 1 O.R. slightly wounded by trench mortar.	
	4th	Enemy Trench mortars fairly active during day, at 9.10 P.M. 16 rockets in our night (followed by firmly bombardment first. No effects of extraneous shells were felt.	Enemy mines were seen. Our sector no mined.
	5th	Enemy trench mortars again active especially on left of our line. Enemy rifle gun very active on communication trenches. Casualties 4 O.R. killed, 2 O.R. wounded.	
	6th	About 10.30 P.M. enemy fired 10 Trench Mortars into uncompleted craters in our right front, from which he was seen sending flares and rifle grenades. Artillery action during day on communication trenches, and dummy M.G. emplacements, but exceptionally quiet after dark.	
	7th	At 1.30 A.M. our Lewis Gun and rifle fire dispersed working party. Trench mortars and artillery very active through the day. About 7 P.m. our lines were drenched with heavy Shrapnel. Casualties 1 O.R. killed, 3 O.R. wounded.	
	8th	Enemy T.M.'s and artillery again active. Our T.M.'s retaliated vigorously.	
	9th	About 6.30 A.M. enemy field guns were active enfilading the night of our front line. Our strokes from completed craters Enemy T.M.'s Trench Quietes than usual. During afternoon Batt. was and Mount H.Q. relieved by 9th Royal Scots 1 Coy and 6 Lewis Guns to ECURIE, 1 Coy Abri Central (A. 28. 8. 15.20) with 1 gun. 1 Coy Abri le Mouton (A.22.a.54.88), 1 Coy Sucreie RJ (A.21.a.98.70) with 1 gun.	
	6/9	A/Col. Graham, O.C. 2/7th Argyle Suth Highrs. was attached.	

[signatures]

WAR DIARY or INTELLIGENCE SUMMARY

Army Form C. 2118.

7th Arg. & Suth. Highldrs.

FRANCE

REF. MAPS 51/3 & 5/5

1916 Hour, Date, Place	Summary of Events and Information	Remarks and references to Appendices
June 10th/11th	In Brigade Reserve. On 11th Reinforcements 1 Officer, 20 O.R. (R.E.)	2 Officers and 66 O.R. taken on the strength
" 12th	Our artillery bombarded Enemy line following explosion of gas mine on our left at 3.29 p.m.	
" 13th/14th	Reinforcements 3 Officers 2/Lts Agstornier, C.M. Hepburn & D. Buchan also 3 O.R. arrived.	
" 15th	In Brigade Reserve.	
" 16th	Relieved 9th R.S. in line. 1 O.R. killed. Enemy shelled lines with heavies during relief.	
" 17th	Enemy's trench mortars very active & artillery shelled our support lines at intervals. Casualties 2 O.R. attack 10.30pm on each Tremor was felt followed by artillery bombardment on our left.	
" 18th	At 6.31am another earth tremor was felt. Enemy's aeroplanes very active several hostilities passing over our line in afternoon & evening. At 5.40 p.m. one of our aeroplanes was brought down after a duel & landed about three hundred yards behind enemy front line & about 500 yds E. of LILLE ROAD. Six Officer Reinforcements joined Battalion 2/Lts Allan, Black, Everitt, Main, Phillit and Robertson.	
" 19th	About 7.15 P.M. a violent earth tremor was felt, and enemy's mortars immediately bombarded battalion on our left. Enemy artillery very active especially during afternoon.	
" 20th	Enemy trench mortars very active on front and intermediate lines. Machine guns very active at night. Heavy artillery active all day, and fell fire during afternoon. Our retaliation was good and effective.	
" 21st	Trench mortars active between 10 am and 11 am chiefly on support line – Artillery quiet. Reinforcements 102 O.R. arrived (from 13th Batn. A & S.H.)	
22/23/24/25th	Battn. was relieved during evening by 9th R.S. and moved to ETRUN.	
26th – 27th	Casualties: Air. Respr. (Prov. W.O.) Capt. R.D. Hunter (2nd S.R.) joined this unit. Reinforcement's 34 O.R. arrived from 37th	

Heavy Bombardment. Is our guard all along the line.

J.H. Hepburn 2/Lt
7th A. & S. Highrs

7th Argyll Suth. Majors Trages / March

Army Form C. 2118.

WAR DIARY
or
INTELLIGENCE SUMMARY

(Erase heading not required.)

Army Form C. 2118.

Instructions regarding War Diaries and Intelligence Summaries are contained in F. S. Regs., Part II. and the Staff Manual respectively. Title pages will be prepared in manuscript.

1916 Hour, Date, Place	Summary of Events and Information	Remarks and references to Appendices
March 29 (Contd)	12 Gas gun shells were fired at Abri Central (A.28.60.6.9) at 11 a.m. and 6 shells at 4.30 a.m. No damage.	
30	A party of 6 or 8 Germans were seen working trench on side house in THELUS from 11 a.m to 1 P.M. Enemy Quiet.	
31	About 3.45 a.m. enemy air torpedo & bomb exploded & mines on our left. Our guns immediately opened fire, and artillery on both sides was very active till 4.30 a.m. Our batteries were shelled throughout the morning. By 6 a.m. 3 enemy Balloons were visible and a hostile aeroplane flying fairly low, patrolled their line undisturbed till 7.30 a.m. At 1.30 p.m. Abri Central received 6 light percussion shells. 2 men wounded	

JG Hyslop Lt. Colonel
Commd. 7. Argyll & Suth. Highlanders

page 4
Jany + Feb High

Army Form C. 2118.

WAR DIARY
or
INTELLIGENCE SUMMARY
(Erase heading not required.)

Ref Map Bruce 51 B

Hour, Date, Place	Summary of Events and Information	Remarks and references to Appendices
1916 March 25 (cont.) 2nd.	A Trench Mortar Battery is suspected to be firing from A.22.6.2.8. Enemy exceptionally quiet – practically no sniping or shelling, weather very bad – Rainy. Subject in early morning.	
26.	Enemy snipers and machine guns rather more active about 10.19.m. at 3.45 PM. two motor ambulances and two cars were seen to enter THELUS from the east; they were followed by 8 bicyclists, and 17 men carrying sandbags.	
26.	Enemy are apparently working on new sap between points 18 + 19 (A.22.6.45;29) at 3 A.m. After a mine had been exploded on our left our guns opened fire on their sector. Snipers active at morning "stand-to". At 6.30 PM a large "canister" bomb exploded and killed one & wounded one, but did no damage. Scattered MG and stokes fire at 1 PM and 1.30 AM (27°) MG's were active firing on Route de Lille. Artillery very quiet on both sides. About 10 PM 2nd Lieut C.C. HARVEY was wounded in knee by bullet.	
27.	At 11.30 AM a party of about 20 was seen coming out of Bois Carre towards WILLERVAL. An enemy's sniping post four trouble till silenced by our snipers — Xroads at A.28.a.6.2 is shelled daily – otherwise enemy artillery has been quiet. At 3.10 PM enemy were seen throwing earth over parapet in trench across Route de LILLE 5 hours from our STOKES MORTAR caused more to cease. Enemy replied by throwing 2 large canister bombs at 3.45 PM which did no damage. Sniper very quiet. A foot patrol reconnoitring was seen in THELUS during afternoon. At 9 PM Batt. war relieved by 9th Royal Scots and proceeded to dug outs and cellars in ECURIE &c.; 1 Platoon & 1 Lewis Gun to Zouave Caves, and 2 Coys to Arras Central. Reinforcements 37 O.R. arrived. (A.28. & 6.9.)	
29.	Hostile aircraft very active all day. At 7 P.M. our artillery opened heavy fire on enemy Trenches A.16.6. as soon as our guns opened fire two planes were sent up in quick succession from one point, shortly afterwards a Green flare [illegible] from whole line that we being bombarded.	

WAR DIARY
or
INTELLIGENCE SUMMARY

(Erase heading not required.)

Army Form C. 2118.

Tay r Sub. Highls.

Hour, Date, Place	Summary of Events and Information	Remarks and references to Appendices
June 27. 28	Reinforcements. 1 Officer (Lt. H.A. Dickie) and 47 O.R. arrived fr S/3. Relieved 9th. R.S. in line. 1 O.R. wounded.	
29	Between 1.15 + 2.15 A.m enemy fired a number of rifle grenades into our front line. Between 3.20 + 4.30 A.m enemy bombards and obstruction to intermediate line, heavily with Stigg Bombs, trench mortars and artillery (4.2's + 5.9's). Considerable amount of damage was done to Communication + fire Trenches. 1 O.R. wounded. From 10.30 to 11.30 A.m we carried out an enemy bombardment of enemy lines — mostly field. From 3 to 3.17 and from 4.3 to 4.25" our enemy lines were again bombarded heavily and Smoke clouds sent over effectively. Retaliation heavy to first phase, but Guns to the second. No casualties. At 4.16 P.m we exploded a mine successfully within German lines. Enemy quiet.	
30	At 3.30 A.m enemy exploded 2 mines about A.22.d.1.15 and A.22.d.25.40. Heavy bombardment followed for half an hour, but no attack. Casualties. 1 Officer (Lt. R.S. Hunter) wounded (slight). 1 OR killed, 8 O.R. wounded. Remainder of morning + afternoon very quiet. During afternoon 2 Coys of 2/10th London Regt. came into the line for instruction, relieving 2 of our platoons, which proceeded to Nuvez.	

J.G. Reynolds Lt Col
cmd 7th/ Sth Highlanders

154th Brigade.

51st Division.

1/7th BATTALION

ARGYLE & SUTHERLAND HIGHLANDERS

JJLY 1916

Vol 20

154/18.L/51

War Diary, July 1916.
7 Arg & Suth. Hrs.

WAR DIARY

7th Bn. Black Watch

INTELLIGENCE SUMMARY

Army Form C. 2118.

(Erase heading not required.)

R. Mails FRANCE 5.1.B. & C.

Hour, Date, Place	Summary of Events and Information	Remarks and references to Appendices
1916 July 1st	Enemy very quiet throughout the day, except for a few sting-bombs and 77mm shells. Reinforcements 1 officer (2/Lt. S.B. MOIR) and 5 O.R. arrived.	✓
2nd	Enemy quiet. An increase in his aerial activity. Major R. LAING, 2nd Seaforth Highrs. arrived.	✓
3rd	Enemy Trench mortars active against our Centre Coy during afternoon & evening. Some firing by machine guns at night. Artillery fairly active with field guns – Reinforcements 1 officer (2/Lt A. ADAM) and 58 O.R. arrived.	✓
4th	Enemy trench mortars active during forenoon – our Stokes guns retaliate. Considerable activity by enemy artillery all day. Stokes gunners of Support Coy. Some afternoon of 30th & 2nd Coys 9/ny London Regt. have been attached to us for training in Trench warfare. During afternoon Batt. was relieved by 9/R.E.S. and proceeded to MAROEUIL.	✓ ✓
5th	In Billets.	
6th 7/8th	Moved to SAVY. (Quarter Master & Stores remaining at ETRUN.)	✓ ✓
9th	Moved to MARŒUIL.	
10th	Relieved 9/ Royal Scots in Trenches as before – less 4 platoons 15 LOUEZ. 2 Coys 2/24th London Regt. attached for training. Some activity by enemy T.M's about 11 P.M.	✓
11th	Enemy T.M's active during afternoon. About midnight one of our patrols bombed a sentry post on near lip of crater on right of our line. Enemy replied with bombs. Enemy artillery seemed to be registering on our support line.	✓

1st Argyle & Sutherland Highlanders

WAR DIARY
or
INTELLIGENCE SUMMARY
(Erase heading not required.)

Army Form C. 2118.

France
Ref. Map, Sheet 11. 1/100,000

Instructions regarding War Diaries and Intelligence Summaries are contained in F.S. Regs., Part II. and the Staff Manual respectively. Title pages will be prepared in manuscript.

1916	Hour, Date, Place	Summary of Events and Information	Remarks and references to Appendices
July	12	At 3.45 p.m. our Stokes guns fired on enemy front line opposite in retaliation. At 10.45 p.m. a patrol under 2/Lt R. Philp went out with intention of entering German Coy and capturing a prisoner; a hostile patrol was seen 40 yds away, but patrol worked to cut enemy party (of 4) retired and were seen dropping into their own [parapet]. Our artillery was also quiet.	A few T.M.S
	13	Some shelling during day. One shell blocking entrance to dugout - Casualties 4 O.R. Killed, 1 wounded. All of 7/4th London Regt. During afternoon Brett rounded up all to line 7th London Regt. and proceeded to billets in MAROEUIL	
	14	Batt. moved to billets in SAVY.	
	15	Batt. moved on short notice to IVERGNY. Starting at 3.40 a.m. Vanderecourt - three by motor lorries; transport following later.	Cross Rds west of V. in
	16	Batt. moved to BERNAVILLE by route march starting at 6.20 a.m. Major R taking left to take command of 2" Enford Regt. 2 Officers (Lt A.E. Stewart and 2/Lt B.? Rowan from Q. A.F. S.M.) Joined as reinforcements.	
	17	In Billets at BERNAVILLE. Capt H.G. Bruce Rathie arrived and took over duties as M.O to.	
	18		
	19	Transport moves at 6 p.m. to FLESSELLES.	
	20	At 1.30 a.m. Battn marches to CANDAS, and entrained for MERICOURT arriving there about 9 a.m.; then marches to dugouts in QUEEN'S WOOD near FRICOURT	BECORDEL (near ALBERT)
	21	At 9.45 p.m. Battn moved forward to dugouts at S.20.a.2.5" (Sheet 57.C) as Bde reserve.	
	22	Heavy bombardment of enemy line from 4 P.M. to 1.30 A.M. - 23rd inst.	

7th Arg & Such. H/R.

Army Form C. 2118.

WAR DIARY
or
INTELLIGENCE SUMMARY
(Erase heading not required.)

Ref Map. 57 C. France

Instructions regarding War Diaries and Intelligence Summaries are contained in F. S. Regs., Part II. and the Staff Manual respectively. Title pages will be prepared in manuscript.

1916. Hour, Date, Place	Summary of Events and Information	Remarks and references to Appendices
July 23rd	At 1.30 am. 9th Royal Scots & 4th Seaforths took part in an attack in neighbourhood of HIGH WOOD. Our A + B. Coys moved to man trenches S.14.D.2.8. as reserve. HQ and 2 Coys remained in old position. Attack failed to gain objectives, and Bat'ns returned to former positions. During attack our area was not shelled to any extent. We provided large carrying parties for RE materials, and 4th Gordons Rations — water. From 7pm to 12.30 am our casualties 17. OR. wounded. During enemy of 23rd we relieved 9th R.S. in front line.	
24th.	Large working parties dug new Trench between S.9.C.4.9. to 4/1a/4 WOOD. This new Trench was shelled in the morning by field guns but little damage done. Casualties 14 OR. wounded. 2 OR. killed.	
	About 6 pm. enemy was seen advancing against our left Company, and reported massing in large numbers along eastern edge of HIGH WOOD. The enemy son were driven back by Rifle fire. But at 8.45 pm. were again reported attacking our left. The Coy Then (C.Coy) went out and swept against them and occupied new trench at S.9.b. whilst has only been held by 10 pr. enemy's our barrage completely checked enemies attack, and by 10 pm. enemy's barrage had stopped. our casualties Killed - Capt H.C. DRUMMOND and 4 OR. Missing 1 OR. Wounded 2/LTs FRASER & ROBB and 40 OR.	
25th.	2nd R. PRUDE reconnoitres enemy positions and located strong post in S.13.C. He shot 2 of the enemy, and is believed to have hit 4 others. M.G. stands were seen in enemy parapet. Casualties 9 OR.	

Forms/C. 2118/11.

7th Any & Suff. Regt.

Army Form C. 2118.

WAR DIARY
or
INTELLIGENCE SUMMARY
(Erase heading not required.)

Ref Map 57C. 62.D

Instructions regarding War Diaries and Intelligence Summaries are contained in F. S. Regs., Part II. and the Staff Manual respectively. Title pages will be prepared in manuscript.

Hour, Date, Place	Summary of Events and Information	Remarks and references to Appendices
1916 July 26.	Any Companies of guard. During running Battn. was relieved by 1st Royal Irish and proceeded first to Bivouacs at S.19.b. and when relieved then to Ger. A. + S.H. to Bivouacs at E.11.25. 3 Coys got down without much trouble, but last Coy (D) was caught in heavy bomb and met with some Shells, at 10 P.m. Before being relieved our B. Coy wounded + captured a German at S.T.6. our casualties 5 Or. killed, 33 Or. wounded.	
July 27th	In Bivouac at E 116 Reinforcements 204 O.R. arrived.	airs[?] arrd [?]
" 28th	"	
" 29th	" Reinforcements 1 O.R. arrived. Capt W.R. Wilson left Battn. for ETAPLES to take up duties as Draft Conducting Officer, also 2nd Lt. J.S. Campbell proceeding to U.K. to be attached to R.F.C.	arrd OR.R.
" 30th	" Battalion found wine field.	
" 31st	" Provided working parties.	

[signatures]
Lindsey 7th Regt Suffolk Highlands[?]

154th Brigade.
51st Division.

1/7th BATTALION

ARGYLE & SUTHERLAND HIGHLANDERS

AUGUST 1 9 1 6 :::::

7th Argyll & Suth. High'rs

WAR DIARY
or
INTELLIGENCE SUMMARY

Army Form C. 2118.
CONFIDENTIAL
No 81 (A)
HIGHLAND DIVISION.

REF MAPS. ALBERT - contind. {57DSE 57cSW / 62DNE 62cNW.

Hour, Date, Place	Summary of Events and Information	Remarks and references to Appendices
1st August 1916	During afternoon Battn moved from bivouac in E12a to support in MAMETZ WOOD and relieved 6th Gordons in area S.19.b. Between 7.30 + 9 pm enemy very heavily shelled the casualties 2 pte's killed, 5 O.R. wounded.	A.R.B. Appendices
2nd " "	Enemy heavily reinforcing. Came up with R.E. and carrying parties at Rue Pottière at 2 am. a few gas shells were fired into Wood. Casualties 2 O.R. wounded	A.R.B.
3rd " "	Supplied parties as above. Heavy shelling 3.5-6.3. 40 pm + 6.30-6.7 pm. Many shellings on left at 10.15 pm. Enemy reported to be making gas attack there. Casualties 2 O.R. wounded.	A.R.B.
4th " "	Battn supplied parties as above, at 12.15 am. Brigade on our right reports S.O.S. whole front, artillery very active till 5 am. Began at 9.40 pm. Casualties 2 O.R. wounded.	A.R.B.
5th " "	Supplied parties as above. Casualties 5 O.R. wounded.	A.R.B.
6th " "	" " " " Wood heavily shelled between 1 and 5 am. Shells	A.R.B.
7th " "	Battn was relieved during afternoon by 2nd Arg. Hth Shghts and proceeded by route march to bivouac in area E.13a via FRICOURT, BECORDEL and VIVIER.	A.R.B.
8th " "	In bivouac at E.13a.	A.R.B.
9th " "	" " " " Transport moved during afternoon to Ponteinville	A.R.B.
10th " "	Battn entrained at EDGEHILL near DERNANCOURT at 9.30 am. and detrained at LONGPRE thence by route march to LIMEUX. Transport moved from POULAINVILLE to LIMEAUX	A.R.B.
11th " "	In billets at LIMEAUX	A.R.B.
12th " "	Battn transferred by Route March to Popt REN'A and entrained there for STEENBECQUE arriving there at 11.30 pm	A.R.B.
13th " "	Battn marched by route about 2 aim. and to billets in WALLON CAPPELL arriving there about 6 am. In Billets at WALLON CAPPELL.	A.R.B.

624

WAR DIARY or INTELLIGENCE SUMMARY

Army Form C. 2118.

7th Army (Light Nighty)

Ref Maps. { ABBEVILLE 5A / HAZEBROUCK 5A / FRANCE SHEET 36 N.W. }

(Erase heading not required.)

Instructions regarding War Diaries and Intelligence Summaries are contained in F.S. Regs., Part II and the Staff Manual respectively. Title Pages will be prepared in manuscript.

Place	Date August 16	Hour	Summary of Events and Information	Remarks and references to Appendices
WALLON CAPPELL	14th		Transport of 154th Bright broke moved by route march to ARMENTIERES starting at 5am. Battr. paraded at 10-15 am. & proceeded by route march to entrain at EBBLINGHEM for STEENWERCK & thence by route march to billets in ARMENTIERES, taking over from 4th Battr. 3rd N.Z. Brigade.	ARR.
ARMENTIERES	15th		In billets. Supplied two parties of trench working about 7pm.	ARR.
"	16th		Two men killed. Casualties 1 O.R. killed 16 O.R. wounded. In billets. Two parties supplied during afternoon moved into billets vacated by 4th Battr. 1st N.Z. Brigade. Supplied parties of trench workers.	ARR.
"	17th		In billets in Armentieres	ARR.
"	18th		2Lt. J.K. Aitken arrived as Officer Reinforcement	ARR.
"	19th		Supplied working parties to 154th Brigade. 2Lt L.R. Rankin ARR. as Officer Reinforcement.	ARR.
"	20th		2Lt. J.C. Tennent arrived as Officer Reinforcement	ARR.
"	21st		Battn. moved to front line trenches and relieved 9th R.S. during the night. There was considerable rifle & machine gun fire.	N.R.
"	22nd		About 1am. while our patrol was examining our wire a German patrol was seen in front of locality 5a. Our patrol was withdrew & Lewis gun fire was brought to bear on enemy patrol. During the afternoon German field guns were active against our front & support line. Aeroplane there also active all day. 2Lt. J.B. Moir left unit to join Machine Gun Corps. 30 o.r. reinforcements arrived. Casualties 14 o.r. at Grantham.	ARR. 14 +
"	23rd		Enemy machine guns & rifle guns were again active. Our working party near T.5.6.75 was disturbed by our snipers. Our Stokes gun practically demolished a house at T.5.6 + 7. Casualties 7 o.r. About 9am. enemy sent over two large minenwerfer which made craters 20 feet wide and 10 feet deep near T.5.6.8.	66 +
"	24th		Enemy sent over T.5.6.8. a German sniper at T.5.6.8. a German sniper was forced to descend from a tree behind their lines. Reinforcement 5 o.r. arrived	4 +

Army Form C. 2118.

WAR DIARY
or
INTELLIGENCE SUMMARY
(Erase heading not required.)

1st Arg Bde. Highland
1st Arg [Hld] Highland
Ref Maps:- France Sheet 36 N.W., Bailleul 28 SW 3

Place	Date August	Hour	Summary of Events and Information	Remarks and references to Appendices
TRENCHES AUGUST	25th		Enemy trench mortars were most active. Our patrol which went to examine German wire in front of our left Coy about 1.5 a 9.9 was prevented from doing so by strong enemy patrol being out. Our Lewis guns fired on this patrol. Our Casualties 1 or. wounded. GAS ALERT received 10.25/pm	AAB. A.B.B.
"	26th		Day very quiet. Casualties 1 or. killed, 1 or. wounded. Reinforcements 30 or. arrived. During afternoon Battn. was relieved by 8th Arg. A&SB. & Suth. Highlrs & therefore proceeded by route march to Brigade Camp.	A.B.B.
NEAR BAILLEUL	27th		Battn. Highlrs & one mile S.E. of BAILLEUL. Combined Church Parade with 4th Seaforth Highlrs.	ABB
"	28th		During forenoon Coys. paraded for Physical & Bayonet training, Specialists were trained under Specialist Officers. In afternoon Brigade paraded at S 22 c to practise formation for following day.	ABB
"	29th		154th Inf. Brigade paraded at S 22 c at 10.40 am. At 11am. G.O.C., 2nd ARMY presented ribbons of decorations awarded for operations in SOMME VALLEY. 2nd LT. R. PHILP was awarded the Military Cross & Pipers T.B. WALLIS the Military Medal. After the presentation the G.O.C. inspected the Brigade. After this the G.O.C of 51st (H.) Divn inspected the whole Brigade marched past at 12.25 pm. G.O.C. Brigade marched past at B 13 d 9.4 from B 23 c & 29 c & B 13 d	6654
"	30th		Battn. marched into billets at Rattray Camp. Transport moved into Camp.	
"	31st		Training under Coy arrangements. Battn. route march in the forenoon & night operations & fought. abbb.	JWJ Hof Cop J/Lt Comdg 7 [or] 1/4 H Hy Sanders

Vol 22

7th Arg. & Suth. High drs.

War Diary

September 1916.

WAR DIARY or INTELLIGENCE SUMMARY

Army Form C. 2118.
4th Bn Black Watch (also Army Form C. 2118)
REF. MAPS: FRANCE SHEET 36 N.W.

6674

Place	Date	Hour	Summary of Events and Information	Remarks and references to Appendices
BAILLEUL	SEPR 1		In Camp continued training	
	2		Battn left Camp at 1.30 pm moved by route march to Hutments at PAPOT B 3 c 8.2. Transport stayed at same place	
PAPOT	3		Battn held Church Parade at Hutments. In the afternoon relieved 13th D.L.I. in the Line of Supports. Transport moved to original position at B 23 c. Battn H.Q. in CHAPELLE - ROMPUE also "B" Coy. H.Q.	
PAPOT CHAPELLE - ROMPUE	4th		"A" Coy in LE TOUQUET STATION REDOUBT, "C" Coy in LYS FARM, "D" Coy in PETITE RABEQUE FARM. In Right Support position, supplying working parties for C. 70. Enemy shelled LE BIZET COUVENT & CHAPELLE ROMPUE about 5-15 pm. Casualties Nil. (Opened a Canteen in Chapelle Rompue)	
	5th	"	"	
	6th	"	Enemy shelled LE BIZET & CHAPELLE 141. ROMPUE about 3.30 pm. Casualties 1st Killed 1 wounded 1 horse killed in Ammunition.	
	7th	"	" Casualties nil	
	8th	"	During January Battn was relieved by 6th Wiltshire Regiment and then moved by route back to Armentières where fresh orders were killed on their first arrival in their area.	
	9th	"	During the afternoon Battn relieved 4/5th Black Watch in the Right Subsector. Battn HQ dugouts at C38 & 10.30. Casualties 2 O.R. wounded	
	10th		In trenches of 153rd Brigade. Day generally very quiet. Machine guns active in the trenches. Enemy went at 8.30 pm then had a demonstration along the whole Bn front. Enemy at 8.35 pm a demonstration of red rockets. Casualties Nil. Enforcement of 50m rifles & rifle grenades. Our rifles retaliated Own trench mortars heavily on German trenches. Enemy fired with Large "minenwerfer" 9 at small trench mortars. Enemy field guns fired on our position locally 9 between 4 & 6pm Casualties 2 O.R. Killed 4 OR wounded.	
	11th			

Copied 7 Sept 1916

Army Form C. 2118.

7th Arg. Knth. Brights
Ref. Map.
France Sheet 36 NW

WAR DIARY
or
INTELLIGENCE SUMMARY

(Erase heading not required.)

Instructions regarding War Diaries and Intelligence Summaries are contained in F.S. Regs, Part II and the Staff Manual respectively. Title Pages will be prepared in manuscript.

Place	Date	Hour	Summary of Events and Information	Remarks and references to Appendices
TRENCHES IN RIGHT SUB SECTOR	12th		About 8 p.m. enemy "minenwerfer" fired on our trenches. Our machine guns fired at 8.30 pm on enemy's 3rd line from emplacements in SS 89 and FRY PAN. Casualties Nil.	M
	13th		Our artillery and trench mortars carried out two minutes bombardments of enemy's lines at intervals during the day. Enemy's retaliation was feeble. One "minenwerfer" being shot over about 10 am. Capt. N. Stanton wounded but not evacuated.	M
	14th		Artillery activity comparatively nil. Casualties nil. Lt. Col. Knights commanding 154th Inf. Brigade. 2nd Brigadier General C.E. STEWART killed by shell fire.	M
SUBSIDIARY LINE	15th		Batt. was relieved during the afternoon by 9th R.S. and thereafter took up position in Subsidiary line vacated by the 9th R.S. Headquarters established in CHATEAU de ROSE, HOUPLINES. Our artillery & T.M. again very active culminating at 8.55 pm in severe bombardment when raiding parties of 7th Black Watch & 7th Gordons attempted entries on enemy's lines at C 29 C 4.8, 7.5 and C 29 a 5.5. The former was successful. Casualties Nil. Reinforcements 30 or. arrived & joined us at B 13 d 9.0.	M
"	16th		Our Subsidiary Line. Day was quiet, but our artillery very active at night. Raids on enemy's trenches were made by 9th Royal Scots assisted by our rifle grenades and the 5th Gordons at T 5 C 7.2 and C 17 a 7.1. Supplied carrying parties for S.A.A. & T.M. ammunition.	M
"	17th		"	
"	18th		In Subsidiary line, supplied working parties for R.E.	
"	19th		3 or. wounded by accidental bursting of a bomb.	Brig. Gen. J.G.H.HAMILTON D.S.O. was in command of 154th Brigade " and " 2nd Lt. J. SHAW and

[signatures]

WAR DIARY or **INTELLIGENCE SUMMARY**

Army Form C. 2118.

7th Army Plat. Hughes
Ref. Map 36 N.W.
HAZEBROUCK 5a.

Place	Date	Hour	Summary of Events and Information	Remarks and references to Appendices
TRENCHES SUBSIDIARY LINE	20th		In Subsidiary Line. Supplied working parties for R.E.	
	21st		" " " " " "	
	22nd		During the afternoon Battn. was relieved by Battn. of 8th Australian Inf. Brigade and thereafter proceeded by route march to hutments and billets one mile West of ERQUINGHEM.	
BILLETS & HUTMENTS	23rd		In billets & hutments	
"	24th		Continued Church Parade with 9th Royal Scots Hamilton being present & after parade was introduced to all officers. Route march and Coy & Specialist drill, also Coys Lewis Coy & specialists & had name tests at Anti-Gas School ARMENTIERES.	
ESTAIRES	25th		Battn. moved by route march with 154th Inf. Brigade to ESTAIRES and Transport followed. Billetted in ESTAIRES. Brigade moved off from road junction Eastern end of RAC-ST MAUR at 9.30 am. 154th Brigade bus transport marched past the	
"	26th		In billets in ESTAIRES. 2nd ARMY COMMANDER during a short route march.	
"	27th		In billets in ESTAIRES. Coyform drill and route marching. Specialist Parades under Specialist Officers	
"	28th		In billets in ESTAIRES. Battn ROUTE MARCH during forenoon round name ESTAIRES. Practised advance guard for road and deployment. Night extension of working parties.	
	29th		In billets in ESTAIRES. Continued training under Coy. arrangements.	
	30th		" " Battn. moved by route to MERVILLE leaving ESTAIRES at 8 p.m. and entrained at MERVILLE STATION for CANDAS about 10 p.m.	

Vol 23

7th ARG. & SUTH. HIG

WAR DIARY

OCTOBER 1916.

WAR DIARY or INTELLIGENCE SUMMARY

Army Form C. 2118.

7th Arg. & Suth. High[rs]

Ref. Maps:- Lens Sheet 11
Sheet 57d

Place	Date	Hour	Summary of Events and Information	Remarks and references to Appendices
FIENVILLERS	Oct 1st		Batt. detrained at CANDAS STATION at 5am. (winter time) and proceeded by Route march to billets in FIENVILLERS. Held Church Parade in forenoon.	App.
"	2nd		In billets. Company training during forenoon.	App.
"	3rd		Batt. proceeded by route march to billets in THIEVRES via BEAUVAL and SARTON. "A" Echelon Transport accompanied Batt. "B" Echelon was See Appendix Brigaded. Roads very bad in places due to recent wet weather. App.	
THIEVRES			Batt. in 5th Corps	
			Batt. proceeded by route march to huts in BUS-LES ARTOIS See App II 1st line Transport accompanies Batt. 2nd line was brigaded. App. Went in huts.	
BUS-LES 4th ARTOIS			In huts. Training. Supplied working party for R.E.s. App.	
	5th		" In the afternoon Batt. practised the attack in conjunction with 9th R.S. App.	
	6th		" In the afternoon Batt. practised the Batt. junction with 9th R.S. on march out. Carried out the attack App.	
	7th		Training in conjunction with 9th R.S. App.	
	8th		1.30 and 152nd Brig. in the line. The Batt. relieved 6 Gordons the Slightly relieved the 1/5 153rd Brig. in bivouacs K25a47 and two coys. App. supplied two coys and Headquarters working parties for R.E.s. Coys in Couvelles supplied	
SUPPORT	9th		In support Supplied working parties for R.E.s Carrying App. parties. Casualties 1 Or. Killed 2 Or. wounded	

J.G.H[?] Lt Col

WAR DIARY or INTELLIGENCE SUMMARY

Army Form C. 2118.

7th Arg. & Suth. High[rs]

Ref. Maps.
Sheet 57d.

Place	Date	Hour	Summary of Events and Information	Remarks and references to Appendices
SUPPORT	Oct R. 10th		In support. Supplied working & carrying parties for R.E's.	" " Reinforcements
	11th		" " Supplied working & carrying parties for R.E's.	" " Reinforcements
	12th		5 Off. 2nd Lts. Gibson, Mayor, Chalmers, Hetherwick, Sutherland, and 10 O.R. arrived. A carrying party in conjunction with 4th Army Operations smoke barrage was released from our Brigade front trenches. Supplied carrying party for smoke bombs. During the afternoon Battn was relieved by 1st Gordon Higrs and proceeded to billets in LOUVENCOURT. Capt J.M. Scott Cavalry 1 O.R. wounded	A.R.8. See Appendix III & IV a.R.8.
LOUVENCOURT	13th		In billets in LOUVENCOURT. Capt J.M. Scott proceeded to ALDERSHOT for two months training. Cause.	a.R.8.
"	14th		" "	a.R.8.
"	15th		" Church Parade in forenoon.	
"	16th		" Attack practice in conjunction with 4th Batn [?] a.R.8.	a.R.8.
"	17th		" and 9th Royal Scots. Battn paraded and proceeded by route march to billets in RAINCHEVAL. Training	a.R.8.
"	18th		" at 10 a.m. Battn paraded and proceeded by route	a.R.8.
RAINCHEVAL	19th		" RAINCHEVAL. Batn proceeded and arrived in billets near LEALVILLERS.	
LEALVILLERS	20th		" Divisional Training. Reinforcements 30 O.R. arrived.	a.R.8.
			" During the afternoon Batn proceeded by route march to billets in FORCEVILLE.	a.R.8.
FORCEVILLE	21st		In billets Training	a.R.8.

WAR DIARY

INTELLIGENCE SUMMARY

1/7th Arg. & Suth High'ders Army Form C. 2118.
Ref Maps:— 57d.

(Erase heading not required.)

Place	Date	Hour	Summary of Events and Information	Remarks and references to Appendices
FORCEVILLE	22nd Oct		Batt" relieved 5th Seaforth Highrs 152nd Inf. Brigade in front line trenches	app IV
TRENCHES			Q 4 b and d and Q 10 b. Three Officers Reinforcements arrived.—	ARB
			2nd Lts. O.G. DAVIES, A.D. MORRISON, and J. ROBERTSON. Our Artillery very active.	
"	23rd		Continued artillery and T.M. activity. Enemy's artillery	ARB
			in trenches active and field guns fired on our trenches. Our	ARB
			were now active and cutting enemy's wire.	
"	24th		Continued artillery activity in cutting enemy's wire.	ARB
			Patrols exploded 13 Bangalore Torpedoes in enemy wire	
			in front of our C.T.'s front & support	
			Heavy enemy shelling on our C.T.'s. 1 O.R. killed, 1 O.R. wounded.	
	25th		Three Officer Reinforcements arrived 2/Lt. J. McLEAN, C.M.T.A.CEWING and T.T. SLOAN, also for	
			the Trenches. Casualties	ARB
			Raiding parties (under 2/Lt Aitken)	
			continued activity & entered German trenches about Q 10.6.7.8	See Appendix VI
			but found no signs of enemy in enemy lines. Another (under 2/Lt Harris)	
			entered German trenches about Q 10.6 and repair parties to	
			enemy. They found a Lewis Gun same brought back to our lines.	
			Wire entanglement about Q 10.6 75 80 but failed to	
			attempted entrance account of thick wire. Casualties 1 O.R. killed	See app VII
			No on account of R.S. Gde Lt. J.W. Hoyle + 2nd Lieutt. attempted to enter German trenches	See app VIII
	26th		Batt" was relieved by through the wire. Casualties 1 O.R. wounded	ARB
			at P 18 b - another thick wire	
			on account of another thick wire.	
MAILLYWOOD	27th 28th		In huts. Flaming & supplying working parties	"Reinforcements 30 O.R. joined ConsB.

J.H.H. HTP P.D. (Colonel)

Army Form C. 2118.

WAR DIARY
INTELLIGENCE SUMMARY

7th Argyll & Sutherland Highlanders

Ref. Maps 57d.

(Erase heading not required.)

Instructions regarding War Diaries and Intelligence Summaries are contained in F. S. Regs., Part II. and the Staff Manual respectively. Title Pages will be prepared in manuscript.

Place	Date Oct.	Hour	Summary of Events and Information	Remarks and references to Appendices
MAILLY WOOD	29th		In huts etc. Supplied working parties and training.	
	30th		" " During the afternoon Battn. proceeded by route march to RAINCHEVAL.	See Appendix No. IX.
RAINCHEVAL	31st		In billets. Training.	

H.Q. 7th A&SH Lt Colonel
Cmdg 7th Bn 7th Sutherland Highlanders

7th Argyll & Sutherland
Highlanders,

War Diary.

November 1916.

Army Form C. 2118.

WAR DIARY
7th Argyll & Sutherland Highlanders
INTELLIGENCE SUMMARY
REF. MAPS - 57d

(Erase heading not required.)

Instructions regarding War Diaries and Intelligence Summaries are contained in F. S. Regs., Part II. and the Staff Manual respectively. Title Pages will be prepared in manuscript.

Place	Date Nov.	Hour	Summary of Events and Information	Remarks and references to Appendices
RAINCHEVAL	1st		In billets in RAINCHEVAL. Training.	
"	2nd		Battn left billets at 8.30 a.m. proceeded by route march to relieve 6th Gordon High'rs in the line but orders were cancelled before Battn reached LEALVILLERS.	AABS
"	3rd		In billets. Training.	
"	4th		Battn vacated billets at 8 a.m. & proceeded by route march to LEALVILLERS, ACHEUX, FORCEVILLE & MAILLY, and reached hqrs two hours via P.17a where dinners were served. During afternoon Battn transport took up standings in P.17 c. ARB relieved 6th GORDON HIGH'DRS. Casualties 1 O.R. wounded	see App. I
TRENCHES	5th		Our artillery were very active especially at 8.30 a.m. Enemy's retaliation was vigorous.	ARB
"	6th		Heavy artillery bombardment of enemy's line at 1 p.m. Patrol under 2/Lt MAYOR & SUTHERLAND examined enemy's line between P.17a where between 9 + 11 p.m. Reinforcements 8 O.R. arrived.	ARB
	7th		2 + 4 a.m. Heavy bombardment of enemy lines at 5.45 p.m. when raiding party of 9th Royal Scots attempted to enter their lines but found strongly held. Enemy artillery retaliation was very vigorous and rifle & m.g. fire of this three Companies entered enemy trenches at Q4 & 31 but were driven out by our depth by counter attack. A party under 2/Lt MAYOR went out to look for two 9th R.S. who were missing.	ARB

WAR DIARY
INTELLIGENCE SUMMARY

7th ARG. & SUTH. HIGHDRS

Ref. Maps:- 57 D.

Army Form C. 2118.

Place	Date Nov.	Hour	Summary of Events and Information	Remarks and references to Appendices
TRENCHES	8th		Slight artillery activity during the forenoon when Battn was relieved by the Royal Scots. This was accomplished under great difficulty as trenches were very muddy owing to heavy rain during the previous 30 hours. Several men had to be dug out of mud. After relief Battn proceeded to hutments in MAILLY WOOD P.18.b. Casualties 2 or wounded.	See App II
MAILLY WOOD	9th		In hutments	ORR ORB
"	10th		"	ORR
"	11th		"	"Reinforcements 190 or aircrafts. ORB
"	12th		"	
"	13th		Battn arr. at 14 hours notice at 11.15am "A+D" Coys under Capts Cunningham & Strang were ordered to reinforce the 152nd Inf. Brigade & took up position in sugar Q.10.a. At 6 pm the See App III "B" & "C" Coys were ordered to reinforce 152nd Brigade and moved into dugouts in Q.10.a. At 8pm "A+D" Coys were moved forward into BEAUMONT HAMEL to reinforce the Batt. Argl & Suth Highdrs. in the old German 3rd line which was being consolidated. At 6.45 am & 15.30 the 51st (H) Divn attacked & took BEAUMONT-HAMEL. Having 152nd & 153rd Brigades in the line and the 154th Brigade in reserve. Simultaneously attacks were made by the 63rd Division on our right and the 2nd Division on our left. Before 6.30 a.m. prisoners were passing through our lines. Our Battn was then utilised to carry in our wounded.	
TRENCHES				

WAR DIARY / INTELLIGENCE SUMMARY

7th Argyll & Sutherland Highlanders
Ref Maps:- 57d
Army Form C. 2118.

Place	Date Nov^r	Hour	Summary of Events and Information	Remarks and references to Appendices
TRENCHES	13th	(contd)	The village was wholly in our possession and third German line completely taken by 6 p.m.	off.
"	14th		At 3 a.m. "B" & "C" Coys under Capts Mitchell and A.L. Stewart were ordered to advance into advanced line E. of BEAUMONT-HAMEL. At 7.30 a.m. "B" & "C" Coys advanced to occupy MUNICH TRENCH. They moved up the hill in file two waves of section in file supported on either flank by bombing parties moving up BEAUMONT ALLEY & LEAVE AVE. The progress was very slow on account of the state of the ground but at 8.30 a.m. MUNICH TRENCH was occupied with slight opposition and some prisoners were sent down. Patrols were at once sent out to connect with each flank, but touch could not be obtained. FRANKFORT TRENCH in front was reported strongly held, but MUNICH TRENCH was very badly damaged by our artillery. At 11 a.m. "D" Coy 9th R.S. (Captain Cowan) was placed under our orders and they were then ordered to support the two forward Coys. At 11 a.m. touch was obtained with the 2nd Dragoons on our left and at the same time a report came to say that our artillery were shelling them very heavily. At 1.30 a.m. forward Coys reported that they had to vacate MUNICH TRENCH on account of the shelling of our own guns and had withdrawn to the first line of advanced trenches where consolidating and getting things out. FRANKFORT TRENCH Pt C Pn a En of pioneers were sent to dig NEW MUNICH Tr. and 6th Cameronians. Casualties: Capt R. STRANG, Killed 2/Lt A.G STORRIER wounded 1 O.R. Killed & 10 O.R. wounded.	See App IV See App V

WAR DIARY
INTELLIGENCE SUMMARY

7th Argyll & Sutherland Highlanders
Ref. Maps:- 57d.
Army Form C. 2118.

Place	Date	Hour	Summary of Events and Information	Remarks and references to Appendices
TRENCHES	Nov. 15		At 4.30 am. "A & D" Coys relieved "C" Coy 9th R.S. who withdrew to dugouts in BEAUMONT-HAMEL. At 9 am. "A" & "D" Coys with "B" Coy in support were ordered to advance and attack MUNICH and FRANKFORT trenches. 5th Divisions on right and left were attacking simultaneously. Our artillery barrage opened short and fell on our jumping off trench but despite this the Coys advanced meeting with heavy bombing and M.G. fire. They advanced across MUNICH TRENCH and some bombers and part of "D" Coy entered FRANKFORT TRENCH and proceeded to bomb outwards. They bombed two dugouts full of Germans and killed many others but as the attacks on the right and left had failed they got no support and eventually had to retire, our Lewis guns covering this movement. We occupied the new MUNICH TRENCH which was still the most advanced part of the British line. During the night "A, B & D" Coys were relieved by two Coys of the 4th Seaforth Highlanders. Casualties 2/Lts J. SCOTT & O.O.G. DAVIES missing believed killed, Capt. Cunningham 2/Lts Rankine and Adam wounded. Casualties 22 or. killed, 97 or. wounded and 19 or. missing. In dugouts in BEAUMONT HAMEL supplied working parties for R.E. Rrepaired wounded, collected salvage between tank & our dugouts on heavily shelled. Casualties 10 or killed 3 or wounded	See App. VI
	16			M Moore M Major

WAR DIARY / INTELLIGENCE SUMMARY

Army Form C. 2118.

1/4 ARG. & SUTH. HIGH.DRS. REF. MAP. 57d.

Place	Date	Hour	Summary of Events and Information	Remarks and references to Appendices
TRENCHES	17th		In dugouts in BEAUMONT HAMEL. Continued Salvage Work. During the afternoon Coys moved back into dugouts in reserve line Q.10+ central to Q.4 central. Casualties 10 Killed 30 wounded.	
	18th		In dugouts in reserve line. Continued Salvage work. Reinforcements arrived BATTN.	
	19th		" " " " During the afternoon the Battn. and thereafter proceeded. See App VII
			was relieved by 152nd Inf. Brigade and proceeded to huttments in MAILLY WOOD (EAST).	
			The following Officers were in action with the Battn:—	
			Lt Col M.J. Haylet D.S.O. Adjt. Capt. A.K. Bain, Sniping Off. 2Lt J.K. Aitken, Signal Officer	
			2Lt S.J. Dobie. Bombing Off. 2Lt W.A. Everitt, M.O. Capt. A.C. Laing R.A.M.C.	
			"A" Coy Capt. J. Cunningham, 2Lts E.P. Rankine, A.L. Gibson, O.G. Dawson & Lt R.G. Hunter.	
			"B" " Capt. Aut. Mitchell, Lt W.V. Macintosh, 2Lt Drummond, R.G.T. Harris.	
			"C" " Capt A.L. Stuart, 2Lts S. Tibbitt, J.D. Allan & J.R. Chalmers.	
			"D" " Capt R. Sturry, 2Lts a. adam, J. Scott, F. Sutherland, C. Hetherwick & T.I.T. Sloan.	
	20th		In hutments in Mailly Wood. Supplied parties for cleaning camp.	
	21st		" " " " " "A" & "C" Coys went as fatigue working party to river in front at Beaussart.	
	22d		" " " " "	
	23d		" " " " " Battn. less (A+C Coys) proceeded by see App VIII route march to billets in HEDAUVILLE leaving at 9.30 a.m. Continued Coys VIII map

WAR DIARY or INTELLIGENCE SUMMARY

Army Form C. 2118.

1/4 Arg'ld & Suth Highrs
R E F. M A P 5'y. D.

Place	Date	Hour	Summary of Events and Information	Remarks and references to Appendices
	24th		In Billets in HEDAUVILLE. Battn less ("A"&"C" Coys) proceeded by route march to billets in PUCHEVILLERS leaving at 9.15am. Continued by Tramway.	see App IX
PUCHEVILLERS	25th		Reinforcements 12 O.Rs arrived. In Billets. Training.	App.
	26th		In Billets. PUCHEVILLERS. Battn less ("A"&"C" Coys) proceeded by route march to Hutments (W.16.a.4.4.) near AVELUY. "A"&"C" Coys leaving at 9.30am Senlis. "A"&"C" Coys joined the Battn at Dinner was served WEST of SENLIS at junction of HEDAUVILLE - BOUZINCOURT ROAD.	see App. X App. App.
	27th		In Hutments near AVELUY. (W.16.a.4.4.) Continued by Tramway	App.
	28th		" " Battn supplies working parties at AVELUY SIDING.	App.
			(W.10.c.1.5.) for unloading trains etc.	
	29th		In Hutments near AVELUY. (W.16.a.4.4.) Continued by Tramway + supplies working parties	App.
	30th		" " Continued by Tramway + supplies working parties.	App.

Vol 27725

"7th" ARG. & SUTH. HIGH^DRS

WAR DIARY

DEC^R 1916.

23.L.

WAR DIARY or INTELLIGENCE SUMMARY

Army Form C. 2118.

1st Arg. & Suth. Highrs.

REF MAP 57D S.E. 2 E ARS.

Place	Date	Hour	Summary of Events and Information	Remarks and references to Appendices
	Dec 1.		In Hutments. BRUCE HUTS. near AVELUY. continued training. Batt supplied working parties.	W.D.
	2		Do	Do	W.D.
	3		The Batt vacated Hutments at 2.45 p.m. & relieved the 9th Black Watch during the night in the front line, left sector of Auverne Front from R.17.b.3.6 to R.13.6.3.4. A Coy. RIGHT. B Coy CENTRE C Coy. LEFT. & D Coy in support. Enemy shelling comparatively quiet. Casualties. 2 Lt. S. SIBERT + 1 O.R. wounded.	see App. No I W.D.
	4		Intermittent shelling with 4.2" & 4.9". A REGINA TRENCH & SUPPORT TRENCH. also 2.7mm & sting bombs on our front line. Intermittent shelling in the vicinity of 7.mm Enemy Snipers particularly active at junction of NEW ST. & SUPPORT TRENCH. Enemy Snipers recognised RED + FLAG. A Stretcher bearer party of our carrying the RED + FLAG was allowed to proceed without being fired at. Casualties. Killed 4 O.R. wounded 5. O.R. Reinforcement arrived 2 Sgts, O.R.s.	W.D.
	5		Enemy shelled intermittently with 4.2" & 4.7mm. In vicinity of NEW STREET + RIGHT Enemy occasional salvoes of 4.7mm shells every 10 minutes on NEW STREET + RIGHT of our front line. Large number of shells fell in vicinity of Batt N.Qrs. during evening. Casualties Killed 2 O.R.	W.D.
	6		Enemy shelling comparatively quiet. The Batt was relieved at night by the 9th Royal Scots + proceeded to Hutments. WOLFE HUTS. X 8 d. The approach/reliefs were difficult owing to no communication trenches + relieves via early boat. Casualties 2 O.R wounded.	see App. No II W.D.

J. F. Gow Major

Army Form C. 2118.

WAR DIARY
1/1 Arg & Suth Hyld*
INTELLIGENCE SUMMARY

(Erase heading not required)

REF. MAP. 57DSE LE SARS & ALBERT

Place	Date 1916	Hour	Summary of Events and Information	Remarks and references to Appendices
X 8 d	Dec 7		In Hutments. WOLFE HUTS. (X 8 d). Cleaning up after tour in R. Trenches. Undernoted N.C.O.s & men awarded MILITARY MEDAL for gallantry on 13 Novr & subsequent days:- Sgt. J. DODDS, L/Cpl. P. WALLS. Bmn. M. WHITTON. PTES. J.G. PATERSON, J. MORRISON, W. MARSHALL, P. WATSON, M. LAIRD, P. McGEACHAN, J. MILLS. D. HENDERSON.	WOD.
"	8		In Hutments. WOLFE HUTS. (X 8 d) Batt. supplied working parties, digging in IRONSIDE TRENCH & carrying stores to front line.	WOD. See App. III
BOUZINCOURT	9		At 10 a.m. Battn. march to Billets in BOUZINCOURT. Transport remained at CROMWELL HUTS. OVILLERS.	WOD.
"	10		In Billets BOUZINCOURT. Continuer Training. Reinforcement of 7 officers arrived viz:- Lt. J.F.C. CONN. 2/Lts. T. D. WILSON, W. DONALDSON, W. A. JENKINS, W. KINROSS, H. GIBSON, J. OLIPHANT.	WOD.
"	11		In Billets BOUZINCOURT. Continued Training & supplied working parties.	WOD.
"	12th		" " " " Capt. A.W.S. MITCHELL & 2/Lt. F. SUTHERLAND awarded the MILITARY CROSS. 755 Sergt. COCKBURN P. awarded D.C.M. CAPT. W. STEWART taken on strength and command "C" Coy. 2.P.S. Reinforcement of 88 o.r. taken on strength. Nº 2080 Sergt. SHANKS awarded bar	Off. O.R.s O.R.s
"	13th		" " Continued Training D.C.M.	
"	14th		" " Continued by route march to Billets in AVELUY.	
"	15th		Battn. proceeded by route march to Billets in AVELUY. C & D Coys to BRUCE HUTS A & B Coys to BRUCE HUTS	O.R.s

J.F. Jones Major

WAR DIARY
7th ARG. & SOTH. HIGH.DRS — Army Form C. 2118.
or
INTELLIGENCE SUMMARY   REF MAPS:- ALBERT, 57D SE, LE SARS.

(Erase heading not required.)

Instructions regarding War Diaries and Intelligence Summaries are contained in F. S. Regs., Part II. and the Staff Manual respectively. Title pages will be prepared in manuscript.

Place	Hour, Date	Summary of Events and Information	Remarks and references to Appendices
OVILLERS	16th OVILLERS	Hd. Qrs. & "B" Coy. proceeded by route march to OVILLERS HUTS. "C" & "D" Coys. in AVELUY ABS.	ABS.
	17th "	Reinforcements 29 or. arrived. Supplied working parties.	
		Supplied Parade in Scotch Chinese tent. Supplies working parties for R.E. etc. Reinforcements 50 or. arrived ABS. Casualties 2 or. wounded.	
	18th "	Supplied working parties	do. ABS.
	19th "	do	do. ABS.
	20th "	do	do. ABS.
	21st "	During the evening Battn. relieved the 7th A. & S. Coys in front line. "C" Coy in Chalk Quarry, "D" Coy at Brigade Hd. Qrs. R.29 central. Some M.G. fire ABS.	Opp. No. IV
	22nd "	Casualties 2 Lt. H. Gibson wounded Intermittent shelling all day, night quiet. Some aerial activity also	ABS.
	23rd "	Intermittent shelling all day. See App. No. V	
	24th "	Battn. unrelieved in front line. By two Coys. of 9 Chalk Mount Battn. Hd. Qr. moved and A&R Coys. to ABS. Casualty 1 or. wounded.	
to	OVILLERS HUTS	REINFORCEMENTS 2 Lts. GREGORY, THOMPSON, HUGHES & GRAHAM 102 or. arrived	J.F. Jones

WAR DIARY or INTELLIGENCE SUMMARY

7th A.R.G. 1 Suth. High. Army Form C. 2118.
Ref. Maps:- ALBERT
57D SE, LE SARS.

Place	Date	Hour	Summary of Events and Information	Remarks and references to Appendices
TRENCHES	DECR 25th		Battn. in support. Supplied carrying parties for front Coys.	O.R.B
	26th		do do do do do do do do	O.R.B
			Reinforcements 2/Lt HISLOP and 47 o.r. arrived	
BRUCE HUTS AVELUY.	27th		7th Bn. A + B Coys were relieved by 5th SEA HIGHDRS and See App. VI	
			thereafter marched to BRUCE HUTS AVELUY, V A + B Coys merely	
			there during the afternoon. Relief was impeded by gas shelling. O.R.B	
SENLIS	28th		Battn. moved by route march to billets in SENLIS	O.R.B
			Reinforcement 2/Lt McLEAY arrived	
"	29th		In Billets. Bn SENLIS Training. Supplied working party for R.E's.	O.R.B
"	30th		do do do do do do do	O.R.B
"	31st		do do 2/Lts R.FRASER do do do do	O.R.B
			do Drafts of 192 o.r. reinforcements arrived	
			Held Church Parade in CINEMA HALL.	

J.F. Jones, Major
Commdg.
7th Arg. Suth. High Cas.

7th Arg. & Suth. Highdrs.

War Diary

January 1917.

WAR DIARY or INTELLIGENCE SUMMARY

7th ARG. & SUTH. HIGHLAND Army Form C. 2118.
REF. MAPS:- 57D ALBERT, LE SARS

Place	Date	Hour	Summary of Events and Information	Remarks and references to Appendices
SENLIS	Jany 1st		In billets in SENLIS. 19 N.C.Os reinforcements arrived	A.C.B.
	2nd		do do do Supplied working parties & continued the strength.	A.C.B.
	3rd		During the forenoon Batt. proceeded by route march to AVELUY — A + B Coys to billets in AVELUY, Hd. Qrs. C + D Coys to OVILLERS HUTS. Supplied working parties. 2 O.R. wounded.	See App. I A.C.B.
AVELUY — OVILLERS.	4th		In AVELUY — OVILLERS Area. Supplied working parties & continued training. Casualties 2 O.R. wounded.	A.C.B.
"	5th		do do do. Supplied working parties & continued training.	A.C.B.
"	6th		do do do do	do A.C.B.
"	7th		do do do do	A.C.B.
"	8th		do do Reinforcements 1/2 on taken on the strength.	do Church Parade A.C.B.
"	9th		Hd. Qrs. C + D Coys relieved 7th Gordon Highlanders in the front line during the evening. A + B Coys. See App. II A.C.B. Coys moved into OVILLERS HUTS. Enemy very quiet. Enemy's artillery fairly active during the day but quiet at night.	A.C.B.
"	10th		Enemy's artillery fairly quiet. During the evening C + D Coys were relieved by "B" & "A" Coys respectively.	A.C.B.
"	11th		At 3.30 am. three German carrying parties were walked into our line & surrendered when challenged & they were poles & belonged to 75th I.R.	A.C.B.

WAR DIARY or INTELLIGENCE SUMMARY

Army Form C. 2118.

7th Arg. y Suth Highdrs. Le Sars, S. d'Albert.
Ref Maps: Lens 11 and Abbeville.

Place	Date Jan.y	Hour	Summary of Events and Information	Remarks and references to Appendices
Trenches	12th		During the evening Battn. was relieved by the 2nd H.L.I. of 2nd Division C & D Coys proceeded to Rubempré in motor lorries, after relief A + B Coys proceeded to Ovillers Huts where they changed, washed and had a hot meal, thereafter going by	See App. III ARB.
Rubempré	13th		Rubempré in motor lorries at arriving at 11.30 a.m. 2/Lt. M. R. Walker arrived as Officer reinforcement.	ARB.
Candas	14th		Battn. proceeded by route-march to Candas via Taumas, La Vicogne and Vert Galande marching brigaded from last place.	at 10.30 a.m. ARB.
Coulonvillers	15th		At 8 a.m. Battn. proceeded by route march to Coulonvillers via Montrelet, Berneuil and Domquer.	ARB.
Bonnelle	16th		Battn. proceeded by route march to Rutments near Bonnelle via St Riquier, Neuilly-Le-Hopital & Nouvion-en-Ponthieu, leaving at 8.15 a.m., and, brigaded between Neuilly and Nouvion.	ARB.
Le Crotoy	17th		Battn. proceeded by route march to Le Crotoy via Favieres.	ARB.
"	18th		In billets	
"	19th		" Training. Reinforcements 69 o.r. arrived.	ORB.
"	20th		" "	ORB.
"	21st		" Held Church Parade	ORB.

J.G. Hyslop 2/Lieut.
for 7/Argyll & Suth Highdrs

WAR DIARY or INTELLIGENCE SUMMARY

Army Form C. 2118.

1st ARG. & SUTH. HIGH DRS.

REF. MAPS:- ABBEVILLE 14.

Place	Date	Hour	Summary of Events and Information	Remarks and references to Appendices
LE CROTOY	JAN^Y 22		In billets. Continued training. Draft of 2 Lts. J.H. HARRIS, H. RANSOM and 32 ort. arrived to J.H. HARRIS, B.S.P. FEARNSIDE A.S.C. attached. H. RANSOM also 32 o.r. inspected in the	ARB
"	23rd		Reinforcement. Continued training. Battn. was inspected in the forenoon by Brig. Gen. J.H. HAMILTON D.S.O.	ARB
"	24th		In billets. Route march during forenoon.	ARB
"	25th		Continued training.	ARB
"	26th		" "	ARB
"	27th		" Lt. LAWSON & 2/Lt. MACKAY attached to R.F.C.	ARB
"	28th		" Held Church Parade in CINEMA HALL. 2/Lt. AITKEN attached to R.F.C.	ARB
"	29th		" Continued training. Held Battn Cross Country	ARB
"	30th		" Inter-Platoon race.	ARB
"	31st		" Continued training. Major General G.M. HARPER C.R.,D.S.O., Commanding 51st (H) Div. and Brig.-Gen. J.G.H. HAMILTON D.S.O. inspected the Battalion doing an attack practice in the forenoon.	ARB

J.W. Sykes Lt. Col.
Commanding
7th Arg. & Suth. Highrs.

S E C R E T.   Copy No...6...

154TH INFANTRY BRIGADE

OPERATION ORDER NO.89.

Reference Map :-
        57.D. 1/20,000.

---

1.   The 154th Brigade (less 4th Seaforth Highlanders detached for work on "Yellow Line") will move independently on 2nd and 3rd January, in accordance with attached march table.
        All moves to be completed by 1 p.m. on 3rd January.

2.   5th Army order issued under my B.242 will be strictly complied with.

3.   Battalions will be prepared to find working parties on the night of 3/4th January.

4.   Billeting arrangements will be made direct by units with Town Majors OVILLERS - AVELUY area.

6.   Completion of all moves to be reported at once to Brigade Headquarters.

7.   Brigade Headquarters will close at BOUZINCOURT at 3-30 p.m. and open at AVELUY at same hour.

        ACKNOWLEDGE.

                                                          Captain,
                                                       Brigade Major,
1st January 1917.   154th Infantry Brigade.

ISSUED AT 12.15/p.m BY ORDERLY.

Copy No. 1 File.
        2 War Diary.
        3 9th Royal Scots.
        4 4th Seaforth Highrs.
        5 4th Gordon Highrs.
        6 7th A. & S. Highrs.
        7 154th M. G. Company.
        8 154th T. M. Battery.
        9 51st (H) Division "G" (For information).
        10 152nd Infantry Brigade.
        11 153rd Infantry Brigade.
        12 Staff Captain.
        13 Brigade Signal Officer.
        14 Brigade Transport Officer.
        15 Town Major, OVILLERS HUTS.
        16 Town Major, AVELUY.

MARCH TABLE.
****

Date.	Unit.	From	To	Time of Starting.	Remarks.
1917. Janry.2nd	4th Gordon Highlanders.	BOUZINCOURT	BRUCE HUTS	---	To be clear of BOUZINCOURT by 10 a.m.
do.	Headquarters, 154th Inf. Brigade.	do.	AVELUY	3-30 p.m.	
Janry.3rd	7th A. & S. Highlanders.	SENLIS	OVILLERS - AVELUY AREA.	10-30 a.m.	2 Coys, AVELUY. H.Q. and 2 Coys. OVILLERS HUTS.
do	9th Royal Scots.	BOUZINCOURT	OVILLERS HUTS	10-30 a.m.	
do	154th Machine Gun Company and 154th Trench Mortar Battery.	do.	OVILLERS - AVELUY AREA.	10 a.m.	

SECRET.

App II.

Copy No. 6.

154TH INFANTRY BRIGADE

OPERATION ORDER NO.90.

Reference Maps :-
    57.D. 1/20,000.
    LE SARS 1/10,000.

1.   The 154th Infantry Brigade will relieve the 153rd Infantry Brigade in the line on 8/9th January, in accordance with attached relief table.

2.   Defence schemes and instructions, aeroplane photos, trench maps and tracings, list of work completed and work in hand will be handed over.

3.   1 Battalion, 152nd Infantry Brigade, will be at disposal of 154th Infantry Brigade. This Battalion is not to be used for the defence of the line except in case of emergency but can be employed on carrying.

4.   The 1/1st (H) Field Co. R.E. will remain in the forward area and will be at the disposal of 154th Infantry Brigade for work in the line.

5.   Headquarters will be as follows :-

        Right Sector   ...   As formerly.
        Left Sector   ...   WEST MIRAUMONT ROAD.
        5th Seaforth Highrs.   ...   CHALK MOUND.
        4th Gordon Highrs.   ...   WOLFE HUTS.
        154th M. G. Company.   ...   R.29 Central.

6.   154th T. M. Battery will remain at WOLSELEY HUTS.

7.   Completion of reliefs will be reported by usual code.

8.   Brigade Headquarters will close at AVELUY at 3-30 p.m. and open at R.29 Central at 5 p.m. on 8th January.

    ACKNOWLEDGE.

Robert Adams
Captain,
Brigade Major,
154th Infantry Brigade.

6th January 1917.

ISSUED AT 7.30 p BY ORDERLY.

Copy No.1 File.
      2 War Diary.
      3 4th Royal Scots.
      4 4th Seaforth Highrs.(For information).
      5 4th Gordon Highrs.
      6 7th A. & S. Highrs.
      7 154th M. G. Company.
      8 154th T. M. Battery.
      9 51st (H) Div."G".
     10 152nd Infantry Brigade.
     11 153rd Infantry Brigade.
     12 5th Seaforth Highrs.
     13 1/1st (H) F. Co. R.E.
     14 Staff Captain.
     15 Brigade Transport Officer.
     16 Brigade Signalers Officer.
     17 Town Major, AVELUY.
     18 Town Major, OVILLERS.

RELIEF TABLE (Part 2).

No.	Date.	Unit.	From.	To.	In relief of.	Remarks.
5.	Jan.8/9th	1 Coy.4th Gordon Highrs. less 1 platoon.	WOLFE HUTS	FRASER POST	1 Coy.6th Black Watch.	} } Guides as for No.3. }
		1 Platoon 4th Gordon Highrs.	do.	Dug-out R.35.c.5.4.	2 platoons 7th Gordon Highrs.	}
6.	Jan.8/9th	H.Q. & 2 Coys. 5th Seaforth Highrs.	BRUCE HUTS.	CHALK MOUND.	H.Q. & 2 Coys. 7th Black Watch.	(1 guide per platoon (will be at Brigade H.C. (R.29.Central at 6 p.m.
		2 Coys. 5th Seaforth Highrs.	do.	WOLFE HUTS.	--	Move at 4 p.m.

NOTE : No buses available.

RELIEF TABLE.

No.	Date.	Unit.	From	To	In relief of.	Remarks.
1.	Jan. 8th	4th Gordon Highrs.	BRUCE HUTS	WOLFE HUTS	5th Gordon Highrs.	March to be completed by 10 a.m. Companies come under orders of 153rd Bde. on arrival. Arrival will be reported to 153rd Bde. direct.
2.	Jan.8/9th	154th M.G. Company.	WOLSELEY HUTS	LINE	153rd M.G. Company.	Rendezvous for guides at rate of 1 per gun will be on BAPAUME ROAD 200 yards W. of junction of COURCELETTE-BAPAUME ROAD at 5 p.m.
3.	Jan.8/9th	H.Q. & 2 Coys. 9th Royal Scots.	OVILLERS HUTS	RIGHT SECTOR.	H.Q. & 2 Coys. 6th Black Watch.	⎫ 1 guide per post for front line ⎪ and 1 per platoon where not for ⎬ front line and 1 per Lewis Gun ⎪ at Dressing Station on COURCEL- ⎭ ETTE Road abo ut R.35.b.5.9 at 5 p.m.
		1 Coy. 9th Royal Scots.	do.	COURCELETTE	1 Coy.6th Black Watch.	
		1 Coy. 9th Royal Scots.	do.	BRIGADE H.Q.	6 platoons, 7th Gordon Highrs.	No, guides.
4.	Jan.8/9th	H.Q. & 2 Coys. 7th A. & S. Hrs.	OVILLERS-AVELUY AREA.	LEFT SECTOR	H.Q. & 2 Coys. 7th Gordon Highrs	⎫ 1 guide per post for front line ⎬ and 1 per platoon where not for ⎪ front line and 1 per Lewis Gun ⎭ on BAPAUME ROAD 200 yards W. of junction of BAPAUME-COURCELETTE ROAD at 6 p.m.
		2 Coys. 7th A. & S. Highrs.	do.	OVILLERS HUTS	2 Coys. 7th B.Watch.	No guides.

S E C R E T.   Copy No. 6

154th INFANTRY BRIGADE
OPERATION ORDER NO. 91.

1.   The following reliefs will take place on 10/11th January :-

  (a)   Headquarters and 2 Companies 4th Gordon Highlanders will relieve Headquarters and 2 Companies 9th Royal Scots in the Right Sub-Sector.
On relief Headquarters and 2 Companies 9th Royal Scots will to WOLFE HUTS.

  (b)   2 Companies 7th A. & S. Highlanders will relieve 2 Companies of that Unit in the Left Sub-Sector.
On relief the 2 Companies from the line will move to OVILLERS HUTS.

2.   All details of relief will be arranged direct by O.C. Units concerned.

3.   Completion of relief will be reported to Brigade Headquarters, by usual code.

ACKNOWLEDGE.

Robert Adam
Captain,
Brigade Major,
154th Infantry Brigade.

7th January 1917.

ISSUED AT. 11/am .... BY ORDERLY.

Copy No. 1 File.
      2 War Diary.
      3 9th Royal Scots.
      4 4th Seaforth Highrs.
      5 4th Gordon Highrs.
      6 7th A. & S. Highrs.
      7 154th M. G. Company.
      8 154th T. M. Battery.
      9 5th Seaforth Highrs.
    10 51st (H) D. "G" (For information).
    11 Brigade Transport Officer.
    12 Brigade Signal Officer.

SECRET.   Copy No...... 6

154TH INFANTRY BRIGADE

OPERATION ORDER NO. 92.

Reference Maps :-
    57.D. 1/20,000.
    LE SARS 1/10,000.

---

1.   The 2nd Division will relieve the 51st (Highland) Division in the line on the 12th and 13th January.

2.   The 5th Infantry Brigade will relieve the 154th Infantry Brigade in the front Brigade Area on the nights 12/13th and 13/14th January, in accordance with attached relief table.

3.   All maps, air photos, defence schemes and instructions, and lists of work completed and work in hand will be handed over on relief.

4.   Troops will be marched back in properly formed bodies of not more than one platoon under an Officer where possible and there must be no straggling.

5.   The following permanent working parties will remain in the area and come under the orders of the 2nd Division at 11 a.m., 13th January.
    They will be relieved by similar parties from 2nd Division by midnight 14/15th January and will be moved back by rail to the BUIGNY Area on 15th January under arrangements to be notified by IVth Corps and orders issued by 2nd Division.
    On the morning of the 14th January an officer from each of the parties will report to A.A.& Q.M.G. 2nd Division at USNA HILL for orders - the Officer of the 2/2nd (Highland) Field Coy. R.E. being responsible for party mentioned in (a).

    (a) 8 officers and 300 O.Rs. 1/4th Seaforth Highlanders working under C.R.E. (YELLOW LINE).

    (b) 2 officers and 60 O.Rs. employed as "Platelayers" and attached to O.C. IVth Corps Tramways at DONNET'S POST, (W.12.d.8.1.).

    (c) 1 officer and 50 O.Rs. temporarily attached to 174th Tunnelling Coy. R.E. as spoil party.

6.   Rendezvous for guides at 4.30 p.m. will be at RED CROSS FLAG, POZIERES (X.9.b.6.5.) at 4-30 p.m. each night. Guides for all positions will be necessary. Guides for line to be at the rate of 1 per post. Those for other places to be 1 per platoon. Guides for Lewis and Machine Guns will be one per gun. Brigade Headquarters will arrange for an officer to see that guides pick up their proper parties at the rendezvous.

7.   Transport details kept back by units will move to RUBEMPRE Area under arrangements to be made by Brigade Transport Officer. Definite arrangements will be notified later.

8.   Separate Administrative Instructions have been issued.

                                                                                                      Continued.

-- 2 --

9. Relief will be reported complete by usual code.

10. Brigade Headquarters will move to RUBEMPRE on completion of relief.

    ACKNOWLEDGE.

Robert Adams
Captain,
Brigade Major,
154th Infantry Brigade.

10th January 1917.

ISSUED BY ORDERLY AT...6.30pm

Copy No. 1 File.
      2 War Diary.
      3 9th Royal Scots.
      4 4th Seaforth Highrs.
      5 4th Gordon Highrs.
      6 7th A. & S. Highrs.
      7 154th M. G. Company.
      8 154th T. M. Battery.
      9 51st (H) Division "G" (For information).
    10 51st (H) Division "G" ("   ")
    11 152nd Infantry Brigade.
    12 153rd Infantry Brigade.
    13 5th Seaforth Highrs.
    14 Staff Captain.
    15 Brigade Transport Officer.
    16 Brigade Signal Officer.
    17 Lieut. Paulin.
    18 Town Major, OVILLERS.
    19 5th Infantry Brigade.

TABLE OF RELIEF.
****

Date.	Unit.	From	To.	Relieved by.	Remarks.
1917 Janry. 12/13th	154th M.G. Company.	Line.	WOLSELEY HUTS.	5th M.G. Company.	1 man per gun and 1 officer will remain for 24 hours to assist incoming unit. This party will return with O.C. 9th Royal Scots on 13/14th Janry.
-do-	H.Q.& 2 Coys.4th Gordon Highrs.	Line, (Right Sub-Sector)	WOLFE HUTS.	H.Q.& 2 Coys.5th Bde.	
-do-	H.Q.& 2 Coys. 7th A. & S. Highrs.	Line (Left Sub-Sector)	OVILLERS HUTS.	H.Q.& 2 Coys.5th Bde.	
-do-	2 Coys. 7th A. & S. Highrs.	OVILLERS HUTS.	---	2 Coys.5th Bde.	
-do-	2 Coys. 9th Royal Scots.	WOLFE HUTS.	---	2 Coys. 5th Bde.	
13/14th	5th Seaforth Highlanders.	CHALK MOUND & WOLFE HUTS.	OVILLERS HUTS.	1 Bn. 5th Bde.	
-do-	H.Q.& 2 Coys. 9th Royal Scots.	WOLFE HUTS, BDE. HQ. and COURCELETTE.	WOLFE HUTS	1 Bn. 5th Bde.	
	1 Coy. 4th Gordon Highrs.	FRASER'S POST and Dug-out R.35.c.3.4.			
12/13th	Brigade Headquarters	Line.	RUBEMPRE	5th Bde. Headquarters.	

SECRET

O.C. 9th Royal Scots
    4th Seaforth do
    6th Gordon do
    7th A & S do ✓
    154 M.G. Coy
    5th Seaforth do
    Lt. PAVLIN.

Dispositions of 5th Bde in the line will be as follows.

Left Battalion

Front Line & Close Support } Right Coy 2½ platoons
                            Left Coy 2½ do.

W. MIRAUMONT Dugouts - Battalion HQ and 1½ platoons of right Coy with 1½ platoons of Left Coy.

Chalk Mound - 2 Companies

Right Battalion

Front Line & close support } Right Coy 2½ Platoons
                             Left Coy 2½ do.

COURCELETTE Dugouts - 3 platoons

Fraser Post
Brigade H.Q.   } 2 Coys.
Dugout at R 35. c 3.4

Robert Adam
BDE. MAJOR 154th INF. BDE.

11 Jany 1917

SECRET

O.C. 9th Royal Scots
4th Seaforth Hrs
4th Gordon Hrs
7th A.D. Hrs ✓
153 M.G. Coy
5th Seaforth Hrs
Lt. PAULIN.

With reference to O.O. 92 & 93.

1. O.C. 7th A.D. Hrs and O.C. 9th R.Scots will each detail an officer to meet buses en route at WOLFE HUTS on 12th Jany and direct parties not going to front line to WOLFE HUTS & OVILLERS HUTS respectively in order to avoid congestion at POZIERES. Buses are due at Red Cross Flag, POZIERES at 4.30 pm. 2 Coys 2/4 Royal Fusiliers will go to WOLFE HUTS and 2 Coys 2 H.L.I. to OVILLERS HUTS.

2. O.C. 7th A.D. Hrs & O.C. 4th Gordon Hrs will leave 1 man per Lewis Gun in the line and 2 orderlies at Battn. H.Q. for 24 hours to assist the 5th Bde.

3. 3 buses will be available for M.G. Coy at OVILLERS HUTS on 12th Jany.

4. O.C. 7th A.D. Hrs and O.C. 4th Gordon Hrs will each detail 1 guide for H.Q. of relieving Battalions. 5th Bde are to put two parties of 1½ platoons each in dug outs at Bn. H.Q. in WEST MIRAUMONT ROAD and O.C. 7th A.D. Hrs will detail 2 guides for these on 12th inst.

5. Coy of 9th R.Scots at COURCELETTE will

2

will be relieved on 12th Jany by 3 platoons of 5th Bde and O.C. 9th R.Scots will detail 3 guides for these. As many of 9th R.S. as accommodation can be found for will proceed on buses on night 12/13th Jany.

6   All guides will have a slip showing the post or position they are to guide parties to.

7   All attached men left behind will proceed by bus on night 13/14 Jany from WOLFE HUTS. They should report there by 7pm.

Acknowledge

Robert Adams
11 Jany 1917 a/BDE. MAJOR 134th INF. BDE

1/7th ARG. & SUTH. HIGHDRS.

WAR DIARY.

FEBRUARY 1917.

WAR DIARY or INTELLIGENCE SUMMARY

7th Arg. & Suth. High'rs Army Form C. 2118.
Ref. Maps:- ABBEVILLE 14.
LENS 11.

(Erase heading not required.)

Instructions regarding War Diaries and Intelligence Summaries are contained in F.S. Regs., Part II. and the Staff Manual respectively. Title Pages will be prepared in manuscript.

Place	Date	Hour	Summary of Events and Information	Remarks and references to Appendices
LE CROTOY	1st		In billets. Continued training.	
"	2nd		" " Football team in Divisional Competition. Played 152nd Bde. Fd. Sec. & beat them 6-0.	A.C.B.
"	3rd		" Continued training.	
"	4th		" Held Church Parade in CINEMA HALL at 10 a.m. During afternoon	A.C.B.
			Battn. marched to BONSILE HUTS.	A.C.B.
BONSILE	5th		Battn. marched to CANCHY starting at 1.30 p.m. 2 Lt. A. Milsom	A.C.B.
			joined Battn. also 30 O.R. reinforcements.	
NOYELLE	6th		" NOYELLE EN-CHAUSSEE starting at 9.15 a.m.	A.C.B.
			(7 miles)	
VACQUERIE	7th		" VACQUERIE-AU-BOUCON starting at 8.45 a.m. 2 Lt A.B. McRae	A.C.B.
			(13¾ miles) joined Battn.	A.C.B.
			NAUGHTON (9¼ miles)	
OEUF	8th		" OEUF starting at 9.45 a.m.	A.C.B.
MONCHY BRETON	9th		" MONCHY BRETON (11½ miles) starting at 9.15 a.m.	A.C.B.
"	10th		In billets.	A.C.B.
ECOIVRES	11th		Training.	A.C.B.
"	12th		Battn. marched to ECOIVRES HUTS (13¾ miles) starting at 10 a.m.	A.C.B.
"	13th		In huts. Supplied working parties & continued training. 2 O.B.	A.C.B.
"	14th		" " " "	A.C.B.
			and also supplied permanent party of 4 Officers & 318 o.r. for 9th Division	A.C.B.
			4 Officers & 158 o.r. for XVII Corps. Artillery	

Army Form C. 2118.

WAR DIARY
or INTELLIGENCE SUMMARY

7th ARG. (SUTH. HIGH)
REF. MAPS LENS 11.
ROLLINCOURT 51B NW1

(Erase heading not required.)

Instructions regarding War Diaries and Intelligence Summaries are contained in F. S. Regs., Part II. and the Staff Manual respectively. Title Pages will be prepared in manuscript.

Place	Date	Hour	Summary of Events and Information	Remarks and references to Appendices
ECOIVRES	15th		In huts. Supplied working parties	APP
"	16th		" at 5.20 a.m. a German aeroplane dropped three bombs on ECOIVRES which wounded some horses	APP
"	17th		" Reinforcement party of 4 Offs + 318 or returned A.B.B.	APP
"	18th		" Batt. Church Parade at 10.30am. 13 or reinforcements joined Batt.	APP
"	19th		" "	APP
"	20th		" "	APP
" + ACQ	21st		During forenoon Batt. marched to billets + huts in ACQ	APP
"	22nd		In billets. Supplied working parties.	APP
"	23rd		" "	APP
"	24th		" " Reinforcements 23 or or joined.	APP
"	25th		" " Bath. Church Parade	APP
"	26th		" "	APP
"	27th		" " During the afternoon Batt. relieved the 5th Arg. & Suth. Highrs. in ECURIE defences, during Offrs. See app.	APP
ECURIE	28th		in ECURIE defences, supplied working parties. (log Annex)	APP

J.W.Sykes?
Lt. Col.
7th Arg. & Suth. Highrs

SECRET.

Appendix I.

Copy No...6..

154th INFANTRY BRIGADE

OPERATION ORDER NO.106.

Reference Maps :-
    Sheet 36 B. 1/40,000.
          51 B. N.W. 1/20,000.
          51 C. N.E. 1/20,000.

1.   The 154th Brigade will relieve the 152nd Brigade in Left Sector on the 27th instant, in accordance with attached Relief Table.

2.   The 152nd Brigade will place one battalion at the disposal of the 154th Brigade for defence of Right Sub-sector.

3.   The relief between M. G. Companies and T.M. Batteries will take place on the 26th., all details to be arranged between C.O's concerned.

4.   In order to maintain definite units for work the following instructions regarding inter-battalion reliefs will be adhered to in future :-

    (a) Relief of battalion lent to Brigade in line will be carried out from ECOIVRES HUTS.

    (b) The battalion in ECURIE will not be employed to hold the line.

5.   The attached working party table shows the work to be undertaken by this Brigade from the night 27/28th inclusive.
     Battalions will arrange to take over all details of these parties from the battalion at present finding them.

6.   Completion of reliefs to be reported to Brigade Headquarters as "Order No.106 complied with".

    ACKNOWLEDGE.

                                                  Captain,
                                                  Brigade Major,
25th February, 1917.   154th Infantry Brigade.

ISSUED AT. /... BY ORDERLY.

Copy No.1 File.
        2 War Diary.
        3 9th Royal Scots.
        4 4th Seaforth Highrs.
        5 4th Gordon Highrs.
        6 7th A. & S. Highrs.
        7 154th M. G. Company.
        8 154th T. M. Battery.
        9 51st Divisional Train.
      10 No-2 Coy. Train.
      11 51st (H) D. "G" (For information).
      12 152nd Infantry Brigade.
      13 153rd Infantry Brigade.
      14 Staff Captain.
      15 Brigade Transport Officer.
      16 Brigade Signal Officer.

RELIEF TABLE.

No. and Date.	Unit.	From.	To.	In relief of.	Remarks.
1. 26/2/17.	154th M.G.Company.	ACQ and ECOIVRES HUTS.	LINE.	152nd M. G. Company.	All details of relief to be arranged between C.O's.concerned.
2. 26/2/17.	154th T.M.Battery.	MAROEUIL.	LINE.	152nd T.M.Battery.	
3. 27/2/17.	Headquarters, 154th Brigade.	ACQ.	MADAGASCAR A.26.d.7.4.	Headquarters, 152nd Brigade.	
4. 27/2/17.	4th Gordon Highrs.	FREVILLERS.	BOIS DE MAROEUIL, F.21.a.2.5.	5th Seaforth Highrs.	Advance party will be sent to take over camp.
5. 27/2/17.	9th Royal Scots.	ECOIVRES HUTS.	Left Sub-Sector.	4th Seaforth Highrs.	All details to be arranged between C.O's. concerned.
6. 27/2/17.	4th Seaforth Highrs.	Left Sub-Sector.	MAROEUIL.	6th Gordon Highrs.	Advance party will be sent to take over billets.
7. 27/2/17.	7th A. & S. Highrs.	ACQ.	ECURIE.	8th A. & S. Highrs.	All details to be arranged between C.O's. concerned.

WORKING PARTY TABLE ISSUED WITH OPERATION ORDER NO. 106.

Location of Battn. furnishing party.	Strength of Party.	Rendezvous and Time.	Working under.	Nature of work.	Remarks.
Battalion at ECURIE. 7th A.& S. Highrs.	1 Officer and 40 other ranks.	To be taken over from 8th A.& S.Hrs. "H" Dump Ecurie Daily 9.15.	A.D.Signals XVII Corps.	Burying Cables.	Details as regards tools etc., to be arranged between C.O's concerned.
Battalion at ECURIE. 7th A.& S. Highrs.	6 Platoons - each of strength not less than 50 other ranks.	HIGH STREET, ECURIE.	C.R.E. C²M20 D10&60	Work on Trenches.	Tools provided by C.R.E. Mid-day rations to be carried.
Battalion at ECURIE. 7th A.& S. Highrs.	Remainder of Battalion.	—	—	—	To work in Left Sub-Sector in advance of GRAND COLLECTEUR under orders of E.C.G. 154th Infantry Brigade.
Battalion at BOIS de MAROEUIL. 4th Gordon Highrs.	410 other ranks.	To be taken over from 6th Gordon Highrs. at MAROEUIL.	A.D.Signals, XVII Corps.	Burying Cables.	Details as regards tools etc., will be sent to 4th Gordon Highrs. by this office.

** 2 **

Location of Battn. Furnishing Party.	Strength of Party.	Rendezvous and Time.	Working under.	Nature of work.	Remarks.
Battalion at MAROEUIL. 4th Seaforth Highrs.	6 Platoons - each of strength not less than 30 other ranks.	ANZIN Church. Officers 9-30 a.m. Other Ranks 10-00 a.m.	Captain MITCHELL, 1/8th Royal Scots.	Work on Trench. 10 a.m. to 4 p.m. (½ hour for dinners).	Tools provided by C.R.E. Mid-day rations to be carried.
Battalion at MAROEUIL. 4th Seaforth Highrs.	2 Platoons.	H.Q. 404th Field Coy. R.E. MAROEUIL at 8-30 a.m.	—	Advanced Divl. Headquarters. 6 hours work excluding interval for dinner.	Tools provided by C.R.E. Mid-day rations to be carried.

S E C R E T.
****

ADDENDUM TO OPERATION ORDER NO.106.
==*=*=*=*=*=*=*=*=*=*=*=*=*=*=*=*=*

Add para. 7 :-

Brigade Headquarters will close at ACQ at 3 p.m., 27th instant, and open at MADAGASCAR, A.26.d.7.4., at same hour.

J a Own
Captain,
Brigade Major,
154th Infantry Brigade.

26th February, 1917.

To all recipients of O.O.No.106.

7th Arg. & Suth. High.drs.

War Diary

March 1917.

WAR DIARY

7th ARG. & SUTH. HIGHrs Army Form C. 2118.

INTELLIGENCE SUMMARY

REF. MAPS :- LENS 11.
ROCLINCOURT 51 B NW 1.

Place	Date MARCH	Hour	Summary of Events and Information	Remarks and references to Appendices
ECURIE	1st		In reserve position supplied working parties.	A.R.B.
"	2nd		" " " " and carrying	
			parties to remove gas cylinders	A.R.B.
"	3rd		from front line	A.R.B.
"	4th		supplied working parties	A.R.B.
"	5th		" " "	A.R.B.
"	6th		" " " casualties 1 or	
			wounded O.R.s	A.R.B.
"	7th		" " "	A.R.B.
"	8th		" " "	A.R.B.
"	9th		" " "	A.R.B.
"	10th		" " " Casualty 1 or wounded O.R.B.	
"	11th		" " " Aircraft very	A.R.B.
"	12th		Enemy Active chiefly in forenoon. D.I. Retaliation forced hostile	A.R.B.
"	13th		Supplied working parties. " enemy artillery activities	A.R.B.
"	14th		" " " on ECURIE.	
			Same as 13th	A.R.B. A.R.B.

2449 Wt. W14957/M90 750,000 1/16 J.B.C. & A. Forms/C.2118/12.

WAR DIARY
or
INTELLIGENCE SUMMARY

7th Arg. ath. Highrs. Army Form C. 2118.
Ref. Maps:- LENS 11
ROCLINCOURT NW 1

(Erase heading not required.)

Place	Date March	Hour	Summary of Events and Information	Remarks and references to Appendices
ECURIE	15th		In reserve position. Supplied working parties. Enemy shelled ECURIE & ROCLINCOURT during day with all Calibres up to 5.9". Casualties 3 or wounded.	
"	16th		During afternoon Batt'n was relieved by 4th Seaforth Highlanders & thereafter proceeded to billets in MAROEUIL.	See App. I.
MAROEUIL	17th		In billets. At 1pm. Batt'n marched off to billets in LA COMTE via AGNIERES, MINGOVAL, BETHONSART & FREVILLERS.	App. 11 " "
LACOMTE	18th		In billets.	App. " "
"	19		" " Training	App. " "
"	20		" " Continued training.	App. " "
"	21		" " "	App. " "
"	22		" " "	App. " "
"	23		" " "	App. " "
"	24		" " XVIIth Corps Commander presented medal ribbons to all officers & men of 154th Brigade at FREVILLERS. Sermon by Field Church Parade 154th Brigade During afternoon Batt'n marched to billets in FREVILLERS.	App. " "
	25th		In billets in FREVILLERS.	App. " "

J.H. Hyslop Lt Col.

Army Form C. 2118.

WAR DIARY
or
INTELLIGENCE SUMMARY

(Erase heading not required.)

7th Argyll & Sutherland Highlanders

REF. MAPS:-
LENS 11
ROCLINCOURT N.W.1
SHEET 36B

Place	Date	Hour	Summary of Events and Information	Remarks and references to Appendices
FREVILLERS	MARCH 26		In billets Continued Training Draft of 140 r. joined Battn.	A/68.
"	27.		"	A/69. Q.D.R.
"	28.		"	
"	29.		" Major Jones died in Hospital Le Touquet	a/68.
"	30.		"	a/68.
"	31.		"	a/68.

H.B. Herbt?
Lt. Col.,
Comdg 7th Highldrs.
7th Arg. & Suth. Highldrs.

Appendix I.

S E C R E T.

AMENDMENT NO.2 TO
154th INFANTRY BRIGADE
OPERATION ORDER NO.109.

Reference Relief Table issued with Operation Order No.109.

No.8:   For "MAROEUIL" to "BAJUS"
        read from "MAROEUIL" to "LA COMTE".

No.9:   Date should read 18.3.17 for 17.3.17.

Acknowledge.

                                      Captain,
                                  Brigade Major,
16th March, 1917.   154th Infantry Brigade.

Copies to :- 154th Brigade Units.
            152nd Infantry Brigade.
            153rd Infantry Brigade.
            51st (H) Division "G".
            Town Majors, BRAY, LA COMTE and BAJUS.

SECRET

AMENDMENT NO.1 TO
154th INFANTRY BRIGADE
OPERATION ORDER NO.109.

Reference Relief Table attached to Operation Order No.109.

No.3: This relief will not take place until the 17th inst.

Acknowledge.

15th March, 1917.

                           Captain,
                       Brigade Major,
            154th Infantry Brigade.

Copies to :- 154th Brigade Units.
            152nd Infantry Brigade.
            153rd Infantry Brigade.
            51st (H) Div. "G".

SECRET.   Copy No... 6 ...

154th INFANTRY BRIGADE

OPERATION ORDER NO.109.

Reference Maps :-
    Sheet 36 B. 1/40,000.
      "   51 C. 1/40,000.

---

1.   The 153rd Brigade will relieve the 154th Brigade in the left sector on the 14th, 15th, 16th and 17th March, in accordance with attached Relief Table.

2.   All details of relief will be arranged between C.O's. concerned.

3.   All distances as laid down in 51st Division No.G.121/4, of 6th March 1917, will be strictly maintained on the march.

4.   The Nos.1 of Vickers gun and Stokes Mortar will remain with incoming teams for 24 hours.

5.   The 4th Seaforth Highlanders will remain in ECURIE after relief and will be at the disposal of the Brigadier General Commanding 153rd Brigade for tactics, but will be under orders of Brigadier General Commanding 154th Brigade for work.

6.   Units will hand over all details of working parties, trench stores, defence schemes, etc, and the 4th and 5th Seaforth Highlanders will submit their handing over report by 15th instant.

7.   Units are reminded that all ranks in the Third Army area must wear their steel helmets when on duty.

8.   All billetting arrangements will be made direct by Units with Town Majors concerned.

9.   The 5th Gordon Highlanders will take over the working parties at present found by 4th Gordon Highlanders at MAROEUIL on the 14th instant.
     The 7th Black Watch will take over working parties at present found by 9th Royal Scots at BOIS DE MAROEUIL on the 17th instant.
     The 5th Gordon Highlanders will take over the working party at present found by detachment 7th A. & S. Highlanders at MAROEUIL on the 17th instant.

10. Completion of all reliefs and moves will be reported at once to Brigade Headquarters by "B.A.B." Code.

11. Brigade Headquarters will close at MADAGASCAR on completion of relief and open at FREVILLERS on arrival.

12. ACKNOWLEDGE.

                                                    Captain,
                                                    Brigade Major,
                                                    154th Infantry Brigade.

13th March, 1917.

ISSUED AT........BY ORDERLY.

```
Copy No. 1  File.
     2  War Diary.
     3  9th Royal Scots.
     4  4th Seaforth Highrs.
     5  4th Gordon Highrs.
     6  7th A. & S. Highrs.
     7  154th M. G. Company.
     8  154th T. M. Battery.
     9  5th Seaforth Highrs.
    10  152nd Infantry Brigade.
    11  153rd Infantry Brigade.
    12  51st (H) Division "G" (For information).
    13  51st Divisional Train.
    14  No.2 Coy. A.S.C..
    15  Town Major, MAROEUIL.
    16  Town Major, BRAY.
    17  Town Major, Frevillers.
    18  Town Major, BAJUS.
    19  Town Major, CAUCOURT.
    20  2nd Canadian Infantry Brigade.
    21  103rd Infantry Brigade.
    22  Staff Captain.
    23  Brigade Transport Officer.
    24  Brigade Signal Officer.
    25  256th Brigade R.F.A.
```

RELIEF TABLE.

No.	Date.	Unit.	From.	To.	Relieved by.	Route.	Remarks.
1.	14.3.17.	4th Gordon Highlanders.	MAROEUIL.	HERMIN.	6th Black Watch.	ACQ-AGNIERES-X Roads D.6.d.95.30.- VILLERS CHATEL-CAUCOURT.	Not to leave MAROEUIL before 2 p.m.
2.	16.3.17.	154th M.G. Coy. LINE.		BRAY.	153rd M.G.Coy.	---	
3.	-do-	154th T.M.Battery.LINE.		BRAY.	153rd T.M.Battery.	---	
4.	-do-	4th Seaforth Highlanders.	Left Subsector.	ECURIE.	6th Black Watch.	---	To come under orders of 153rd Brigade after relief.
5.	-do-	7th A. & S. Highlanders.	ECURIE.	MAROEUIL.	4th Seaforth Highrs.	---	To arrange with 4th Seaforths so that this move does not interfere with the relief.
6.	-do-	9th Royal Scots.	BOIS DE MAROEUIL.	FREVILLERS.	7th Black Watch.	ACQ-CAPELLE FERMONT-AGNIERES-X Rds. D.6.d.1.3.- MINGOVAL.	Rear of column to clear X Roads ACQ E.12.c.1.7. at 2-30 p.m.
7.	-do-	Headquarters, 154th Brigade.	MADAGASCAR.	FREVILLERS.	Headquarters, 153rd Brigade.	No restrictions.	
8.	17.3.17.	7th A. & S. Highlanders.	MAROEUIL.	BAJUS.	7th Gordons.	ACQ-CAPELLE FERMONT -AGNIERES-X Roads D.6.d.1.3.- MINGOVAL.	Rear of column to clear X Roads ACQ, E.12.c.1.7. at 2-30 p.m.
9.	-do-	154th T.M.Battery.	BRAY.	CUVIGNY. COMMY.	---	No restrictions.	To be clear of BRAY by 9-30 a.m.
10.	-do-	154th M.G.Company.	BRAY.	CAUCOURT.	---	-do-	To be clear of BRAY by 10 a.m.
11.	-do-	5th Seaforth Highlanders.	Right Subsector.	BOIS DE MAROEUIL.	5th Gordons.	---	

O.C.
   9th Royal Scots.
   4th Seaforth Highrs.
   7th A. & S. Highrs. ✓
   154th M. G. Company.
   154th T. M. Battery.

Reference Operation Order No.109.

Arrangements for transport of blankets and baggage are being made, and will be issued later.

Quartermasters Stores in ACQ should not be entirely vacated without orders from this office.

13th March, 1917.

                      Captain,
                  Staff Captain,
          154th Infantry Brigade.

Vol. 29

War Diary.

7th Argyll & Sutherland Highrs.

April 1917.

Chapter II

The Crushing of Serbia.

7th Argyll & Sutherland
Highlanders

War Diary

April 1917.

WAR DIARY or **INTELLIGENCE SUMMARY**

Army Form C. 2118.

1st Argyll & Sutherland Highlanders 11/518

LENS • ROCLINCOURT/N.1

(Erase heading not required.)

1917. Hour, Date, Place		Summary of Events and Information	Remarks and references to Appendices
APRIL	1st FREVILLERS	In billets. Held Church Parade	AAB
"	2nd "	Continued training.	AAB
"	3rd "	"	AAB
"	4th "	"	AAB
"	5th CAMP MAROEUIL	at 9.45 am. Battn. marched off to camp at Bois-de-MAROEUIL, via BETHONSART – MINGOVAL – AGNIERES – ACQ – ECOIVRES – BRAY.	AAB
"	6th "	In Camp. Completing equipment for offensive action.	AAB
"	7th "	"	AAB
"	8th "	Held Church Parade at 7.45 am. Battn. moved at 11.30 am. to trenches in A.23.c in preparation for the Offensive attack on the Maître Scottish Churches. Army. The following Officers went with Battn:- Lt. Col. N.G. Hopkin D.S.O., 2nd Capt Cockburn 2nd in Co. Lt. Col. Doolie, Intelligence Officer 2/Lt. Adj. & S.M. L. Oliphant Sig. Off A. Greer "A" Coy. Capt D.J. Robertson, Lts. J.H. Stedman, W.H. Erskine, H. Hislop "B" " Capt W Mitchell M.C. 2/Lts R.N. McLean, R.G.J. McIvor & W.F. King "C" " Capt W Stewart, 2Lts W. Bell, 2Co W. Kenso and A.B. Macnaughton "D" " Cpt R.J.P. Harle, 2Lts C. Hetherwick, A Hughes and J.H. Harris.	See Appendix A AAB J.B. Brown Major

WAR DIARY
INTELLIGENCE SUMMARY

5th Arg. y Suth. High Drs.
Army Form C. 2118.
Ref Maps: LENS 11
ROCLINCOURT 51B NW 1

Hour, Date, Place	Summary of Events and Information	Remarks and references to Appendices
1917 APRIL 9th LINE	At 5:30 a.m. the attack on the VIMY RIDGE was launched by the 9th R.S. on right & 4th Seaforths on left of 152nd Infy Bde. These Battns. were detailed to capture the BLACK LINE. At 7:10 a.m. A & B Coys advanced from their assembly positions to attack the BLUE LINE having two Coys of 4th Gordon Highldrs on left & 5th Seaforths of 152nd Bde on right. Owing to heavy machine gun fire the 9th R.S. had their right & left in no doing lost touch with the Coys on right & left & in no doing lost touch with the Black Line reinforcements. Barrage which was emptying towards the BLUE LINE. Consequently considerably experienced rally but out of action & both these were finally captured. Black and Blue Lines. At 11:25 a.m. C & D Coys advanced from their assembly position the BLUE LINE. In the vicinity of the BROWN LINE where they reached the BLUE LINE they found this line to capture it after they top of the Ridge and advancing to near the top of the Right they found the 152nd Brigade on their right were killed up near the BLUE LINE and our Coys experienced very heavy machine gun and rifle fire from direction of ZEHNER WES. Lay forming mounted attacked & captured three lines of trenches there taking two machine guns & some 10 prisoners including one Regimental Commdr all highly cultivated & was considered & and their patrols were pushed out to near the railway. a.k.b.	See Map Append I. " Append II. " Appx to Appx III.

WAR DIARY

7th ARGYLL & SUTHERLAND HIGHRS Army Form C. 2118.

INTELLIGENCE SUMMARY

REF. MAPS __LENS 11__
__ROCLINCOURT 51B NW.1__

Hour, Date, Place	Summary of Events and Information	Remarks and references to Appendices
1917 APRIL 10th VIMY RIDGE	The 4th Gordons on our left had lost touch with the CANADIANS on their left and patrols found our BROWN LINE objective to be strongly held by the enemy. Two attempts were made to occupy this line by bombing at TOMMY OUSE. Bangalos and also by a flank attack on the right of OUSE. Heavy resistance was experienced & all attempts were unavailing. The wire in front of these lines was found to be uncut. After a few hours heavy artillery bombardment, for the 9th R.S. were ordered to attack this line in conjunction with	A.R.B.
APRIL 11th "	"D" Coy 7th A&S.H. on right & one Coy of 4th Gordons with 7th A&S.H. on left. Two tanks were to assist our [?]attack at 5.30 p.m. but patrols sent out until later and these found that the trench had been evacuated during the preceding bombardment. We at once shared "D" Coy Captured one field gun. Consolidated it. 51st Divn was relieved at night by the 2nd Divn + Battn marched back to huts on ARRAS – ST POL Road of Junction with HABARCQ Road. Casualties Rev. W. JARDINE reported at duty 8th Capt & RO Mitchell M.C. & 2nd Lt A. Jenkins J. Wilson reported from 10th 9th Lt W. BELL wounded.	A.R.B.

Killed -
Wounded - 135
Missing - 10

WAR DIARY / INTELLIGENCE SUMMARY

7th Aug & Suth High'ders
Ref. Maps: Lens 11
France 51 9 N.W.

Army Form C. 2118.

Date	Hour	Place	Summary of Events and Information	Remarks and references to Appendices
1917 APRIL 12th		Lakesset Huts	In Huts on Arras – St. Pol. road.	ORB
13th		"	Refitting & equipping	ORB
14th		"	24 or reinforcements arrived	ORB
15th		"	"	ORB
			At 1 pm Battn left Huts & marched to position in Brown Line near Athies in H15a. No dugouts available, shelters in H14.b and trenches and made with QM Stores moved to ACQ + Bancourt to St Nicholas	See App III ORB
16th		Support Posn	In above shelters. Major E.S.T. Lindsay arrived and assumed command.	ORB
17th		"	In above shelters. A+B Coy moved forward & occupied Sunken Road through H.15a & H.15d from the river Cavalry 4 or killed 18 or wounded	See App IVa ORB
18th		Front Line & Rd Support	A+B Coys in front line C+D in rest in H15a Casualties 4 or killed 1 or wounded	ORB
19th		do do	A+B Coys were relieved by remaining Coys of 9th Royal Scots during the evening During the afternoon 2Lt Donaldson carried out a very successful bombing raid on Ceylon + Colne Trench killing about 30 of the enemy. After relief Coys proceeded to dugouts & shelters in Railway Embankment in H13d. 2Lt Ranson wounded 2 or Casualties 9 or wounded ORB	

7th ARGYLL & SUTHERLAND HIGHRS. O. B. Rs.
Army Form C. 2118.
Ref. Maps:- LENS 11
51/5 N.W.

WAR DIARY
INTELLIGENCE SUMMARY
(Erase heading not required.)

Instructions regarding War Diaries and Intelligence Summaries are contained in F.S. Regs., Part II. and the Staff Manual respectively. Title pages will be prepared in manuscript.

Place	Date 1917 April	Hour	Summary of Events and Information	Remarks and references to Appendices
ATHIES	20th		In Brigade Support in dugouts & shelters in H 13d and H 15 a. Casualties 3 or. wounded.	O.R.B.
	21st		In Support in above place. Major Rinking ordered to proceed to 4th S.A. Infantry. Casualties 2 or. wounded.	O.R.B
	22nd		In above position. Capt. D.F. Bickmore (Norfolks) arrived as 2nd in Command. Casualties 1 or killed, 2 or wounded. At 6.30 pm after all preparation for action had been made the Battn. moved forward to assembly position in # SUNKEN ROAD in H 24 c and d. Battn Hd. Qrs. established at H 24 c 8.0. This move was complete by 11.30 pm. The following Officers went into action with the Battn:— The 2nd in C.O. Lt. Col. A.G. Hyslop D.S.O., Adjt Capt abays, Med. Off. Capt. A.C. Laing, Signal Off. Lt. Sir Donald Cabell, & Liaison Off. Lts. F. Sutherland & J.B. Gregory. "A" Coy. Lt. R.G. HUNTER, Lts. A. Milligan, J. Oliphant & F.L. Philp. "B" " Lt. J.C. Conn, Capt. M.R. Walker, R.G.T. Mavor and W. Donaldson. "C" " Lt. F. Cameron, Lts. A.C. Gibson, J.D. Wilson and A.B. Macnaughton. "D" " Capt. R.J.P. HARLE, Lts. T.I.T. Sloan, A. Hughes and H.W. MUNRO.	O.R.B

App |
| FRONT LINE. | | | | O.R.B. |
| " | 23rd | | At Zero 4.45 a.m. our artillery barrage opened on enemy's line. The 154th Brigade were ordered to attack to capture the BLACK LINE from river to railway & BLUE LINE from river to RAILWAY including the village of ROEUX and the CHEMICAL WORKS on the S. side of RIVER SCARPE, the 17th Divn. having on their left on after fifty & the 153rd Brigade on the left. | See App IV |

Army Form C. 2118.

7th ARGYLL & SUTHERLAND HIGH. DRS.

REF MAPS. LENS 51 NW
FAMPOUX 51 NW 4.

WAR DIARY
INTELLIGENCE SUMMARY
(Erase heading not required.)

Place	Date	Hour	Summary of Events and Information	Remarks and references to Appendices
FRONT LINE	1917 APRIL 23rd (contd)		The 7th A.& S. Highrs with 2 Coys 9th Royal Scots for consolidation purposes were to take the BLACK LINE from River to I.19 a.8.6, the village of ROEUX and BLUE LINE from RIVER to I.20.9.4.6. The 4th Gordons being on the left & the 4th Seaforths in Brigade Reserve. The first wave consisting of two Platoons B Coy on right, two platoons "A" Coy on left were to capture the BLACK LINE. The second wave of two platoons "D" Coy on right, one Platoon "A" Coy in centre & two Platoons "C" Coy on left were to take line of road from river to I.19.B.3.6. At 4.45 a.m. the barrage started and at the same time the Battn which had previously got into assembly positions moved off in the first wave unfortunately pushed into it & had considerable casualties. The German barrage consisting almost entirely of heavy shells was very quick in opening & was very dense. On the left the continuation of CEYLON trench to CORONA trench and Mt PLEASANT WOOD were found to be full of Germans with some machine guns which just behind the rise from near Mt PLEASANT WOOD to ROEUX WOOD a rough trench if joined up shell holes running I.19.c.6.4 was also strongly held and ROEUX WOOD itself was full of snipers & two or five machine guns. Our barrage seemed to support them after their intent doing much harm and the whole attack was delayed at least 1½ hours while our losses particularly in Officers were very heavy.	See App V.

WAR DIARY

7th Arg. ... Highlanders Army Form C. 2118.

INTELLIGENCE SUMMARY

REF. MAPS. LENS 11
57 B NW
FAMPOUX 57 B1 NW 4.

Place	Date 1917	Hour	Summary of Events and Information	Remarks and references to Appendices
FRONT LINE	APRIL 23 (cont'd)		Our men advanced firing from the hip and our Lewis guns were employed to trickle away and and about 6.30am the Germans began coming out from principally CEYLON & COROPA trenches. at this time turned mattero & the BLACK LINE of the railway about Consolidation of stopping points began at once. About 5.30am. 1 & 9 Royal Scots had been drawn into the village of ROEUX in support. Our men now pushed forward into the Cemetery bombarded and the Tank following then to the N.W of the village of ROEUX & snipers from houses which were troublesome. They then went towards the railway bridge & the S. front of our men got into ROEUX WOOD & into the outskirts of the village but this wood had not been properly cleared & snipers & stationary Machine guns gave much trouble & Particularly to runners at the time the Officers became casualties & by this time 2nd Batty... had become very much mixed up. & two villages bombing parties began to clear the houses & cop. & a considerable number were cleared, but the Germans left the houses gardens seemed to be connected as the next still machine guns were acting from many of the upper stories. All this took a considerable time & the advance on the left had meanwhile not come in line with us.	RR.B [signature]

7th ARG. & SUTH. HIGH'DS
REF MAPS:- LENS 11
51B NW
FAMROUX 51B NW 4

Army Form C. 2118.

WAR DIARY
INTELLIGENCE SUMMARY
(Erase heading not required.)

Instructions regarding War Diaries and Intelligence Summaries are contained in F.S. Regs., Part II and the Staff Manual respectively. Title pages will be prepared in manuscript.

Place	Date 1917	Hour	Summary of Events and Information	Remarks and references to Appendices
FRONT LINE	APRIL 23RD cont?		At about 10.30am a strong counter attack from direction T.14 a forced us out of the northern end of the village but the pattrols parties dug themselves into shell-holes near the light railway through T.19 central and held this line till evening when they were relieved. Meanwhile strong points had being constructed in front of MT. PLEASANT NG'D near T.19.g.8.0 and T.19.c.7.8. When the attack of the 4th Leafridge developed on our left we had no organised parties to support them. that new Germany there were up to subject them the village had machine gun fire from the southern part of the River seriously hampered any movements and fell up of platoon which had been sent round by the right bank of the river to assist on that bank. Our counter attack during the forenoon became somewhat accounted for. Casualties: Killed:- Lts Hunter Cameron, Hg Mevel, Sloan, Munro & Walker 148 or. Wounded:- Capt Harle, Lts Cameron, Otto, Killeen, Gibson, Milligan, Sutherland M.C., ALB. Oliphant, Hughes Macnaughton and 220 or. Missing 2Lt F.C. Hislop & 39 or.	
SUNKEN RD.	24th		The Battn was relieved during the evening by the 9th N. Fusiliers and thereupon withdrew to the Sunken Road. Shelling was intermittent during the night. Some enemy snipers from posts to northern edge of Mt. Pleasant (one was captured but the remainder took refuge in a small wood in upon) have bothered us very much about T19.C.14 and were effectively dealt with by our Stokes guns. Our Lewis guns places in	

WAR DIARY
INTELLIGENCE SUMMARY

7th Arg. & Suth. High'rs.
Army Form C. 2118.
Ref. Maps. LENS 11 51/2 NW
FAMPOUX 51/3 NW 4.

Place	Date	Hour	Summary of Events and Information	Remarks and references to Appendices
SUNKEN Rd	24th/25th Cont'd		in shellholes on river bank accounted for nine of these & the remaining two gave themselves up. Casualties 2 or. killed 50 or. wounded	A.R.B.
ARRAS	25th	2 a.m.	Batt'n was relieved by 11th Suffolks & thereafter proceeded to billets in ARRAS.	See App. III
		6.30pm	Batt'n entraining at ARRAS, detrained at LIGNY-ST-FLOCHEL they proceeded fifty by motor lorry & half by route march to PENIN. Transport had marched direct from ARRAS during the day.	A.R.B.
		11.30pm	billets in PENIN	A.R.B.
PENIN	26th		Res. in billets. Bathing parades held at TINCQUES.	A.R.B.
"	27th		" " Refitting.	A.R.B.
"	28th		" " Resting off 38 ors. arrived. C.E. Hyslop took over command of 157th Brigade during Brigadiers above on short leave.	A.R.B.
"	29th		" " Held Church Parade.	A.R.B.
"	30th		" " Company intensive training. Total strength 25 Off. 605 or.	A.R.B.

J.A. Birkmore Major
Commanding
7. Arg. & Suth. Highrs

S E C R E T.

Copy No. 8

Appendix II.

331/2

NOT TO BE TAKEN INTO THE TRENCHES.

154th BRIGADE INSTRUCTIONS WITH REGARD TO FORTHCOMING OFFENSIVE OPERATIONS.

These instructions cancel all previous instructions which should be at once destroyed.

1. OBJECT OF THE OPERATION.

The primary object of the forthcoming offensive is to capture the Southern portion of the VIMY RIDGE in conjunction with the Canadian Corps on the North.

The XVIIth Corps objective is to establish a line along the German Third Line System which runs from LE POINT DU JOUR on the South - MAESON DE LA COTE - to COMMANDANT'S HOUSE on the North.

2. TROOPS AVAILABLE.

There are four Divisions available for the operation and on Zero day they will be disposed as under :-

On the Right of XVIIth Corps = 9th Scottish Division.
On the centre   - do -   = 34th Division.
On the Left   - do -   = 51st (H) Division.
In Reserve   = 4th Division.
On the left of the 51st Division will be the 1st Canadian Division.

3. THE 51st DIVISION'S OBJECTIVE.

The final objective for the 51st Division is to capture MAISON DE LA COTE - COMMANDANT'S HOUSE line.

Before arriving at this line there are four complete systems of trenches to capture. These systems will be known as follows :-

(a) THE BLACK LINE.
This includes the German front line system of trenches, viz. Firing Line, Support Line and Reserve Line.

(b) THE BLUE LINE.
The enemy's second line system organised into two trench lines.

(c) THE BROWN LINE.
The enemy's third line which is rapidly growing into a strong defensive line, and is behind the crest of the hill.

(d) THE GREEN LINE.
Which is the line of observation.

** 2 **

These lines, frontages and boundaries of the Division, Brigades, and Battalions of this Brigade, are shown on Map No.1 (issued with previous instructions).

4. METHOD OF ATTACK.

(a) The attack of the 51st (H) Division will be carried out as follows.

152nd Brigade plus 1 Battalion 153rd Brigade on the Right.

154th Brigade plus 1 Battalion 153rd Brigade on the Left.

2 Battalions 153rd Brigade Divisional Reserve.

152nd and 154th Brigades with 5 Battalions each, will both carry attack right through to the BROWN LINE, supplying their own carrying parties, etc.

The attack of the 154th Brigade will be carried out as follows :-

The 9th Royal Scots on the Right and the 4th Seaforth Highrs. on the Left will capture and consolidate the BLACK LINE.

The 7th A. & S. Highrs. less 2 Companies on the right and the 4th Gordon Highrs. less 2 Companies on the Left will capture and consolidate the BLUE LINE.

2 Companies 7th A. & S. Highrs. on the Right and 2 Companies 4th Gordon Highrs. on the Left, supported by 2 Companies 7th Black Watch will capture and consolidate the BROWN LINE.

2 Companies 7th Black Watch will be retained as Brigade Reserve.

The method of attack will be the "Leap Frog" system, as already laid down in Divisional instructions for the attack.

(b) The 9th Royal Scots will be formed up in the old French trenches in front of BONNAL between Saps 20 and 22 inclusive on a 2 Company front with Companies on a 2 platoon front thus making 4 double waves.

The 4th Seaforth Highrs., less 5 platoons, will form up in the old French trenches in front of BONNAL between Saps 22 and 23 with 3 platoons in front forming 1 double wave, the remaining 2 Companies forming 2 double waves thus making 3 double waves in all.

Each double wave will be responsible for the clearance of the line allotted to it, special men being told off in each wave to deal with dug-outs.

The half Battalions for the capture of the BLUE LINE will assemble in BONNAL and will remain there until it is time for them to move off in order to catch up the protective barrage in front of the BLACK LINE. They will then move off, using artillery formations if possible, with Companies on a 2 platoon front thus making 2 double waves when deployed.

The half Battalions detailed to capture the BROWN LINE will assemble in GRAND COLLECTEUR and will remain there until it is time for them to move off in order to catch up the protective barrage in front of the BLUE LINE. They will then move off in artillery formations as long as possible with Companies on a 2 platoon front thus making 2 double waves when deployed. Cont on

Addenda No 2 of 6th April

3

The 2 Companies 7th Black Watch detailed to support the troops assaulting the BROWN LINE will assemble in trenches below the ridge running through ABRI CENTRALE. They will move off in artillery formations 200 yards in rear of the rearmost troops assaulting the BROWN LINE AND will consolidate 8 strong points each consisting of one Lewis Gun and one platoon. The positions of these strong points will have to be decided by the officers on the spot but they should be on the West of the Ridge and the line of TOMMY TRENCH would appear to be the most satisfactory. When these points are consolidated the right Company will be at the disposal of the 7th A. & S. Highrs. and the left Company at the disposal of the 4th Gordon Highrs.

The remaining 2 Companies 7th Black Watch and Headquarters will remain in the trenches under the Ridge running through ABRI CENTRALE under Brigade orders.

The positions of assembly of troops are shown on attached plan "A".

Each wave after it has taken its objective must be prepared to render assistance to the wave in front of it if that wave is in difficulties, but only such men as are not employed in "mopping up" are available for this duty.

A tracing will shortly be issued to Battalions showing the positions of known German Headquarters. Special men should be detailed to search these Headquarters and send back to Brigade Headquarters all documents, maps, etc. found therein. If possible, a man who can read German should be one of this party and it should be explained to him roughly what is of value.

(c) The attack on the Salient on the LILLE ROAD will form a separate operation but will be carried out simultaneously with the remainder of the attack and in close touch with the 1st Canadian division.

The O.C. 4th Seaforth Highrs. will therefore detail one Company and one Platoon to attack this Salient from the South and establish themselves on a line from A.22.b.35.40. along FUNK, FOB, and LAY TRENCHES to the trench junction A.23.a.2.6.

When the BLACK LINE has been taken this party will be available for carrying parties, etc.

The remainder of the 4th Seaforth Highrs. will move with their left on the WITTELSBACHER WEG.

(d) The objectives of the 1st Canadian Division on the left will not coincide exactly with the various lines and objectives allotted to the 154th Brigade.

Both on the BLACK and BLUE LINES the 1st Canadian Division objectives are in advance of those of the 154th Brigade.

In order to ensure proper connection the 4th Seaforth Highrs. on reaching the BLACK LINE will push forward posts so as to connect with the 1st Canadian Division at A.17.d.4.2.

Similarly on reaching the BLUE LINE the 4th Gordon Highrs. will throw forward posts to connect with the 1st Canadian Division at A.18.b.9.1.

** 4 **

(e) In order to allow troops on the South to advance simultaneously to the assault of the BLUE LINE there must be a considerable halt on the BLACK LINE. The advance on the BLUE LINE will, therefore, not commence until Zero plus 2 hours and 6 mins. but the 4th Seaforth Highrs. will push forward posts to connect with the 1st Canadian Division on their left at Zero plus 1 hour and 20 mins.   Z+1.40

The assault of the SWISCHEN STELLUNG on the 1st Canadian Division's front and our attack on the BLUE LINE will be carried out simultaneously, the barrage lifting off this trench at Zero plus 2 hours and 40 mins. The 4th Gordon Highrs. will then push out their posts to connect with the 1st Canadian Division on their left at Zero plus 2 hours and 55 mins.

As at present the subsequent advance to the BROWN LINE will not take place till Zero plus 6 hours and 46 mins.

(f) In all cases where a stationary and protective barrage is placed 200 to 300 yards in front of a trench battle posts with Lewis Guns or Bombing Squads should be pushed forward as close to the barrage as possible. On reaching the BROWN LINE they must be pushed well in advance to exploit success.   Z+5.55

(g) In the advance to the BROWN LINE when the crest of the hill is reached patrols should be pushed quickly forward as close as possible to the barrage to report on the state of the wire in front of the BROWN LINE before the main body expose themselves over the crest.

6. **CONSOLIDATION.**

After each objective has been captured and cleared up the work of consolidation must commence at once.

After the capture of the BLUE LINE the Os.C. 9th Royal Scots and 4th Seaforth Highrs. will reorganise their Battalions in order to supply carrying parties from the troops who have captured the German front and support lines to feed the BLUE LINE.

Between the BLACK and BLUE LINES at least one strong point capable of accommodating one platoon and 2 Vickers guns should be constructed and garrisoned by the troops who have taken the BLUE ~~BLACK~~ LINE. A good position for this post would be about A.24.a.10.85. *it will be made & garrisoned by the 7th A.& S.H.*

The troops who have captured the BROWN LINE will consolidate a line just West of the Ridge as the main line of resistance, the BROWN LINE itself then being occupied by posts and becoming the line of observation.

As soon as possible special parties R.Es. and Pioneers will be detailed to move forward for the consolidation of these posts and the opening up of communications.

As soon as it is quite certain the troops have reached the various lines notice boards marked "BLACK LINE", etc., and also squares of tin will be sent up under Brigade arrangements. These will be placed on the line taken so that they are easily visible from the rear.

** 5 **

7. **HEADQUARTERS AND COMMUNICATIONS.**

    Communication trenches are arranged as follows :-

<u>Main In.</u>   ANZIN - BARRICADE TUNNEL - BLANCHARD.

<u>Front System In.</u>   AVENUE "A" and BIDOT AVENUE.

<u>Main Out.</u>   OLD FANTOME - ECURIE AVENUE - MADAGASCAR.

<u>Front System Out.</u>   OLD FANTOME - AVENUE "G" - RIPPERT.

152nd Brigade Area.

<u>Main In.</u>   GENIE AVENUE - TRENCH 40 - THURSDAY AVENUE.

<u>Front System In.</u>   FISH AVENUE - WEDNESDAY AVENUE.

<u>Main Out.</u>   THURSDAY AVENUE - NEW TRENCH - FILATIERS AVENUE - GENIE AVENUE as far as junction of Trench 40.

<u>Front System Out.</u>   THURSDAY AVENUE - SEAFORTH AVENUE.

    Advanced Divisional Headquarters, MAROEUIL, F.27.b.9.5.

152nd Brigade.
Advanced Brigade Headquarters, A.29.a.6.1.
2 Right Battalions "I" Work A.29.b.7.5.
2 Left Battalions "L" Work A.29.b.20.75.
Fifth Battalion : ROCLINCOURT.

153rd Brigade.
Advanced Brigade Headquarters, A.28.b.20.50.
Battalion Headquarters, FERME DES CAVES and A.28.a.40.45.

154th Brigade.
Advanced Brigade Headquarters, A.28.b.65.80.
2 forward Battalions, A.23.c.4.5.
4th Gordon Highrs. A.22.d.80.25.
7th A. & S. Highrs. A.23.c.2.1. 4.2
Fifth Battalion : ABRI CENTRALE.
    7th Black Watch A.22.d.40.30

    Battalion Headquarters should be marked by a flag for assistance of Orderlies.

    Commanding Officers will on no account leave their Headquarters or move their Headquarters without reference to Brigade Headquarters. Before Battalion Headquarters are advanced an Officer must go forward and select the new Headquarters, position of which must be reported at once to Brigade Headquarters and the Units on either flank and as clearly marked as possible.

8.   Administrative Instructions have been issued separately by the Staff Captain.

9. Police arrangements, Stragglers' Posts, etc., will be issued separately. The Brigade will have to find 1 officer, 1 N.C.O. and 15 privates for this duty. They should be found from regimental police and ear marked at once. The allotment is as follows :-

	Officer.	N.C.O.	Privates.
9th Royal Scots.	-	-	4.
4th Seaforth Highrs.	-	-	4.
4th Gordon Highrs.	1.	-	3.
7th A. & S. Highrs.	-	1.	4.

The Officer in charge of Trench Traffic Control in this Brigade Sector will be 2/Lt. W. G. MURRAY of the 4th Gordon Highrs. and his Headquarters will be in the BARRICADE TUNNEL.

10. Officers and Other Ranks must be left out of action in accordance with S.S.135 "Instructions for the Training of Divisions for Offensive Action" amended.

11. Artillery barrage table will be issued later. *See Amendment*

12. ACTION OF MACHINE GUNS.

There are 48 Machine Guns available in the Division, and these will be employed as follows :-

(a) In creating a barrage fire during the advance and to and consolidation of the BLACK and BLUE LINES.

(b) In assisting in defence of the various lines by a barrage fire if attack fails.

(c) In strengthening the various lines or posts when consolidating.

(d) In harrassing the enemy behind the BROWN LINE from new positions.

At the commencement of the operation the 48 guns will be employed as follows :-

On barrage = 36.
Under each Brigade's orders for strengthening lines and strong points = 6.

On the consolidation of the BLACK LINE 4 more guns from the barrage come under Brigade orders.

On consolidation of strong points between BLACK and BLUE LINES 2 more guns from the barrage come under Brigade orders.

On consolidation of the BROWN LINE 4 guns from the barrage come under Brigade orders.

The remaining 16 guns will fall into reserve, 4 guns being under the orders of each Brigade and 8 being in Divisional Reserve.

13. CARRYING PARTIES.

Up to the time the BLACK LINE has been captured and cleared the 2 Companies 7th Black Watch in Brigade Reserve will provide all necessary carrying parties.

As soon as the BLACK LINE has been captured and cleared troops not required for consolidating the BLACK LINE will be organised into carrying parties and will carry from Advanced Brigade Dumps in BONNAL Trench to the BLACK LINE and later to the BLUE LINE when it has been taken, the 2 Companies, 7th Black Watch continuing to fill the Dumps in BONNAL.

14. SIGNAL COMMUNICATIONS.

The 1st Canadian Division are using BLUE and YELLOW flags to denote their position in the trenches. These will be waved to and fro.

(a) WIRELESS.

One trench set is allotted to the Brigade. During the attack this trench set will be working.

As soon as the situation is cleared up this set will be sent forward and allotted to a definite Sector Commander.

(b) POWER BUZZERS AND AMPLIFIERS.

2 Power buzzers and 1 amplifier are allotted to the Brigade. Their range is restricted to 1200 yards.

During the attack they may be employed as an emergency means of communication between Battalions and Brigade. When the situation is cleared up power buzzers should be sent up to strong points in the BLUE and BROWN LINES about B.13.c. The amplifier will be sent up to selected Battalion Headquarters in the BLACK LINE.

Co-operation between power buzzers, amplifiers and trench wireless sets should be arranged.

Carrying parties and necessary guides must be provided by the Sector Commander to whom the sets may be allotted by the Brigade.

(c) PIGEONS.

3 stations of 2 birds each are allotted to the Brigade. These will be allotted as follows :-

    (a) Troops for the BLACK LINE.
    (b) Troops for the BLUE LINE.
    (c) Troops for the BROWN LINE.

(d) VISUAL.

A central visual receiving station will be established at the Divisional O.P. in TRENCH 40 about G.4.a.6.5. This station will be equipped to receive messages from the whole Divisional front. Battalions should take up with them discs, shutters and lamps.

Secret:

To o/c
1/7 Argyll & Sutherland Highlanders

13

Amendment to
154th Brigade Instructions with regard to forthcoming offensive operations

Para. 14. Signal Communications

(e) Runners.
During the attack Runners from Companies should return straight to their respective Battalions.

As soon as Battalion Headquarters move the Brigade will establish a relay station at the head of the buried cable. Position of this station will be the end of the tunnel which starts from Avenue "C" to the left of the Bonnal trench and runs direct towards the enemy's front line.

Runners from forward area should strike this Relay Station on route.

A. Kemp.
2/Lt. R.E.(+)
Sigs. 154th Inf. Brigade

3.4.17

8

D.D. messages to be sent and each message sent at least three times. The central receiving station will not send forward or acknowledge messages and will not be manned by night.

(e) **RUNNERS.**

During the attack Runners from Companies should return straight to their respective Battalions.

As soon as Battalion Headquarters move the Brigade will establish a relay station at the head of the buried cable. Position of this station will be Sap 21, A.23.c.7.7.

Runners from forward area should strike this relay station on route.

(f) **LIGHT SIGNALS.**

Light signal communication between the front line and Batteries through any intermediate station which can be established. The code of signals will be issued later. These signals will be fired from Very Pistols and will be continued until the required response is made by the Artillery. *These signals come into force at 12 noon of on 7th April & they are not to be used during the barrage covering the assault.*

These Signals do not come into force until orders to that effect are issued from Brigade Headquarters and they are not to be used during the barrage covering the assault.

The S.O.S. Signal which has hitherto been given by rocket only will, when this system comes into force, consist of a succession of green lights of any kind whatsoever. This fact should be made clear to all personnel carrying any means of signal lights so that there may be no misunderstanding. Care will have to be taken that with so many individuals in possession of means of giving the S.O.S. Signal it is not used unnecessarily. *The S.O.S. Signal laid down in 22867 will not be used after 12 noon 7th April*

The signal for lengthening ~~for lengthening~~ range is premarily intended for use by Artillery personnel and should only be used by Infantry when urgently necessary.

The Code Signals will probably be :-

Succession of GREEN Lights --- S.O.S.
Succession of WHITE Lights --- Lenghhen Range.

by
The increment which the range will be increased or decreased will be 100 yards.

15. **LIAISON.**
    Artillery.

A senior Artillery Officer will be with Brigade Headquarters throughout the operation, who will be in direct telephonic communication with the C.R.A. and the Group Commander, also the O.P. Exchange.

9

A selected Officer will be with each Battalion Headquarters. This Officer will not leave the O.C. Battalion without an express order, or permission of the latter. He will have a direct line to the Brigade Liaison Officer and the O.P. Exchange.

Infantry.

Each Battalion will keep one of its surplus officers at Battalion Headquarters to act as Liaison Officer between Battalion and Brigade and between Battalions on right and left as the case may be.

Machine Guns.

The O.C. 154th Machine Gun Company will detail one officer of his surplus officers to act as Liaison Officer with Brigade Headquarters. This Officer will join Brigade Headquarters at least an hour before Zero.

R.E's.

There will be an R.E. Liaison Officer at Brigade Headquarters who will arrange to open up communications as in 4 when the B.G.C. 154th Brigade considers this can be done.

16. USE OF GAS PROJECTORS.

100 guns for firing Liven's Gas Projector have been allotted to the Division.

These are to be employed against the Salient on the LILLE ROAD as follows :-

Target "I". Sunken Road about A.22.b.7.3. to A.22.b.9.7. - 25 guns - placed in disused trenches A.23.c.5.8.

Target "J". As above. Guns in disused trenches A.22.d.8.6.

Target "K". Group of dugouts in the German line about A.23.a.80.55. to A.23.a.25.60. - 50 guns.

See page 3 Amendment

The discharge from projectors will take place 15 minutes before the Artillery bombardment begins.

If the wind is unfavourable at that time, the discharge will take place between the time fixed and Zero - 6 hours, at first favourable opportunity.

The following precautions will be taken by all troops :-

(a) "Gas Alert" precautions will be maintained while the gas bombs are in the trenches.

(b) Bombs will not be discharged over the heads of our troops.

One Section of 4" Stokes Mortars for firing gas shell have been allotted to the Division.

These will be used against the tunnels, dug-outs and Company Headquarters opposite extreme right of the 152nd Brigade.

17. **CO-OPERATION WITH AIRCRAFT.**

    (a) The following procedure will be adhered to in the matter of lighting flares for indicating the positions reached by Infantry in the various stages of the assault.

    (b) Infantry will be prepared to light flares (RED) and will be on the look-out for the contact aeroplane at :-

    (1) Zero plus 1 hour, i.e., after BLACK LINE should be captured.

    (2) Zero plus 3 hours 10 mins., i.e., after BLUE LINE should be captured.

    (3) Zero plus 8 hours 10 mins., i.e., after BROWN LINE should be captured.

    The flares will be lighted when the aeroplane actually calls for them.

    (c) Contact aeroplanes working with the Division are marked with one black band under the left plane (when looking in direction in which aeroplane is travelling). The black band is prolonged to the rear by a black streamer.

    In addition to above, Battalions will be prepared to use the ground signal panels and lamps for communication with aeroplane.

    All information thus obtained will be dropped at the Corps Dropping Station at F.29.a.3.3., when it will be transmitted to the Division.

18. **R.E. AND PIONEERS.**

    Working parties will be held in readiness as stated below :-

    (a) Making communication trench from mouth of FISH TUNNEL, A.30.a.0.4. to German lines.

    (b) Making communication trench from tunnel L.21.a. (A.23.c.3.8.) to the German lines.

    (c) Making communication trench from the tunnel L.27.b. (A.22.b.4.3.) to the German lines.

    In cases (b) and (c), the parties with necessary materials and tools will be accommodated in the tunnels mentioned during Y/Z night.

    (d) Opening up direct road from ROCLINCOURT towards THELUS.

    This road will be completed as far as BONNAL TRENCH on or before the night Y/Z.

    (e) Sufficient R.E. will be held in readiness to move forward and consolidate strong points as follows :-

    After /-

11.

After capture of BLACK LINE.

Trench at A.24.d.10.80.
Trench junction at A.24.a.2.9.
Trench junction with THELUS ROAD A.17.d.70.15.

After capture of BLUE LINE.

Trench junction at B.19.d.5.9.
Trench junction at B.19.b.3.9.
Trench junction at B.13.c.6.9.

On completion of work on strong points the R.E. Officer in charge will report to senior Officer on the spot that work is finished and return via Brigade Headquarters bringing details of work.

(f) 184th Tunnelling Company will send forward parties of Officers and men, as soon as the situation permits, to search the German lines for the purpose of discovering and clearing dug-outs for use, etc.

19. ACTION OF STOKES MORTARS.

12 Stokes Mortars, ie. 154th Trench Mortar Battery plus half 153rd Trench Mortar Battery, are allotted to the Brigade. They will be employed on Zero day as follows :-
(a) Bombardment of front line trenches from Zero till Zero plus 3 minutes.
(b) Bombardment of support line (where possible) from Zero plus 3 minutes till Zero plus 6 minutes. At Zero plus 6 minutes all Mortars will cease fire.

The O.C. 154th Trench Mortar Battery will select emplacements for these 12 Mortars and will arrange for storage of ammunition up to 200 rounds per Mortar.

After the above 6 minutes bombardment the guns of the 153rd Trench Mortar Battery will come under orders of the B.G.C. 153rd Brigade.

The guns of the 154th Trench Mortar Battery will become available to support any portion of the attack where they may be required. The O.C. 154th Trench Mortar Battery will at once get in touch with Brigade Headquarters and await further orders.

20. ACKNOWLEDGE. *See also amendment page 3*

J A Devine
Captain,
Brigade Major,
154th Infantry Brigade.

1st April 1917.

A

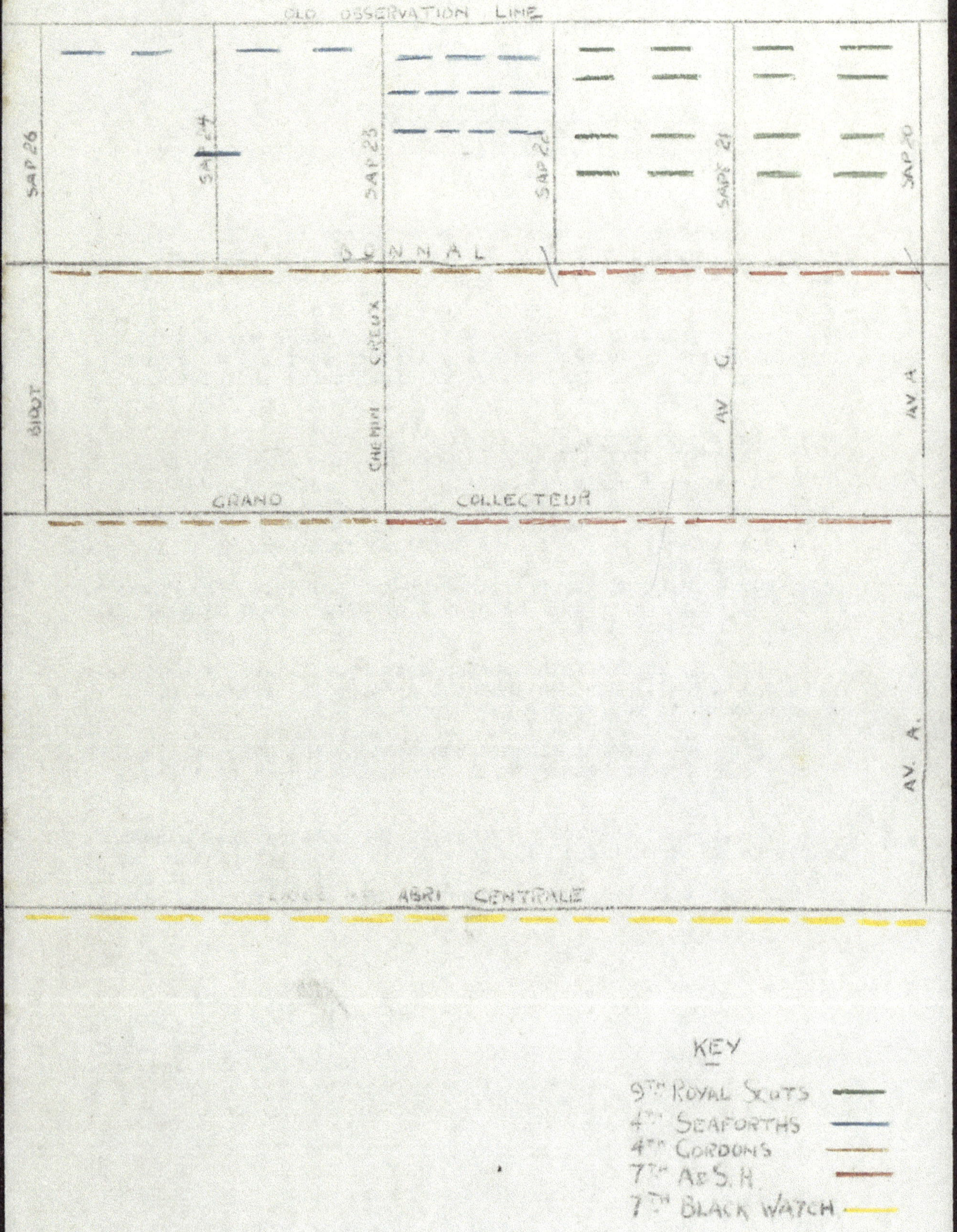

OLD OBSERVATION LINE

SAP 26 | SAP 24 | SAP 23 | SAP 22 | SAP 21 | SAP 20

BONNAL

BIDOT | CHEMIN S. REUX | AV. C. | AV. A.

GRAND COLLECTEUR

AV. A.

ABRI CENTRALE

KEY
9TH ROYAL SCOTS ───
4TH SEAFORTHS ───
4TH GORDONS ───
7TH A & S.H. ───
7TH BLACK WATCH ───

S E C R E T.
****

Copy No. 4

154th INFANTRY BRIGADE
OPERATION ORDER NO.112.
****

Reference Map :-
Sheet 51.B.N.W.1 Ed.6A. 1/10,000.

In continuation of 154th Brigade Instructions No.ZZ.1/2.

1.   On ZERO day at an hour to be notified later (called ZERO hour) the XVIIth Corps on the left of the Third Army and the Canadian Corps on the Right of the First Army will attack the VIMY RIDGE and establish a line beyond the German third line system from the River SCARPE northwards through MAISON de la COTE - COMMANDANT'S HOUSE to the East of THELUS.

The 154th Brigade will attack on the extreme left of the XVIIth Corps in conjunction with the 1st Canadian Division on the left and the 152nd Brigade on the right.

2.   The final objective of the 154th Brigade is to capture the MAISON de la COTE - COMMANDANT'S HOUSE line and establish a line of observation to the EAST of this line.

The attack will be carried out in three stages :-

(a) 1st Objective - The enemy's front line system up to and including the BLACK LINE.

(b) 2nd Objective - The enemy's second line system, i.e., the BLUE LINE.

(c) 3rd Objective - The enemy's third line, i.e., the BROWN LINE.

These lines are shown on Map No.1 already issued.

3.   The frontage of the 154th Brigade is from AVENUE "A" inclusive to ARRAS - LILLE ROAD inclusive.

The boundaries of the attack will be :-

On the SOUTH.
From AVENUE "A" to A.23.b.9.0. - trench junctions at Points 11 and 66, both inclusive - B.13.d.24.00. - B.14.c.0.2. - B.14.d.1.1.

On the NORTH.
LILLE ROAD inclusive where it cuts the front line at A.22.b.2.2. - trench junction A.23.a.47.87. inclusive - trench junction A.17.d.37.20. exclusive - trench junction A.18.c.98.78. xxxxxxxxx exclusive - thence in a straight line to Southern boundary of FARBUS WOOD.

4. The 154th Brigade plus 1 Battalion 153rd Brigade will attack on a frontage of 2 Battalions.

The 9th Royal Scots on the Right and the 4th Seaforth Highrs. on the Left will attack and capture the BLACK LINE.

The 4th Seaforth Highrs. will also detail 5 platoons to attack and capture the German front and support lines in the Salient from where the German front line crosses the LILLE ROAD inclusive to trench junction at A.23.a.2.6.

The 7th A. & S. Highrs. less 2 Companies on the Right and the 4th Gordon Highrs. less 2 Companies on the Left will attack and capture the BLUE LINE.

2 Companies 7th A. & S. Highrs. on the Right and 2 Companies 4th Gordon Highrs. on the Left, supported by 2 Companies 7th Black Watch, will attack and capture the BROWN LINE.

The 7th Black Watch less 2 Companies will be in Brigade Reserve.

The dividing line between Battalions will be :-

On the BLACK LINE - A.23.b.0.4.

On the BLUE LINE - A.24.a.1.9.

On the BROWN LINE - B.14.a.65.40.

The attack will be carried out in the "Leap Frog" system Battalions being deployed on a 2 Company front, Companies on a 2 platoon front.

The assault on the BLACK LINE will take place at ZERO plus 34 mins.

The assault on the BLUE LINE will take place at ZERO plus 2 hours and 43 mins.

The assault on the BROWN LINE will take place at ZERO plus 7 hours and 24 mins.

All other details of the attack have been laid down in ZZ.1/2.

5. After the capture of the BROWN LINE the main line of resistance to be consolidated will be on the Western side of the crest of the RIDGE running Southwards through B.13. and B.19., the BROWN LINE then becoming the line of observation.

6. The attack will be preceded by a 4 days' bombardment and wire cutting commencing on "V" day.

Detailed Artillery arrangements, barrage table, etc., have already been issued.

7. The 3 Machine Gun Companies will cover the attack with a barrage as far as the BLUE LINE.

6 guns of 154th M. G. Company will be at the disposal of B.G.C. 154th Brigade for use during the attack or for consolidation.

** 3 **

8. Prior to or during bombardment when wind is favourable 200 guns firing gas drums and 8 4" Stokes Mortars firing in all 1600 gas shells will be used.

9. The action of R.E. and Pioneers has already been detailed in ZZ.1/2.

10. Contact patrols will fly over captured lines about ZERO plus 1 hour, ZERO plus 3 hours 10 mins., ZERO plus 8 hours 10 mins. Infantry will be prepared to light RED flares at these hours. *Zero + 9 hours 15 minutes.*

11. All Battalions of the 154th Brigade and 7th Black Watch will be in Assembly Positions by 2-30 a.m. and code words as under will be sent to Brigade Headquarters by 3 a.m. to denote that all is ready :- *9 R S & 4 S.H. to be clear of Roussal by 2 a.m.*

   9th Royal Scots --- GREEN.
   4th Seaforth Highrs. --- UNTHANK.
   4th Gordon Highrs. --- McCLINTOCK.
   7th A. & S. Highrs. --- HYSLOP.
   7th Black Watch. --- SUTHERLAND.

12. Lieut. Lindsay, Brigade Intelligence Officer, will be at MADAGASCAR at 6 p.m. on "Y" day and midnight Y/Z night to synchronise watches with an Officer of the Divisional Staff. Representatives from each Unit of the Brigade and 7th Black Watch will meet Lieut. Lindsay at Brigade Headquarters at 7 p.m. on "Y" day and 1 a.m. on Y/Z night.

13. Brigade Headquarters will open in Battle Position in SABLIERE A.28.b.65.80. at 8 p.m. on X/Y night.

  ACKNOWLEDGE.

              J A Dunn
                Captain,
                Brigade Major,
4th April, 1917.   154th Infantry Brigade.

ISSUED AT 7-30 a.m. BY ORDERLY.

Copy No. 1 9th Royal Scots.
   2 4th Seaforth Highrs.
   3 4th Gordon Highrs.
   4 ~~4th Seaforth~~ 7th A. & S. Highrs.
   5 7th Black Watch.
   6 154th M. G. Company.
   7 154th T. M. Battery.
   8 1st Canadian Infantry Brigade.
   9 2nd Canadian Infantry Brigade.
  10 51st (H) Division "G" (For information).
  11 152nd Infantry Brigade.
  12 153rd Infantry Brigade.
  13 51st Division Artillery.
  14 Staff Captain.
  15 Brigade Transport Officer.
  16 Brigade Signal Officer.
  17 Brigade Intelligence Officer.
  18 Capt. Herrick.
  19 War Diary.
  20 File.

SECRET.
****

O.C.
    9th Royal Scots.
    4th Seaforth Highrs.
    4th Gordon Highrs.
    7th A. & S. Highrs.
    7th Black Watch.

Reference Operation Order No.112.

Please amend para.11 as follows :-

All Battalions, 154th Brigade, and 7th Black Watch will report that they are in assembly positions by 3 a.m., the code word being the name of the O.C. Battalion.

The 9th Royal Scots and 4th Seaforth Highlanders will be all EAST of BONNAL by 2 a.m.

The greatest care must be taken that no indication of the assembly is given to the enemy either by rattling of equipment, noise of any kind or moonlight shining on bayonets, mess tins, etc.

                                            Captain,
                                      Brigade Major,
5th April, 1917.   154th Infantry Brigade.

SECRET.   Copy No. 8

The following amendments and addenda to ZZ.1/2 are issued.

Plan "B" showing units on either flank of this Brigade at the different objectives is attached.

HEADQUARTERS: page 5 para.7.

154th Brigade, amended as follows :-

7th A. & S. Highrs. A.23.c.2.1. read A.23.c.4.2.
For "Fifth Battalion : ABRI CENTRALE" read
"7th Black Watch A.22.d.40.30."

Add para.11 as follows :-

ARTILLERY PLAN.

The 51st Divisional zone will be divided into 6 sectors or lanes, one Field Artillery Brigade being allotted to each lane.

Each Brigade will carry out a preliminiary bombardment of wire-cutting within the bounds of its own lane.

One selected Battery cutting wire and bombarding trenches up to and including the BLACK LINE.

One Battery bombarding trenches from BLACK LINE up to and including the BLUE LINE.

One Battery bombarding trenches from BLUE LINE up to and including the BROWN LINE.

Similarly the 28 Medium Trench Mortars will be grouped into 6 batteries and will cut wire and bombard trenches as far as they can reach in the 6 lanes.

9 9.45" Trench Mortars will be grouped into 3 groups of 3 Mortars and will bombard trenches each group covering 2 lanes.

The 3 Brigades covering 154th Brigade will be known as "No.2 Group" with Headquarters in the old battery position A.26.a.2.6., and will be in command of Lieut.Col. DYSON, 256th Brigade, R.F.A.

No.2 Group will consist of :-

256th Brigade, R.F.A.
84th Army Field Artillery Brigade.
315th Army Field Artillery Brigade.

BARRAGES.

The 3 types of barrage are as follows :-

(1) Creeping.
(2) Standing and trench.
(3) Searching.

Approximately two thirds of the 18-pdrs. form the creeping barrage and one third the standing and searching barrage.

As the creeping and standing barrages are the same up to the BLACK LINE and as throughout the whole attack the H.A. and 4.5" Hows. are on trenches and strong points in rear it will be seen the standing or trench barrage is much the more formidable.

The main functions of the creeping barrage are :-

(a) To act as a guide to the Infantry.
(b) To keep down the heads of the defenders until the last possible moment.

The creeping barrage commences at ZERO on the German front line and creeps forward at uniform paces by lifts of about 100 yards. Wherever possible this barrage remains on objective trench for about 8 minutes before lifting to allow time for the Infantry to form up and go into the trench with one rush.

The times of the various lifts are shown on the barrage map.

The lift off the BLUE and the BROWN LINES is more than 100 yards so as to make absolutely certain that the "tail" of the barrage is well clear of the trench.

The standing barrage is formed at ZERO on the Support line and the hostile front system, the lifts from trench to trench being joined on each objective trench by the creeping barrage, both barrages lifting off the objective trench together.

The searching barrage searches the ground from 500 to 1000 yards in front of the creeping barrage.

The 4.5" Hows. will be 200 yards or more ahead of the creeping barrage, and will be specially on communication trenches, strong points, trench junctions and the next trench.

H.A. will be on the next trench as far as is safe, moving at least 300 yards ahead of the creeping barrage.

60-pdrs. will be employed to search and sweep all the ground in rear of each objective.

When the creeping barrage lifts off the final objective of each stage of the attack, it will move forward for 300 yards where it will halt and form a protective barrage.

Barrage during consolidation will be H.E. It is intended to use a shrapnel barrage as far as possible, the fuzes being set at such a length as to ensure 1 in 3 bursting on graze.

Barrage maps 1/5,000 will be issued as follows :-

             Brigade Headquarters   6.
             Battalions   10
             M.G.Company.   2.
             T.M.Battery.   2.

In addition probably barrage maps 1/10,000 will be issued on the same scale.

The following points will receive special attention from Howitzers :-

A.24.a.40.55.	=	O.P.
A.24.a.65.70.	=	Trench junction.
A.24.b.2.9.	=	Trench junction.
A.24.a.05.95.	=	Battalion Headquarters.
A.18.c.75.25.	=	Trench junction.
A.18.d.55.38.	=	O.P.
B.13.c.6.9.	=	Trench junction.
B.13.d.10.80.	=	O.P.
A.23.a.3.7.	=	Trench junction.
A.23.a.5.9.	=	Trench junction.
A.17.d.35.20.	=	Trench junction.
A.18.c.9.8.	=	Dugout.
A.18.d.65.68.	=	O.P.

At intervals from ZERO - 10 hours to ZERO - 15 minutes bombardments of lachrymatory and lethal shell will take place on command posts, trench telephone exchanges and important groups of dugouts.

The preparatory bombardment will now commence 96 hours before ZERO on "Z" day. The bombardment will no longer be continuous for the last 24 hours but will be continuous throughout "Y" day.

The attention of the 4th Seaforth Highrs. and 9th Royal Scots is drawn to the fact that the 1st Canadian Division will assault after the 3 minutes' barrage on the German front line whereas the 51st Division do not assault until after a 4 minutes' barrage on the German front line. Great care will have to be taken that the troops on the left, particularly the 5 platoons 4th Seaforth Highrs. for the attack on the salient, do not advance to the assault too soon.

Page 9 para.16 erase lines 11 to 15 inclusive and substitute-

The discharge of gas drums will take place on April 4th at 6-15 a.m., i.e., 15 minutes before the hour fixed for the bombardment. If the wind is unfavourable, the discharge will take place as soon as the direction of the wind makes it possible, and battalions in the line will be informed with at least 4 hours warning, following code being used :-

    DRESDEN   =   Discharge postponed.

    BERLIN (time) =   Discharge will take place at (time).

Page 11 para.19: ACTION OF STOKES MORTARS: add :-

During the preliminary bombardment there will be rehearsals of the 18-pdr. barrage :-

    (a) On the 5th April at 8 a.m.
    (b) On the 6th April at 1-30 p.m.
    (c) On the 7th April at 11-15 a.m.

** 4 **

Stokes Mortars will bombard front line trenches as the barrage lifts off the front line for 3 minutes intense bombardment.

The orders for these Stokes Mortar bombardments will be issued by B.G.C. 153rd Brigade in the case of (a) and (b), and B.G.C's. 152nd and 154th Brigade in the case of (c).

MAPS, PAPERS TO BE TAKEN INTO ACTION.

Para.20 erase "Acknowledge" and substitute :-

In order to avoid any chance of information falling into the hands of the enemy, no documents, maps showing our trenches, secret maps or papers (including private letters) will be taken into action with the exceptions noted below :-

(1) Map - ROCLINCOURT - 1/10,000 5A. or 6A. (not showing our trenches.

(2) Map - S.20 Ed.2 1/10,000.

(3) Maps- Showing barrage 1/5,000 and 1/10,000.

(4) Company, platoon and section rolls.

(5) A.B.64.

With the exception of the above all papers will be collected and stored under unit arrangements previous to the attack.

All Unit Commanders down to platoon commanders should be in possession of Map S.20 Ed.2 which will be issued on the following scale :-

    Brigade Headquarters 20.
    Battalions 50.
    M.G.Company. 10.
    T.M.Battery. 10.

Acknowledge.

                Captain,
                Brigade Major,
4th April, 1917.   154th Infantry Brigade.

"B" SECRET

DIAGRAM SHOWING UNITS ON EITHER FLANK OF 154TH INF. BDE. AT THE DIFFERENT OBJECTIVES.

BROWN LINE

| 3RD CAN. INF. BATT. | ½ BATT. 4TH GORDONS | ½ BATT. 7TH A. & S.H. | 5TH SEAFORTHS |

BLUE LINE

| 1ST CAN. INF. BATT. | ½ BATT. 4TH GORDONS | ½ BATT. 7TH A. & S.H. | 5TH SEAFORTHS |

CANADIAN RED LINE
5TH CAN. INF. BATT.

BLACK LINE

| 5TH CAN. INF. BATT. | 4TH SEAFORTHS | 9TH ROYAL SCOTS | 6TH SEAFORTHS |

ASSEMBLY POSITION

| 5TH CAN. INF. BATT. | 4TH SEAFORTHS | 9TH ROYAL SCOTS | 6TH SEAFORTHS |

KEY

154TH INF. BDE :
152ND DO :
CANADIAN TROOPS :

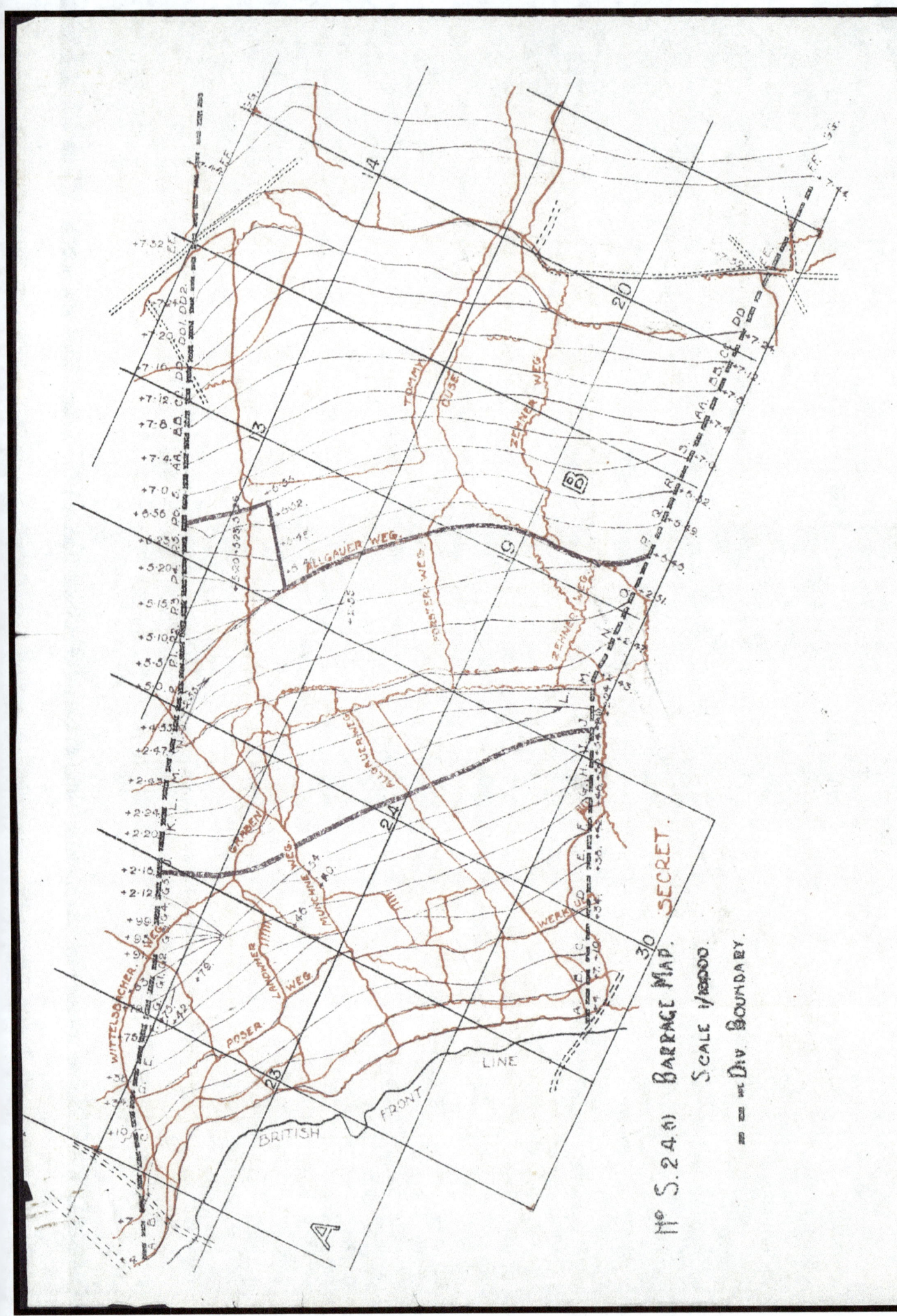

S E C R E T.

O.C. 9th Royal Scots.
4th Seaforth Highrs.
4th Gordon Highrs.
7th A. & S. Highrs.
154th M. G. Company.
154th T. M. Battery.

WARNING ORDER.

The 51st Division will relieve the 9th Division to-morrow. The 154th Brigade will be in support in BROWN and BLUE LINES. Details later.

14th April, 1917.

Captain,
Brigade Major,
154th Infantry Brigade.

SECRET.   Copy No. 4

154th INFANTRY BRIGADE

WARNING ORDERS.

Reference Maps :-   3
      FAMPOUX 1/10,000. S.A.
      51.B.N.W. 1/20,000. X 6.A.

---

1.   The 51st (Highland) Division will take over the battle front from the 9th Division on night 15/16th April.

        Dispositions as follows :-

        1 Brigade in Line.
        1 Brigade in Support (BROWN and BLUE LINES).
        1 Brigade in Reserve (BLACK LINE and OLD BRITISH
                                              TRENCHES).

2.   Frontage to be taken over is from RIVER SCARPE H.24.a.4.7. thence through H.19.d. and b. and a, H.12.c. to the HYDERABAD REDOUBT H.12.c.1.9. exclusive.

3.   153rd Brigade will take over the front line. 154th Brigade will march to-morrow and take over Support Area. 152nd Brigade will take over Reserve Area.
                                bus
4.   One Battalion will be at "Y" Huts to-morrow morning at 8 a.m. to take Officers forward to reconnoitre, vacancies are allotted as follows :-

        Each Battalion   5.
        M.G.Company   3.
        T.M.Battery   2.

5.   Details later.

        ACKNOWLEDGE.

                                              Captain,
                                              Brigade Major,
14th April, 1917.   154th Infantry Brigade.

Copy No.1 9th Royal Scots.
        2 4th Seaforth Highrs.
        3 4th Gordon Highrs.
        4 7th A. & S. Highrs.
        5 154th M. G. Company.
        6 154th T. M. Battery.
        7 Brigade Transport Officer.
        8 Brigade Signal Officer.

Appendix IV

SECRET.

No. ZZ/2/2.
Copy No. 4.

154th INFANTRY BRIGADE

INSTRUCTIONS NO.1.

Reference Maps :-
   Sheet 51.B.N.W.   1/20,000, Ed. 6A.
   and tracing for map T.S. No. M,.8.b. attached.

---

1. ENEMY'S POSITION.

The enemy is holding the GAVRELLE - OPPY LINE to the North of HYDERABAD REDOUBT and to the S.E. of this point a newly dug system which runs through squares H.12., H.18., I.13., to the West of MOUNT PLEASANT WOOD (I.19.c.).

A support line appears to be dug on the general line of the ROEUX - GAVRELLE ROAD.

2. INTENTION.

The First Army is to advance on the GAVRELLE - OPPY LINE and the XVIIth Corps on left of Third Army will advance simultaneously.

XVIIth Corps attack will be carried out by 51st Division on the right and 4th Division on the left.

The 17th Division will advance on the right of the 51st Division South of the SCARPE.

3. BOUNDARIES.

   Divisional Boundaries.

      On the North.
   Communication Trench running East from HYDERABAD REDOUBT (inclusive to 51st Division).

      On the South.
   River SCARPE.

   Brigade Boundary.

Railway as far as I.13.c.95.80. (inclusive to 153rd Brigade) thence due EAST.

   Battalion Boundary.

German trench through I.19.a. to its junction with track at I.19.a.7.7. (inclusive to 7th A. & S. Highrs.) thence due EAST.

4. OBJECTIVES.

   (a) Trenches in H.12., H.18., I.13., and I.19. called BLACK LINE.

   (b) ROEUX - OPPY ROAD North of railway and trenches S.W. of Chemical Works in I.13. and 19. called BLUE LINE.

   (c) Village of ROEUX called BROWN LINE.

      These are shown on attached tracing.

"A" Form.
MESSAGES AND SIGNALS.

Army Form C.2121 (in pads of 100).

| TO | · | PINK | app. IVa. |

Sender's Number.	Day of Month.	In reply to Number.	AAA
*BM383	17		

You will occupy the sunken Rd through H24 B+D East of the SCARPE tonight with 2 Coys aaa 2 Coys 8th Roy al Scots pioneers will be available for consolidation of this position aaa You will send guides to River bridge at FEUCHY H21a37 at 6pm to guide these two Coys to position to be consolidated. aaa You will move your 2 Coys along the tow path on the S bank of the river as far as possible by daylight & not move onto the railway till after dusk. aaa A report on the situation giving full details will reach BHQ not later than 12 midnight aaa acknowledge by bearer

RED

(Z) Jardine Capt

SECRET.

154th Inf. Bde. No. ZZ.3/2.

Copy No. 4.

154th INFANTRY BRIGADE

INSTRUCTIONS NO.2.

Reference Maps :-
    Sheet 51.B.N.W. 1/20,000 Ed.6A.
    Map attached 1/10,000.

---

1. These instructions cancel paras.3, 4, 5 and 6 of Instructions No.1.
    Para.2 sub-para.2 of Instructions No.1 for 4th Division read 37th Division.
    In continuation of Instructions No.1 the objectives of the attack have been altered and are shown on the attached map. (Tracing already issued will be destroyed).

    It is the intention to secure the whole of the high ground on GREENLAND HILL and the spur running S.E. through HAUSA and DELBAR WOODS.

    Boundaries are shown on attached map.

2. PLAN OF ATTACK.

    The 51st Division will attack with 2 Brigades.
    (a) 154th Brigade plus 1 Battalion 152nd Brigade (6th Gordon Highrs.) on right.
    (b) 153rd Brigade (less 5th Gordon Highrs.) plus 1 Battalion 152nd Brigade (6th Seaforth Highrs) on left.

    The remaining 3 Battalions will be held in Divisional Reserve.

    One Brigade 34th Division will probably relieve BLACK and BLUE LINES during night Z/Z plus 1 and may take over the whole battle front on the night Z plus 1/Z plus 2. *The final objective of 154 Bde will be the BLUE LINE*

    The 154th Brigade will attack as follows :-

    Attack as far as BLUE LINE will be carried out by 2 Battalions each supported by 2 Companies.

    (a) 4th Gordon Highrs. plus 2 Coy. 9th Royal Scots on left.
    (b) 7th A. & S. Highrs. plus 2 Coy. 9th Royal Scots on right.

    The attack on the RED LINE will be carried out by 6th Gordon Highrs. on left and 4th Seaforth Highrs. on the right.

    There will probably be one Battalion 34th Division as Brigade Reserve. *The 4th Seaforth Hrs will be in Bde Reserve*

    The Battalions for the BLUE LINE will assemble in the vicinity of the sunken road through H.24.b. and d. on a 2 Company front, Companies on a 2 platoon front.

    The assault will be carried out in 3 waves :-

After the BLUE LINE is taken the 153rd Brigade will swing Southwards from the Railway taking first the BROWN LINE and then CYPRUS TRENCH with patrols pushed out through DELBAR and HAUSA Woods.

The 7th A. & S. Highrs. will arrange to connect up with 153rd Brigade along the tracks through I.20.b.

** 2 **

Objective of 1st wave - BLACK LINE.

Objective of 2nd wave - Road from I.19.d.9.2. to I.13.c.95.85.

Objective of 3rd wave - BLUE LINE.

The remaining 2 platoons in each Battalion will act as Battalion Reserve and be used for any minor operations that are necessary.

The 4 Companies 9th Royal Scots will also assemble in the vicinity of the sunken road through H.24.b. and d. and will move forward in rear of the last wave for the BLUE LINE and consolidate the BLUE LINE. Everyman will carry a tool in the proportion of 4 shovels to 1 pick.

The 7th A. & S. Highrs. will detail one platoon to follow the assault made on either bank of the River and connect up with the 51st Brigade at the Bridge I.19.d.90.15. at Zero plus 60 mins.

In the event of considerable resistance in ROEUX the 7th A. & S. Highrs. will have to push forward on the North and endeavour to envelope the village. Touch will be gained with 17th Division on Eastern edge of ROEUX at Zero plus 100 mins.

There will be a halt on the BLUE LINE till probably Zero plus 7 hours, when the protective barrage will lift.

As soon as the BLUE LINE has been taken the O.Cs. 7th A. & S. Highrs. and 4th Gordon Highrs. will reorganise their Battalions to provide carrying parties to carry from Brigade store at sunken road H.23.b.4.1. to BLUE and RED LINES.

The 2 Battalions for the RED LINE will assemble in the vicinity of the Railway through H.23.b. and d., H.22.d., the 4th Seaforth Highrs. in front and will advance in artillery formations so as to catch up the artillery barrage in front of the BLUE LINE in time to advance with it to the RED LINE.

These Battalions will deploy into 3 waves when necessary :-

Objective of 1st wave - German trench through I.14.b. and d.

Objective of 3rd wave - RED LINE.

Remaining wave will work round the flanks in event of the enemy putting up strong resistance in DELBAR and HAUSA WOODS.

On reaching the RED LINE a firing line will be consolidated to the East of both Woods with posts in front for observation and the German trench through I.14.d. and b. will be consolidated as a support line.

Touch will be gained by the 4th Seaforth Highrs. with the 51st Brigade on the River. When the RED LINE has been taken strong patrols must be pushed forward towards PLOUVAIN to exploit success.

3. ARTILLERY.

The assault on the BLACK LINE will take place at Zero plus 19 mins.; after that barrage will move at 100 yards in 6 mins.

The assault on the BLUE LINE will take place at Zero plus 100 mins. and protective barrage will lift at Zero plus 7 hours.

The assault on the RED LINE will take place at Zero plus 8 hours.

Barrage table will be issued later.

Gas shell will be fired on CHEMICAL WORKS and ROEUX during X/Y and Y/Z nights and from Zero smoke will be used along SCARPE S. of ROEUX.

-- 3 --

4. HEADQUARTERS.

O.C's. 7th A. & S. Highrs. and 4th Gordon Highrs. will arrange to have a combined Headquarters in Sunken Road.

9th Royal Scots Headquarters with Brigade Headquarters.

~~The other 2 Battalions will fix a Headquarters forward during the long pause on the BLUE LINE.~~

5. INFORMATION.

The vital importance of accurate reports on the situation being continually sent back is again impressed on Commanding Officers. An Officer who can be relied on must be kept at Battalion Headquarters to go forward and report on any obscure or doubtful situations.

The importance of all Officers using their compasses cannot be over estimated.

6. TANKS.

It is proposed to use two Tanks on this Brigade front to deal with MOUNT PLEASANT WOOD and buildings South of the Railway and ROEUX Village.

Tanks will use the bridge under the Railway at H.18.d.2.1. Any damage to this Bridge will be immediately reported to Brigade Headquarters by 9th Royal Scots.

7. GAS.

300 LIVENS PROJECTORS are being installed in the Sunken Road about H.24.b.6.3. These will fire gas bombs on MOUNT PLEASANT WOOD and ROEUX on X/Y night.

8. STOKES MORTARS.

O.C. 154th Trench Mortar Battery will arrange to attach 2 Stokes Mortars and teams to each of the front Battalions. These Battalions will place a carrying party of 10 men for ammunition at the disposal of the Officer in charge of each detachment.

The remainder of the 154th Trench Mortar Battery will take up position near Brigade Headquarters and send an Officer to Brigade Headquarters to await orders.

9. "Z" day will probably by Monday, 23rd April.

Acknowledge.

J A D....
Captain,
Brigade Major,
154th Infantry Brigade.

20th April, 1917.

Copy No. 1 9th Royal Scots.   Copy No. 10 51st Infantry Brigade.
        2 4th Seaforth Hrs.   11 C.R.A. 51st Division.
        3 4th Gordon Hrs.   12 Staff Captain.
        4 7th A. & S. Hrs.   13 Brigade Signal Officer.
        5 154th M. G. Company.   14 Bde. Transport Officer.
        6 154th T. M. Battery.   15 Bde. Intell. Officer.
        7 51st (H) Div. "G".   16 Brigade Major.
        8 152nd Infantry Brigade.   17 6th Gordon Highrs.
        9 153rd Infantry Brigade.   18 War Diary.

SECRET   154TH BDE. O.O. No 114   COPY No. 4

REF. MAPS:-
    SHEET 1/20,000 51B N.W. ED. 6A.

1. The enemy is holding the GAVRELLE - OPPY line in the NORTH & some recently dug trenches which connect with the above line and run through H.12, H.18, H.13, to WEST of MOUNT PLEASANT WOOD to I.19.a.

   His support line appears to be in the general line of the ROEUX - GAVRELLE RD.

   There is a third line just WEST of HAUSA & DELBAR WOODS.

2. The troops taking part in the attack, the boundaries and objectives, have already been notified to all concerned in the 154TH BDE INSTRUCTIONS No 1 & 2.

3. The 154TH Bde will attack the enemies trenches, between the railway and the RIVER SCARPE as far as the BLUE LINE which will be strongly consolidated and touch gained with the 153RD Bde on the RED LINE & the 51ST Bde on the RIVER.

4. The situation at present being, that we hold the SUNKEN RD. through H.24 B. & D. as far as its junction with CEYLON TRENCH, thence up CEYLON TR. to its junction with COLNE TR. thence along COLNE TR.

   The 4TH GORDON HDRS will assemble with first 2 waves in the new trench in front of the SUNKEN RD. remaining waves in SUNKEN RD. and 2 COYS 9TH ROYAL SCOTS (attached) in SUNKEN RD.

   The 7TH A. & S. HRS. will assemble with their first wave along CEYLON & COLNE TRS. the remaining waves & 2 COYS 9TH ROYAL SCOTS (attached) in SUNKEN RD.

   The dividing line between Battalions for assembly will be the point H 24 b 5.5.

   The O.C 7TH A & S. HRS. will push the ~~te~~ platoon which is to follow the attack on either side of the river, as far SOUTH as possible before ZERO.

2.

The 7th A. & S. Hdrs. & 4th Gordon Hdrs. will report that everything is ready by code letter O.K. by 3.30 a.m.

The attack will be carried out as laid down in 154th Bde Instructions No. 2.

Strong points will be constructed by 9th Royal Scots at I 20 a.7.3 & I 4. c 0.4.

5. Heavy Artillery will barrage at least 500 yds in front of Infantry.

4.5" Hows. will fire on strong points at least 260 yds in front of Infantry.

18 pdr. barrage will be in accordance with barrage MAP No. 2. already issued.

Smoke will be used against ROEUX.

6. Machine Gun Coys. will form a barrage during advance.

7. Two Tanks will operate S. of railway.

8. Gas will be liberated as detailed in 154th Bde. Instructions No. 2.

9. Watches will be be synchronised as follows:—

Lt. LINSDAY & representative 154th M.G. Coy will synchronise with Division at L'ABBAYETTE FARM, ATHIES at 7 P.M. on 22nd.

Each Batt. & T.M. Batty. will send representatives to synchronise with Lt. LINSDAY at Bde. Battle H.Q. at 8.30 pm.

10. Times at which contact aeroplanes will call for flares will be notified later.

11. The B.G.C. wishes Commanding Officers to impress most strongly on all ranks, that the whole secret of success is to keep up to the 18 pdr. barrage.

12. Every use must be made of visual signalling for transmission of information as the country lends itself to this, and wire communications cannot be relied on to hold out for any length of time.

ACKNOWLEDGE.
22/4/17

J A Dunn
CAPT.
BDE. MAJOR.
154 INF BRIGADE

Appendix T.

OPERATION ORDERS
by
Lt.Col.H. G. HYSLOP, D.S.O.   22/4/17.

INTENTION. The 51st Division will attack the enemy's position on the front from HYDERABAD WORK H.12.C.5.2. to RIVER SCARPE I.25. A.3.8. The 153rd Brigade will be on the left and the 154th on the right.

The 17th Division will advance on the right of the 51st Division.

The 154th Brigade attack will be carried out by two Battalions, the 4th Gordon Highlanders on the left and the 7th Arg.& Suth.Hldrs. on the right. Each if these Battalions will be supported by two Companies of 9th Royal Scots.

The 4th SeafrthHldrs. will be in Brigade reserve. Battalions will assemble in SUNKEN ROAD through H.24.B. & D.

BATTALION BOUNDARY. German trench through I.19a to its junction with track at I.19.a.7.7. (inclusive to 7th A & S.H.)thence due EAST.

OBJECTIVES. The attack will be carried out in three waves.

   Objective of First Wave   The BLACK Line.
   "   " Second "   Read from I.19.d.9.2. to I.13.c.95.25.
   "   " Third "   The BLUE Line.

FORMATIONS FOR THE ATTACK. The Battn. will attack and capture the village of ROEUX.

First Wave, two platoons of "B" Coy. will attack and establish themselves on the BLACK Line from I.25.a.8.8. to I.19.c.7.4.

Two platoons of "A" Coy. will attack and establish themselves on the BLACK Line from I.19.a.7.8. to I.19.c.6.9. taking in the whole of MOUNT PLEASANT WOOD position. At the same time one platoon of "B" Coy. will jump the new German trench through I.19.c.

2ND.WAVE. Two platoons of "D" COY. from bridge at I.19.d.9.2. to cross roads I.19.d.6.6. inclusive.

One platoon "B" Coy. to join up with two platoons of "C" Coy who will take from I.19.b.3.9. to I.19.b.3.6.

After advance of 2nd wave one platoon each from "A" and "B" Coys. on BLACK Line will follow the wave and mop up in rear.

One platoon of "B" Coy. will advance by the southern bank of the River keeping slightly in advance of the waves and will assist waves by flanking fire.

This platoon on reaching BRIDGE I.19.d.9.2. will consolidate position under orders of O.C. "D" Coy. and will join hands with the 17th Division.

3RD WAVE. On the right two platoons of "D" Coy., centre two platoons of "A" Coy., left two platoons "C" Coy.

Platoons of "C" and "D" Coys. will work round the flanks of the village of ROEUX and will join hands about I.20.a.8.2. while the two platoons of "A" Coy. go through the village and mop up.

As the village of PELVES is not being attacked by the 17th Division until after the capture of BLUE Line "D" Coy. will have to form a protective flank along the RIVER.

The two companies of 9th Royal Scots will follow the third wave and consolidate the BLUE Line.

RED LINE. The 153rd Brigade will attack from the north of the railway and attack and capture the RED Line.

Os.C. "C" and "D" Coys. will be responsible that touch is obtained with the 153rd Brigade along the tracks running eastwards from ROEUX.

ARTILLERY. The assault on the BLACK Line will take place at ZERO & plus 12 minutes. Assault on BLUE Line at Z plus 100 minutes. Barrage will move from BLUE to RED Lines at Z plus 7 hours. Barrage table will be issued later.

The absolute necessity of keeping close up to BARRAGE is again impressed on all ranks.

TANKS. A tank will probably operate against MOUNT PLEASANT WOOD and may be called on to help with the capture of strong points in the village of ROEUX.

STOKES MORTARS. Two Stokes mortars are at the disposal of the Battalion and can be called for when required. They will first of all be in position against MOUNT PLEASANT WOOD.

BATTALION HEADQUARTERS. will be in SUNKEN ROAD about H.24.b.7.2.

BATTALION AID POST. This will first of all be under RAILWAY BRIDGE at H.18.d.3.1. and after attack has commenced will move to SUNKEN ROAD near Battalion Headquarters.

Acknowledge.

Capt. & Adjt.
9th Arg. & Suth. Highdrs.

"A" Form.
MESSAGES AND SIGNALS.

Army Form C.2121 (in pads of 100).

SECRET

Appendix VI

TO	26th North Fusiliers	51st Div
	4th Seaforth Hrs	153rd Bde
	7th A & S Hrs	50th Bde

Sender's Number: BM 445
Day of Month: 23
AAA

The 26th North Fusiliers will take over the Battle front at present held by 7th A & S Hrs and dispositions as follows 3 Coys in front line from I.19.B.3.7 to the river about I.25.A.7.8 using commanding ground and making a chain of Lunettes aaa one Coy in support in CEYLON TRENCH aaa None of the 154th Bde will be relieved but O.C. 4th Seaforth Hrs & 7th A & S Hrs will reorganise the remnants of 12 Coys who attacked this morning and form them up in Sunken road and occupy it and the remainder of CEYLON trench aaa 50th Bde on right of river and 153 Bde N of railway will cooperate aaa Strong patrols will be pushed out through

From: Village of ROEUX to try & occupy it aaa
Place: 154 Inf Bde
Time:

(Z)

Bde Major

"A" Form.
MESSAGES AND SIGNALS.

Army Form C.2121 (in pads of 100).

TO { 2

respectively aaa OC 7th A&S Hrs will be responsible for relief of all details of his own Battn 4th R Scots & 4th Gordon Hrs in SUNKEN road and they will march under his orders when relieved aaa The whole Bde will march to ARRAS on completion of relief by Towpath to bridge at G 16 D 5 3 where guides from transport lines will meet units and guide to billets. All outgoing troops will use bridge under railway only aaa The Bde will move off to an unknown destination by train at about 4 pm tomorrow aaa 26th NF on relief will rejoin 103 Bde immediately N of railway guides will be at H 18 D 25 15 by 10 pm aaa Completion of all reliefs will be reported at once to Bde HQrs by code OK aaa All bomb ammunition lights &c will be handed over aaa acknowledge /154 Inf Bde

From: OK
Place:
Time:

Bde Maj Capt

"A" Form.
MESSAGES AND SIGNALS.
Army Form C.2121 (in pads of 100).

SECRET

Append. VII

TO: 7th A&S Hrs 9th R.Scots 26 NF CORN
4th Gordon Hrs 152 TM Batty 50 Bde 101 Bde
5th Seaforth Hrs 152 M.G. Coy R.O.E.

Sender's Number: BM 460
Day of Month: 24

AAA

34th Division will relieve 51st Div tonight aaa 101 Bde will relieve 152 Bde with 2 Battalions as follows aaa 11th Suffolks will relieve 4th Seaforth Hrs on left with 2 Coys in CEYLON from railway to 119 a 7 6 and 2 Coys in sunken road from railway to junction with CEYLON aaa 16th Royal Scots will relieve 26th NF on right with 2 Coys in New trench from 119 a 7 6 to river and 2 Coys in CEYLON and sunken road to S of CEYLON aaa Relief of 152 M.G. Co & 152 T.M.B. will be arranged between COs concerned aaa Guides at ratio of 1 per platoon & 1 per HQ from 4th Seaforth Hrs & 26th NF will be at Bde HQ at 10 pm & 10.30 pm

SECRET.   ADJ 4-246.

1.   Neither Battalion nor Transport will leave here before 11a.m.

2.   Advance parties however are as previously arranged.

3.   Reveille will now be 6a.m., sick parade 6.30a.m. breakfasts 7a.m.   Cook Sgt. will inform cooks.

4.   Companies however must ensure that advance parties have their breakfast and are at Orderly Room by 7a.m.

5.   Qr.Mr. will send a man to Brigade Hdqrs. to be there at 7.30a.m. who can guide back one motor lorry for stores. This lorry will not leave for new area till noon.

6.   There will be a Coy. Commanders' conference at 8.15a.m. Qr.Mr., and Transport Officer (or representative) will attend.

                                              C.A. Marchant
                                              Capt. & Adjt.

Issued at 3A.m.
29.4.18.

Distribution. All Coy — Cook Sgt — T.O. — QM —
              RPM — C.O. — File — C.A.M.

SECRET

AR.4-245.

TO:-

All Coys.

1. The Brigade will move back to the R.ARRAS Sector to-morrow and will probably take over the line North of the SCARPE. on.

2. Nothing is known of times.

3. Personnel will proceed by train. Transport by march route.

~~[struck through line illegible]~~

4. DRESS: Full Marching Order. Steel Helmets. Kilt Aprons. No extraneous Stores allowed to be carried on the men. Blankets will be carried rolled on top of pack.

5. Transport will probably move off about 8 a.m., possibly earlier.

6. Provisional Routine: Reveille 5 a.m. Breakfast 5.45 a.m. Sick parade 6.15 a.m.

7. Valises to be packed and stacked in Company dumps outside Company messes at 6.30 a.m.

8. Lewis gun limbers 6.30 a.m. will call at Companies when Lewis gun Magazines etc. must be ready for packing.

9. Maps will will be re-issued at earliest opportunity.

10. Advance Section. The following personnel will be ready to move off at 7 a.m. [margin: 7 am Coy], and will report at Battalion Headquarters at that hour (in default of further orders) to reconnoitre the line. Battalion Headquarters. Lt. MacKay and one N.C.O. for H.Q. Coy. Each Coy. one officer and one N.C.O.

To take over accommodation:- Lt. Stratford and one N.C.O. per Coy. (including H.Q. Coy.)

11. Dixies with dry tea and sugar and tins of milk will be carried by cooks on the march. Meat rations and one cook per Coy. will go with Cookers. Officers should carry trench Mess Kit on train with them.

12. All other stores will be at Quartermaster Stores by 6.30 a.m.

13. Battalion must be ready to move at two hours' notice.

14. All Battalion Routine Orders requiring action to-morrow are cancelled.

15. Acknowledge, stating time received.

[signature]

SECRET.   COPY NO........

45th Infantry Brigade Operation Order No. 91.

Reference :-   Headquarters, 45th Inf. Bde,
    LENS.11. 1/100,000.   29th April, 1918.
    Sheet 36B. 1/40,000.

1. (a).   The 15th Division is moving to-day to ARRAS area
    by march and train route and is being transferred to the
    XVII Corps.

    (b).   On the night of 30th April/1st May the Brigade
    is relieving a Canadian Brigade N. of the SCARPE.

2.   The 45th Infantry Brigade Group will move as
    follows :-

        Mounted Portion.   By March Route.

        Dismounted Portion.   Train from CALONNE RICOUART
                                Station I.19.d.5.1. to ACQ Station
                                (3 miles N. of AGNEZ - LES - DUISANS)

3. (a).   The 13th Royal Scots and 6th Cameron Highlanders
    with advance parties of Brigade Signal Section, 47th Field
    Ambulance and 73rd Field Company R. E., will proceed by the
    1st train leaving CALONNE RICOUART at 9 a.m.

    (b).   The march to the Station will be carried out as
    follows :-

        Starting Point.   Cross Roads. C.30.d.2.3.

        Time.   13th Royal Scots.   7.50 a.m.
                            6th Cameron Highlanders. 8 a.m.

    (c).   Advance parties consisting of 1 officer and
    4 N.C.Os. from Brigade Signal Section, 47th Field Ambulance
    and 73rd Field Company R. E. will report to an officer of the
    13th Royal Scots at the R.T.O's office CALONNE RICOUART STATION
    at 8 a.m.

4. (a).   The 11th A & S. Highlanders, 73rd Field Company
    R. E. 47th Field Ambulance, 45th Trench Mortar Battery and
    Brigade Headquarters will proceed by the 2nd train leaving
    CALONNE RICOUART at 2 p.m.

    (b).   The march to the Station will be carried out as
    follows :-

        Starting Point.   Cross Roads.   C.30.d.2.3.

        Time.   11th A & S. Highlanders. 12.45 p.m.
                            Brigade Headquarters.   12.57 p.m.
                            45th Trench Mortar Batty. 1 p.m.
                            73rd Field Coy. R. E.   1.5 p.m.
                            47th Field Ambulance.   1.10 p.m.

5. (a).   An officer from each unit proceeding by train
    will report to the R. T. O. CALONNE RICOUART one hour before
    their train is due to depart (i.e. they will report at 8 a.m.
    or 1 p.m.) and will hand to him a parade state of their unit.

    (b).   Units will NOT enter the station yard until
    permission has been obtained from the R. T. O. by the officer
    sent forward with the parade state.

- 2 -

      (c). Units will move to the entraining station by companies at 100 yards distance. There will be NO halt after passing the Brigade Starting Point except for those due to traffic blocks.

      (d). An officer is being detailed by Brigade Headquarters to be on duty during the entraining and he will have a cyclist orderly with him.

6.   (a). Two lorries will be at Brigade Headquarters at 7.30 a.m. and will take on a party to reconnoitre the front of the Canadian Brigade to be relieved composed as under :-

        1 Officer and 1 N.C.O. per Battalion H.Q.
        1   "   " 1 "   per Company.
        1   "   " 1 "   from 45th T.M. Battery.
        1   "   " 1 "   from 45th Inf. Bde. Hd. Qrs.

and an advance party to reconnoitre billets and meet units at the detraining station (ACQ) composed as under :-

        1 Officer and 4 N.C.Os. per Battalion.
        1 N.C.O. from 45th Trench Mortar Battery.
        1 N.C.O. from 45th Inf. Bde. Headquarters.

      (b). Captain MacLEAN, 11th A & S. Highlanders attached 45th Infantry Brigade Headquarters will be in charge of the party to reconnoitre the forward area, and the Staff Captain of that to reconnoitre accommodation and provide guides.

7.   (a). 1 lorry per unit will be available to move surplus stores under separate instructions which have been issued by the Staff Captain.

      (b). Blankets will be carried on the man to the entraining station. Application has been made for lorries to meet units of the Brigade at the detraining station to convey the blankets to billets in ARRAS.

8.   The Staff Captain will be on duty at ACQ during the detraining and the Brigade Signal Officer will arrange for a motor cyclist to report to him at ACQ Station at 11 a.m.

9.   Transport will move as follows :-

    (a). 13th Royal Scots   ) Head of column to pass Cross
        6th Cameron Highlanders.) Roads C.30.d.2.3. at 8.30 a.m.

      Destination.   AGNEZ - LES - DUISANS.

    (b). 11th A & S. Highlanders.) Head of column to pass Cross
        Brigade Headquarters   ) Roads C.30.d.2.3. at 12.15 p.m.

      Destination   AGNEZ - LES - DUISANS.

    (c). Transport of the 47th Field Ambulance and 73rd Field Company R.E. may move to their destination when convenient as long as they do not pass cross roads C.30.d.2.3. at hours when the dismounted personnel are passing it (vide paras 3 (b) and 4 (b).

      Route for all Transport.

        DIVION - HOUDAIN - ESTREE CAUCHEE - CAMBIGNEUL - AUBIGNY - HAUTE AVESNES.

      BRUAY is NOT to be entered.

10. Brigade Headquarters will close at MARLES - LES - MINES at 12 noon to-day and open at ARRAS on arrival when location will be notified to all concerned.

Issued through 4 a.m.
Signals at 3 a.m.

Capt. Ryan
Captain,
Brigade Major, 45th Infantry Brigade

DISTRIBUTION :-
All recipients of O. O.

Copy No.	
13.	15th Division.
14.	15th Division "Q".
15.	44th Infantry Brigade.
16th	46th Infantry Brigade.
17.	73rd Field Company R. E.
18.	47th Field Ambulance.
19.	C. R. E.
20.	A. D. M. S.
21.	15th Div. Train.
22.	No. 3 Company Train.
23.	Town Major, MARLES-LES-MINES.
24.	Town Major, ARRAS.
25.	R. T. O. CALONNE RICOUART.

S E C R E T. 45th Infantry Brigade No. A/1/153.

13th Royal Scots.
6th Cameron Highlanders.
11th A & S. Highlanders.
45th Trench Mortar Battery.

Adminstrative Arrangements.
(to accompany 45th I.B.Operation Order No.91.).

Reference :-
Sheet. LENS 11, map 1/100,000.

---

1. First Line Transport of 45th Infantry Brigade Group is moving to AGNEZ - LES - DUISANS by march route. The Brigade Transport Officer will detail a small advance party to arrange billets and allot standings.

2. Five lorries will be available and are allotted as follows :-

    Brigade Headquarters..........1.
    Each Battalion................1.
    45th T. M. Battery............1.

    Each unit will send a guide to meet the lorries at Brigade Headquarters at 7.30 a.m.

    After loading, lorries will rendezvous at the junction of the RUE DE PERNES and RUE DE BRUAN and proceed to the Town Commandant's Office, ARRAS as follows :-

    13th Royal Scots.   )
    6th Cameron Highlanders.   )   proceed at 8.30 a.m.

    Bde. Headquarters.   )   1.30
    11th A & S. Highlanders.   )   Proceed at 1 p.m.
    45th T. M. Battery.   )

    Arrangements will be made by Staff Capt for

    Guides from the advanced billeting parties will meet the lorries at the Town Commandant's Office, ARRAS.

    Lorries will be unloaded and sent to Brigade Headquarters at ARRAS as early as possible after arrival there.

3. XVII Corps have been asked to detail 2 lorries to meet each train at ACQ to carry units blankets to ARRAS.

4. Receipts will be obtained for any area or trench stores handed over and duplicates forwarded to Brigade Headquarters.

    Lists of stores taken over on arrival at ARRAS will be forwarded to Brigade Headquarters.

5. A list of billets occupied at ARRAS will be forwarded in duplicate to Brigade Headquarters.

                                    A Ryan Capt for
                                    Captain,
29th April, 1918.   Staff Captain, 45th Infantry Bde.
            Copy to :- Brigade Transport Officer.
                       Brigade Major.

11th (S) Bn Argyll
& Sutherland Highrs

SECRET.   COPY NO......

45th Infantry Brigade Defence Scheme.
(Provisional).

GAVRELLE SECTION, 15TH DIVISIONAL SECTOR, XVII CORPS.

Reference:-   Headquarters, 45th Infantry Brigade,
51B.N.W.1/20,000.   5th May, 1918.
Trace attached.

I.   BOUNDARIES & LINES OF DEFENCE.

(a).   Boundaries and dispositions are shown on map issued with 45th Infantry Brigade No. 224/2 G. dated 3/5/18 (to units only).

(b).   Lines of defence are shown on the attached trace.

II.   Location of headquarters are as follows:-

Brigade Headquarters.................G.3.b.80.30.
Brigade Report Centre................
Right Front Battalion................H.4.c.50.50.
Left Front Battalion.................H.3.c.40.60.
Support Battalion....................H.1.d.35.55.
Trench Mortar Battery................H.1.c.75.55.
Right Flanking Battalion.............H.16.b.70.90.
Left Flanking Battalion..............

A new Brigade Headquarters is under construction at G.12.b.90.20.

III.   PRINCIPLES OF DEFENCE.

(a).   All lines of defence will be held at all costs. No ground will be given up, there will be no withdrawal and every shell hole and trench is to be fought for to the last.

(b).   In the event of any portion of a trench being lost troops still holding on will form a defensive flank and will not withdraw. Battalions in line will use their reserves to counter-attack, and if they are not successful, the Brigade will counter-attack with the support battalion.

(c).   Touch with flanking units must be maintained irrespective of Brigade boundaries. Flanking posts will be inter-locked with those of flanking Brigades.

(d).   Experience has shown that the flanks of units are particularly vulnerable. Front line battalions will take special steps to arrange for the defence of their flanks should the enemy penetrate on their flanks.

IV.   ACTION IN CASE OF ATTACK.

(a).   The front line battalions will act in accordance with the principles laid down in the previous paragraph. Under no circumstances will there be any withdrawal.

P.T.O.

(2).

(b). The support battalion will move at once one of its two rear companies to reinforce the two already in position in the BLUE and PINK lines, and one to the area D.2.central. The companies occupying the BLUE and PINK lines will defend it to the last if necessary, and the whole battalion will be prepared on receipt of orders from Brigade Headquarters, but not before, to carry out an attack on any portion of the Brigade front.

(c). All working parties East of the ARRAS - DOUAI RAILWAY will be accompanied by a Lewis gun section for every platoon in the party. They will man the nearest fire-trench and will report to the nearest officer of the battalion garrisoning the area in which they are working. The latter will then be responsible for informing his next senior commander (Company or Battalion) who will issue orders to the officer in charge of the working party as may be necessary.

V.   S. O. S. ARRANGEMENTS.

(a). The S. O. S. Signal is a No.32.Grenade.i.e.

RED over GREEN over RED.

(b). This will be repeated at Company, Front Battalion and Support Battalion Headquarters and also at the Artillery Brigade O. P.

(c). When the S. O. S. Signal is received artillery and machine guns will open on their S.O.S. Lines.
Rates of fire will be:-

For first) 18-pdr. 4 rounds per gun per minute.
5 minutes)4.5"-How. 2   "   "   "   "   "

For next) 18-pdrs. 3 rounds per gun per minute.
5 minutes)4.5"-How. 1½   "   "   "   "   "

After this the rates of fire will be normal (2 rounds - 18-pdr. and 1 rounds - 4.5" How. per gun perminute), and will be continued until the situation is clear, when it will either stop or be increased according to circumstances.

Should another S.O.S. be sent up, the artillery will immediately increase to the rates given above.

(d). Artillery S.O.S. lines have been forwarded to units on trace "A" (45th Infantry Brigade No. 227/I.g. dated 5/5/18).

VI.   MACHINE GUNS.

(a). The front is covered by "A" Company, 15th Bn. Machine Gun Corps.

(b). The positions of machine guns have been forwarded to units on Trace "C" (45th Infantry Brigade No. 227/I.g. dated 5/5/18).

3..........

VII.   COMMUNICATIONS.

(a).   All battalions are connected by buried cable direct to Brigade.

(b).   The Left Front Battalion has a loop set (wireless) working back to H.1.d.35.65. (close to Support Battalion H. Q.). A trench wireless set works from this point back to Brigade.

(c).   The Right Front Battalion works visual (DD) to the Left Front Battalion, and the Left Front Battalion works direct to Brigade.
A transmitting station is being placed at G.6.a.3.3. to work to the Left Front and the Support Battalion (both ways working). This transmitting station will work to Brigade both by visual and buried cable.

(d).   Two pairs of piggeons are allotted to the Right Front Battalion and 1 pair to the Left Front Battalion daily. These birds must be released before 7.30 p.m. except in unfavourable weather.

(e).   A Brigade runner and lineman's station is situated at H.1.d.35.55. in a dugout next to the Support Battalion Signal Office. D.R.L.S. leaves Brigade at approximately 7 a.m., 1 p.m. and 8 p.m. for all units. A special run will leave Brigade Report Centre for Brigade at 10.30 a.m. If summaries are not there by that hour the Battalion runner must himself take the summary on to Brigade.
S.D.R.'s. for Brigade will be accepted at this Relay Station but all correspondence must be sent by the D.R.L.S. as far as possible.

C. Ryan

Issued through
Signals at 8 p.m.

Captain.,
Brigade Major, 45th Infantry Brigade.

DISTRIBUTION:-

Copy No. 1.   War Diary.
        2.   File.
        3.   13th Bn. The Royal Scots.
        4.   6th Cameron Highlanders.
        5.   11th A & S. Highlanders.
        6.   45th Trench Mortar Battery.
        7.   15th Division.
        8.   15th Division "Q".
        9.   44th Infantry Brigade.
        10.   46th Infantry Brigade.
        11.   2nd D. A.
        12.   48th Army Brigade R.F.A.
        13.   Staff Captain.
        14.   Brigade Signals.

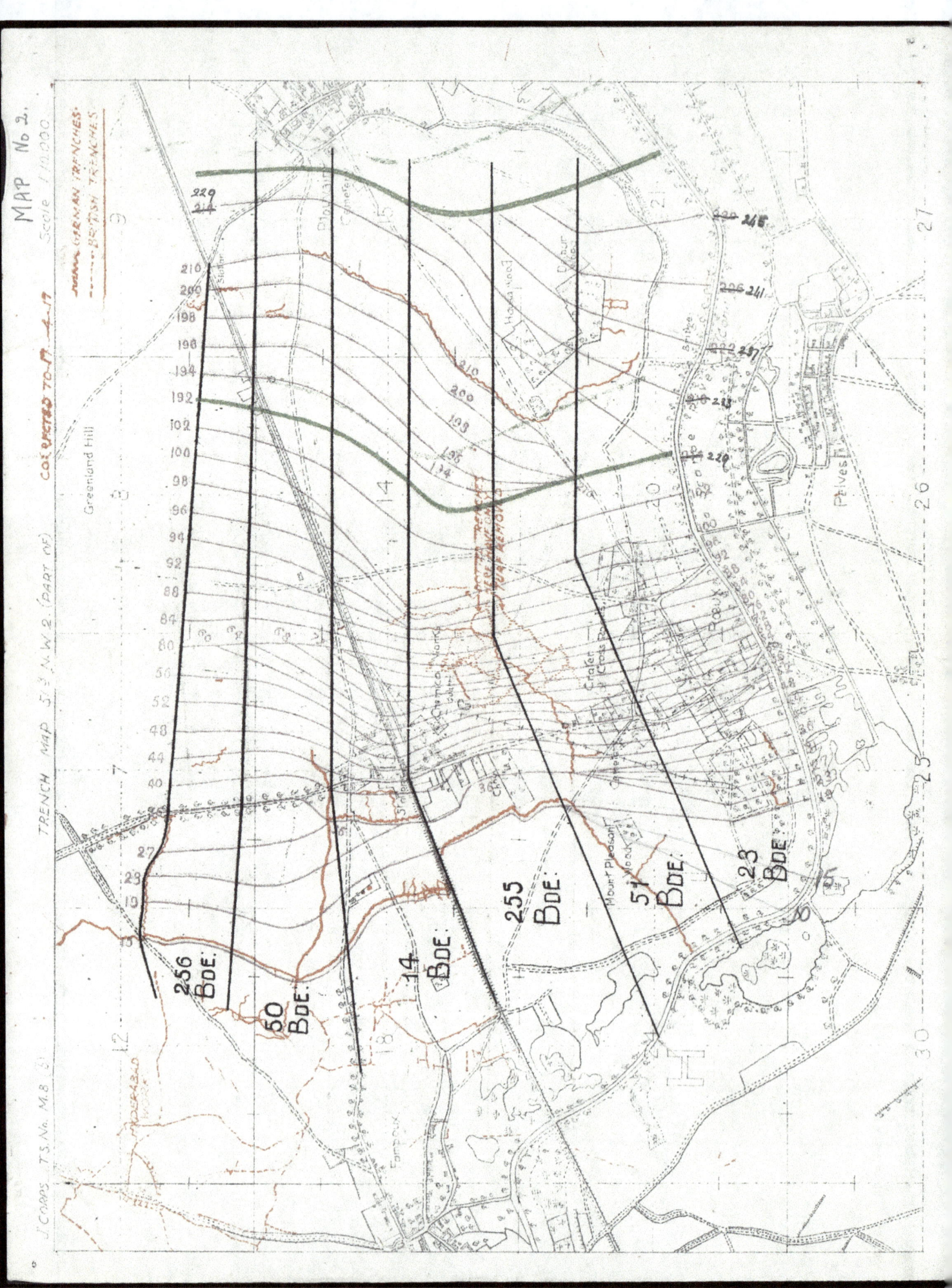

TRENCH MAP.
ROCLINCOURT.
51B N.W. 1.
EDITION 5.A
Scale 1:10,000.

Appendix I

MAP No. 1

INDEX TO ADJOINING SHEETS.

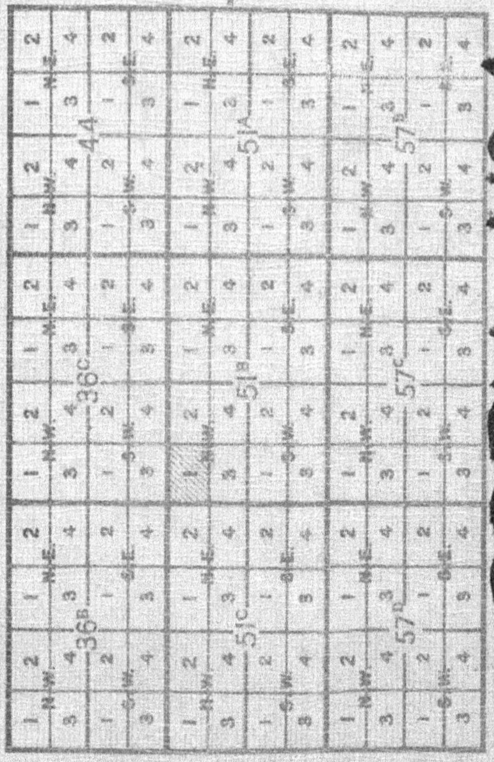

COPY No. 4

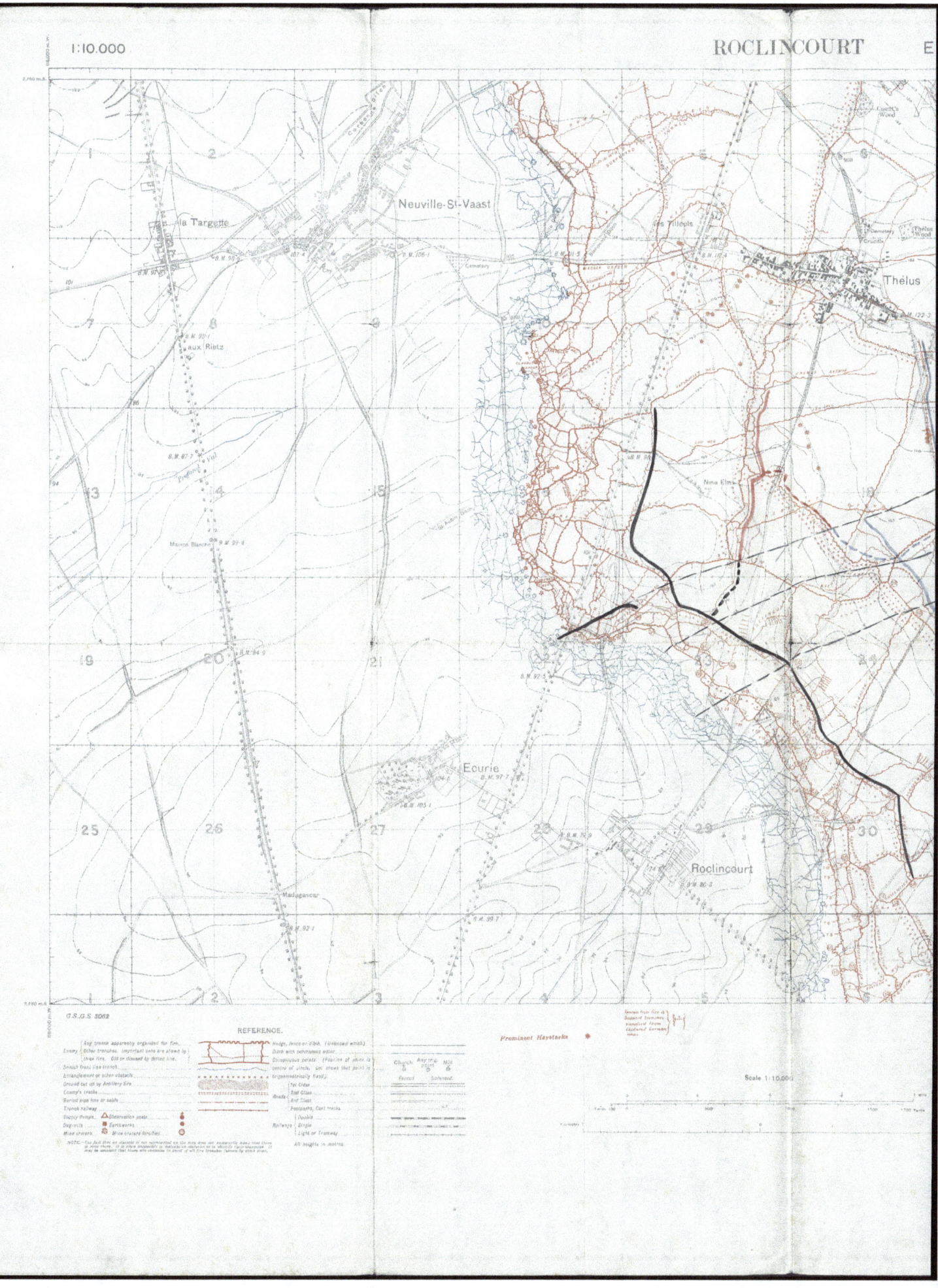

GLOSSARY.

Abbaye, Abbⁱᵉ	Abbey.
Abreuvoir, Abʳ	Watering-place.
Abri de douaniers	Customs-shelter.
Aciérie	Steel works.
Aiguilles	Points (Ry.)
Allée	Alley, Narrow road.
Ancien - ne, Ancⁿ⁻ⁿᵉ	Old.
Aqueduc	Aqueduct.
Arbre	Tree.
,, éventail	fan-shaped.
,, déclassé	bare.
,, fourchu	forked.
,, isolé	isolated.
,, penché	leaning.
Arbrisseau	Small tree.
Arc	Arch.
Ardoisière, Ardⁱᵉ	Slate quarry.
Arrêt	Halt.
Asile	Asylum.
,, des aliénés	Lunatic asylum.
,, d' ,,	
,, de charité	
,, des pauvres	Asylum.
,, de refuge	
Auberge, Aubᵍᵉ	Inn.
Aune	Alder-tree.
Bac	Ferry.
,, à traille	
Bains	Baths.
Place aux bains	Bathing place.
Balise	Boom, beacon.
Banc de sable	Sand-bank.
,, ,, vase	Mud-bank.
Baraque	Hut.
Barrage	Dam.
Barrières	Gate, Stile.
(Machine à) Bascule	Weigh-bridge.
Bassin	Dock, Pond.
,, d'échouage	Tidal dock.
Bassin de radoub	Dry dock.
Bateau phare	Light-ship.
Blanchisserie	Laundry.
B.M. (borne milliaire)	Mile stone.
Bⁿᵉ (borne kilométrique)	
Boulangerie	
Fabᵗ de boulons	Bolt Factory.
Bouée	Buoy.
Brasserie, Brassⁱᵉ	Brewery.
Briqueterie, Briqᵗᵉ	Brickfield.
Brise-lames	Breakwater.
Bureau de poste	Post office.
,, de douane	Custom house.
Butte	Butt, Mound.
Cabane	Hut.
Cabaret, Cabᵗ	Inn.
Câble sous-marin	Submarine cable.
Calvaire, Calvᵉ	Calvary.
Canal de dessèchement	Drainage canal.
Canal d'irrigation	Irrigation canal.
Fabᵗ de caoutchouc	Rubber factory.
Carrières, Carrᵉˢ	Quarry.
,, de gravier	Gravel-pit.
Caserne	Barracks.
Champ de courses	Race-course.
,, ,, manœuvres	Drill-ground.
,, ,, tir	Rifle range.
Chantier	Building yard.
,, ,, Ship yard.
,, ,, Dock yard.
Chantier de construction	Slip-way.
Chapelle, Chᵖᵉ	Chapel.
Charbonnage	Colliery.
Château d'eau	Water tower.
Chaussée	Causeway.
Chemin de fer	Railway.
Cheminée, Chᵉᵉ	Chimney.
Chêne	Oak tree.
Cimetière, Cimʳᵉ	Cemetery.
Clocher	Belfry.
Clouterie	Nail factory.
Colombier	Dove-cot.
Coron	Workmen's dwellings.
Cour des marchandises	Goods yard.
,, aux ,,	
Couvent	Convent.
Crassier	Slag heap.
Croix	Cross.
Darse	Inner dock.
Démoli - e	Destroyed.
Détruit - e, Détᵗ	
Déversoir	Weir.
Digue	Dyke, causeway.
Distillerie, Distⁱᵉ	Distillery.
Douane	Custom-house.
Bureau de douane	
Entrepôt de douane	Custom warehouse.
Dynamitière, Dynamⁱᵉ	Dynamite magazine.
Dynamiterie	Dynamite factory.
Écluse	Sluice, Lock.
Écluvette, Eclᵗᵉ	Sluice.
École	School.
Écurie	Stable.
Église	Church.
Emaillerie	Enamel works.
Embarcadère, Embʳᵉ	Landing-place.
Estaminet, Estamᵗ	Inn.
Étang	Pond.
Fabrique, Fabᵗ	Factory.
Fabᵗ de produits chimiques	Chemical works.
Fabᵗ de faïence	Pottery.
Faïencerie	
Ferme, Fᵐᵉ	Farm.
Filature, Filᵗʳᵉ	Spinning mill.
Fonderie, Fondⁱᵉ	Foundry.
Fontaine, Fonᵗⁿᵉ	Spring, fountain.
Forêt	Forest.
Forme de radoub	Dry dock.
Forge	Smithy.
Fosse	Mine, Pit.
Fossé	Moat, Ditch.
Four	Kiln.
,, à chaux	Lime-kiln.
Four à coke	Coke oven.
Glacerie	Glass Factory.
Gare	Station.
Garenne	Warren.
Garnison	Garrison.
Gazomètre	Gasometer.
Glacerie	
Fabᵗ de glaces	Mirror Factory.
Glacière	Ice factory.
Grue	Crane.
Gué	Ford.
Guérite	Sentry-box, Turret.
,, à signaux	Signal-box (Ry.)
Halte	Halt.
Hangar	Shed, Hangar.
Hôpital	Hospital.
Hôtel-de-Ville	Town hall.
Houillère	Colliery.
Huilerie	Oil factory.
Imprimerie, Impʳⁱᵉ	Printing works.
Jetée	Pier.
Laminerie	Rolling mills.
Ligne de haute marée	High water mark.
Laisse de basse marée	Low ,,
Maison Forestière, Mⁿ Fⁿᵉ	Forester's house.
Malterie	Malt-house.
Marbrerie	Marble works.
Marais	Marsh.
Marais salant	Saltern.
,, ,, Salt marsh.
Marché	Market.
Mare	Pool.
Meule	Rick.
Minière	Mine.
Monastère	Monastery.
Moulin, Mⁿ	Mill.
,, à vapeur	Steam mill.
Mur	Wall.
,, crénelé	Loop-holed wall.
Nacelle	Ferry.
Orme	Elm.
Orphelinat	Orphanage.
Oseraies	Osier-beds.
Ouvrage	Fort.
Ouvrages hydrauliques	Water works.
Papeterie	Paper-mill.
Parc	Park, yard.
,, aéronautique	Aviation ground.
,, à charbon	Coal yard.
,, à pétrole	Petrol store.
Passage à niveau P.N	Level-crossing.
Passerelle, Psˢᵉ	Foot-bridge.
Pépinière	Nursery garden.
Peuplier	Poplar tree.
Phare	Light-house.
Pilier, Pilʳ	Post.
Plaine d'exercices	Drill ground.
Pompe	Pump.
Ponceau	Culvert.
Pont	Bridge.
,, levis	Drawbridge.
Poste de garde	Coast-guard station.
Station côte	
Poteau Pᵘ	Post.
Poterie	Pottery.
Poudrière, Poudʳᵉ	Powder magazine.
Magasin à poudre	
Prise d'eau	Water supply.
Puits	Pit-head, Shaft, Well.
,, artésien	Artesian well.
,, d'arrêtage	Ventilating shaft.
,, ventilateur	
,, de sondage	Boring.
Quai	Quay, Platform.
,, aux bestiaux	Cattle platform.
,, aux marchandises	Goods platform.
Raccordement	Junction.
Raffinerie	Refinery.
,, de sucre	Sugar refinery.
Râperie	Beet-root factory.

War Diary
7th Arg. & Suth. Highrs.
May 1917.

Army Form C. 2118.

7th ARS. 1 Soth. HIGH'RS
Ref. Maps :- LENS 11
 51C

WAR DIARY
or
INTELLIGENCE SUMMARY.
(Erase heading not required.)

Place	Date	Hour	Summary of Events and Information	Remarks and references to Appendices
PENIN	1917 MAY 1st		In billets Training	ARB
"	2nd		" Continued training	ARB
"	3rd		" Reinforcements 129 or. arrived	ARB
"	4th		" "	ARB
"	5th		" Major MacBain 9th joined Battn.	ARB
"	6th		" Held Church Parade	ARB
"	7th		" Continued training	ARB
"	8th		" "	ARB
"	9th		" " Held into Battn Sports with 6th bn by	ARB
"	10th		" " Replaced highly. ARB bands 4th Alberta. War Cairns	ARB
"	11th		" " Old Alberta's War Cairns I.A. Raus joined Battn	ARB
"	12th		" At 10 a.m. Battn moved off & marched by Y'Huts via DOFFINE, IZEL-LEZ-HAMEAU-HERMAVILLE Reinforcements	ARB
"	13th		93 O.R. joined Battn. Held Clinical Parade.	ARB

WAR DIARY or INTELLIGENCE SUMMARY

Army Form C. 2118.

7th Argyll & Sutherland Highlanders

REF. MAPS. LENS 11
51B NW, PLOUVAIN & FAMPOUX

Place	Date 1917 MAY	Hour	Summary of Events and Information	Remarks and references to Appendices
ARRAS	14th		At 2.15pm Battn. marched off from "Y" Huts to billets in ARRAS	A&S See App.
"	15th		In billets, training	A&S
"	16th	7.30 am	orders were received to proceed at once to bivouacs – Divisional front that morning. Position was attacked by 9.45 am. At 10 pm Battn. moved into dugouts in RAILWAY EMBANKMENT H.13.d. Very heavy rain during afternoon & evening. Embankment was shelled about 11.30pm. Casualties 1 or. wounded.	A&S
EMBANKMENT H.13.d.	17th		In Divisional Reserve – Continued training. Embankment shelled at intervals throughout day.	A&S
do.	18th		" " " "	
do.	19th		Continued training. A&S	
do. to do	20th		" " Embankment heavily shelled today. 5.7" from Cambrai. 2 of Coys & Bn. HQ moved up. A&S	
do	21st		A & B Coys moved up to H.18.d in support of 1/5th R.Scots. Casualties 1 or. killed 5 or. wounded	A&S
do	22nd		" C & D Coys training 1 or. " 2 or. wounded + 1 or. missing	A&S
do	23rd		" A & B Coys were relieved by night + joined Battn.	A&S
do	24th		Battn. Cont'd training. Casualties 1 or. wounded	A&S
Support Battn.	25th		Battn. moved into Support position relieving 9th R.S. HQ A & B Coys in Railway Cutting H.13.c C & D Coy in H.24.b in CRUMP TRENCH. Casualties 1 or. killed 10 or. wounded. Supplied working parties for front line. Casualties 5 or. wounded	A&S

Army Form C. 2118.

WAR DIARY

7th Argyll & Sutherland Highlanders

REF MAPS. LENS II, 51 S.T. N.W
PLOUVAIN & FAMPOUX.

INTELLIGENCE SUMMARY

(Erase heading not required.)

Instructions regarding War Diaries and Intelligence Summaries are contained in F. S. Regs., Part II. and the Staff Manual respectively. Title pages will be prepared in manuscript.

Place	Date 1917	Hour	Summary of Events and Information	Remarks and references to Appendices
SUPPORT POSITION H.23.c. H.24.b.	MAY 26th		In support position. Supplied working + carrying parties for front line. A&B.	
do	27th		" " " " " " Capt. J. Cunningham " A&B	
do	28th		Relieved the 9th Royal Scots in front line & Right Sector. Battn Joined Battn H.Q. at I.9.c.9.2 A&B. Enemy aircraft active. Casualties 9 o.r wounded.	See Map App. I a
do	29th		In front line. Enemy artillery very active on front during the day. A German patrol lines at intervals during the night; attempted to reach No.1 Post Right Coy. from the near. Three enemy own lines and the Capt. was taken prisoner. A&B. Casualties 1 o.r killed 4 o.r wounded.	
do	30th		Enemy artillery very quiet during the day. Hostile aircraft very active, attempting to fly over our lines at low altitude but were driven off by Lewis machine gun fire. Casualties 8 o.r wounded. A&B Very heavy rain in the afternoon and evening. Enemy very quiet.	
do	31st		Enemy artillery comparatively quiet. During the night Battn was relieved by 8th Black Watch, 26th Infy Brigade + after relief proceeded to billets in ARRAS arriving there about 4am. Strength 31 Offs + 766 o.r.	See App. II

J. G. Taylor
Lt. Col.
7th Arg. Suth.ᵈ Highlanders

App. I.

SECRET. Copy No. 6

154th INFANTRY BRIGADE
OPERATION ORDER NO. 117.

Reference Maps :-
    51.C. 1/40,000.
    51.B.N.W. 1/20,000.

----

1.   The 154th Brigade will move from "Y" HUTS to ARRAS on the 14th May in accordance with attached March Table.

2.   Battalions will move by platoons, Machine Gun Company and Trench Mortar Battery by sections, at 50 yards distance. Distances as laid down in 51st Division No. G.121/4 of 6th March will be maintained between Battalions and transport.

3.   Staff Captain will make all billetting and administrative arrangements.

4.   Completion of all moves to be reported to Brigade Headquarters.

5.   Brigade Headquarters will close at "Y" HUTS at 2-30 p.m. and open at RUE DONCRE, ARRAS, on arrival.

    ACKNOWLEDGE.

                                            Captain,
                                      Brigade Major,
13th May, 1917.   154th Infantry Brigade.

ISSUED AT 3/... BY ORDERLY.

Copy No. 1 File.
      2 War Diary.
      3 9th Royal Scots.
      4 4th Seaforth Highrs.
      5 4th Gordon Highrs.
      6 7th A. & S. Highrs.
      7 154th M. G. Company.
      8 154th T. M. Battery.
      9 152nd Infantry Brigade.
    10 153rd Infantry Brigade.
    11 51st (H) Division "G".
    12 No. 2 Company A.S.C.
    13 51st Divisional Train.
    14 Camp Commandant, "Y" Huts.
    15 Town Commandant, ARRAS.
    16 Staff Captain.
    17 Brigade Transport Officer.
    18 Brigade Signal Officer.

MARCH TABLE.

No.	UNIT.	FROM.	TO.	ROUTE.	Remarks.
1.	7th A. & S. Highrs.	"Y" HUTS.	ARRAS.	ST.POL - ARRAS Road.	To march off at 2 p.m.
2.	154th Brigade Headquarters.	do.	do.	do.	To march off at 2-30 p.m.
3.	154th M. G. Company.	do.	do.	do.	To march off at 2-40 p.m.
4.	154th T. M. Battery.	do.	do.	do.	To march off at 3 p.m.
5.	9th Royal Scots.	do.	do.	do.	To march off at 3-10 p.m.
6.	4th Seaforth Highrs.	do.	do.	do.	To march off at 3-40 p.m.
7.	4th Gordon Highrs.	do.	do.	do.	To march off at 4-10 p.m.

App II.

SECRET.

Copy No. 6

154th INFANTRY BRIGADE
OPERATION ORDER NO.118.

Reference Maps :-
    Trench Maps 51.B.N.W. 1/20,000.
                 51.C.N.E. 1/20,000.
    LENS Sheet 11 1/100,000.

1.   The 26th Infantry Brigade will relieve the 154th Infantry Brigade in the Right Sector on the 31st May and night 31st May/1st June in accordance with attached relief table.
       Relief to be complete by 3-20 a.m. on 1st June.
       Command of Right Sector will pass to B.G.C. 26th Infantry Brigade on completion of relief.
       On 1st June the 154th Brigade will move, personnel by train, transport by road, to CHELERS area.
       Transport of units will move independently by road under orders of Brigade Transport Officer on 1st June, a distance of 100 yards to be maintained between units. No restrictions as to roads West of ARRAS.
       Details as to entraining and location of billets will be issued later.

2.   All details of relief in the line will be made between the O.C. 8th Black Watch and O.C. 7th A. & S. Highlanders.
       26th Machine Gun Company will relieve the 154th Machine Gun Company on the 30th.

3.   The infantry attached to 184th Tunnelling Company R.E. will be relieved by a similar party from 9th Division by mid-day, 1st June. These parties will rejoin their Battalions and move back with them.

4.   The 4th Gordon Highlanders will find a working party for A.D.A.S., XVII Corps of 8 officers and 400 other ranks on night of 29th/30th May, details later.

5.   Movements in forward area will be carried out by :-

    (a) Overland tracks where possible.
    (b) Tow path RIVER SCARPE.
    (c) Road ATHIES-ST.LAURENT BLANGY to cross roads G.18.c.5.4. thence South across the River through BLANGY to ARRAS.

6.   The Brigade Transport Officer will point out billets in ARRAS to representatives of each unit and units will make their own arrangements for guides.

7.   On arrival at CHELERS the Brigade Group will be formed as under :-

            154th Infantry Brigade.
            154th Machine Gun Company.
            154th Trench Mortar Battery.
            401st Field Company R.E.
            2/1st Field Ambulance.
            No.2 Coy. Divisional Train.
            1/8th Royal Scots (Pioneers).

** 2 **

8.   Completion of all reliefs and moves, giving positions of Headquarters, will be reported at once to Brigade Headquarters as "O.K".

9.   Brigade Headquarters will close at H.14.a.1.9. on completion of relief and open in ARRAS on arrival.

Acknowledge by wire.

Captain,
Brigade Major,
154th Infantry Brigade.

27th May, 1917.

ISSUED AT 7.30 BY ORDERLY.

Copy No.1 File.
   2 War Diary.
   3 9th Royal Scots.
   4 4th Seaforth Highrs.
   5 4th Gordon Highrs.
   6 7th A. & S. Highrs.
   7 154th M. G. Company.
   8 154th T. M. Battery.
   9 No.2 Coy. A.S.C.
   10 401st Field Company R.E.
   11 2/1st Field Ambulance.
   12 8th Royal Scots.
   13 51st (H) Division "G".
   14 152nd Infantry Brigade.
   15 153rd Infantry Brigade.
   16 51st Divisional Train.
   17 88th Infantry Brigade.
   18 26th Infantry Brigade.
   19 51st Divisional Artillery.
   20 Staff Captain.
   21 Brigade Transport Officer.
   22 Brigade Signal Officer.
   23 Town Commandant, ARRAS.

RELIEF TABLE.

No.	Date.	UNIT.	FROM.	TO.	RELIEVED BY.	REMARKS.
1.	1917 30th May.	154th Machine Gun Co.	LINE.	ARRAS.	26th Machine Gun Co.	All details to be arranged between C.O's. concerned.
2.	31st May.	4th Gordon Highrs.	STIRLING CAMP.	ARRAS.	8th Black Watch.	Relief will take place during morning. Battalion of 26th Brigade to come under orders of B.G.C. 154th Brigade. on arrival.
3.	do.	9th Royal Scots.	do.	do.	5th Cameron Highrs.	--- do ---
4.	do.	4th Seaforth Hrs.	SUPPORT.	do.	5th Cameron Highrs.	(The 26th Brigade may only put one Battalion across the River in which case the 2 Coys. 4th Seaforths in CRUMP and CRETE will be relieved under O.C. 7th A.& S. Hrs. arrangements and 2 Coys. 5th Camerons will relieve remaining 2 Coys. 4th Seaforths in Support.
5.	do.	7th A. & S. Highrs.	LINE.	do.	8th Black Watch.	
6.	do.	154th T. M. Battery.	LINE & SUPPORT.	do.	26th T.M. Battery.	All arrangements to be made by O.C's. concerned.
7.	do.	154th M. G. Company.	ARRAS.	HOUVELIN.	---	Personnel by bus. Transport by road.
8.	1st June.	154th Brigade less 154th M. G. Company.	ARRAS.	CHELERS AREA.	---	Personnel entrain ARRAS. Detrain LIGNY ST. FLOCHEL. Transport by road.

7th "ARG. & SUTH. HIGH^DRS."

WAR DIARY

JUNE 1917.

7th Argyll & Sutherland Highlanders
REF. MAPS LENS//11 Army Form C. 2118.
HAZEBROUCK 5a

WAR DIARY
or
INTELLIGENCE SUMMARY.
(Erase heading not required.)

Place	Date JUNE	Hour	Summary of Events and Information	Remarks and references to Appendices
ARRAS	1st		In billets. Battn entrained at station at 3 pm. detrained at TINCQUES and marched to billets in CHELERS. Transport moved by road. A.R.B.	
CHELERS	2nd		In billets. Reinforcements 119 or. joined Battn. A.R.B.	
"	3rd		Capt A. L. STEWART rejoined Battn. Church Parade. A.R.B.	
"	4th		At 7.30 am Battn marched to billets in BOURS about 7 miles. A.R.B	
BOURS	5th		Battn marched off at 8.30 am to billets in VERCHIN. Owing to heat & dust march was very trying. Dinners were taken on road & Battn reached billets 4 to 5 pm. A.R.B.	
VERCHIN	6th		In billets in VERCHIN. At 7.45 am. transport moved off A.R.B. to WIZERNES.	
"	7th		At 8 am. Battn moved off in motor buses to billets. ZOUAFQUES via WIZERNES — TILQUES & NORDAUSQUES. Transport moved by road to same place. A.R.B.	
ZOUAFQUES	8th		In billets. Training in training area A.R.B	
"	9th		" " " " Draft of 35 or. joined Battn A.R.B.	
"	10th		" " " " " 46 " " " A.R.B.	
"	11th		" " " " Practising Bde. attack A.R.B.	
"	12th		" " " " " on range. Held rifle A.R.B	
"	13th		" " " " near village. Competitions for NCOs & men A.R.B	

WAR DIARY
INTELLIGENCE SUMMARY

Ref. Maps:- HAZEBROUCK 27a N.E. 27a S.W.

Army Form C. 2118.

Place	Date 1917	Hour	Summary of Events and Information	Remarks and references to Appendices
ZOUAFQUES	June 14th		In billets. At 10.30 a.m. Battr. marched off at 10.30 a.m. to RANGE "A" Q.8.d. via NORDAUSQUES and main ST OMER ROAD. for range practice.	A.R.B.
"	15th		In billets. Continued training. 2/Lt. J.A. BLACK, R.E. joined Battr.	A.R.B.
"	16th	"	"	A.R.B.
"	17th		" Held Church Parade. Party of 103 o.r. for fortnights Course at Second Army Musketry School, NORTBECOURT	A.R.B.
"	18th		In billets. Continued training in NORTLEULINGHEM area.	A.R.B.
"	19th		" " Practised the attack on NORTLEULINGHEM area.	
"	20th	8 a.m.	Battr. marched to "B" range Q.7a arriving there at 8 a.m. & carried out stage 5 1st Diff. "Batmyth" and Rand Byr a 51st Diff. "Balmoyth" and Rand Byr a performance at Enemy. There was heavy Thunder performance at the Laryet evening. 20/Lt. R. CLARK joined Battr.	A.R.B.
"	21st		In billets. Continued training in billets in CROME STRAETE	A.R.B.
"	22nd	7.45 a.m.	At 7.45 a.m. Battr. marched off via NORDAUSQUES, MONNECOVE, GANSPETTE, WATTEN and LE BERSTACKS,	
CROME STRAETE	23rd		Continued training.	A.R.B.
"	24th		In billets. Held Church Parade.	A.R.B.

WAR DIARY or INTELLIGENCE SUMMARY

Army Form C. 2118.

Ref. Maps. HAZEBROUCK 27a NE 27a SW

Place	Date	Hour	Summary of Events and Information	Remarks and references to Appendices
CROMBE STRAETE	JUNE 25th		In billets. Battn carried out an attack practice on VOLKERINCKHOVE training area.	AKS
"	26th		In Billets. Battn moved off at 8.30 a.m. for Tontenam At 10 p.m. patrol practice was carried out.	AKS
"	27th		In billets. Continued training.	AKS
"	28th		" " "B" Coy is detailed for special training at 18th Corps School	AKS
"	29th		VOLKERICKHOVE. In billets. Training on Volkerinckhove Area in forenoon Capt A. STEIN joined Battn also 160 or reinforcements	AKS
"	30th		In billets. Continued training Battn Strength 32 Off. + 1004 or.	AKS

J.G. Stephens
Lt. Col.
Comg.
7th Arg & Suth Highlanders

7th Argyll &
Suth. Highrs.
War Diary.
July 1917.

WAR DIARY
or
INTELLIGENCE SUMMARY

7th Arg. & Suth. Highdrs.
Ref Maps: Sheet 27 } 28 N.W.

Army Form C. 2118.

Place	Date	Hour	Summary of Events and Information	Remarks and references to Appendices
CROMB-STRAETE	July 1st 2nd 3rd 4th 5th 6th 7th 8th		In Lillets	
"	9th		Continued training	
"	"		Lt W.R. Blair & 2nd Lt W. Scott joined Battn on 4th Capt W.W. Mitchell joined Battn on 8th	O.C.B.
A 30 central	10th		Battn marched off at 1.30 p.m. & entrained at St Omer, detrained at POPERINGHE and marched to Camp at A.30 central In Camp supplied working party for R.Es at Canal Bank.	O.C.B. O.C.B.
"	11th		" " " " " "Battn"	"
"	12th		Capt. D.S. Robertson rejoined "Battn". In Camp. During the night Battr relieved 9th Royal Scots in the front line E.14.d and C.15.c. About 11pm some enemy gas shells landed near the WILLOWS C.20.b. Battn from 11th Entrenching Battn. The following Officers joined the Battn from 11th Entrenching Battn. 2/Lts. D.W. Anderson, E.R. Sinclair, W.B. Fraser-Campbell, and J.P. Purves. 10 p.m. 1200 or were left in A.30 central in echelon "B".	See App. I
R.F. Trenches	13th		Between 10 and 11am some trench mortars fell near the Willows. Enemy 5.9" artillery were very active especially against TURCO FARM and Causeway over Canal. At 9.15pm enemy shelled our front line, some rounds dropped short & five yellow rockets were sent up from enemy 2.30am lines and immediately range was lengthened. About 2.30am gas shells were fired on which Canal. This is a new type of gas when violent bridging.	

7th ARGYLL & SUTHERLAND HIGHLANDERS.
REF MAPS:- 28 N.W.

Army Form C. 2118.

WAR DIARY
or
INTELLIGENCE SUMMARY.
(Erase heading not required.)

Place	Date	Hour	Summary of Events and Information	Remarks and references to Appendices
A.30 central and trenches (cont)	JULY 13th		About 5 am. one enemy aeroplane flew along our front line about 1,000 feet high. It was engaged by our Lewis guns & turned. Officers patrols reconnoitring our front. Saps at C.15.c.6.9 and C.15.c.8.6 were found to be deserted. Enemy were in loose and well concealed by vegetation but no get could be found. Sounds of trench tramways in enemy's lines were heard. Casualties 1 or. killed.	
"	14th		Enemy's artillery was very quiet during the day. Between 9.30 & 10 p.m. and 10.45 p.m. & 11 p.m. enemy shelled front support & Canal Bank trenches with all calibres. Our aircraft were very active, 29 machines seen over enemy lines at 7.45 p.m. Casualties 1 killed 9 or. wounded. ORB	
"	15th		At 2.35 a.m. our heavy T.Ms. bombarded enemy's support lines, BELOW & HURST FARMS with gas shells. Gas shells were again used by enemy about 1 am. on our battery positions west of CANAL. Incendiary shells were also freely used by enemy west of CANAL. A left side arm seen wearing a green cap with badge on left side was seen at C.14.d.9.1. Our Officers patrols again examined the enemy's wire. Casualties 2 or. killed 8 or. wounded. Battn was relieved by 9th Sherwood Foresters R.R.B. Joined Reinforcements. See App. II.	

7th Argyll Sutherland Highlanders

Army Form C. 2118.

WAR DIARY
or
INTELLIGENCE SUMMARY
(Erase heading not required.)

Ref. Maps:- 28 NW

Place	Date 1917 July	Hour	Summary of Events and Information	Remarks and references to Appendices
A.30 a.n.d	16th		Relief of Battn. was completed at 1.40 a.m. and Battn. marched back to E. Camp. Supplied working parties of 410 or.	aSH
"	17th		In Camp. Training. Supplied working parties. Capt. W. Nicol + working party of 175 or went to Canal Bank Def-	aSH
"	18th		" " Supplied working parties. Casualty 1 or. wounded	aSH
"	19th		" " " Casualty 1 or. wounded.	aSH
"	20th		" " Supplied working parties	aSH
"	21st		Capt. Cunningham + 135 or. relieved permanent pty in Canal Bank	aSH
"	22nd		Supplied working parties. Casualties 3 or. killed 30 or. wounded	aSH
"	23rd		" " 30 or. wounded.	aSH
"	"		Lt. Baxter, 2Lts Drummond + Park carried out a successful see App. III raid on German lines capturing four wounded prisoners + killing seventeen. Casualties 3 or. killed 4 or. wounded	" III
"	24th		Casualties:- Lt. Drummond wounded, 1 or. wounded	" IV
"	25th		In Camp. Supplied working parties for front line.	
"	26th		" " Casualty 1 or. wounded	
"	27th		" " Supplied working parties. Casualties aSH 4 10 or. Left Camp at 8.15 a.m. under Capt. Stein M.C. for Kortepyne Reserve aRHS

4th Arg. & Suth. Highrs
Ref. Maps 28 N.W.
PILCKEM

WAR DIARY
INTELLIGENCE SUMMARY.
(Erase heading not required.)

Army Form C. 2118.

Place	Date July	Hour	Summary of Events and Information	Remarks and references to Appendices
Camp. A.30 central	28th		In Camp at Mifton, an enemy aeroplane flew over Camp and fired his machine gun wounding one man.	
"	29th		In Camp. Lt. Col. Hyslop took over command of 153rd Inf. Bde. a&B as G.O.C. was wounded.	
"	30th		In Camp. Completing equipment and organisation of Coys for Operations under 2Lts. A.D. MORRISON and R. CLARK a&B. Two platoons attached to 401st Coy. R.E.	
"	31st	At 3.50 a.m.	51st Divn attacked and captured their objectives up to the GREEN LINE with 153rd Brigade on right and 152nd Brigade on left; 154th Brigade being in reserve. a&B	See appx.

JG Hyslop Lt/Colonel
Comdg. 7th Ary Suth Highlanders.

Appendix No. I

SECRET   154 Inf. Bde   Copy No.
                 Operation Order No 123

Ref. Map 57 I/NW 1/10,000

1.   The 7th Arg. & Suth'd Hrs and 4th Gordon
H'rs will relieve the 9th Royal Scots and
4th Seaforth H'rs respectively in the front line
on the night 12/13th July

2.   All details of relief to be arranged
direct between C.O.s concerned

3.   Guides at the rate of 1 per HQ, 1 per
platoon or post and 1 per Lewis Gun will
rendezvous at RIDGEWNSBURG CHATEAU at 10 pm

4.   Companies will meet guides in the
following order:—
       2 front line Coys — 7th A. & S. Hrs } 1 Offr from each
       3   4th Gordon Hrs } Batt will
       2 support Coys   7th A & S Hrs } go to rendezvous
       3   4th Gordon Hrs } and guide
                                       } the officers
                                       } to proper unit

5.   The Battalions in the line will take
over billets vacated by Battalions relieving them

6.   Petrol tins for water will be handed
over under Battalion arrangements.

7.   All air photos, defence schemes, complete
lists of working parties etc will be handed over
on relief

8.   200 yards between Companies will be
maintained on the march

9.   All reliefs will be reported as O.K.

       Acknowledge

11 July 1917   J. A. Dinwid, Capt
Issued at 5 pm by orderly.   Brigade Major
                                           154 Inf Bde

OPERATION ORDERS
by
Lieut.Col.H.G.HYSLOP, D.S.O.,
Commanding 7th Arg. & Sutherland Highrs.

12th July, 1917.

RELIEF. The Battalion will relieve the 9th Royal Scots in the line to-night.

Guides at the rate of one per post or per platoon will meet Companies at REIGERSBURG CHATEAU at 10 p.m.

Companies will leave here in following order:-
Three front platoons "C" Coy. start at 8 p.m.)
Reserve Platoon "C" Coy.   " " " ")
"D" Coy. start at 8-15 p.m.
2 Coys. 4th Gordon Highrs.   " " 8.30 and 8.45 p.m.
"B" Coy.   " " 9 p.m.
"A" ",   " " 9.15 p.m.

Two hundred yards distance.

Officers commanding "C" and "D" Coys. will each detail four runners for duty at Battalion Headquarters.

Two of those runners will go up in the afternoon with the advance parties to find out location of all Headquarters etc.

Officers commanding "A" and "B" Coys. will each detail two runners for duty at Battalion Headquarters; these will parade under 2/Lt. Dobbie.

Advance parties will take over all trench stores and 24 magazines for each Lewis gun, also detail of work parties.

Receipted lists of trench stores taken over will be sent to Battalion Headquarters in GORDON TERRACE by 10 a.m. on 13th inst.

Completion of relief will be reported to Battalion Headquarters by runner.

Lewis guns will be loaded on a limber at 7-30 p.m. and taken to REIGERSBURG CHATEAU.

10 Camp kettles, one for each ____ on in Canal Bank will be taken up, and Q.M. will arrange for fue_ ations made up in bags of 8 and 80 tins of water will be taken to REIGERSBURG CHATEAU to be drawn as follows:-

4 Tins per platoon.
2 "   " Company H.Q.
8 "   for Battalion H.Q.

C.Q.M.Ss. will go on with limbers and make all arrangements.

A limber for Officers' mess stores will be loaded at 7-30 p.m. and taken to Canal Bank.

Officers' valises and mess stores will be stored in No. 2 Hut, which will be shown to Officers servants this afternoon

Packs, greatcoats and blankets will not be taken into the trenches, these will be stored in huts in afternoon.

Blankets will be rolled in bundles of ten, and greatcoats will be in packs.

All ranks must take shaving kit in their haversacks, also water-proof sheets.

All reserve personnel not going into the line will parade at 7 p.m. in full marching order under Captain D.I.Robertson.

By order,
(Signed) A. R. BAIN, Lieut. & Adjt.,
7th Arg. & Sutherland Highlanders.

Operation Orders
by
Lieut. Col. H.G. Hyslop, D.S.O,
Commanding 7th Arg. & Suth. Highlanders,
15th July, 1917

The Battalion will be relieved in the line by the Sherwood Foresters tonight.

One guide per post of "D" Coy, and one guide per platoon from other Coys, along with one for Battalion H.Q. will be at Reigersburg Chateau at 9 p.m. under 2/Lt Dobbie.

On relief Coys will march by platoons to "E" Camp A.30. CENTRAL.

Completion of all reliefs is to be notified personally by Coy Commanders to Battalion Hd.Qrs.

Lewis Gun teams of "C" & "D" Coys will move out with "A" & "B" Coys on completion of relief.

2/Lt. Drummond and one reliable N.C.O. from "C" & "D" Coys will remain for 24 hours with incoming Coys. O.C. Coys will arrange for their rations.

"A" & "B" Coys will not be relieved by the Sherwood Foresters, but will not move from their present positions until they receive orders to do so from Battn. Hd. Qrs.

A Lewis Gun limber will be at Reigersburg Chateau at 12 midnight.

A limber for Officers' Mess Stores will be at Red Hart Estaminet at 10/30 pm

All platoons going out will cross the canal and go along the Essex Farm — NOORD HOFWIJK ROAD, thence by No. 5 route to REIGERSBURG CHATEAU.

All trench Stores will be handed over to relieving Coys, and receipts obtained.

Empty petrol tins must be sent down to Battn. Hd. Qrs. by runners and guides before relief.

A.K. Bain
Lieut. & Adjt.
7th ARG. & SUTH. HRS.

154 Inf. Bde Operation Order No 124   App No II

Ref Maps: Poperinghe & France Sheet 27 & 28 N.W.S.O.

1. 154 Inf Bde will be relieved on the night 13/14 July by two Battalions
33rd Inf Bde 11th Division. On the same night two Battalions 32nd Inf Bde
118 Inf Bde
will relieve 154 M.G. Coy (less 4 guns) and 154 T.M. Battery will be relieved on night
14/15 July.
1 M.G. Coy will leave 4 guns in position.

2. On completion of relief the 154 Inf Bde will be disposed as follows:-
Bde HQ, 9th R.Scots, 4th Sea Hrs, 154 T.M.B. — HOUTKERQUE area.
7th A & S Hrs, 8th Gor Hrs, 154 M.G. Coy (less 4 guns) — A30 central.
Detailed orders for relief will be issued later.

3. The following moves will take place on 13th and 16th July
respectively:-
(a) On 13th July
9th R. Scots will leave Inf lines from A30 central to HOUTKERQUE
taking over camps from 8th W. Riding & 5th Y. Lancs respectively (32nd Inf Bde)
Battalions will move off by Coys at 200yds distance, 9th R.Scots
followed by 4th Sea Hrs first Coy to move off at 1pm.

(b) On 16th July
154 Bde HQ and 154 TMB from A30 central to HOUTKERQUE
taking over accommodation vacated by 32nd Bde HQ & 32nd T.M.B.
Bde HQ to move off at 1pm, TMB to follow at 200 yards distance
On completion of all reliefs and moves giving position of HQrs to
be as detailed above as possible to Bde HQn.

4. Bde HQrs will close in CHIPS BARN on completion of relief
and open at A30 central on arrival, close at A30 central at 12noon
16th July and open at HOUTKERQUE at same hour.

5. Lorries
3 lorries will report at A30 central at 9am on 13th to take
blankets etc of 9th R.Scots and 4th Sea Hrs to HOUTKERQUE (1½ lorries
9th R.Scots, 1½ lorries 4 Sea Hrs).

6. Ammunition bombs and stores not required will be left in
present transport lines under guards.

Acknowledge

J A D---
Capt
Brigade Major
154th Inf Bde

12 July 17
Issued at 3pm Copied by

Copy No			Copy No	
1	Bde		15	51st Bde?
2	War Diary		16	152 Inf Bde
3	9th R. Scots		17	153
4	4th Sea Hrs		18	51st Divl Train (for R.O.S to AS)
5	8th Gor Hrs		19	33 Inf Bde
6	7th A & S Hrs		20	33
7	154 M.G.Coy		21	Staff Capt
8	154 T.M Batty		22	Bde Sig Off
9	118 Inf Bde		23	Bde Tr. Off
10	32			
11	C.R.E.			
12	Area Commdt CHIPS BARN			
13	C.R.A.			
14	Cdt 11th Sig Coy A30 Cent			

SECRET   Copy No 6

Amendment No 1
to 154 Inf Bde Operation Order No 124.

From :—
       Bde HQ will close at CANAL BANK
on completion of relief and open at Bde
Transport lines "G" at 9 pm on arrival, close
at Bde Transport lines at 12 noon 16th July
and open at HOUTKERQUE at same hour.
       Acknowledge.

14 July 1917   J A Davies
Issued at 1 pm by orderly   Capt
                                            Brigade Major
                                            154 Inf Bde.

_____

Copy No 1 — File
      2 — W. Diary
      3 — 9th R. Scots
      4 — 4th Sea Hrs
      5 — 6th Gor. Hrs
      6 — 7th A & S Hrs
      7 — 154 M.G. Coy
      8 — 154 T.M. Batty
      9 — 51st Div. G.
      10 — 51st Divl Train for No 3 Co A.S.C.
      11 — Camp Commdt A 30 central
      12 — Staff Capt
      13 — Bde Sig. Off
      14 — Bde T.R. Off.

SECRET   154 Inf Bde Operation Order No 125   Copy No 6

Ref Maps ST JULIEN 1/10000
         BELGIUM Sheet 28 N.W. 1/20000.

1. In continuation of O.O. No 124, the relief will take place as follows:-
9th Sherwood Foresters relieve 4th Gordons & 7th A&S.Hrs on night 15/16
32nd Machine Gun Coy relieve 154 M.G.C. (less 8 guns) " 14/15
33rd T.M. Batty relieve 154 T.M.B. " 14/15
Lewis Guns-9th Sherwood Foresters relieve Lewis Guns 7th A&S Hrs & 4th Gordons " 14/15

Each Battalion will leave an officer at HQ & a NCO at Coy HQ. in front line for 24 hours after relief as liaison.

2. All details of relief will be arranged between C.Os. concerned but guides will rendezvous at RAIGERSBURG CHATEAU as follows:-
On night 14/15 at 11.30 pm. - 1 guide per gun or mortar team, 1 guide per HQ.
" 15/16 " 9.30 pm. - 1 guide per platoon or post, 1 guide for HQ.
An officer will be sent with each Battn's guides to allot them to incoming units.
As the 9th Sherwood Foresters are taking over the 7th A.&S. Hrs Hqrs, the guides will be supplied by this Battn.

3. Commanding Officers will ensure that the Reserve platoons on Canal Bank, which will not be relieved by 9th Sherwood Fors, do not leave their positions till the whole of the front system relief is complete.

4. O.C. 9th Sherwood Foresters will visit Battn HQrs during morning of 15th to arrange details.
Coy Commanders & 2 NCOs per Coy will come to Bttn HQ. at about 3.30 pm on 15th and Battns will guide them up to Coys they are to relieve.
O.Cs 154 M.G.Co. & 154 T.M.B will meet O.C. 32nd M.G.C & 33 T.M.C at 118th Bde Hqrs at 9.30 am. 15th to arrange details.

5. ~~All details of all daily working parties found by Bt-~~ ~~tn will be handed over~~ Working parties from A30 central will continue to be found by 4th Gor Hrs & 7th A&S Hrs as at present.
Defence schemes, aeroplane photos & maps as taken over from 152nd Bde will be handed over.

6. Left Bttn will use HALIFAX TRENCH and Right Bttn STRAND BOAR LANE for relief.
All outgoing units will cross the Canal by the ESSEX FARM – NOORDHOFWYK Rd and not move along the Canal Bank.

7. Completion of all reliefs will be reported at once to Bde HQ. as "OK"

Acknowledge
                                              J A Davis Capt
13 July 1917.   Issued at 10 am   Brigade Major
                                            154 Inf. Bde.

Copy No 1 - File	Copy No 7 - 154 M.G.Coy	Copy No 13 - CRA	Copy No 19 - 32nd Bde
2 - W. Diary	8 - T.M. Bty	14 - Camp Commdt	20 - 33 Bde
3 - 9th R. Scots	9 - 118 Bde	- Bde Post	21 - Staff Capt
4 - 4 Sea Hrs	10 - HQS	15 - 51 Div G	22 - Bde
5 - 4 Gor Hrs	11 - CRE	16 - 152 Bde	23 - Bde H.Q.
6 - 7 A&S Hrs	12 -	17 - 153 Bde	
		18 - 51 Div Engineers	

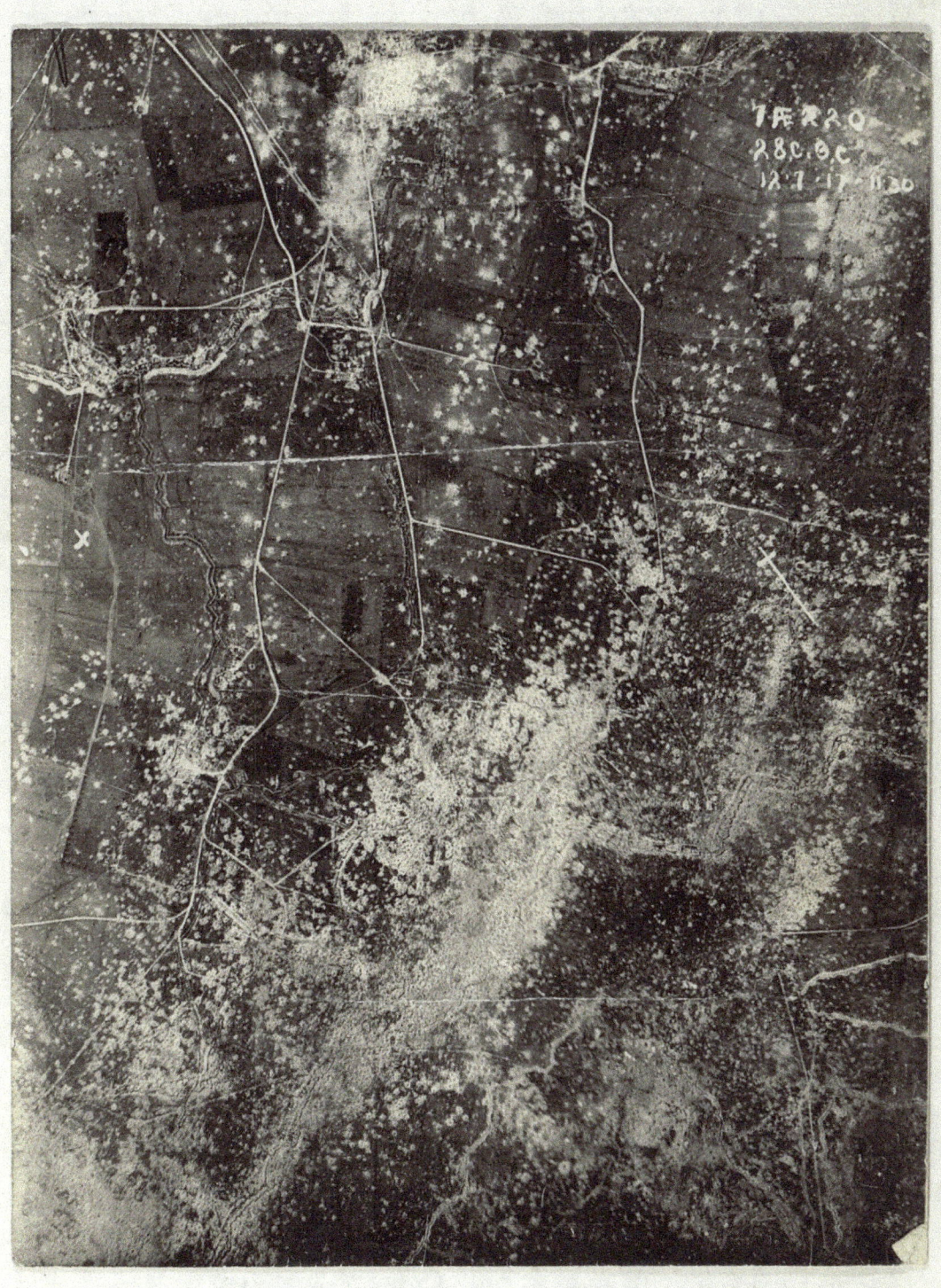

Appendix No. III

OPERATION ORDERS No. 2.
by
Lieut.Col. H.G.HYSLOP, D.S.O.

Copy No. 1...

22nd July, 1917.

Ref.Sheet 28.N.W. 2. 1/10,000.

1. **INTENTION.**

A Daylight Raid will be carried out by the Battalion on 24th July, 1917, on the enemy trenches from C.15.d.25.75. to C.15.a.72.05. with the object of obtaining identifications and of finding out what lines the enemy are holding.

2. **OBJECTIVES.**

German Front Line.
CALENDAR Trench from C15.d.25.75 to C.15.a.72.05.

Support Line.
CALENDAR SUPPORT. from C.15.d.18.90 to C.15.a.80.15.

Reserve Line.
CALENDAR RESERVE at junction with CALEDONIA LANE C.15.a.85.40 to 90.40.

3. **BARRAGE.**

To open on German Front line from C.15 d.65.30 to C.15.a.10.10 at ZERO and lift to form Box barrage at ZERO plus 4 minutes (See Artillery Operation Orders issued separately).

4. **STRENGTH.**

Raiders to consist of :-
"A" Party Lieut. A.R.Baxter and 30 o.r. of "A" Coy.

"B" Party 2/Lt. D. Drummond and 30 o.r. of "B" Coy.

Covering Party. 2/Lt. R.M.Park and 16 o.r. with two Lewis guns of "B" Coy.

5. **OPERATIONS.**

Covering Party less Lewis guns will go out before dawn and occupy MORTELDJE SAP C.15.d.03.60. They will leave a party of one N.C.O' and three men to hold the Sap head while the remainder of party withdraw to our trenches.

They will follow the Raiding Party from the trenches taking up position on the rising ground near MORTELDJE EST. C.15.c.85.60. with Lewis guns covering flanks of raiders and two rifle grenadiers (with No.24 grenades) on either flank. They will remain in position until raiders have all returned through them.

Raiders will leave our trenches at ZERO advancing under barrage and storming trenches when barrage lifts.
Party "A" will take trenches East of BOUNDARY ROAD exclusive to C.15.d.25.75.
(1) 1 Sergeant and 16 o.r. will advance on CALENDAR TRENCH to North of trench junction C.15.d.25.80 moving with their right on MORTELDJE SAP. On reaching trench 1 Sergeant and 8 o.r. will advance down trench to corner C.15.d.30.70. where they will establish a temporary post.
1 N.C.O. and 3 men will push up CALENDAR LANE C.T. as far as barrage will permit.
1.N.C.O. and 3 Men will examine the trench they have entered North of trench junction C.15.d.25.80.
XXX
(2) 1 Sergeant and 7 men will enter trench on either side of corner C.15.d.20.90 joining hands with parties on either flank and examining Eastern end of CALENDAR SUPPORT.

5. OPERATIONS (Continued).

(3). 1 N.C.O. and 4 men will enter trench East of BOUNDARY ROAD near C.15.d.06.85.
Lt. Baxter will accompany No.(1) Party and when he has satisfied himself that nothing more is to be gained by staying longer will give the signal (A whistle blast repeated by N.C.Os. in charge of Parties) to withdraw the whole of Party "A".

Party "B" will take trenches West of BOUNDARY ROAD inclusive to C.15.a.72.05.

(1) 1 Sergeant and 7 men will enter trench from Salient C.15.c.95.80 to BOUNDARY ROAD inclusive.

(2) 1 N.C.O. and 5 men will enter trench on either side of point C.15.c.85.90.

(3) 1 N.C.O. and 5 men will enter trench near junction of CALEDONIA LANE and Front Line.

(4) 1 Sergeant and 9 men will enter trench near same spot as (3) and if Front Trench is found unoccupied will at once push on to CALENDAR RESERVE moving over the open near CALEDONIA LANE. They will enter CALENDAR RESERVE obtain any indentifications and return as soon as possible without allowing themselves to become heavily engaged. Should Front Line be found strongly held this Party will not endeavour to push on further but will assist there.
2/Lt. Drummond will accompany (No.3) Party and on return of (No.4) Party will give the signal (A whistle blast repeated by N.C.Os. in charge of Parties) to withdraw all Party "B".

6. GENERAL INSTRUCTIONS.

All Parties will examine trenches and dug-outs they may find. Prisoners will be at once sent back under escort to our trenches. No bombs are on any account to be thrown except on extreme flanks or if necessary into dug-outs.
Parties "A" and "B" will withdraw independently of one another.

7. DIRECTING OFFICER.

Major Bickmore will be in our Front Trenches near C.15.c.5.7. and will direct operations. He will check raiders on return and will send up one or more golden rain rockets as a signal to the Artillery that the raid is over. He will be accompanied by a special Officer from the 282nd Army Brigade R.F.A.
4 Runners will be detailed to go with Major Bickmore.
A special report will be at once despatched to Battalion Hd.Qrs. on completion of Raid, and Major Bickmore and Officers of Raiding Parties will report personally at Bn. Hd.Qrs. as soon as possible after Raid.

8. STRETCHER BEARERS.

A party of 8 stretcher bearers with 2 stretchers will be detailed and will remain in our Front Line during Raid.

9. DRESS.

Raiders and Covering Party will wear trousers and puttees. No badges or identifications. No equipment for Raiders except Box Respirators will be worn. One man in every two will carry wire cutters either Rifle or Hand. Covering Party will wear equipment.

10. ARMS.

Raiders Bayonet and Rifle. 10 Rounds in magazine and two spare clips in pocket.
Each bomber will carry 4 Mills' bombs.
Covering Party will carry 120 rounds S.A.A. Officers will carry revolvers.

11. **TIME.**

Watches will be synchronised by the Adjutant at 5-30 p.m. on 23rd and again at 12-30 a.m. on the 24th July before Parties leave Camp.

12. **ZERO HOUR.**

ZERO Hour will be at 6 a.m.

13. **BATTN. HD. QRS.**

Bn. Hd. Qrs. will be in Bn. Hd. Qrs. of Right Sector of Division on East side of Canal Bank about C.25.a.9.7.

14. **MARCH ORDERS.**

Orders for departure from and return to Camp will be issued separately.

                                                              Lieut. Col.
Commanding 7th Arg. & Sutherland Highlanders.

```
Copy No. 1 to War Diary.
  "    "  2  " 51st (H) Divn.
  "    "  3  " 154th Inf. Bde.
  "    "  4  " 33rd Inf. Bde.
  "    "  5  " Bn. Hd. Qrs.
  "    "  6  " O.C. "A" Party.
  "    "  7  " O.C. "B" Party
               & Covering Party.
```

War Diary

Appendix No. IV

REPORT on DAYLIGHT RAID carried out by
7th ARGYLL & SUTHERLAND HIGHLANDERS
on 24th JULY, 1917.

STRENGTH - 3 Officers and 70 O.R.

OBJECTIVE.

The part of the German Front Line raided was from C.15.d.25.75 to C.15.a.72.05.

OPERATIONS.

Previous to the Raid MORTELDJE SAP (C.15.d.03.60) was occupied without opposition.

The barrage opened at 6 a.m., at which time the Raiders left our trenches and crept up under the barrage. At 6-4 a.m. the barrage lifted off the line to be raided and the trench was stormed.

The only part of the trench found occupied was at C.15.a.75.05, where 8 Germans were found, 3 of them in a small concrete shelter, the remainder in the trenches. As one or two of these showed fight by attempting to throw bombs, three were shot, the remaining five being brought back as prisoners, one being wounded.

Just previous to the Raid some Germans with full packs had been seen near C.15.a.70.89, and the 6th LINCOLNS had been requested to train a Lewis gun on that spot. When the barrage lifted off the Front Line these Germans, numbering seven or eight, attempted to run back; the Lewis gun open on them and four or five were seen to fall.

The scrap with the Germans in the Front line had taken up some little time and absorbed the party of 10 o.r. who had been specially detailed to go to CALENDAR RESERVE. This party therefore, only got to junction of CALENDAR Support and CALEDONIA LANE, where they saw a small concrete shelter, but no Germans. A few shots were fired at them from CALENDAR RESERVE, but these appeared to come more from one or two snipers than from an organised garrison.

The Raiding Party returned to our trenches about 6-28 a.m., and five rockets were at that time sent up to stop the barrage.

WIRE.

The wire is blown to pieces all along the Front of the trench and affords no obstacle at any place, and the same may be said of MORTELDJE SAP.

TRENCHES.

With the exception of two small portions at C.15.a.75.05 and C.15.d.00.85 the trenches can hardly be recognised as such. They are completely blown to pieces, and even the concrete shelters are smashed.

At C.15.a.75.05 there were three small concrete shelters which had not been much damaged. At C.15.d.00.85 the trench had not been greatly damaged and afforded about 6 feet of cover mostly breastwork. In this portion of the trench there were two square steel look-out posts with steel doors which were shut and could not be opened. The inside was, however, examined through a slit and appeared quite empty, and as if they had not been used for some time.

There was no sign of a travel trench or a trench railway.

The C.Ts. CALEDONIA LANE and CALENDAR LANE had been very much damaged for some distance back and were hard to recognise. The same may be said of CALENDAR SUPPORT.

NO MAN'S LAND.

No Man's Land is very much broken up, principally by old, deep shell holes with water in them.

MISCELLANEOUS.

No identifications were seen anywhere in the broken up Front Line.

At C.15.d.00.85 a quite new bit of tape was found running out from trench some little way into No Man's Land.

BARRAGE.

A special report on the barrage is being sent in by the R.F.A. Liaison Officer. A good many of the 18 pounder shrapnel were very short, and it is believed caused practically the whole of our casualties.

The Germans put down no barrage, and only a few shells were fired by them during the whole raid.

CASUALTIES.

One Officer, 2/Lt. Drummond, wounded, two o.r. killed, one o.r. died of wounds, four o.r. wounded (two at duty).

Lieut.Col.,
Commanding 7th Arg. & Sutherland Highlanders.

24th July, 1917.

SECRET.   Extracts from   App. V.   War Diary

INSTRUCTIONS FOR OFFENSIVE OPERATIONS.

GENERAL INSTRUCTIONS.

On a date and hour to be notified later (known as Z day and zero hour) the Fifth Army will attack the enemy's trenches E. and N.E. of YPRES.

The 51st Division will attack with:-
- 152nd Infantry Brigade on Right
- 153rd   "   "   Left.
- 154th   "   "   in Reserve.

Objectives and boundaries of Division and Brigades are shown on ~~attached tracing "A".~~ PILCKEM MAP.

The BLUE line consisting of the German first line system.

The BLACK line consisting of the German Support line system.

The GREEN line which is an undefined line and represents the best tactically defensive line covering the River STEENBEEK.

PLAN OF ATTACK.

The final objective for the first day will be the GREEN line.

After the capture of the GREEN line the 51st Division will push forward 2 Companies across the River STEENBEEK, the Company of the 152nd Brigade on the Right forming a Company post at MON DU RATA and the Company 153rd Brigade forming a similar post on MILITARY ROAD.

These posts are to form "rallying points" for a Cavalry Squadron which will come under orders of Division.

The 154th Brigade will be in Divisional Reserve and will be formed up with Two Battalions on the CANAL BANK, i.e.
- 9th Royal Scots on right.
- 4th Seaforths on left.
- 2 Battalions in "D" and "E" Camps A.30 central

If the 152nd and 153rd Brigades succeed in capturing the whole of the first day's objectives, the 154th Brigade will be used either to relieve these Brigades probably on Night Z plus 1, or for a further advance on Z plus 1 day.

9th Royal Scots and 4th Seaforth Highlanders will be under orders of 152nd and 153rd Brigades respectively to continue the advance to the GREEN line and across the River STEENBEEK in the event of serious fighting on the BLACK line having absorbed the whole of the troops of the 152nd and 153rd Brigades.

Infantry will not move by roads but by double cart track across country which is being made as far as our front line and continued beyond after Zero hour.   Artillery will have precedence over all roads and tracks after Zero hour.

HEADQUARTERS.

152nd Brigade	...	Dugout - The WILLOWS, C.20.b.65.65.
154th Brigade	...	Two in CANAL BANK.
	...	Two in Camps "E" and "D".

ARTILLERY.

The attack of the 51st Division will be supported by:-
> 51st Divisional Artillery.
> 11th   "   "
> 2 Army Field Artillery Brigades, viz:-
> 77th A.F.A. and 282nd A.F.A. Brigades.

The attack will be preceded by a bombardment lasting, as far as is known at present, 7 days.

Barrage maps will be issued down to Platoon Commanders.

CO-OPERATION WITH AIRCRAFT.

The 7th Squadron R.F.C. will provide contact aeroplane during the forthcoming operations. This will be marked with two black rectangular flags (2 feet x 1'3") attached to and projecting from lower plane on each side of the fusilage.

The signal for contact plane for Infantry to light flares will be either:-
> (1) A series of white lights.
> (2) A succession of A's on Klaxon horn or daylight lamp.

Infantry will show their position to the Contact Plane by lighting flares. As far as possible these flares should be lighted in bunches of three. White flares will be used until a change to red is ordered.

Each Brigade and Battalion headquarters will be marked by ground sheets of authorised shape with the code letters of the Unit laid out with white stripes alongside. Signalling to aeroplane will be done by panels.

PRISONERS OF WAR.

Prisoners taken will be collected in bunches and sent down under Battalion escort to the Prisoners' Collecting Post XXXXXXX at C.25.a.5.6., reporting en route to Brigade Headquarters. At Collecting Post they will be taken over by XXXXXXXXXXX the Divisional A.P.M.

Only weapons will be removed from prisoners.

DOCUMENTS.

Arrangements will be made by Battalions for a systematic search of German corpses. The German indentity disc is in two halves and is easily broken. One half of the identity disc and all documents will be collected.

SIGNAL COMMUNICATIONS.

Brigade Forward Stations.

These stations will be marked by Blue and White flags.

Whenever a Battalion Headquarters moves forward its position must be marked by a distinctive flag. (The flag for this Battalion is dark blue mounted on two sticks with BATTALION HEADQUARTERS and four pale blue stripes painted on it). These positions will then become advanced Report Centres.

SIGNAL COMMUNICATIONS CONTINUED

LIGHT SIGNALS.

From ZERO onwards the S.O.S. signal on the whole Army Front will be a series of four lights, two RED, two GREEN, fired rapidly in that order.

It will be acted on by the Artillery or Machine Gun Barrage, if made in any one of the three following ways:-

    (1) S.O.S. Signal Rifle Grenade - One signal bursting into two RED and two GREEN balls

    (2) Rockets - Two RED, two GREEN, fired rapidly in that order.

    (3) Very Lights (1½" and 1") - Two RED, two GREEN, fired rapidly in that order.

Messages transmitted by other means than wireless, are whenever possible, to be sent in B.A.B. They may, however, be sent in clear if the tactical situation is sufficiently critical or circumstances sufficiently urgent to warrant no waste of time.

Messages by Pigeon Post will be sent in clear

EMPLOYMENT OF R.E. AND PIONEERS.

Assisting Infantry in making strong points.

Marking tracks and fixing sign boards in captured trenches.

INSTRUCTIONS FOR CAVALRY SQUADRONS.

The role of the Cavalry is to establish themselves under cover of the Infantry posts at MON DU RASTA and the Bridgehead covering Military Road and thence to sent out patrols.

In the event of counter-attack, the Cavalry will act dismounted in defence of the Infantry posts.

ACTION OF TANKS.

8 Tanks have been allotted to 51st (H) Division on ZERO day.

They will be divided into two Echelons.

The First Echelon, will be used to mop up on the BLUE line if necessary and the BLACK line, the objectives aimed at being the ones where the assistance of the tanks would most likely be required. These tanks will advance with the Infantry to the GREEN line, and assist in covering the consolidation of it, and cover the crossing of the STEENBEEK by the Infantry told off to form the Bridgeheads.

The Second Echelon, will have the special task of crossing the STEENBEEK at the points shown and covering the consolidation of the bridgeheads.

Crossing the STEENBEEK.
Infantry must be prepared to give material assistance to the tanks in helping to prepare the crossings at the points shown on map.

Signals between Tanks and Infantry.
The following signals (disc) will be used between Tanks and Infantry
    GREEN DISC ....Wire Cut.
    RED..................................Wire Uncut.

    RED   )........................... Have reached my objective.
    GREEN)

ACTION OF TANKS CONTINUED.

    RED   )
    WHITE) .... Enemy is in dug-outs.
    RED   )

The location of any Tank becoming derelict will be sent to Brigade Headquarters.

The position of Tanks will be marked on Maps as follows:-

                             Tank in Action.

                             Tank out of Action.

A Tank out of Action displays -

    (a) A WHITE Square 18"x 18" on top of the Tank for aeroplanes to see.

    (b) 3 RED Discs for TANKS or INFANTRY to see.

Whenever possible when marking Tanks on Maps the Battalion Letter and number of Tank should be stated.

A.L.Bain
Lieut. & Adjt.,
7th Arg. & Sutherland Highlanders.

21st July, 1917.

7th "ARG. & SUTH. HIGHDRS."

WAR DIARY

AUGUST 1917.

9th ARG. & SUTH. HIGHDRS.
REF MAPS:- 28 N.W., ST. JULIEN Army Form* C. 2118.

WAR DIARY
INTELLIGENCE SUMMARY.
(Erase heading not required.)

Place	Date 1917 Aug.	Hour	Summary of Events and Information	Remarks and references to Appendices
TRENCHES	1st		In dugouts, three Coys in the Div. at 1st British front line C.14.d. CASAL BANK C.9.5.E. One Coy in old British front line C.14.d. Casualty 1 or. wounded	A+B
"	2nd		do Very wet weather.	A+B
"	3rd		do Casualties 3 or. wounded, 1 or. killed.	A+B
"	4th		do During the night the Battn relieved the 9th Royal Scots in the front line of the right sub-sector, C.5.C. Casualties 6 or. wounded.	see App. I
FRONT LINE	5th		Enemy artillery very active at periods throughout the day commencing at 9.30 am on C.10.C and along BLACK LINE. Seven Enemy aircraft flew low over our lines at 11.30 am and about 7.30 & 6 pm. Heavy barrage from just down on our trenches about 9.30 pm. Casualties 5 or killed 9 or. wounded.	A+B
"	6th		Enemy artillery very active about 5 am particularly around C.4.d.8.H. S.O.S. signals were seen by artillery on left, but owing to mist they were not clearly seen by artillery. S.O.S. was fired back from Battn H.Q. by wireless and light signals. Artillery then opened. An Officer's patrol reconnoitred C.5.a.8.1, C.5.a.8.0.35 and C.5.a.74.40 but no enemy were seen. Enemy was putting up flares about C.5.a.70.65, and appeared to be holding small posts about 300 yards from the LANGEMARCK ROAD. Movement was also seen in LANGEMARCK. Casualties 3 or. killed 5 or. wounded.	Ref H. Harris enquiry
"	7th		All during the day enemy were exceptionally active with shrapnel & H.E. barrage on our area. An E.A. flew over our lines and fired a M.G. during the night. Battn were relieved by 9th Wind Yorks. 32nd Bde Relief was speedy carried out by heavy enemy shelling & mist. Casualties Lt. C. Scott wounded 2 or. killed 14 or wounded.	see App. II A+B

WAR DIARY

INTELLIGENCE SUMMARY

7th ARG. & SUTH. HIGHDRS.
REF. MAPS 28 NW
27
HAZEBROUCK 5a.

Army Form C. 2118.

Place	Date 1917 Aug	Hour	Summary of Events and Information	Remarks and references to Appendices
CANAL BANK	8th		On completion of relief Battn. moved into dugouts in the CANAL BANK & left there at 8 a.m. marched to VLAMERTINGHE and proceeded by train to POPERINGHE. Battn. then marched from there to Tincilling Camp. L. 36. c. Reserve personel from HOUTKERQUE and a draft of 100 r. joined Battn. Casualties 8 or. wounded.	a/R.B.
ST JANSTER BIEZEN	9th		In Camp.	a/R.B.
GANSPETTE - HELLEBROUCQ	10th		Battn. proceeded by train from PROVEN to WATTEN leaving PROVEN at 6 p.m. & marched from WATTEN to billets in GANSPETTE and HELLEBROUCQ. Transport proceeded by road to WORMHOUDT.	a/R.B.
"	11th		In billets. Transport arrived in GANSPETTE	a/R.B.
"	12th		Held Church Parade. Major W. Frew & Lt. G.W. Tickell joined Battn.	a/R.B.
"	13th		Lts. F. Cameron and J. Miller also Rev. J.S. Leishman joined Battn.	a/R.B.
"	14th		Training.	a/R.B.
"	15th		Co-operating with other three Battns. ex Brigade attack Practice was carried out. 190 r. reinforcements joined Battn.	a/R.B.
"	16th		Training. 2/Lt. D.R. WATSON joined Battn.	a/R.B.
"	17th		"	a/R.B.
"	18th		"	a/R.B.

WAR DIARY
or
INTELLIGENCE SUMMARY.
(Erase heading not required.)

7th ARGYLL & SUTHERLAND HIGHDRS

Army Form C. 2118.

REF MAPS HAZEBROUCQ 5a SHEETS 27 and 28 NW

Place	Date August 1917	Hour	Summary of Events and Information	Remarks and references to Appendices
GANSPETTE HELLEBROUCQ	19th		In billets. Held Church Parade. "B" Coy Sports were held in the afternoon.	A.R.B a.R.B
"	20th		" Continued training. D. Coy reinforcements joined Battn.	a.R.B
"	21st		" " a platoon attack competition was won by "B" Coy.	
"	22nd		" " D. Coy + a guard mounting competition by "B" Coy. Battn transport moved off to NOORDPEENE leaving a.R.B	
"	23rd		Battn moved by train leaving WATTEN at 12.30 p.m. and detraining at AREELE, thence by route march to TUNNELLING CAMP, St JANSTER BIEZEN.	a.R.B
ST JANSTER BIEZEN	24th		In Camp. Training. Rev W. Jardine rejoined Battn.	a.R.B
"	25th		" "	a.R.B
"	26th		" " Lt. Col. N.G. Hyslop D.S.O. left Battn to Command 59th Inf. Bde.	a.R.B
"	27th		" " Very strong gale + heavy rain.	a.R.B
"	28th		" "	a.R.B
"	29th		Battn marched off at 5.30 a.m. to MURAT CAMP B. 30. 4.2. via SWITCH ROAD round POPERINGHE see App. III.	a.R.B
MURAT CAMP B.30.4.2 BRIELEN	30th		VLAMERTINGHE and BRIELEN. Transport moved to rear of Battn to HOSPITAL FARM.	a.R.B
"	31st		In Camp. Training.	a.R.B

D.F. Buchanan, Major,
7th Arg. Suth. Highrs.

Ref Map ST. JULIEN   SECRET   54 Inf. Bde   Copy 06
1/10000   ...tion Order No 131.

1.   The 7th Arg & Suth'd Br and 4th Gordons
       will relieve the 9th R. Scots and 4th Seaforth Br
       respectively in the front line tomorrow the 20th inst.

2.   All details of relief will be arranged
       between ... Os. concerned.

3.   Relieving battalions will move by platoons
       at 50 yards interval, companies at 100 yards
       interval as far as battalion H.Q. on one line
       (If the weather clears this may have to be
       modified).

4.   Guides and rendezvous will be arranged
       between battalions concerned, but a guide to take
       relieving battalions to Battn H.Q. in the line
       can be arranged by Brigade if required.

5.   BLACK and BLUE lines will be relieved
       by daylight as far as possible.

6.   The 4th Seaforth Br may accommodate
       the company of LANCASHIRE Fus in Canal Bank
       if accommodation can be found for them there.

7.   Ingoing battalions will carry two days'
       rations in with them. The greatest care must be
       taken to have reliable guides for all the forward posts.

8.   Before relief O.C. 4th Seaforth Br will arrange
       to send all the WELSH in his area back to their battalion.

9.   Every endeavour will be made to collect all
       tools, S.A.A. bombs and petrol tins into dumps and handed
       over to relieving units and a duplicate list forwarded to Bde HQ.

10.   Completion of relief to be reported to Bde HQ
       in B.A.B.

       ACKNOWLEDGE

                                                    H.W. Paulin Lt
                                                        for Capt
                                                    Brigade Major
                                                   154 Inf. Bde.

5.30p

Copies to all Bde Units, 51st Div, Recce right and left ..., ...
... Cmdt, Bde Staff, Area Comdt Canal Bank.

SECRET

Warning Order

O.C. 9th Royal Scots
    4th Seaforth Hrs
    6th Gordon Hrs
    7th A. & S. Hrs

1. The 154 Inf. Bde will be relieved by the 32nd Brigade in the line on the 6th inst. and night 7/8 as follows:

On 6th inst.
    9th West Yorks relieve 9th Royal Scots
    8th Duke of Wellington's Reg. relieve 4th Seaf Hrs

These battalions on relief move by train to ST. JANSTER BIEZEN.

On the night 7/8th
    9th West Yorks relieve 7th A.S. Hrs
    8th Duke of Wellington Reg. relieve 6th Gordon Hrs

These battalions on relief will move to CANAL BANK to accommodation occupied by 9th R. Scots & 4th Seaf. Hrs respectively.

On the 8th inst
    7th A. & S. Hrs & 6th Gordon Hrs move by train from BRIELEN to ST. JANSTER BIEZEN, leaving at 9 A.M.

Details later.
Acknowledge.

J.E. Dine
CAPT.
BDE. MAJOR 154th INF. BDE.

5 Aug 1917

Copy No. 6

Ref Map ST JULIEN 1/10000
Sheet 27.28 1/40000

184 Infantry Bde. Operation Order No. 132

1. In continuation of Warning Orders issued yesterday the relief of the 75th Bde by the 32nd Bde will take place in accordance with attached relief table.

2. On completion of relief the 184 Bde will concentrate on the ST JANSTER BIEZEN area in accordance with attached march table.

3. All details of relief including times and rendezvous for guides will be arranged between the COs concerned.

4. All plans, maps, and photos etc will be handed over.

5. Sappers malos will rejoin the Brigade at DIRTY BUCKET CAMP to be completed by 3 pm on 7th inst.

6. Garrisons of P.L.9 posts will be withdrawn on night 7/8th and rejoin the Brigade at DIRTY BUCKET CAMP reporting to Major _____ 9th R. Scots under orders to be issued by _____ with HQ.

7. During all moves a distance of 100 yards to be maintained between Companies and units of equivalent will exist.

8. Every endeavour will be made to collect all trench stores into dumps before handing over, duplicate list to be forwarded to Staff Capt.

9. Completion of all relief and moves, giving position HQ will be reported to 184 HQ Brief on P.R.P.

10. Bde HQ will close at Corn Farm on completion relief and open at V.13.d. on arrival, close at A.27.d.4.3 at 5 am on 8th inst and open at Tournesing Camp, ST JANSTER BIEZEN by 8.30 am.

Acknowledge.

ack

5 August 1917
Issued at 7.30 am 6/8

J. Dennis Capt.
Brigade Major
184 Inf. Bde.

RELIEF TABLE

DATE	No	UNIT	FROM	TO	RELIEVED BY	ROUTE	REMARKS
Aug 6	1	9th Royal Scots	OLD BRITISH LINE & CANAL BANK	DIRTY BUCKET CAMP (A 30 CENT)	9th W YORKS	ESSEX FM - CROSS RDS B 29 d 7.5 - CROSS RDS B 22 c 6.9 - SIEGE JUNT - BRIDGE JUNT - HOSPITAL FM - DIRTY BUCKET CORNER	
- DO -	2	4th Sea Hdrs	BLUE LINE & CANAL BANK	- DO -	8th Duke Wellingtons Regt	- DO -	
- DO -	3	1/2 154 M.G. Coy, 1/2 232 M.G. Coy, 154 T.M. Batty	CANAL BANK	- DO -	32nd M.C. Coy, 32nd T.M. Batty	- DO -	
Night 7/8th	4	4th Gor Hdrs	LINE	CANAL BANK	8th Duke Wellingtons Regt		} All 4 Coys will be Accommodated in Canal Bank
- DO -	5	7th A & S Hdrs	LINE	- DO -	9th W YORKS		- DO -
- DO -	6	1/2 154 M.G. Coy, 1/2 232 M.G. Coy	- DO -	- DO -	32nd M.C. Coy		
- DO -	7	154 Bde H.Q.	FOCH FM	A 27 d 4.3	32nd Bde H.Q.	AS PER No 1	

March Table

Date	No.	Unit	From	To	Starting Point and Time	Road	Remarks
August 5th	1	15th R.W.F.	27th R.F.A.	Smelting Works Tram Junction (Hove-Crowhurst Rd)	5 a.m.	Church Road – Offington Hollett – Poppering Road – Dozing Road	March to be completed by 7:30 am. Advance parties to report to Camp Commandant St Janvier re sites for camps. Shelter trenches to be dug if time permits for men & horses. Shelters to be dug for the Cap & Pots Ready
do	2	2nd Royal Scots	D.H.Q. Bowers Camp	do	do	do	
do	3	46 Infy Bde	do	do	5.20 a.m.	do	
do	4	432 M.G.C. 150 K.T.M.B.	do	do	5.40 a.m.	do	
do	5	46 Div Amn Coln 156 & 114 M.G.C. 2nd & 11 M.G.C. 4 M.G.C.	Crown Bank	do	—	—	By lightly Going except orders to be issued by S.O. Extra Brigade Train west of Poperinghe

Administrative Orders
154th Inf. Bde. O.O. 182

1. Echelon B and transports of 7th A. & S. Hrs. 4th Gordon Hrs, 154th M.G. Coy., and 154th T.M. Battery will march to St JANSTER BIEZEN on 8th inst. under orders of Bde Transport Officer, leaving A.27.d. at 5.15 a.m.

2. Cookers may move independently under Battalion arrangements.

3. Baggage wagons will report to T.Os. on evening of 7th.

4. Tents at A.27.d. will be taken to new Transport Lines.

5. One bus will start from A.27.d. at h.hr. on 7th inst. with the following billeting parties, who will stay overnight at St JANSTER BIEZEN
   Each Battn.   5.
   M.G. Coy.   1.
   T.M. Battery   1.
reporting to Major Thorburn 1/8th Royal Scots Tunnelling Camp.

                                A Scott
                                Captain
                                Staff Captain
6th August, 1917.   154th Inf. Brigade

Copies to:-
   All Units
   All T.Os.

S E C R E T.

Copy No. ..6....

App III

154th INFANTRY BRIGADE
OPERATION ORDER NO. 134.

Reference Maps :-
    Sheets 27 & 28 1/40,000.
    Sheet 28.N.W. 1/20,000.

---

1.   In continuation of Warning Order KK307, the 154th Infantry Brigade Group consisting of 154th Infantry Brigade and 232nd M. G. Company will move from TUNNELLING CAMP, ST. JANSTER BIEZEN, to MURAT CAMP, B.30.b. on 29th inst. in accordance with attached march table.
    The starting point will be the road junction L.4.b.7.2.

2.   Echelon "B" will proceed to HOUTKERQUE on 29th by march route under Battalion arrangements.
    The senior officer in the Brigade Surplus Personnel will be in command of the whole Brigade detachment and report to COMMANDANT on arrival.

3.   First Line Transport will accompany Units and take over Transport Lines at HOSPITAL FARM.

4.   Administrative Instructions have been issued by Staff Captain.

5.   Completion of move will be reported at once to Brigade Headquarters.

6.   Brigade Headquarters will close at TUNNELLING CAMP at 5.30 a.m. and open at CHATEAU DES TROIS TOURS on arrival.

    ACKNOWLEDGE.

ack?

J C Durie
Captain,
Brigade Major,
154th Infantry Brigade.

ISSUED AT 11 a.m. BY ORDERLY.

Copy No. 1 to File.
        2   War Diary.
        3   9th Royal Scots.
        4   4th Seaforth Highrs.
        5   4th Gordon Highrs.
        6   7th A. & S. Highrs.
        7   154th M. G. Company.
        8   154th T. M. Battery.
        9   232nd M. G. Company.
       10   No. 2 Coy. A.S.C.
       11   51st Divl. Train.
       12   51st (H) Division "G".
       13   152nd Infantry Brigade.
       14   153rd Infantry Brigade.
       15   Camp Commandant, TUNNELLING CAMP.
       16   Camp Commandant, MURAT CAMP.
       17   Staff Captain.
       18   Brigade Transport Officer.
       19   Brigade Signal Officer.
       20   Area Commandant, HOUTKERQUE

M A R C H   T A B L E.

No.	Unit.	From.	To.	Time of passing Starting Point.	Route.	Remarks.
1.	154th T.M. Battery.	TUNNELLING CAMP.	MURAT CAMP.	5.20 a.m.	SWITCH ROAD - Main POPERINGHE - VLAMERTINGHE Road to H.8.b.4.9. - POTTENHOEK-BRIELEN.	
2.	232nd M.G. Company.	-do-	-do-	5.30 a.m.	-do-	
3.	154th M.G. Company.	-do-	-do-	5.40 a.m.	-do-	
4.	154th Brigade Hd. Qrs.	-do-	CHATEAU DES TROIS TOURS.	6.00 a.m.	-do-	
5.	7th A. & S. Highrs.	-do-	MURAT CAMP.	6.10 a.m.	-do-	
6.	4th Gordon Highrs.	-do-	-do-	6.35 a.m.	-do-	
7.	9th Royal Scots.	-do-	-do-	7.00 a.m.	-do-	
8.	4th Seaforth Highrs.	-do-	-do-	7.25 a.m.	-do-	

200 yards between Companies and units of similar road space to be maintained throughout, greater distances EAST of VLAMERTINGHE can be made at discretion of C.O's.

PROVISIONAL.

154th INFANTRY BRIGADE
ADMINISTRATIVE INSTRUCTIONS No. S.S. 58.

In the event of the Brigade moving to MURAT CAMP, the following will come into force :-

BILLETING PARTIES.

A bus will start from entrance to "M" Camp on ST. JANSTER BIEZEN Road at 2 p.m. on 28th and take the following parties to MURAT CAMP; there they will report to Staff Captain at Camp Commandant's Office. They will be prepared to stay over-night.

            Each Battalion   ... 5.
            Each M. G. Company ... 1.
            T. M. Battery   ... 1.

LORRIES.

2 Lorries for each Battalion, 1 for M. G. Coys and T. M. Battery combined will arrive at "N" Camp about 8 p.m. to-morrow, to take blankets, etc., on 29th. Baggage wagons will report to units to-morrow night and be returned to No. 2 Coy. A.S.C. immediately move is complete. After taking blankets, etc., to MURAT CAMP, lorries will return to their Park. Arrangements for transport of baggage, etc., of Echelon "B" to HOUTKERQUE will be notified later, also details about rations.

TRANSPORT.

Transport Lines and Q.M. Stores will be at HOSPITAL FARM. Transport Officers or representatives will report to Bde. Transport Officer at Bde. Transport Lines, 9 a.m. on 28th and proceed to HOSPITAL FARM to be allotted ground.

The tents and bivouac sheets allotted to units for Transport will be taken to HOSPITAL FARM. 154th M. G. Company will draw 4 tents from Bde. H.Q. T. M. Battery Transport will move with Bde. H.Q.

TENTS.

Units will check numbers of Tents and Tent Shelters before vacating present Camps, and obtain a receipt from the Area Commandant, forwarding a duplicate to this office by 9 a.m. on the 30th inst.

The Tents and Tent Shelters in possession of First Line Transport will not be included in these numbers.

ACKNOWLEDGE.

ack

A. Scott
Captain,
Staff Captain,
154th Infantry Brigade.

27th August, 1917.

Copy to 9th Royal Scots.
       4th Seaforth Highrs.
       4th Gordon Highrs.
       7th A. & S. Highrs.
       154th M. G. Company.
       154th T. M. Battery.
       232nd M. G. Company.
       No. 2 Coy. A.S.C.
       51st Divl. Train.
       Camp Commandant, Tunnelling Camp.
          "   "   MURAT, Camp.
       Supply Officer, No. 2 Coy. A.S.C.
       Brigade Transport Officer.
       File.

SECRET.

154th INFANTRY BRIGADE
AMENDMENT TO O. O. No. 134.

Para. 2 of O. O. No. 134 is cancelled.

Echelon "B" will accompany units and not proceed to HOUTKERQUE.

One officer and a party from each unit will remain behind to clean up Camp and Transport Lines; a certificate to be obtained from Camp Commandant that lines are clean and forwarded to Bde. H.Q. by 30th inst.

ACKNOWLEDGE.

A Scott
Captain,
Brigade Major,
154th Infantry Brigade.

28th August, 1917.

To all recipients of O.O. No. 134.

7th Argyll & Sutherland
Highlanders.
War Diary.
September 1917.

4th Arg'll & Suth'd Highlanders
Ref Maps 28 N.W.

WAR DIARY
or
INTELLIGENCE SUMMARY

Army Form C. 2118.

34

Place	Date Septr 1917	Hour	Summary of Events and Information	Remarks and references to Appendices
MURAT CAMP B.30.c.	1st		In Camp. At 1 a.m. an enemy aeroplane flew low over Camp & was fired on by our Lewis gun. It came down at B.N.C. Continued training.	a.b.8.
"	2nd 3rd		In Camp. Hell Church Parade. Continued training. 3 o.r. ad	a.b.8.
"			" Camp. Continued training. In forenoon two enemy shells burst near Camp killing 3 o.r. and wounding 4 o.r.	a.b.8.
DIRTY BUCKET CAMP A.30.central	4th		Battn. marched off at 8.40 a.m. to Dirty Bucket Camp A.30.central Supplied working parties. Casualties 2 o.r. killed 17 o.r. wounded a.b.8.	
"	5th		In Camp. Continued training. Major E.E. Hill-Whitson took over Command of Battn.	a.b.2.
"	6th		Battn. relieved the 6th Gordon Highlanders in the Canal Bank Echelon "B" remained in Camp and 81 o.r. excess personnel proceeded to MURAT CAMP.	a.b.8.
CANAL BANK	7th		In dugouts. Continued training. Considerable shelling during the night. 2/Lt. J.A. Black and 10 o.r. wounded 1 o.r. killed. Supplied parties. Excess personnel moved back to A.3 Dental R.S.	
"	8th		In dugouts. Enemy working hearty to strike Camp at Murat. Canal Bank was shelled heavily during night. Casualties 5 killed 13 o.r. wounded.	
"	9th		In Canal Bank. At 6.15 p.m. Battn. moved off from Canal Bank to relieve 9th R.S. in front line. Owing to a raid carried out by the Division on our right & heavy shelling, relief was delayed	32. l.

7th Arg. High[rs]
Ref Maps:- 28 NW.
POELCAPPELLE 1/10,000

WAR DIARY
INTELLIGENCE SUMMARY

Army Form C. 2118.

Place	Date SEPT	Hour	Summary of Events and Information	Remarks and references to Appendices
FRONT LINE (Conto)	9th 10th		"A" Coy were on right C.6.b and d. "C" Coy on left N.30.c and C.6.d. "B" Coy in support C.5.a and "D" Coy in reserve at C.4.b. C.10.a and C.10.b. Casualties 5 or. killed 11 or. wounded. A.O.S.	
" "	11th		In line. Enemy artillery very active each overnoon. Hostile sniper's fire very active in evening. A.O.S. If Casualties 8 or. wounded.	
			Our artillery very active all day. also enemy at periods. Our Patrols examined enemy wire along whole front. located two working parties & dispersed same by rifle & L.G. fire. Two enemy aeroplanes and one of ours were brought down, there was exceptional activity of enemy aeroplanes at night. Two prisoners of 5th Grenadier Regts were taken by our left Coy. at 8.15 p.m. while attempting to get out of our artillery fire. Casualties nil. A.O.S.	
" "	13th		Shelling was ... heavy during the day, but great aerial ... was again during the evening signalling by ... was stopped about N.27.a.05 Latter was ... night by 5th Gordon Hldrs and marched to ... Casualties 3 or. killed 3 or. wounded. A.O.S.	

7th Argyll Sutherland Highlanders

WAR DIARY
or
INTELLIGENCE SUMMARY.

Army Form C. 2118.

Ref Maps :- 28 NW 1/20,000
POELCAPPELLE 1/10,000

Place	Date Sept	Hour	Summary of Events and Information	Remarks and references to Appendices
SIEGE CAMP	13th		In Camp training	
	14th		" " " Hostile aircraft dropped bombs in Camp about midday Causing casualties in Gordon Lines.	APP. A.B.B. A.B.B
	15th		" " "	
	16th		" " "	APP.
	17th		" " " Practical Brigade attack.	
	18th		" " "	
	19th		" " " Commencing at 5.30 a.m. A.B.B.	App
		At 9.30pm	Leaving equipment etc. Batt. marched off to the assembly positions near British Front Line. Heavy rain between 10pm & 12 midnight made ground very slippery and delayed Completion of assembly. Some shelling was experienced and 1/Lt Clark & 4 o.r. were wounded.	
Line	20th	At Zero hour 5.40 a.m.	intense barrage opened and Ref Off attack commenced. This Battn followed 9th Royal Scots and leap-frogged through them to the Final objective which was reached up to time. Prisoners 3 Off. & 56 or also 4 machine guns. Objective was consolidated and all went well until 5 pm when Enemy Counter-attack developed on the right Sr 4 fronts, this was well met developed on a severe loss to the enemy.	

A 5834. Wt. W 4973/M687 750,000 8/16 D.D.&I. Ltd. Forms/C.2118/13.

7th Army. Auth. Mights
Ry. Mylo.
BELGIUM 28 NW
POELCAPPELLE

WAR DIARY
INTELLIGENCE SUMMARY.
(Erase heading not required.)

Army Form C. 2118.

Place	Date	Hour	Summary of Events and Information	Remarks and references to Appendices
LINE	Sept Cont'd 20th		This counter attack pushed along to the Batn on our left & their front line was forced to withdraw. Our left front Coy formed a defensive flank facing north & inflicted very severe casualties on the enemy. After 8.15pm the night was quiet and SAA + water was sent up to forward Coys. 8th Argylls. Owing to casualties one Coy of two Platoons HLI was attacked as reinforcements - the left Coy were sent forward to assist the left Coy & other two Platoons were retained as local reserve at BUXTON FARM.	
	21st		There was intermittent enemy artillery fire during the day generally was quiet but night's enemy notifying which prevented the evacuation at 6.30pm enemy counter-attacks on our front but were completely repulsed. During the night the Batn was relieved by	

7th Aug Sheet 28NW
Ref. Maps: POELCAPPELLE

WAR DIARY
or
INTELLIGENCE SUMMARY.

Army Form C. 2118.

Place	Date	Hour	Summary of Events and Information	Remarks and references to Appendices
LINE	Sept 21 (Cont⁴)		This Coy of 6th Seaforth Highrs and thereafter proceeded to SIEGE CAMP which was reached at 6 am. Total Casualties:— 2/Lt E.R.SINCLAIR wounded, 23 or killed 162 or wounded 16 or missing Officers with Battn going into action:— Hd. Qrs. Lt. Col. E.E. Hill-Whitson. Capt A.Bain, H⁵ Lt Dobbie & A.D.Morton A Coy Capt J. Cunningham, 2/Lt J. Bayne and 2/Lt Andrew B „ 2/Lt W⁵ Menzies 2/Lt R.M.Park and 2/Lt J. Miller C „ Lt W.V. Macintosh 2/Lt W. Scott and 2/Lt E.R. Sinclair D „ Capt A. Stein M.C. 2/Lt R.C. Clark and R. Freer Campbell M.O. Capt J.R. Hunter R.A.M.C. Chaplain Rev⁴ W.S. Jardine C.F.	
	22ⁿᵈ		In Camp.	A.F.F.
	23ʳᵈ		Held Church Parade.	A.F.F.
POPERINGHE	24ᵗʰ		At 9 am Battⁿ marched off 6 billets in Poperinghe.	
"	24ᵗʰ		In Billets Poperinghe. Received draft of 160 or from A.F.F. 10th Entrenching Battalion.	W.O.S.

WAR DIARY
or
INTELLIGENCE SUMMARY.
(Erase heading not required.)

7th Argyll & Sutherland Highlanders
Army Form C. 2118.

Ref Maps – 28 N.W. HAZEBROUCK
LENS

Place	Date	Hour	Summary of Events and Information	Remarks and references to Appendices
POPERINGHE	25th		In Billets – Training under Company arrangements. Reinforcements 9 Officers (CAPT A.T. ARKOL, LT D.V. THOMSON, 2/LTS W.L. MUIR-KAY, M.C, A.M. NEISH, W. BATTISON, J.B. LAMONT, T. GEMMELL, W. RUSSELL, I.H.G. TUCKWELL.) and 222 O.R. reported	WORS WORS
"	26th		In Billets – Training	WORS
"	27th		Do Do Do	
"	28th		Do Do Do	WORS
"	29th		Battalion including transport entrained at HOPOUTRE Stn. (1 mile W of POPERINGHE) at 6.15 a.m. & proceeded by rail to BAPAUME, where they detrained at 4 p.m. thence by march route to Camp at COURCELLES-le-COMTE, arriving about 6 p.m.	
COURCELLES & COMTE	30th		In Camp. Field Church Parade. 1 Officer LT W A EVERITT, and 7 O.R. reinforcements reported	WORS

Lewis-[illegible] Lt Col
Commanding
7th Argyll & Sutherland Highlanders

SECRET.   App. I   Copy No. ....1....

OPERATION ORDER No. 3,
by
Lieut-Col. E.C. HILL-WHITSON,
Commanding 7th Arg. & Suth. Highrs.

Ref.Maps:- POELCAPPELLE Ed. 3, 1/10,000, Q4 Attached.

1. GENERAL. On a date to be notified later the XVIIIth. Corps will resume the offensive.
The 154th. Infy. Brigade will attack on 51st. Div. front.
Boundries as shown on Map "A" (attached) WINCHESTER RD. and LEKKERBOTERBEEK both inclusive to this Battn.
The 7th. Arg. & Suth. Highrs. will form the right Bn. of the second wave, with 4th. Gordon Hrs. on left, and 2nd. London Rifle Brigade on their right.

2. ATTACK. The attack will be carried out by this Battn. as follows:-
"D", "A", and "C" Coys. in line forming two waves each on a two platoon frontage with "B" Coy. less one and a half platoons in reserve.

3. OBJECTIVE. These three Coys. will leap-frog through the 9th Royal Scots who will occupy and hold up to the DOTTED BLUE LINE, mopping up to as near protective barrage as possible.
The objective of the first wave is the BROWN LINE shown on Map A. The objective of the second wave is a tactical line approximately on the BLUE LINE.
Companies will consolidate in depth taking up dispositions as shown on attached table B.

4. ZERO. ZERO DAY and Hour will be notified later.

5. ASSEMBLY. On Y/Z night the Battalion will march off from Camp at 9.10.30 p.m.

Order of March.
"D" Coy.
"A" "
"C" "
"H.Q"
"B" Coy. less
1 Platoon.

Companies at 200 yards distance West of CANAL and 100 yards distance between platoons East of CANAL
All Companies will be clear of the CANAL BANK by 12 midnight and will form up in assembly positions in accordance with instructions already received; roughly on the line U.30.c.5.5 to C.6.b.0.4 which will be marked by luminous stakes.
One Officer per Company and 1 N.C.O. per platoon will go on in advance and meet 2/Lt. Morrison at CANAL BANK at 5 p.m. This party will be shown the forming up positions of the platoons and meet the Battalion at MON DURASTA and guide their platoons to assembly positions. Companies will report having reached assembly positions immediately to Battn. Headquarters.

6. ADVANCE. The three attacking Coys. will move forward at Z plus 10 minutes in Artillery formation halting during the pause of the barrage on the BLUE DOTTED LINE, in vicinity of PHEASANT and NEW Trenches.
They will move forward from here at Z plus 58 minutes catch up the protective barrage in front of the BLUE DOTTED LINE, first wave. opening into assault formation on crossing the STROOMBEEK.
At Z plus 35 minutes "B" Coy. less one and a half platoons will move forward in Artillery formation to a position of readiness in support, in the vicinity of V.25.c.50.30
Compass Bearings. Companies will march on a magnetic bearing of 97½°.

7. REORGANISATION. On reaching objectives all Companies will consolidate and reorganise and Os.C. "A" and "C" Coys. will hold one platoon each in readiness to be at the disposal of O.C. "B" Coy. for immediate counter-attack in the event of the front line being penetrated at any point.

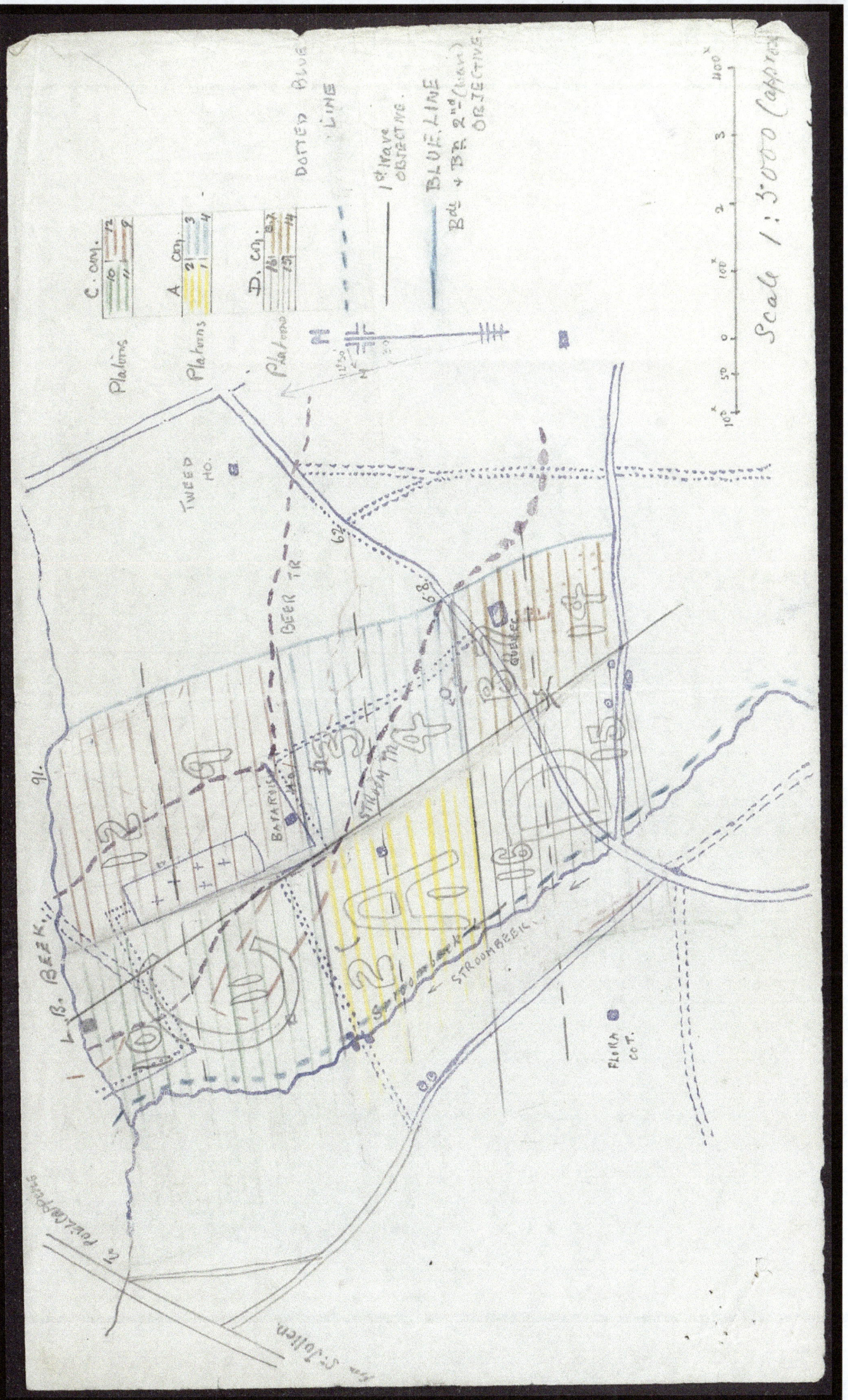

1:10 000   Q.4. MAP "A" FOR WAR DIARY

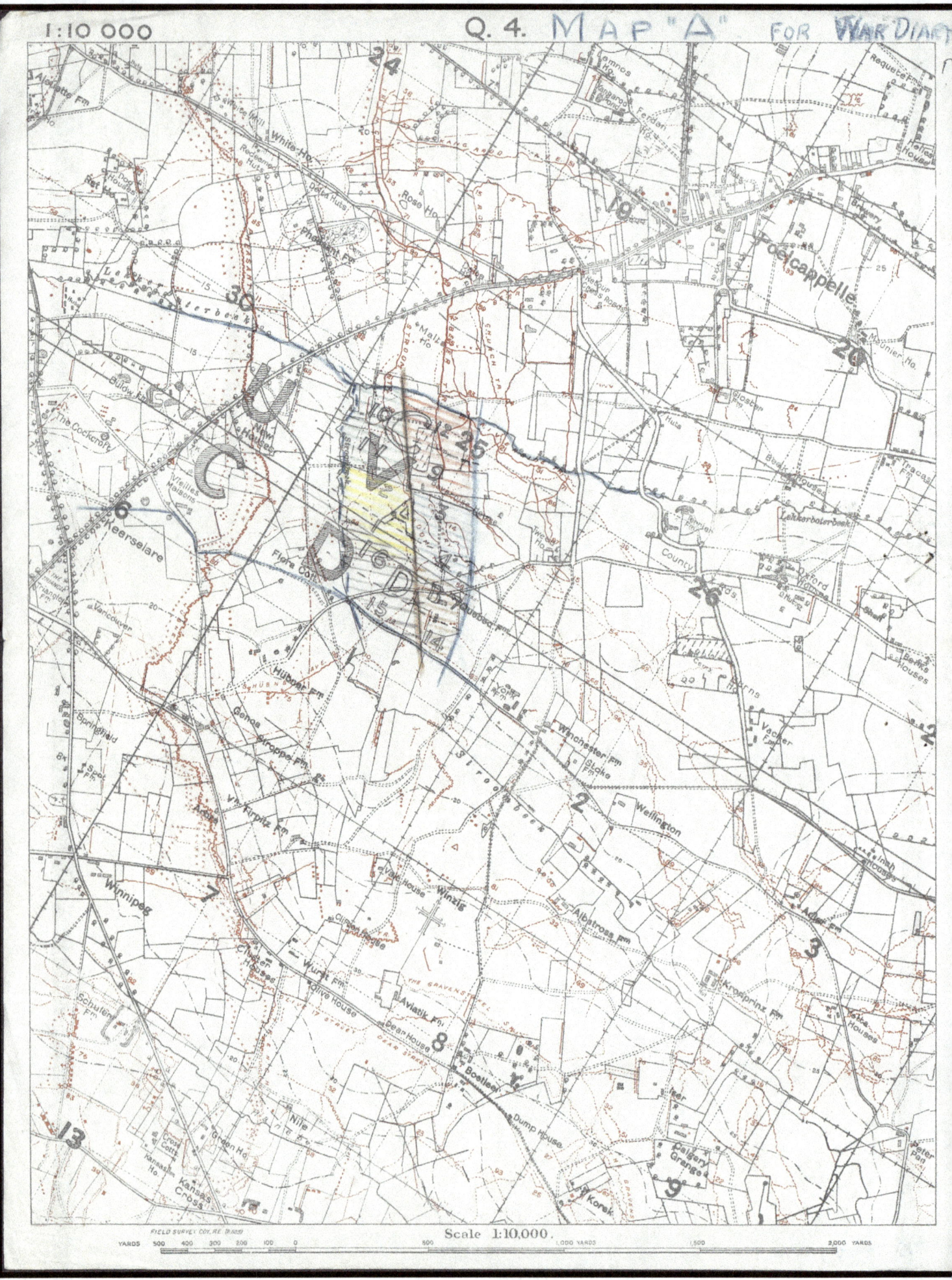

Scale 1:10,000.

SECRET.

7th ARGYLL & SUTHERLAND HIGHLANDERS.

Dispositions and Objectives for forthcoming Operations.
(See attached Sketch).

"D" Coy. (Right).

1st Wave
(No.15 Platoon will take D.1.b.5.5 and cluster of houses.
(No.16 Platoon will ~~take~~ MAKE Strong Point South of road at D.1.b.2.6.

2nd Wave
(No.14 Platoon will take Quebec Defences between road and Southern
(Building of Farm.
(No.13 Platoon will take all buildings of Quebec Farm.

"A" Coy. (Centre).

1st Wave
(No.1 Platoon will consolidate line from V.25.d.07.00 to
(V.25.c.90.30.
(No.2 Platoon will consolidate from V.25.c.90.30 to V.25.c.72.50

2nd Wave
(No.4 Platoon will take M.G. emplacements at V.25.b.15.10 and
(V.25.b.20.10, also from point "58" to V.25.d.40.30.
(No.3 Platoon will take from V.25.d.40.30 to V.25.d.30.55 and
(make one section Strong Point at M.G. emplacement at
(C of Cemetery Trench.

"C" Coy. (Left).

1st Wave
(No.11 Platoon will take from V.25.c.72.50 to V.25.c.55.80.
(No.10 Platoon will take from V.25.c.55.80 to V.25.a.30.09,
(detailing one section, or two if necessary to mop up
(Strong Points in vicinity of point "39".

2nd Wave
(No. 9 Platoon will take from V.25.d.30.55 to V.25.d.10.90
(No.12 Platoon will take V.25.d.10.90 to V.25.a.95.25 (20 yards
(East of point "91".

"B" Coy. (Reserve).

No. 7 Platoon will be under orders of O.C. "D" Coy.

Two sections of No. 5 Platoon will act as carriers for Trench
Mortar Battery.

SPECIAL GARRISON.

No. 6 and No.8 Platoons also No. 5 less 2 sections will be in
reserve at COCKROFT.

The Reserve will move forward in accordance with Operation
Orders immediately East of the STROOMBEEK.

aR Bain

Capt. & Adjt.,
7th Arg. & Suth. Highrs.

18th September. 1917.

Sheet 2.

It must be impressed on all ranks that a counter-attack by the enemy is inevitable and it must be expected and every man fully prepared to meet it. The direction from which it will come cannot be foretold, but, if only the men will use their rifles there is nothing to be feared from it. If, however, it does break through, the troops detailed for counter-attacking must act with speed and determination. It is of the utmost importance that we retain possession of BAVAROISE HILL.

8. MACHINE GUNS. When it is known that the BLUE LINE has been captured one section of 154th Machine Gun Coy. will go forward to QUEBEC FARM and come under orders of O.C. "D" Coy. & 1 Secton £ BAVAROISE HQ.

9. TRENCH MORTARS. One Stokes Mortar will be allotted each to O.C. "D" and "C" Coys.

Carrying parties of 7 O.R. for each gun will be detailed by O.C. "B" Coy. These parties are to march from Camp at the head of the Coy. to which they are detailed and will draw their ammunition ready filled in YUKON PACK from O.C. 154th. T.M.Battery at BULGAR DUMP.

On reaching their position the ammunition will be dumped under the orders of the O.C. Coy. concerned and the men return to Battn. Headquarters with empty packs.

This party will carry rifles and 50 rounds S.A.A. only.

10 ARTILLERY. The attack will be preceded by 24 hours intense bombardment.

Up to DOTTED BLUE LINE lifts will be xxxxx 50 yards every three minutes, from here to BLUE LINE, 50 yards every 4 minutes.

11 TANKS. It is hoped that Tanks will assist in capture of BAVAROISE HOUSE,.
SIGNALS:-
RED)
WHITE) DISC = Enemy in concrete emplacement.
RED)

RED)
RED) DISC = Tank broken down.
RED)

RED DISC = Position captured.

If infantry require the help of Tanks they will signal to them by waving their Steel Helmets on top of their rifles.

Position of Tanks must be marked on situation report Maps as under :-
Tank in Action.= ▲
" out of Action.= △

Whenever possible the Battn. letter and Number of tank should be stated.

Owing to difficulties of the ground the tanks can only be expected to act as Moppers Up if required and it is to be clearly understood that the Infantry are on no account to await the arrival of tanks.

12 CONTACT AEROPLANES The 7th. Squadron R.F.C. will detail a Contact Machine to fly over the objectives at Z plus 2 hours 30 minutes, and at Z plus 4 hours, also when ordered by Corps H.Q..

Companies will arrange to light RED Flares in small bunches by most advanced troops along the whole line when called for by KLAXON Horn, or the dropping of WHITE Lights.

If Hostile Air-craft fly over our lines at low altitude they must be fired on immediately by rifles and lewis guns.

Sheet 3.

13. **LIAISON.** In order to ensure close touch with flanking Units "D" Coy. will arrange to join hands with 2nd London Rifle Brigade at Concrete Houses, D.1.b.3.3, and "C" Coy. with 4th Gordon Highrs. at V.25.a.2.1 also at V.25.a.9.1.

14. **SIGNALS.** The Signalling Officer will arrange the following alternative schemes for visual signalling.
   (a) From forward Company Headquarters by daylight lamp or signalling shutter transmitting station at C.6.b.15.48 and thence to BULOW FARM.
   or (b) From Coy. Headquarters to a point WEST of FLORA COTTAGE at D.1.a.1.3. and thence to Battalion Headquarters.
   S.O.S.Signal will be two RED and two GREEN rockets fired in rapid succession. This must only be used in case of grave emergency from heavy counter-attack.

15. **HEADQUARTERS.**
   154th Bde. Adv.Report Centre:- FERDINAND FARM.
   154th Bde. Headquarters:- CANE POST.
   4th Gordon Highrs. Bn.Hqrs:- U.29.d.82.58.
   7th Arg.& Suth.Hrs. " " BULOW FARM.
   O.C.Coys. will report exact location of their Hd.Qrs. immediately on reaching their objectives.

16. **REPORTS.** Situation reports will be rendered by all Companies at least every two hours, and estimated casualties as soon as possible.

17. **SYNCHRONISATION.** One Officer per Coy. will synchronise at least two watches with the Signalling Officer at 2 p.m. and 9 p.m. at Officers' Mess Huts.on Y day.

18. **OBSERVATION.** Company Commanders will endeavour to establish good Observation Posts on commanding ground and have these manned by specially detailed Scouts whose reports will be sent immediately to Battn. H.Q.

A.R.Bain

Capt. & Adjt.,
7th Arg & Suth. Highrs.

18th September, 1917.

Copy No.1.....War Diary.
"   "   2......Qr.Mr. and T.O.
"   "   3.....O.C. "A" Coy.
"   "   4..... "   "B" "
"   "   5..... "   "C" "
"   "   6..... "   "D" "
"   "   7...... Signalling Officer.
"   "   8...... Brigade Headquarters.

ADMINISTRATIVE INSTRUCTIONS FOR OFFENSIVE OPERATIONS
issued with OPERATION ORDERS No.3.

Fighting Kit, including flares, grenades, etc. to be carried during forthcoming Operations.

1. Fighting dress will be worn as follows:-

   (a) Clothing as issued. Officers will wear the same as men.
   (b) Arms as issued.
   (c) Accoutrements as issued except pack. Haversacks to be worn on back and entrenching tool carried.
   (d) The following articles will be carried in haversack:-
   Towel, soap and razor, spare oil tin, iron ration, one tin Solidified Alcohol, one complete days ration and special Breakfast ration carried in mess tin slung outside haversack, one pair dry socks, waterproof sheet carried on top of haversack under flap. Dry socks will be put on on Z/Z plus 1 night and the dirty pair carried down in the haversack.
   (e) Greatcoats, cardigans and Balmorals to be left in packs.
   (f) Three sand bags will be carried by each man tied neatly on to braces of equipment.
   (g) Mills' hand grenades; one will be carried by each man in pocket.
   (h) S.A.A. 170 Rounds will be carried by all except bombers, Signallers, Scouts, Runners and Lewis gunners, who will carry 100 rounds.
   (i) Water bottles must be full and their contents kept for consumption on Z day.
   (j) 3 Men out of every 5 will carry two aeroplane flares.
   (k) 24 Lewis gun magazines per gun will be taken, also one sling per gun.
   (l) Rifle Bombers will carry 6 Mills' rifle grenades No.23 in bucket and 100 rounds S.A.A. and two smoke grenades. Rifle Grenadiers will carry 8 No.24 grenades in special bucket and 120 rounds S.A.A.
   (m) Every second man of first and second waves will carry a shovel, Entrenching Tools will be used as picks if required.
   (n) VERY LIGHTS.
       30 WHITE 1 inch lights per Coy. H.Q.
       6 RED   1   "   "   "   "   "   "
       6 GREEN 1   "   "   "   "   "   "
   (o) Dumps.
       Forward Dumps Right Sector, BULOW FARM C.6.a.7.8. Containing
           60 Boxes S.A.A.
           30 Boxes Mills Rifle Grenades.
           30 Boxes No.24 Grenades.
           4 Boxes 1 inch Very Lights.
   Ration and Water Dump is at BULOW FARM.
   Water will be carried to forward Coys. on Z night by "B" Coy.

   (p) Special equipment will be issued as follows:-
           Wire cutters hand, Mk.V
   (p) Battn. Headquarters will be at BULOW FARM.
       Aid Post will be at MON DURASTA.
   (q) Special Equipment will be issued as follows:-
           Wire Cutters Hand Mark V, two per platoon.
           "   "   S.A. Rifle,   "   "   "
           Cups grenade four per platoon.
           Very Pistols 1 inch, five per Coy.
           Periscopes Vigilant, eight per Coy.
           Compasses N.P. six per Coy.
           Bin oculars N.P. two per platoon.
       O.C. Coys. will keep a careful note of men to whom those are issued and all articles will be recovered as far as possible from casualties.
   (r) CARRYING PARTIES.
       (i) O.C. "B" Coy. will arrange to attach one man per platoon to "A", "C" and "D" Coys. to carry up hot food containers from MINTY'S FARM, to assembly positions. These men will wait until food is consumed and take back empty containers

Sheet 2.

to Battn. Headquarters at BULOW FARM. The haversacks of these men will be carried at their sides. Two N.C.Os. will be sent with these men.

(s) 1 N.C.O. and 6 men will be attached to both "C" and "D" Coys. as carriers for T.M. Ammunition with YUKON Packs. Packs will be drawn ready filled at MON BULGAR. These Packs will be returned to Battn. H.Q. when carrying has been completed by the party concerned. O.C. "B" Coy. will arrange for these men to carry rations and water. Rifles and bandoliers must also be carried.

(s) HOT MEAL. The tea brought up in hot food containers will be consumed along with breakfast ration at ZERO - 1 hour 30 mins.

Os.C. "C" and "D" Coys. will arrange that the T.M.personnel and carriers attached to their Coys. are given a share of the tea.

Owing to shortage of hot food containers the Qr.Mr. will arrange to give "B" Coy. an extra supply of tea, sugar, and solidified alcohol.

(t) DIRECTION MARKERS. The Adjutant will arrange for a party to put out WHITE wooden direction sticks from Battn. H.Q. to Concrete House at V.26.c.75.35. "D", "A" and "C" Coys. will be issued with 5 tracing tapes each,which must be mudded and laid between Coy.H.Q. and this point.

PRISONERS.

(u) All ranks must be warned that prisoners should be collected in batches under Coy. arrangements, and sent back to Battn.H.Q. under escort of only 5 per cent. Runners can be used for this

Prisoners are to be disarmed, but their pay-books must be left in their possession.

(v) WOUNDED. All ranks must be specially warned that if they become casualties they must bring back arms and equipment to the Dressing Station with them. Lightly wounded men found returning to Aid Post without arms and equipment will be sent back to recover these.

Wounded will be evacuated from MON DURASTA to Tramway Line near FERDINAND FARM via Duckboard track and tramway.

(w) TRANSPORT. The T.O. will arrange for limbers to be loaded at Camp at 6 p.m. to carry up Lewis guns, magazines and buckets of Mills' rifle grenades and Signalling Stores to (but not the buckets of No. 24s which are to be carried on the man) and Signalling stores to ADAMS' FARM. Limbers to move off from Camp at 10.15 p.m. and be unloaded at ADAMS' FARM in time to issue stores to Coys. as they pass. Two men per Coy. will go with these limbers to take charge of their Coy. Lewis guns, bomb buckets etc.

The Quartermaster will arrange to have hot tea ready in hot food containers also to go up in limbers to the same place.

O.C. "B" Coy. will detail an Officer and 14 o.r. of a carrying party to go with this limber to ensure the correct distribution of same.

aRBain
Capt. & Adjt.,
7th Arg. & Suth. Highrs.

Addenda to be read after para.(r) sub.para(2).
"O.C. "B" Coy. will draw 48 tins of water from BULOW FARM in passing on way to assembly positions. This will be carried forward by "B" Coy. to their position of readiness about V.25.c. and issued on Z night to all Companies by O.C."B" Coy."

"B" Coy. will also carry up to Battn. Hd. Qrs. five jars of Rum in Sandbags which the Q.M. will arrange to load at the Stores on limbers proceeding to ADAM'S FARM.

ADMINISTRATIVE INSTRUCTIONS.

Addenda No. 1.

Ref. Administrative Instructions para.(r) CARRYING PARTIES.

Hot Food Containers will be issued to Companies as follows :-
                4 Each to "C" and "D" Companies.
                3   to "A" Company.
                2   to "B" Company.

O.C. "C" and "D" Companies will ensure that Trench Mortar personnel, Trench Mortar Carrying party, and men who carry these Hot Food Containers all get a share of this hot meal.

O.C. "B" Coy. will detail this Carrying Party accordingly, and not as laid down in para.(r) sub.para.(1).

"B" Coy. will also carry up to Battalion H.Q. Five jars of Rum in sand bags which the Quartermaster will arrange to load at the Stores on limbers proceeding to ADAMS' FARM.

Para.(v) WOUNDED. All ranks are to be warned that on no account are unwounded men to be allowed to come back with wounded comrades. The evacuation of Wounded must be left entirely to Stretcher-bearers and special parties during operations.

A.R. Bain Capt & Adjt
7th Argyll & Sutherland Highlanders

Copies to: [handwritten annotations]

SECRET.

7th ARGYLL & SUTHERLAND HIGHLANDERS.

Dispositions and Objectives for forthcoming Operations.
(See attached sketch)

"D" Coy. (Right)

1st Wave
- No.15 Platoon will take D.1.b.3.3. and cluster of houses.
- No.16 Platoon will take Strong Point South of road at D.1.b.3.6.

2nd Wave
- No.14 Platoon will take Quebec Defences between road and Southern Building of Farm.
- No.B7 Platoon will take all buildings of Quebec Farm.

"A" Coy. (Centre).

1st Wave
- No.1 Platoon will consolidate Line from V.25.d.07.00 to V.25.c.90.30.
- No.2 Platoon will consolidate from V.25.c.90.30 to V.25.c.72.50.

2nd Wave
- No.4 Platoon will take M.G. emplacements at V.35.b.15.10 and V.35.b.30.10, also from point "58" to V.35.d.40.30.
- No.3 Platoon will take from V.25.d.40.30 to V.25.d.30.55, and make one section Strong Point at M.G. emplacement at C of Cemetery.

"C" Coy. (Left).

1st Wave
- No.11 Platoon will take from V.25.c.72.50 to V.25.c.55.80.
- No.10 Platoon will take from V.25.c.55.80 to V.25.a.30.00, detailing one section, or two if necessary to mop up Strong Points in vicinity of point "39".

2nd Wave
- No.9 Platoon will take from V.25.d.30.55 to V.25.d.10.90.
- No.12 Platoon will take V.25.d.10.90 to V.25.a.95.25 (20 yards East of point "91".

"B" Coy. (Reserve)

No.7 Platoon will be under orders of O.C. "D" Coy.

Two sections of No.5 Platoon under an Officer will make a third wave 20 yards in rear of "C" Coy. second wave. Their duty will be to occupy and consolidate BAVAROISE HOUSE and Block House at V.25.c.75.85. The remaining two sections of this Platoon will act as carriers for Trench Mortar Battery.

Special Orders: No.6 and No.8 Platoons will be in reserve at ~~MON BULGAR~~ COCKROFT + No 5 less 2 sections

* The Reserve will move forward in accordance with Operation Orders immediately East of the STEENBEEK.

a.R.Bain
Capt. for + adjt
~~Commanding~~ 7th Arg. & Suth. Highrs.

15/9/17.

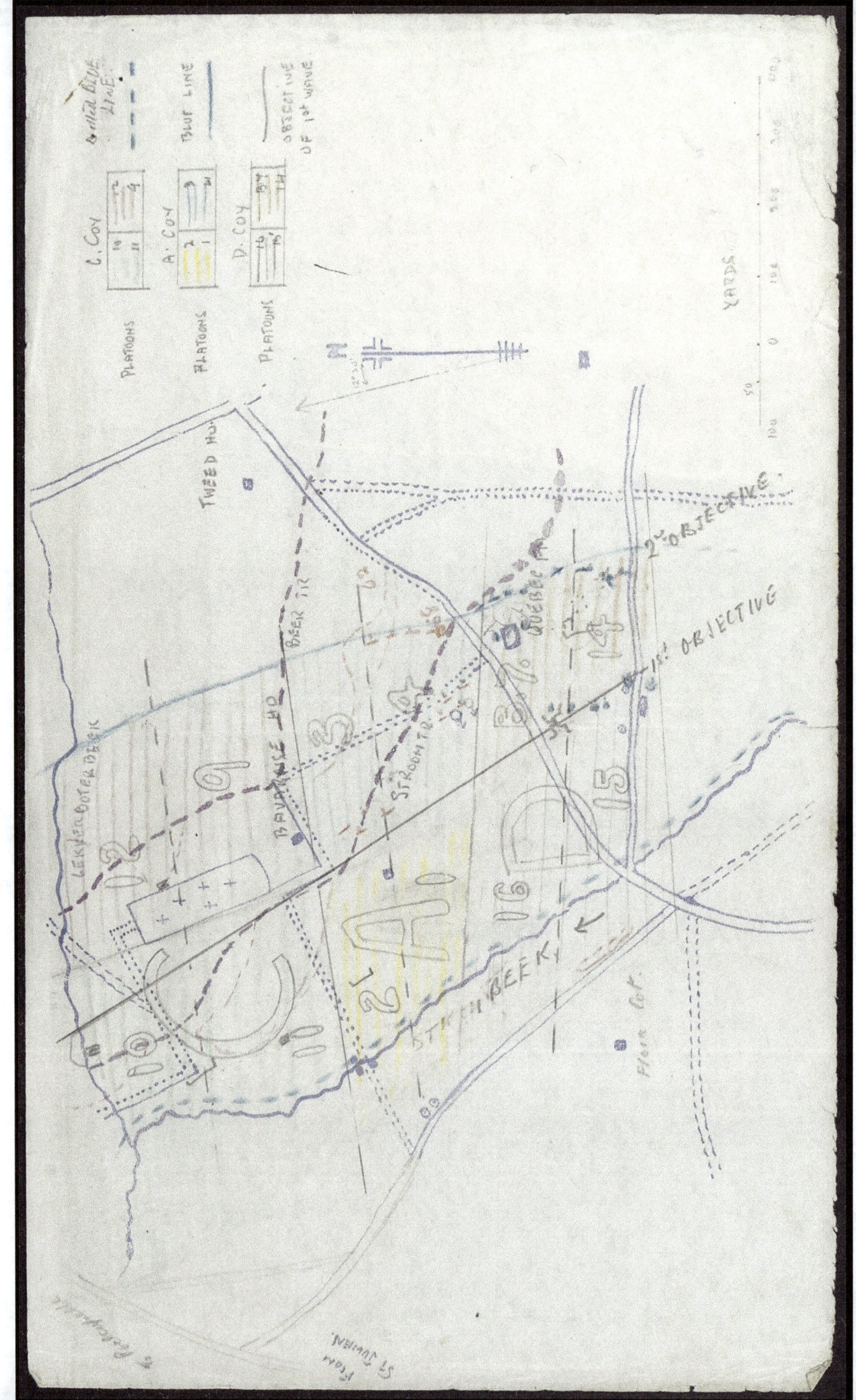

Visual Scheme for Communication
between BLUE LINE AND BULOW FARM

1. From the different Coy. Hqs. in
the BLUE LINE the messages will
be sent by Daylight Lamp or
Signalling Shutter to transmitting station situated at
C6 b 15.40. from whence they will
be sent to BULOW FARM.

Alternative:— From BLUE LINE messages
will be sent visually to a point WEST
of FLORA COT at D1 b 1.5. & transmitted
visually to BULOW FARM.

Reference Map — POELCAPPELLE
Edition 3, 1·10,000.

F.H.Dobbie 2/Lt.
Sig. Officer

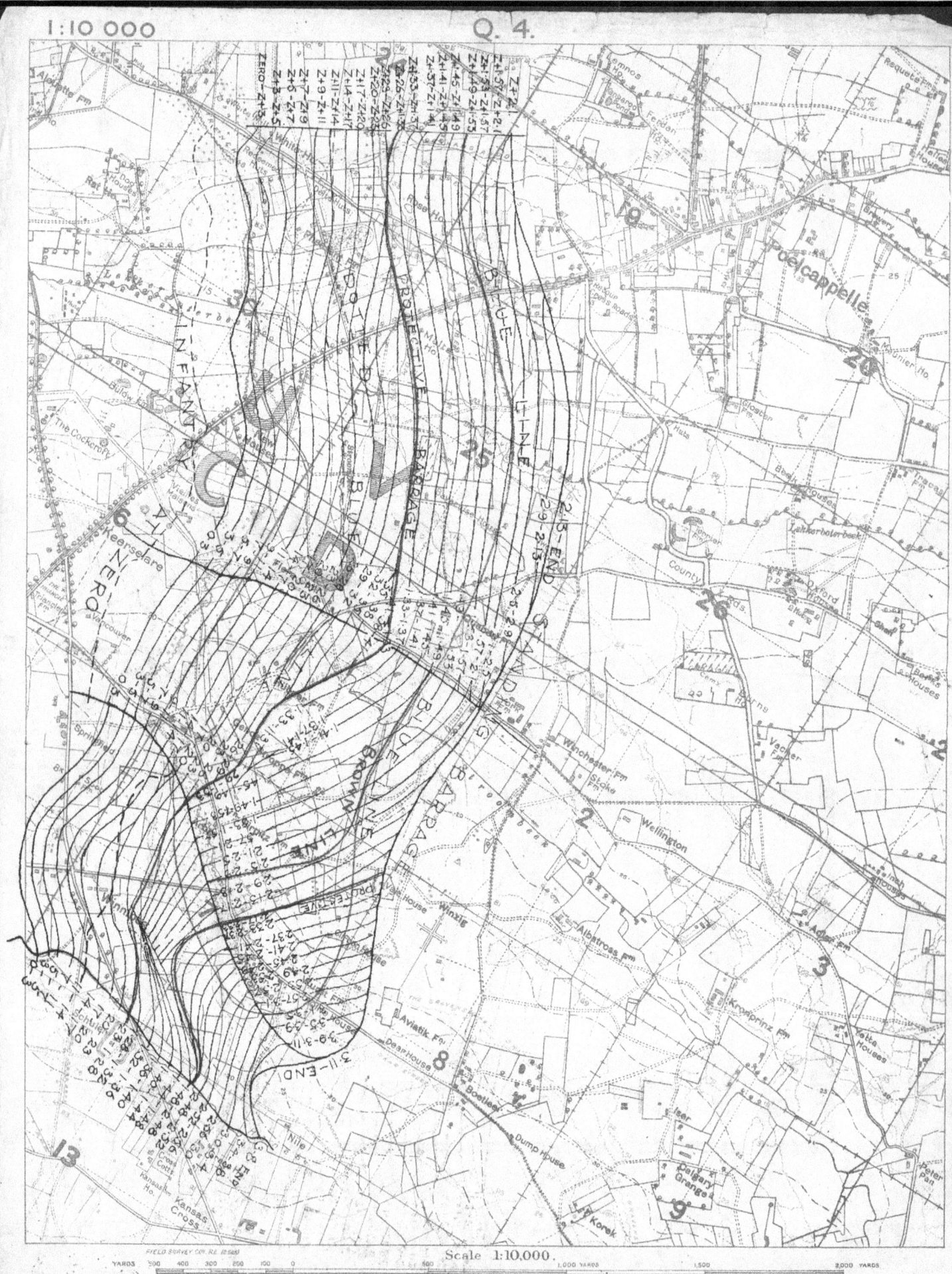

7th Argyll & Sutherland Highlanders.
War Diary.
October 1917.

WAR DIARY
INTELLIGENCE SUMMARY

Army Form C. 2118.

7th Canadian Inf. Bde. HQs
Ref. Maps - LENS.
51B N.W.

Place	Date	Hour	Summary of Events and Information	Remarks and references to Appendices
COURCELLES	1st		In Camp - Training	W.W.B.
"	2nd		Do.	W.W.B.
CONTE	3rd		Do.	W.W.B.
"	4th		Do. Lt.Col. J.R. McALPINE-DOWNIE, 8th A.I.S. Hrs., taken on strength (attached)	W.W.B.
"	5th		2/Lt. T.J. MACKENZIE, reported for duty.	W.W.B.
"	6th		The Batt'n moved by march route to YORK LINES M.22.6.8.3. at 10 a.m.	W.W.B.
M.22.6.8.3.	6th		In Camp Training	W.W.B.
"	7th		" Held Church Parade.	W.W.B.
"	8th		" Training.	W.W.B.
"	9th		" "	W.W.B.
"	10th		" Lt.Col. E.C. HILL-WHITSON, relinquished Command of this Batt'n, Major D.F. BICKMORE, assumes command, Capt. E.R. ORR reported for duty.	W.W.B.
"	11th		"	W.W.B.
"	12th		In Camp Training.	
June	13th		The Battalion relieved the 4th Seaforths Highrs. in the line, taking over the left Battalion frontage of the Right Brigade of 51st Division front. Dispositions — A Coy Right front bay, "B" Coy left front bay, "C" Coy Support Coy, "D" Coy Reserve Coy, Two officers and "D" Coy prmtd working parties wiring in front of Coy, and during the night — one from each front line Coy digging Rs. At 4.55 pm the Division on our left made a successful raid on the enemy lines opposite their front. The enemy Bomb. our men on the planted of the raid extended to our front at the same time.	See App. I
"	14th		successful. Enemy Art. Heavy Shelled our lines the following two in retaliation, causing light damage — 2 known rifle hits reported.	W.W.B.

WAR DIARY
or
INTELLIGENCE SUMMARY.

Army Form C. 2118.

4th Canadian Infantry Bde
Ref. Maps. LENS
51/3. S.W.

Place	Date	Hour	Summary of Events and Information	Remarks and references to Appendices
Line	14th		Two officers patrols went out on our front during the night. Casualties 1 O.R. killed 12 wounded.	W.R.B.
"	15th		In the line. The ground by R.E. party was cleared for from Enemy Snipers at 8.30 pm. There were no casualties by the enemy working parties prevented - enemy appearing to be using dummies out from our lines during the night. Two patrols went out. Two officers patrols.	W.R.B.
"	16.		In the line. Working parties forward. Casualties 1 O.R. killed 3 wounded. Two officers patrols out during the night.	W.R.B.
"	17		In the line. Working parties out - saw little enemy activity. Carried out - shelled by Krauts by 5.9s. Shelled left front relieved. Night spent by Krauts. One officers patrol out. Two working parties arrived out. Casualties nil.	W.R.B.
"	18		In the line. Working parties co working during the night. One officers patrol carried out. Two officers patrols during the day. Two officers activity unusual.	W.R.B.
"	19.		In the line. Artillery activity quiet. Enemy obtained a direct hit on our four post with a slug bomb. Working parties carried on at night. Two officers patrols at night. Our numbers clear lit during the day. Aerial activity quiet. Casualties 5 O.R. wounded.	W.R.B.

WAR DIARY
INTELLIGENCE SUMMARY.

4th Army Intr / Army Form C. 2118.
Ref. Maps. LENS
51 B S.W.

Place	Date	Hour	Summary of Events and Information	Remarks and references to Appendices
Line	20		In the line. Artillery activity normal. Working parties supplied. Our officer's patrol went out during the night. Enemy sent 8 "Stanezer" shells in HOPE SUPPORT R.T. Casualties 1 O.R. killed.	Corps
"	21		Battalion was relieved by the 4 Seaforth Hrs. about 4 p.m. and B & D Coys proceeded to CARLISLE LINES. A & C Coys proceeded to dugouts at N.16.C Camp M.17.a. Casualties 1 OR wounded.	Corps
CARLISLE LINES. M.17.a.	22		In Camp training.	Corps
"	23		Do.	Corps
"	24		Do.	Corps
"	25		Do.	Corps
"	26		Do.	Corps
"	27		Do.	Corps

7th Army & 6th Bns.
Army Form C. 2118.
Ref. Maps LENS 11
51 C

WAR DIARY
INTELLIGENCE SUMMARY
(Erase heading not required.)

Place	Date	Hour	Summary of Events and Information	Remarks and references to Appendices
CARLISLE LINES M(?)a LATTRE-ST-QUENTIN.	28th		Battalion entrained at STONE SIDING (M23d) Noreux Goug Railway at 12.30 p.m. and detrained at SIDING between WANQUETIN and GOUY at 5.35 p.m. and proceeded by march route to LATTRE-ST-QUENTIN W.R.B arriving there about 7 p.m. Battalion in Billets.	WRB
"	29th		In Billets; training under Company arrangements.	ABB
"	30th		Do. 16 o.r. reinforcements joined Battn. with ABB	ABB
"	31st		Do. 3 " " " " ABB	ABB
			Strength of Battn. 47 Off. and 1038 o.r.	

J.J. Bickmore
Major
Commanding
7th Arg & Suth. Hrs

app. I.

S E C R E T.

COPY No. 6

154th INFANTRY BRIGADE ORDER No.143.

Reference Maps:-
    FRANCE - Sheet 51B. S.W. 1/20,000.
    VIS-EN-ARTOIS 51B. S.W.2, 1/10,000.

---

1. The 4th Gordon Highrs. and 7th Argyll and Sutherland Highrs. will relieve the 9th Royal Scots and 4th Seaforth Highrs.respectively, in the Line on 13th October. The 4th Gordon Highrs.will complete their relief by 1 p.m. The first Platoon of the 7th Argyll and Sutherland Highrs. will not arrive at MARLIERE CAVE before 1 p.m.

2. On relief 9th Royal Scots will proceed to YORK LINES; 4th Seaforth Highrs.(less two Companies) to CARLISLE LINES; two Companies 4th Seaforth Highrs. to Shelters vacated by 4th Gordon Highrs.

3. All details of the relief will be arranged between Os.C. concerned.

4. Surplus personnel of 9th Royal Scots and 4th Seaforth Highrs. will proceed to the area allotted to their units on afternoon of 13th inst. and will vacate their present accommodation by 2 p.m. That accommodation will be available for surplus personnel of 4th Gordon Highrs. and 7th Argyll and Sutherland Highrs. Accommodation at CARLISLE LINES will be allotted by the Staff Captain.

5. The two Companies of 4th Seaforth Highrs. at N.15.a will remain under their own Unit for training but will come under Brigade Headquarters for tactical purposes.
   They will take over all guards at present found by the 4th Gordon Highrs.

6. Battalions in the Line will hand over to relieving Battalions
   (a) All maps, Defence Schemes, photographs, etc, taken over from 150th Brigade.
   (b) Details of Working Parties, policy of work and work in hand.
   (c) All Trench Srores; copies of Trench Store Lists will be sent to Brigade Headquarters by Units handing over by 9 a.m. 14th October.

7. There will be no cessation of work on night of relief.

8. Completion of relief will be wired to Brigade Headquarters by Code word RIGHT.

    ACKNOWLEDGE.

                                    J. M. Henderson Lieut
                                    for Capt.
                                    Brigade Major.
11th October, 1917.   154th Infantry Brigade.

    Issued at..........by Orderly.

154th Brigade.

51st Division.

7th BATTALION

ARGYLE & SUTHERLAND HIGHLANDERS

NOVEMBER 1917.

Attached:-   Report on Operations

7th Arg. & Suth. Highlrs.
Army Form C. 2118.
REF. MAPS :- LENS 11
FRANCE 51c

WAR DIARY
INTELLIGENCE SUMMARY.
(Erase heading not required.)

Place	Date Nov R	Hour	Summary of Events and Information	Remarks and references to Appendices
LATTRE-ST-QUENTIN	1st		In billets. Continued training.	aCB
"	2nd		" " " Capt. J. McLaren joined Battn	aCB aCB
"	3rd		" " "	
"	4th		" " "	aCB
"	5th		Held Church Parade.	
			Capt. J. A. Duric M.C. Brig. Major 154th Inf. Bde. took over Command of Battn. Continued training	aCB
"	6th		Continued training.	aCB
"	7th		" " 40 or reinforcements taken on strength	aCB
			Lt. J. McLaren evacuated to Hospital	aCB
"	8th		" "	aCB
"	9th		" " + supplied working party for R.F.C.	aCB
"	10th		" " In Brigade Boxing Competition	
			welter & light weight events were won by Serg. G. Walker	aCB
			and Drummer McCagin	aCB
"	11th		In billets. Held Church Parade.	aCB
"	12th		" XVIIth Corps Commdr. Lt. Gen Sir C. Ferguson Bt., KCB, MVO, DSO.,	
			presented medal ribbons to members of 154th Brigade	aCB
"	13th		In billets. As anniversary of Regymant Day a holiday was	
			granted to the men. In 154th Bde Sports this unit won the tug-of-war and Five-a-side Football Competitions	aCB

7th Aug Lth Highrs
Ref. Maps. LENS 11
FRANCE 5/c

Army Form C. 2118.

WAR DIARY
or
INTELLIGENCE SUMMARY.
(Erase heading not required.)

Place	Date	Hour	Summary of Events and Information	Remarks and references to Appendices
LATTRE-ST-QUENTIN	14th		In billets. Continued training.	AKB AKB
	15th		" " "	AKB
	16th		" " "	
	14th		for BEAUMCOURT at 10:15 PM traveling during the night. Batt. entrained at BEAUMETZ-lès-LOGES at 4 PM and detrained at BAPAUME at 6:30 PM. Proceeded by march route 10 mile near BEAUMENCOURT	AKB
BEAUMENCOURT	19th		Held Church Parade. Batt proceeded by march route to Camp near YTRES at 5 PM.	AKB
			Bivvie equipment received.	
	19th		Batt proceeded to Billets in METZ at 10 PM.	AKB
METZ	20th	9AM	Battalion was assembled in Q. 30.a in full fighting kit ready to go into action 14 Off. + 588 O. Ranks in strength. C.O. Lt. Col. J.A. Duncan M.C. 2nd i/c Bapt. A.M. Bain M.C. Off. cmdg. J/c Off. g'nd of "D" Morrisons M.C. Adj. Off. Lt. S.H. Gilchrist. I/c Off. Hunter R.A.M.C. M.O. Capt. J.H. Thomson. Lewis ?? W.B. Sterson
"A" Coy Capt. G. to Orr
"B" " " J. McLaren 2nd Lt. W.A. Burnett 2nd Lt. J.B. Irving
"C" " Major W. Green 2nd Lt. A.M. ?? of The Kings
"D" " Capt. A.J. Arnold 2nd Lt. B.T. Maddox 2nd Lt. B. Shaw	

Army Form C. 2118.

74 Arg. Rhth. Klub
Ry. Mylo
57 c.

WAR DIARY
or
INTELLIGENCE SUMMARY.

(Erase heading not required.)

Instructions regarding War Diaries and Intelligence Summaries are contained in F. S. Regs., Part II. and the Staff Manual respectively. Title pages will be prepared in manuscript.

Place	Date	Hour	Summary of Events and Information	Remarks and references to Appendices
METZ	20"	10.30am	Batty had arrived in Assembly positions in the Bosch front line in front of TRESCAULT. The attack by 152 & 153 Brigs. was reported going well. Red flash in front of FLESQUIERES as all tanks had been disabled by Anti-Tank guns.	
		6pm	38 off and 1411 O.R. prisoners had passed through Divnl hqrs. Alb
TRESCAULT	21"		At 152 & 153 Brigade continuing the attack on FLESQUIERES at 6.15am. Batty moved off from TRESCAULT at 6 am. in column of Rte. to railway cutting R 23 to see app. I. The enemy had evacuated FLESQUIERES during night and it was occupied and the other Bdes pushed on to their final objective RED LINE	
		8.30am	The Batty in conjunction with 4th Gordons on right moved forward from Railway on Artillery formation but left was held up by fire from ANNEUX at 10.10am 2 right by CANTAING. "C" Bdy was detailed to go and assist 62nd Divn with attack on ANNEUX which was captured at 11.20am.	

7th Arg & Sup Illus
Map
Ref. 57c

WAR DIARY
or
INTELLIGENCE SUMMARY.
Army Form C. 2118.

(Erase heading not required.)

Place	Date	Hour	Summary of Events and Information	Remarks and references to Appendices
FONTAINE NOTRE DAME	21/11		Advance was then continued towards FONTAINE by Companies on two platoon frontage in two waves	
			"B" Coy on right in touch with 4th Gordon Hdrs.	
			"A" " Left " " 62nd Division	
			"D" " right Support	
			"C" " Left "	
			Companies were held up by heavy rifle and M.G. fire from CANTAING and at 12 noon 2 Companies had to dig in there	
		2 PM.	Tanks advanced and reached CANTAING line about 2.55 PM. when line was captured and about 80 prisoners taken.	
			Tanks proceeded through FONTAINE-NOTRE-DAME followed by "A" "B" + part of "D" Coy.	
			One Coy of 4th Seaforths reached FONTAINE as they had been sent on to fill a gap which had occurred on our right.	
			Our Companies consolidated defence of the Village on N & W sides. Some prisoners were taken and many civilians were sent back.	
			The night was quiet and defence securely consolidated	

7th Arg. Rxth Highldrs
Rxf Nch 57c

Army Form C. 2118.

WAR DIARY
—or—
INTELLIGENCE SUMMARY.
(Erase heading not required.)

Place	Date	Hour	Summary of Events and Information	Remarks and references to Appendices
LINE near FONTAINE NOTRE DAME	22nd		"B" & three platoons of "A" Coy were relieved by 4th Seaforths during the morning took up positions shown in Appendix II. Before the fourth Platoon of "A" Coy could be relieved the enemy delivered a very strong counter Attack about 10.30 a.m. on FONTAINE compelling the 4th Seaforths to evacuate it. Our Companies held on to consolidated positions and checked the Counter Attack. Some difficulty was experienced in getting forward supplies of S.A.A. but the 154th F.M. took parties under 2nd Lieut. R. M. Park rendered invaluable assistance in taking forward S.A.A. under heavy fire. During the night the Batten was relieved by the 4th Black Watch "HQ" "A"+"B" Coys going to divisional line pits in L/42 A.R.S "C"+"D" Coys to Quarry at LA JUSTICE L.1.a.9.8.	
	23rd		"C"+"D" Coys took up positions in L.Y.6 and came under orders of O.C. 4th Black Watch.	
		3 PM	"HQ" "A"+"B" moved back to Billets in METZ, "C"+"D" moved at 6.30 P.M. to METZ	

7th Aug 1917
Ref Map 57c
AMIENS 17.

Army Form C. 2118.

WAR DIARY
or
INTELLIGENCE SUMMARY.
(Erase heading not required.)

Place	Date	Hour	Summary of Events and Information	Remarks and references to Appendices
			Total Casualties. Capt J McLaren Killed, Capt. to McCrie Missing 2nd Lt. A Law & 2nd Lt. J J McKenzie wounded & Major W J Ypres wounded at Duty	
	24th		8 O.R. killed, 122 O.R. wounded & 21 O.R. Missing	A.R.B
			At 3.15 P.M. Battn marched off to YTRES Str. via EQUANCOURT & ETRICOURT, entrained at YTRES and detrained at EDGEHILL near DERNANCOURT and marched to billets in RIBEMONT	A.R.B
			Transport moved by route march to BEAULENCOURT Transport completed journey at 5.30 P.M.	A.R.B
RIBEMONT	25th		In Billets	A.R.B
"	26th		" Training	A.R.B
"	27th		" "	A.R.B
"	28th		" "	A.R.B.
"	29th		" " At 3pm. orders were received to move at once to ALBERT to entrain there as enemy had broken through to GOUZEAUCOURT	
"	30th		Orders were subsequently amended & Battn entrained at 8.30pm at EDGEHILL near DERNANCOURT and proceeded to BAPAUME, the marching from there to ROCQUIGNY. Batn of Transport proceeded by route which leaving at 6.30pm	A.R.B

J A Druid Lt. Col.
7th Arg Hulth 1/9/1917.

A5834 Wt. W4973/M687 750,000 8/16 D. D. & L. Ltd. Forms/C.2118/13.

ACCOUNT OF ACTIVE OPERATIONS CARRIED OUT BY 7th A. & S.H.
on 20th, 21st, 22nd & 23rd November, 1917.

Ref. Map attached
Sheet 57C 1/40,000.

20th. 8-20 a.m.   Battalion was formed up in a position of assembly in Q.30.b.
9-50 a.m.   Battalion was ordered to move forward to old British Front Line.
10.30 a.m.   Reported arrival in old British front line.

21st. 1 a.m.   Received orders to move up to Railway cutting in K.23.b.& d., and to follow 153rd Brigade when situation in FLESQUIERES permitted, and to capture the CANTAING LINE and Village of FONTAINE, and to consolidate the high ground beyond the village. It was stated that ANNEUX and CANTAING were both in our hands.
6 a.m.   Battalion marched off in column of route.
7-20 a.m.   Arrived at Railway cutting without incident.
7-45 a.m.   Intelligence Officer reported FLESQUIERES to be in our hands and 153rd Brigade moving on to BROWN Line. I arranged with COL. ROWBOTHAM that we should both advance in Artillery formations at 8-30 a.m.
8-30 a.m.   Battalion moved off in Artillery formation, "B" Coy. on Right, "C" Coy. on Left, followed by "D" Coy. on Right and "A" Coy. on Left.
9-45 a.m.   Battalion reached a line parallel to Southern edge of ORIVAL WOOD.
I called on Col. McTaggart Commanding 5th Gordon Hrs. who informed me that ANNEUX was not in our hands, but he believed that it was only held by a rear-guard consisting of a company of M.Gs. and some snipers. I decided to detach "C"Coy. to take on this village from N.W.and S.E. while the remainder of the Battalion passed on to its original objective.
10-10a.m.   "C" Coy. extended in Sunken Road through K.6.b., L.1.a.& 6. and advanced over the crest where they were met with very heavy M.G. and rifle fire. Parties were immediately detached to work round the flanks. About simultaneously the 62nd Division attacked the village from N.W. with the aid of Artillery and Tanks. As "C" Coy. obviously would not advance from the position they were in, and the village was not in our area, I ordered Major Frew to withdraw if he could do so. The withdrawal was effected with the exception of one party of a Sergeant and 6 men who were working round the Southern flank; this party got mixed up with the attack of the 62nd Division, and is still missing.
11-20 a.m.   ANNEUX reported taken and Battalion continued its advance in extended order, "A" Coy. having replaced "C" Coy. in front.
12 noon.   Battalion was completely held up by M.G. and rifle fire about 300 yards short of CANTAING Line. The Battalion lay here under very heavy enfilade fire from CANTAING MILL and BOURLON WOOD.
I took up my H.Q. at LA JUSTICE with Col.Unthank 4th Seaforths.
On the Right the 4th Gordons found that CANTAING was also strongly held by the enemy and as their Left Company had been drawn away from me in an attack on that village, Col. Unthank ordered up one of his Companies to fill the gap between the 4th Gordons and my Battalion.
As no tanks appeared to be forthcoming I ordered my Battalion to dig in where they were.
I should like to emphasise very strongly the fact that

- 2 -

from the time my Battalion reached this position until the end of the day 2 enemy aeroplanes flying at about 150 feet patrolled up and down our lines dropping lights and firing at the men causing some 30 casualties. None of our aeroplanes appeared the whole of this day.

2 p.m. 7 Tanks passed LA JUSTICE on their way to the CANTAING Line, I ordered my leading Companies to advance under cover of the Tanks to their final objective.

3-50 p.m. The CANTAING Line was taken, and my Battalion was advancing on FONTAINE under cover of Tanks.
The advance of the Infantry was greatly hampered by enfilade fire from BOURLON WOOD and the advance of the tanks by the above mentioned aeroplanes who followed them dropping lights and directing the enemy's battery.

5-5 p.m. The village of FONTAINE was captured, and my Battalion was disposed as follows:-
"B" Coy. held from Sunken Road in F.16.a. to Sunken Road F.15.a.95, three platoons "D" Coy. which had been sent up to reinforce "B" Coy from Sunken Road F.15.a.95 to F.14.b.9.3, "A" Coy. from F.14.b.9.3 to CAMBRAI - BAPAUME Road, "C" Coy. had formed a defensive flank across the CANTAING Line in F.20.c. with two platoons - Sunken Road in F.26.c.
The Eastern half of the village had been taken and held by three Coys. 4th Seaforths.
"D" Coy. H.Q. and 1 Platoon were in Sunken Road F.26.c.

9 p.m. Ordered to reorganise the defence, 4th Seaforths being responsible for defence of FONTAINE, 7th A.& S.H. both flanks in rear of FONTAINE.
I arranged with COL. Unthank that he should send up his fourth Coy. to relieve my "B", "A" and three platoons of "D" Coy., and that these should come back to position in Sunken Road in F.21.c.

22nd - 6 a.m. Two platoons "C" Coy. from Sunken Road F.26.c. relieved No.3 Coy. 4th Seaforths in touch with 62nd Division about F.25.b.
H.Q. and 1 platoon "D" Coy. moved from Sunken Road in F.26.c. to Sunken Road in F.21.c.
No.3 Coy. 4th Seaforths relieved "B" Coy., three platoons "D" Coy. and "A" Coy. one platoon which it was not possible to relieve by daylight. These units on relief moved back to Sunken Road in F.21.c. where they consolidated positions as follows:-
"B" and "D" Coys. facing N.W. and "A" Coy.(less 1 platoon) facing W. and S.W.
This relief and the subsequent consolidation was greatly hampered by 7 enemy aeroplanes which patrolled our lines from dawn onwards and by enfilade M.G. fire from BOURLON WOOD. My Battalion saw nothing of any counter-attacks till about 12 noon when they observed parties of 4th Seaforths retiring through the village.

12 noon. I ordered Capt. Arrol, who commanded the 3 Companies (less 1 platoon) in F.21.c. to reorganise his dispositions so as to face the village and to stop all stragglers, and to prevent the enemy from breaking through beyond the village. These orders were carried out, all men of the 4th Seaforths were stopped and reorganised, and the enemy was heavily engaged by L.G. and rifle fire whenever he attempted to debouch from the village or to work round the flanks.
These positions were maintained till relief by 7th Black Watch which was complete by 1-12 a.m. on 23rd. "C" and "D" Coys. were left at LA JUSTICE in support of 7th Black Watch

27th November, 1917.

Lieut.Col.
Commanding 7th Arg.& Suth.Highrs.

REMARKS.

The work of the Tanks was magnificent; without them no advance beyond the CANTAING Line would have been possible.

Maps issued should either be properly contoured or not at all, the gross mistakes in contouring in the 1/20,000 maps issued were most misleading.

The Artillery were very late indeed opening on the S.O.S. sent up by 4th Seaforths. I myself, standing at L.1.b.7.5.at about 11-45 a.m. saw 2 S.O.S.rockets go up and the batteries immediately behind me made no response. Eventually I found an Artillery liaison Officer and made him get through to his battery and get them started.

Our aeroplanes were conspicuous by their absence from the 21st to end of 23 rd.

The advance to FONTAINE should never have taken place till BOURLON WOOD was captured, but unfortunately the order cancelling this advance (your K.B.22) did not arrive till the Battalion was well on its way.

Total prisoners captured by the Battalion -
1 Officer and 200 O.R.

27th November, 1917.   Commanding 7th Arg. & Suth. Highrs.
                                                      Lieut.Col.

"A" Form
MESSAGES AND SIGNALS.

Army Form C.2121
(In pads of 100.)

No. of Message..........

Prefix....... Code.......m. | Words. | Charge. | This message is on a/c of: | Recd. at.........m.
Office of Origin and Service Instructions | Sent At.......m. | | ....Service. | Date.
.... | To. | | | From
.... | By. | (Signature of "Franking Officer.") | | By

TO— { 4/E.H. | 7/A+S. | 9/R.S. | 4/S.A.
154 M.G.Coy | 154 T.M.B. | K.E.H. | Coops Gchts

Sender's Number | Day of Month | In reply to Number |
*K.B.8 | 20. | | AAA

(1) At Zero on morning 21st Nov: 152 & 153 Brigades will continue attack on FLESQUIERES Six Tanks cooperating On capturing the village these Brigades will capture & consolidate the BROWN LINE & GRAINCOURT PREMY CHAPEL Sunken Road Line.

(2) Artillery barrage will rest on (a) BROWN LINE from Zero to Zero + 45 min.
(b) Line through S edge of ORIVAL WOOD from Zero + 45 to Zero + 90.
(c) Line through N edge of ORIVAL WOOD from Zero + 90 to Zero + 105
(d) GRAINCOURT — PREMY CHAPEL Line from Zero + 105 to Zero + 120.

From
Place   No barrage by F.A will be possible
Time   beyond this line until the guns are moved
forward

The above may be forwarded as now corrected. (Z)

Censor.   Signature of Addressor or person authorised to telegraph in his name.
*This line should be erased if not required.

"A" Form
MESSAGES AND SIGNALS.

Army Form C. 2121
(In pads of 100.)

(3) 154 Brigade will pass through 152 & 153 Brigades & capture the BOURLON - CANTAING line & FONTAINE NOTRE DAME.

(4) 4/Gordons on right & 7/A and S High[rs] on left will capture the objectives assigned to the Brigade, the existing Boundary between 152 & 153 being the Battalion boundary. These Batt[alion]s will be assembled on the line of the Railway in K.24.c & d & K.23.a and d at zero + 1 hour & will advance as soon as the situation at FLESQUIERES permits. This must be decided by observation & reconnaissance on the spot. 152 & 153 will probably not be clear of the Railway before Zero + 1 hour.

"A" Form
MESSAGES AND SIGNALS.

Army Form C. 2121
(In pads of 100.)

(5) 4/G.H. & 7 A&S H'rs will pass through 152 & 153 Brigades on the BROWN LINE or between it & the GRAINCOURT-PREMY CHAPEL line should these Brigades be hung up.

(6) 4/S.H. & 9 R.S. each with 2 Vickers guns attached will assemble in the HINDENBURG Front System, 4/S.H on the Right & 9 R.S. on the left, they will cross our front trench at Zero + 15 min.

(7) Remainder 154 M.G Coy & T.M By will assemble at the H.Q. of Q 4 a 5.5 at Zero.

"A" Form
MESSAGES AND SIGNALS.

Army Form C. 2121
(In pads of 100.)

(8) On the 4/G.H & 7/A&S clearing their starting position on the Railway 4/S.H & 9/R.S will move forward there. The last named Batt will keep touch with 4/G.H & 7/A&S during the action.

(9) "A" Sqdn K.E.H & 2 Coys IV Corps Cyclists will be attached to the Brigade — They will be assembled at Q.10.A.2.1 at Zero – 15 min, the respective C.O's reporting to Brigade H.Q. at that hour.

(10) Brigade H.Q is now at Q.10.A.2.1 & will move forward to K.35.9.8 at an hour to be notified

(11) Zero hour will be 6.15 A.M.

From 154/14/B
Place
Time 12.5 A.M

(12) Acknowledge

R.J. Buchanan

MESSAGE FORM.

..................Divisio
..................Map

1. I am at ....

2. I am at .... { are
                         al
                         an

3. Am held up at ....

4. I need :-   S.A.A.
                     Rifle Gre
                     Water.
                     Very Ligh
                     S.O.S. S
                     Stokes Sh

5. Enemy forming up for count

6. Enemy troops strength esti

7. I am in touch with ....

8. I am not in touch on   Righ
                           Lef

9. I estimate my present str

10. Hostile Battery }
    Machine Gun   }   act
    Trench Mortar   }

    Time .... a.m.
                      p.m.

    Date ../../1917.

MESSAGE FORM.

..........................Division.

............................Map reference, or own position on map.

1. I am at ....

2. I am at .... { am consolidating and have consolidated and am ready to advance to .... { by M.G. at .... { by wire at ....

3. Am held up at ....

4. I need :-
   S.A.A.
   Rifle Grenades.
   Water.
   Very lights.
   S.O.S. Signals.
   Sandbags.

5. Enemy forming up for counter attack at .... { advance retire

6. Enemy troops strength estimated at ...., on Right at .... Left

7. I am in touch with .... Right Left

8. I am not in touch on Right Left

9. I estimate my present strength at ....

10. Hostile Battery }
    Machine Gun   } active at ....
    Trench Mortar   }

Time .... a.m. Name ....
                   p.m. Rank ....

Army Form W. 3091.

Cover for Documents.

Nature of Enclosures.

7th Argyll & Sutherland
Highlanders.
War Diary.
December 1917.

Notes, or Letters written.

WAR DIARY
or
INTELLIGENCE SUMMARY.
(Erase heading not required.)

Army Form C. 2118.

7th Arg. & Suth. Highrs.
Ref. Mypo - 57c

Place	Date Decr.	Hour	Summary of Events and Information	Remarks and references to Appendices
ROCQUIGNY	1st	4.30am	Batt. arrived in huts after marching from BAPAUME.	
BERTINCOURT	2nd	~~6am~~ 10.15am	Batt. marched off to RUGLIGNY BERTINCOURT arriving there at 11.40am. At 2.15pm Batt. less transport & Echelon B marched into position in old British front line near BOURSIES. C Coy in J.6.d. A Coy in J.6.a. & b. "D" Coy in J.5.b. Hd. Qrs. + B Coy in SUNKEN ROAD J.5.C. in Night transport moved up Brigade was Taken up by 9.35pm. O.R.s	App. I
"	3rd		Day was spent in support in position near LEBUCQUIERES. At 6pm "B" Coy moved up to position in MOEUVRES Reserve Line in support to 4th Seaforth Highrs. Enemy shelled BOURSIES intermittently during the day. At 11.30pm Patrol Bombing aeroplane crashed at J.6.C.9. R.F.C. that filed Returns were unfit the belonged to 101st Squadron R.F.C. also	App. II
"	4th	11am	"D" Coy moved up to position in E.25.G. Our trenches in E.25 were heavily shelled. Casualties 5 o.r. wounded.	
"	"	8.30pm	5th Seaforths come at to relieve Bn. A "C" Coys also proceeded back to billets in BEVGNY. B + D Coys came back under orders of O/c. 4th Seaforth Highrs	App. III
BEVGNY	5th		Batt. arrived back in billets by 4:30am	O.R.B.
"	6th		At 12.45am a hostile aeroplane dropped two bombs in the village	O.R.B.
"	7th		In billets training	O.R.B.
"	"		"	O.R.B.

1st Argyll Sutherland Highlanders
Army Form C. 2118.
Ref. Napo:- 57 c

WAR DIARY

INTELLIGENCE SUMMARY

(Erase heading not required.)

Place	Date	Hour	Summary of Events and Information	Remarks and references to Appendices
BEUGNY	DEC 8th		In billets. Continued training.	A.R.B.
"	9th		Owing to rain Church Parade was cancelled.	A.R.B.
"	10th		Continued training. Batt'n. was placed at half-an-hour's notice to move to support position near HAVRINCOURT. FLESQUIERES.	A.R.B.
"	11th		Continued training.	A.R.B. A.R.B.
"	12th		"	J.P.C.
"	13th		"	J.P.C.
"	14th		"	J.P.C.
"	15th		"	
"	16th		Held Church Parade. At 4.15 p.m Battalion less transport moved up the Line over the lines from 9th BLACK WATCH. "A" Coy on right holding front line from J.6.a. 55.25 to K.1.c. 05.35 and "C" Coy on right from 15.1.c. 05.30 to K.7.a. 6.2. "D" Coy in support in the front /Labour at Quarry J.6.d and two Platoons at J.12.c.6.1 and J.12.c.8.1. "B" Coy in Reserve in SUNKEN ROAD J.7.9.	App IV

WAR DIARY or INTELLIGENCE SUMMARY

(Erase heading not required.)

Army Form C. 2118.

Place	Date Dec.	Hour	Summary of Events and Information	Remarks and references to Appendices
J.17.a.5.7.	16th contd		Battalion H.Q. at J.17.a.5.7. Night fairly quiet. Relief complete by 10 p.m.	J.M.B.
	17th		Day was fairly quiet. Lt. Col. J.A.D.R.I.E. was admitted to Hospital. Casualties 1 O.R. wounded.	J.M.B.
	18th		Enemy used Trench Mortars & shells, some of the shells of heavy type 7 from map sqs. A.65.25 & T.6.a.3.13. Casualties 1 O.R. killed and 3 O.R. wounded. Intermittent shelling all day.	J.M.B.
	19th		Day was generally quiet. Intermittent shelling. Corpse post "X" established and Battn H.Q. Casualties 1 O.R. wounded.	J.M.B.
	20th		Day quiet. Casualties 1 O.R. killed and 1 O.R. wounded	J.M.B.
	21st		do Casualties 2 O.Rs wounded	J.M.B.
	22nd		Intermittent shelling. Relieved by 6th London R. Casualties 3 O.Rs wounded. Battalion moved back in camp at MIDDLESEX CAMP by 11.30 p.m.	a/16V
	23rd		In camp. Relief complete by 5 p.m. Between 15th & a number of T.A. hospital many Trench all wound about Camp. Casualties 2 O.Rs killed and 25 O.Rs wounded.	J.M.B.
	24th		In camp – During making walls round the huts and drying out trenches.	J.M.B.
	25th		In camp. General holiday. Held Church parade at 10 a.m.	J.M.B.
	26th		do	
	27th		Continued training & making walls round huts etc	Baker?

Army Form C. 2118.

WAR DIARY
or
INTELLIGENCE SUMMARY.
(Erase heading not required.)

Instructions regarding War Diaries and Intelligence Summaries are contained in F. S. Regs., Part II. and the Staff Manual respectively. Title pages will be prepared in manuscript.

Place	Date	Hour	Summary of Events and Information	Remarks and references to Appendices
FRICOURT	27th Dec		Batt'n moved at 3 p.m. from MIDDLESEX CAMP to CAMP marked by 64 BLACK WATCH in LINDOP CAMP, FRICOURT	
do	28th		In camp. Combined training and digging off trenches.	
do	29th		do	
do	30th		Batt'n less transport moved at 1.30 p.m. to take over the line from 6th GORDON HIGHLANDERS. "B" Coy on right holding front line from K.7.a.9.1 to J.6.d.95.25 and "D" Coy on the left holding front line from J.6.d.95.25 to J.6.a.9.1. "C" Coy in support with two platoons at Quarry J.6.d. and two platoons at J.12.c.6.1. and J.12.c.6.1 and J.10.d. Battalion "A" Coy in Reserve in SUNKEN ROAD J.17.a. and J.10.d. Battalion H.Q. at J.17.a.5.9. Night was very quiet and relief was complete by 7 p.m. Casualties NIL.	
	31st		Day was very quiet. Casualties NIL.	

D A Bidmore
Major
Commanding
1/7 Arg. & Suth. Highrs.

War Diary G

S E C R E T.   Copy No. 4

154th INFANTRY BRIGADE
OPERATION ORDER NO. 152.

Reference Maps :
    57.C. 1/40,000.
    57.C.N.E.1. 1/10,000.

1.   154th Infantry Brigade will relieve 169th Infantry Brigade (56th Div.) on nights 1st/2nd December and 2nd/3rd December. 2nd Division will be on our right; 153rd Infantry Brigade on our left.

2.   Moves of 9th Royal Scots and 4th Gordon Highrs. into old British front line on night 1st/2nd December have already been arranged.

3.   On night 2nd/3rd December 9th Royal Scots will relieve London Rifle Bde. in Right Sector, 4th Gordon Highrs. will relieve 3rd Londons in Left Sector.
     All details regarding this relief to be arranged by Commanding Officers concerned. The necessary reconnaissance to be carried out by daylight on 2nd inst.

4.   On night 2nd/3rd December 4th Seaforth Highrs. will replace 9th Royal Scots on right in old British front line, and 7th Argylls will replace 4th Gordon Highrs. on left in old British front line.

5.   4th Seaforth Highrs. and 7th Argylls will march from BERTINCOURT at 1.45 p.m. and 2.15 p.m. respectively to reach Western end of DOIGNIES (J.16.a.1.5.) about dusk - route BERTINCOURT - X Roads O.5.d. - thence N. to X Roads I.30.d.2.4. - thence Road and Railway crossing J.25.a.9.4. - BEAUMETZ - DOIGNIES. From X Roads I.30.d. movement will be by platoons at 150 yards interval; previous reconnaissance of this route is necessary.

6.   To-morrow morning each Coy. 4th Seaforth Highrs. and 7th Argylls will send one Officer to 169th Bde. H.Q. (J.17.a.2.6.) in Sunken Road, to reconnoitre the line, and have situation explained. These Officers will be back at 169th Bde. H.Q. one hour before battalion reaches J.16.a.1.5. to pick up platoon guides provided by 169th Bde.

7.   154th M. G. Coy. will leave BEUGNY at 1.45 p.m. to-morrow and proceed to 169th Bde. H.Q. (J.17.a.2.6.) with 16 guns. Guns will be off-limbered there and guides provided by 169th M. G. Coy. Route as already given to O.C. 154th M. G. Coy.

8.   154th T. M. Battery will send 3 Mortars to 169th Bde. H.Q. (J.17.a.2.6.) leaving BERTINCOURT at 1.30 p.m. 2 Mortars are for Left Sector, one for right. Guides will be provided by 169th T. M. Battery. One Officer T. M. Battery will make previous reconnaissance of line, reporting to 169th Bde. H.Q. as early as possible to-morrow. Remainder of T. M. Battery will move to transport lines BEAUCOURT, leaving BERTINCOURT at 2.45 p.m.

- 2 -

9. All transport will concentrate near BERTINCOURT to-morrow: a representative from each transport will meet B.T.O. at X Roads I.28.b.5.2. at 9.30 a.m. to-morrow.

10. Units leaving BERTINCOURT to-morrow will go into the line in fighting kit plus <u>greatcoats</u>: blankets will not be carried.

11. Orders regarding Echelon "B" will be issued later.

12. On completion of relief on 2nd/3rd December B.G.C., 154th Bde. will assume command of the line.

13. Bde. H.Q. will close at BEUGNY at 2 p.m. to-morrow and open at J.17.a.2.6. on arrival.

14. ACKNOWLEDGE.

ack?

a Scott
Captain,
Staff Captain,
154th Infantry Brigade.

1st December, 1917.

ISSUED AT........BY O.D.R.L.?

Copy No. 1 9th Royal Scots.
         2 4th Seaforth Highrs.
         3 4th Gordon Highrs.
         4 7th A. & S. Highrs.
         5 154th M. G. Company.
         6 154th T. M. Battery.
         7 51st (H) Div. "G".
         8 51st (H) Div. "Q".
         9 169th Inf. Brigade.
        10 152nd   "   "
        11 153rd   "   "
        12 No. 2 Coy. A. S. C.
        13 H.Q. 51st (H) Div. Train.
        14 401st Field Coy. R.E.
        15 2/1st (H) Field Ambulance.
        16 Brigade Transport Officer.
        17 Brigade Signal Officer.
        18 File.
        19 War Diary.

SECRET.   Copy No...6...

154th INFANTRY BRIGADE
OPERATION ORDER NO. 153.

Reference Map 57.C. 1/40,000.
----

1.   To-night 3rd/4th December 154th Brigade will extend its right to the CANAL inclusive, frontage about 1000 yards. 4th Seaforths will take over the front from the CANAL to Sap at E.20.c.6.3., Sap exclusive; 9th Royal Scots will extend their present right to Sap at E.20.c.6.3. inclusive.

2.   4th Seaforths will relieve B and C Companies H.L.I. and C and D Coys. South Staffords with Headquarters at E.23.b.1.2.

        9th Royal Scots will relieve A and D Companies H.L.I.

        Guides are being arranged by Units concerned.

3.   7th Argylls will move one Coy. into MOEUVRES Reserve in E.26.c. replacing troops of 186th Brigade there. O.C. Coy. to get into touch with Seaforth's Battalion H.Q.

        Remainder of 7th Argylls will be disposed in old British front line, with Battalion H.Q. in its present position.

4.   Completion of relief to be reported to Bde. H.Q.

5.   B.G.C. 154th Brigade will assume command of extended sector on completion of relief.

6.   Acknowledge by bearer.

                                                    A Scott
                                                    Captain,
                                                    Brigade Major,
3rd Decr. 1917   154th Infantry Brigade.

ISSUED AT...6.15pm...BY ORDERLY.

Copy No. 1 File.
        2 War Diary.
        3 9th Royal Scots.
        4 4th Seaforth Highrs.
        5 4th Gordon Highrs.
        6 7th A. & S. Highrs.
        7 154th M. G. Company.
        8 154th T. M. Battery.
        9 51st (H) Division "G".
       10 6th Infantry Brigade
       11 152nd   "   "
       12 153rd   "   "
       13 No. 2 Coy. A.S.C.
       14 51st Divisional Train.
       15 Brigade Signal Officer.
       16 Brigade Transport Officer.

SECRET.

154th Inf. Bde. No.K.K.457

O.C.
    9th Royal Scots.
    4th Seaforth Highrs.
    4th Gordon Highrs.
    7th A. & S. Highrs.
    154th M. G. Company.
    154th T. M. Battery.
H. Q. 51st (H) Division "G".
    152nd Inf. Brigade.
    153rd " "

1.   There has been considerable fighting in the neighbourhood of MOEUVRES and TADPOLE COPSE during the last four days and the enemy may be expected to renew his efforts to regain the HINDENBURG LINE, more especially the high ground on which TADPOLE COPSE lies.

2.   The loss of the HINDENBURG SUPPORT TRENCH on the 30th Nov. endangers our present front line as follows :-

(a)   There is no adequate or immediate support line.

(b)   The portion of the line N.W. of TADPOLE COPSE is in the air.

(c)   The numerous communication trenches leading from our front line to the enemy blocks someway up them are a source of danger.

(d)   The old German Outpost Line which was dug out as a support trench is in some places 500 yards behind our present front line, the next line of defence being the old British Line some 1500 yards in rear.

3.   To provide a better system of defence the following work will be carried out forthwith :-

(a)   To dig a line of posts immediately in rear of the wire which is in rear of our front line.

(b)   Fill in all C.T's leading to the German lines as far forward as possible, thereby doing away with numerous garrisons detailed to hold them, and allowing our Artillery to shell the German front line, concentrate Stokes Mortars and Rifle Grenades on portions of these C.T's held by the enemy.

(c)   As soon as the new support line posts are dug, to hold the old German outpost line as thinly as possible and chiefly with machine guns.

(d)   Gaps in the three rows of wire in rear of our front line must be cut, and marked to facilitate counter-attack and the moving up of reinforcements.

4 (a)   With regard to 3 (a).

Centre Battalion (at present 9th Royal Scots) will construct 4 posts from about E.26.a.5.8. to ALDGATE inclusive and 3 posts from about E.19.d.5.3. to C.T. at E.19.c.7.7. exclusive. Left Battalion (at present 4th Gordons) will construct 4 posts from C.T. at E.19.c.7.7. to trench junction at E.19.a.3.8. This Battalion will also deepen and make fit for holding a garrison the portion of trench from E.19.a.3.8. to the left boundary of the Brigade.

(b)   With regard to 3 (b)

Front Battalions will use all possible means to fill in all C.T's., etc., now held as bombing posts. Experiments are now being made with Bengalore Torpedoes and if successful the R.E. will blow in lengths of these trenches. Wherever it is possible, filling the C.T. with wire is to be avoided.

** 2 **

5.   Until it is possible to withdraw the bombing posts from the forward C.T's each Unit holding the front will have reserve bombing squads in readiness to reinforce the existing posts or to counter-attack should the enemy succeed in gaining a footing in our line. These reserve squads, which must each have a definite task and area allotted, may be placed in the dugouts which exist in the front line. Arrangements must be made, however, to ensure their leaving the dugouts instantly they are required.

        Reserve Companies in the old German Oupost Line and elsewhere will be given routes to be followed by O.C. Battalions in event of their being required for counter-attack.

        Until such time as the defence of the old outpost line is completed by the moving forward of additional M.G's into it, Battalion Commanders will arrange that not less than one platoon which is to be detailed by name remains as garrison of the line.

        The centre Battalion may call on the Company of the Reserve Battalion (at present 7th A. & S. Highrs.) in MOEUVRES Reserve for counter-attack on his right front and will issue instructions to the Company Commander. One platoon will remain as garrison of the trench as laid down above.

        The right Battalion (at present 4th Seaforths) will be organised in depth.

6.   The Brigade Reserve, 3 Coys., (at present 7th A. & S. Highrs.) in old British Front Line will be used under orders from Bde. H.Q. for counter-attack. These Coys. must know the best routes over the open to assembly positions in the old German Outpost Line.

        On the Right Battalion Front i.e. East of ALDGATE.

        On the Centre Battalion Front i.e. between ALDGATE and HOUNDSDITCH

        On the Left Battalion Front i.e. NORTH of HOUNDSDITCH.

7.   After relief on night 3rd/4th December Divisional Eastern Boundary will run from North of the CANAL, inclusive to 51st Division, to junction of CANAL and BAPAUME - CAMBRAI Road, thence to K.7.d.4.5.; thence to J.23.Central.

8.   Acknowledge.

3rd December, 1917.

Captain,
Brigade Major,
154th Infantry Brigade.

S E C R E T.   Copy No. 6

154th INFANTRY BRIGADE
OPERATION ORDER NO. 154.

1.   It has been decided to withdraw the British Line on the CAMBRAI battle front to-night, 4th/5th December.

2.   As far as the 51st Division is concerned the line will be withdrawn to the old British front line in the following manner :-

(a)   At dusk to-day, 152nd Inf. Brigade will move forward and take over the new Divisional front in old British front line, i.e. from K.1.c.40.25. (road inclusive) to D.21.d.70.35. This front line will be held by 3 Battalions, the 4th Battalion, 152nd Bde. being in intermediate line with Battalion H.Q. at present 154th Brigade H.Q. J.17.a.5.6.

        152nd M.G. Company will take over positions of 153rd and 154th M.G. Companies in old British Front System.

        M.G's of 154th Brigade Company in positions in rear of old British Front Line will stand fast.

(b)   The withdrawal of troops of 154th Inf. Brigade holding present line in advance of old British Front Line will be carried out in following manner.

(i)   At dusk each Battalion in front line will detail special parties to carry back as much S.A.A., Grenades and Stores as possible and dump in old British Front Line at following points :-

   Parties of 4th Seaforth Highrs. and 2 Coys. 7th A. & S. Highrs.
                        at K.1.c.4.2.
   Parties of 9th Royal Scots at J.6.d.4.9.
   Parties of 4th Gordon Highrs. at J.6.a.4.2.

        Having dumped parties will move back to billets as detailed in para. 4 of this order.

        As soon as possible after dusk Bde. T.O. will arrange for limbers to be sent up to Dump at E.26.d.3.2. and to HOUND Dump at D.30.b.9.9. to remove stores there.

        7th A. & S. Highrs. and 4th Gordon Highrs. will each detail 20 men to load up these limbers., 7th A. & S. Highrs. at E.26.d.3.2. and 4th Gordon Highrs. at D.30.b.9.9. O.C. 4/S.H will detail 7/A&S party from the 2 Coys in MOEUVRES RESERVE under him

        7th A. & S. Highrs. will detail an unloading party of 20 men to be at J.6.c.7.6. (Cross Roads). Stores to be concealed as much as possible. Limbers will do 2 journeys. On completion loading and unloading parties will move back to billets.

(ii)   The withdrawal of front line Battalions will be carried out as follows :-

As soon as the carrying parties detailed in above para. are clear, supporting troops of 4th Seaforth Highrs., 9th Royal Scots and 4th Gordon Highrs. will commence withdrawing. The 2 Coys. 7th A. & S. Highrs. in MOEUVRES RESERVE withdrawing under orders of 4th Seaforth Highrs.

By 3 a.m. on 5th December all troops of 4th Seaforth Highrs., 9th Royal Scots, 4th Gordon Highrs. and 7th A. & S. Highrs will be through and clear of the old British Front Line, except a rear guard as detailed below.

4th Seaforth Highrs., 9th Royal Scots and 4th Gordon Highrs. will maintain a rear guard under specially selected Officers as follows :-

In the present front line, sufficient men to hold the Bombing Saps.

In the support line (old German Ourpost Line) one platoon per Battalion with one Vickers gun.

At 4 a.m. on 5th December all troops in front line will withdraw passing through the supporting platoons in the old outpost line.

At 4.45 a.m. on 5th December the supporting platoons and Vickers guns in old outpost line will withdraw.

The following routes will be used in the withdrawal :-

 4th Seaforths and 2 Coys. 7th A. & S. Highrs.
  CAMBRAI - BAPAUME ROAD.

 9th Royal Scots ... ALDGATE - CAMBRAI - BAPAUME ROAD.

 4th Gordon Highrs.... HOUNDSDITCH - BISHOPSGATE -
  CAMBRAI - BAPAUME ROAD.

All troops on reaching Cross Roads at J.9.F.7.2. will move by any track South of main Road but not on Main Road.

Everyman will carry some article of store or ammunition, dumping same in old British Front Line when crossing.

4th Seaforth Highrs. will synchronise time with the Battalion of 2nd Division on his right.

An Officer of 4th Seaforth Highrs. Rear Guard will gain touch with this Battalion at LOCK 6 where a post of an outpost line is being maintained by 2nd Division.

4th Gordon Highrs. will synchronise time with 5th Gordon Highrs., 153rd Brigade, at 7 p.m. to-night at junction of HOUNDSDITCH and BARBICAN.

3. Stokes Mortars in the line will withdraw at 7 p.m. to-night.

Vickers guns in front of old British Front Line, except those remaining with the Rear Guard, i.e. 4, will commence withdrawal at 11 p.m.

** 3 **

4. On withdrawal of the Brigade, it will move into billets in BEUGNY and FREMICOURT now occupied by 152nd Brigade.
Billeting parties from Echelon "B" have been sent to take over from various Units.
7th A. & S. Highrs. to BEUGNY; remainder of Brigade to FREMICOURT.

5. As soon as each Unit's Rear Guard has completely passed through old British Front Line, a report will be sent to Bde. H.Q. at J.17.a.5.6., where Brigade will remain until all troops are clear.

6. 4th Seaforth Highrs. will be responsible for warning M.G's of 6th Inf. Brigade at present covering his front to withdraw in accordance with para. 4. Also any Stokes Mortars of 6th Bn. in his line

7. Absolute secrecy is to be maintained regarding the withdrawal to-night. On no account is any reference to be made of it on the telephone. When arranging details in the front line, no mention is to be made of it, and O.C. Battalions will see that instructions to N.C.Os. are written out and given them to read.

8. H.Q. and 2 Coys. 7th A. & S. Highrs. now in old British Front Line, as soon as replaced by 5th Seaforth Highrs, 152nd Brigade, will move back to BEUGNY.

9. Battalion Signal Officers will each arrange for telephone lines to be reeled up and brought back to old British Front Line – units will provide the necessary carrying parties – work to begin at 11 p.m.
Visual will be maintained till Battalion H.Q's move.

10. Should the withdrawal be cancelled for to-night, 4th/5th, the following code message will be wired to all concerned :-

        BON ACCORD = Withdraw.
        E.F. = Night 5th/6th.
        E.G. = Night 6th/7th and so on.

11. Acknowledge by bearer.

4th December, 1917.

Captain,
Brigade Major,
154th Infantry Brigade.

ISSUED AT........BY ORDERLY.

Copy No. 1 File.
     2 War Diary.
     3 9th Royal Scots.
     4 4th Seaforth Highrs.
     5 4th Gordon Highrs.
     6 7th A. & S. Highrs.
     7 154th M. G. Company.
     8 154th T. M. Battery.
     9 51st (H) Division "G".
    10 152nd Inf. Brigade.
    11 153rd   "   "
    12 153rd   "   "
    13 6th   "   "

SECRET.   War Diary G   IV

Copy No. 4

154th INFANTRY BRIGADE
OPERATION ORDER NO. 155.

Reference Maps :-
    Trench Map 1/10,000.
    Sheet 57.C.1/40,000.

----

1.   154th Inf. Brigade will relieve 153rd Inf. Brigade in the line on night 16th/17th December, as under :-

    7th A. & S. Highrs. will relieve 7th Black Watch.
    9th Royal Scots   "   "   7th Gordon Highrs.
    4th Seaforth Highrs. "   "   6th Black Watch.
    4th Gordon Highrs.   "   "   5th Gordon Highrs.
                                     (in Reserve)
    154th M.G. Company   "   "   153rd M.G. Company.
    154th T.M. Battery   "   "   153rd T.M. Battery.

2.   All arrangements for relief will be made direct between Commanding Officers concerned, including rendezvous for platoon and company guides.

    Guides for M.G. Company and T.M. Battery will be arranged direct.

3.   All maps of trenches, Defence Schemes, programmes of work in hand, Air Photos, Stores, etc. will be taken over on relief.

4.   Battalions will leave their present billets at the following times :-

    4th Gordon Highrs.   3 p.m.
    4th Seaforth Highrs. 4 p.m.
    7th A. & S. Highrs.   4.15 p.m.
    9th Royal Scots   4.30 p.m.

7th A. & S. Highrs. will not enter main BAPAUME - CAMBRAI ROAD till 4th Gordon Highrs. are clear of BEUGNY.

5.   153rd M.G. Company will leave one man per gun in line for 24 hours after relief.

6.   Mining platoons will go up with Battalions and will commence work on respective dugouts, as under, at noon on 17th inst. They will work in three 8 hour shifts of twelve men each. First shift will report at the dugout at which it will work at 10 a.m. on 17th inst. so as to commence work at 12 noon.

    Work will be carried out under 252nd Tunnelling Coy., a representative of which will meet parties.

    7th A. & S. Highrs. at J.6.d.3.0.) Under Capt. DONALD,
    9th Royal Scots at D.29.c.3.1.) 252nd Tunnelling Coy.

    4th Gordon Highrs. at D.28.a.9.8.) Under Capt. HUTCHEONS,
    4th Seaforth Hrs. at D.27.b.9.9.) 252nd Tunnelling Coy.

~~Both~~ Officers can be found at J.21.d.3.4.

** 2 **

7. 154th T. M. Battery will take over mining work on dugout J.7.b.9.1. from 153rd T. M. Battery. They will work under O.C. 401st Field Coy. R.E. First shift, consisting of 1 N.C.O. and 8 men, will commence work at 12 midnight 16th/17th December.

8. Details of daily working parties and mining parties required from Battalions will be communicated later.

9. Echelon "B" will be accommodated in the Transport Lines.

10. Lists of Trench Stores taken over will be forwarded to Brigade H.Q. by 6 p.m. on 17th inst.

11. Units will report relief complete to this Brigade H.Q. by code word "DUB" and will come under orders of B.G.C. 153rd Inf. Brigade until 8 a.m., 17th inst, when B.G.C. 154th Inf. Brigade will assume command of the Sector.

["DUG" BOOK — handwritten margin note]

12. Headquarters 154th Inf. Brigade will close at LINDOP CAMP, FREMICOURT, at 7 a.m. on 17th December and will open at I.12.b.3.3. at 8 a.m. same date.

13. From noon on 17th December the S.O.S. signal will be

2 GREEN and 2 WHITE Very Lights or Rifle Grenades.

These will be issued.

14. 51st Division come under orders of IV Corps from 12 noon on 15th December.

The tactical boundary between 51st Division and the 2nd Division on the right will remain as at present.

The tactical boundary between 51st Division and 25th Division on the left will be CENTRAL AVENUE and LARK POST, inclusive to 51st Division. This new portion of front will be taken over by 153rd Inf. Brigade during 16th December and will be handed over by 6th Black Watch to 4th Seaforth Highrs on night 16th/17th December.

A map showing the above tactical boundary will be issued later.

15. ACKNOWLEDGE.

E.C. Hunt.
Captain,
Brigade Major,
154th Infantry Brigade.

15th December, 1917.

ISSUED AT..4/*...BY ORDERLY.

Copy No. 1 9th Royal Scots.
2 4th Seaforth Highrs.
3 4th Gordon Highrs.
4 7th A. & S. Highrs.
5 154th M. G. Company.
6 154th T. M. Battery.
7 51st (H) Division "Q".
8 51st (H)   "   "A".
9 152nd Inf. Brigade.
10 153rd   "   "
11 5th   "   "
12 74th   "   "

No. 13 2/1st (H) Field Ambulance.
14 No. 2 Coy. A.S.C.
15 401st Field Coy., R.E.
16 B.G.C.
17 Bde. Transport Officer.
18 "   Signal Officer.
19 Staff Captain.
20 War Diary.
21 File.

SECRET.   Copy No. 4

154th INFANTRY BRIGADE
OPERATION ORDER NO.156.

Reference Maps :-
   Trench Map 1/10,000.
   Sheet 57.C. 1/40,000.
---

1.   154th Inf. Brigade will be relieved in the line on night 22nd/23rd December as under :-

   (a)   By the 152nd Inf. Brigade taking over with 2 Battalions the front now held by 7th A. & S. Highrs and 9th Royal Scots.

   (b)   By the 153rd Inf. Brigade taking over with 2 Battalions the front now held by 4th Seaforth Highrs. and 4th Gordon Highrs.

2.   Relief will be carried out in accordance with relief table attached.

3. (a)   If the visibility is low on 22nd December relieving Battalions of 152nd and 153rd Inf. Brigades will move up during the afternoon and the times in the attached relief table have been drawn up on this supposition.

   (b)   If the weather is thick Battalion Commanders will arrange to guide relieving Battalions by the most direct route to the front line and incoming Battalions will not use the communication trenches.

   (c)   If the weather is very clear the relief will be postponed by two hours and this information will be sent by means of the code word "SUNLIGHT" to all concerned.

NOTE: In (a) and (b) above relieving troops will move by half platoons at intervals of 200 yards.

4.   154th M. G. Company will be relieved by 152nd and 153rd M. G. Companies after dark on 22nd December. Details will follow.

5.   154th T. M. Battery will be relieved by 152nd T. M. Battery after dark on 22nd December except for two gun positions at D.21.c.9.6., which will be relieved by 153rd T. M. Battery.

6.   Mining platoons of relieving Battalions will go into the line with their Battalions taking over the shifts from 154th Brigade mining platoons at 12 noon on 23rd December as follows -

Location of Dugout.	Unit working at present.	Relieved by.
J.6.d.3.0.	7th A. & S. Hrs.	6th Gordon Hrs.
J.6.d.1.5.	9th Royal Scots.	6th Seaforth Hrs.
D.28.a.9.8.	4th Gordon Hrs.	5th Gordon Hrs.
D.27.b.9.9.	4th Seaforth Hrs.	7th Black Watch.

7.   Completion of relief will be reported to Brigade H.Q. - Code word, name of O.C. Unit.

** 2 **

8.   Lists of Trench Stores handed over will reach Brigade H.Q. by 6 p.m. 23rd December.

9.   Command of the line will pass at 9 a.m., 23rd December. Until this hour all troops of 152nd and 153rd Inf. Brigades in the line will come under orders of B.G.C. 154th Inf. Brigade.

10.   Headquarters, 154th Inf. Brigade, will close at I.12.b.3.3. at 9 a.m. on 23rd December and will open at LINDOP CAMP, FREMICOURT, on arrival.

11.   ACKNOWLEDGE.

                                                   Captain,
                                                  Brigade Major,

21st December, 1917.   154th Infantry Brigade.

ISSUED AT..7 p...BY ORDERLY.

Copy No. 1 9th Royal Scots.
        2 4th Seaforth Highrs.
        3 4th Gordon Highrs.
        4 7th A. & S. Highrs.
        5 154th M. G. Company.
        6 154th T. M. Battery.
        7 51st (H) Division "G".
        8 51st (H)   "   "A".
        9 152nd Inf. Brigade.
      10 153rd   "   "
      11 5th   "   "
      12 74th   "   "
      13 2/1st (H) Field Ambulance.
      14 No. 2 Coy. A.S.C.
      15 401st Field Coy. R.E.
      16 404th   "   "   "
      17 Right Group Arty.
      18 Left   "   "
      19 252nd Tunnelling Coy. (Adv.H.Q.)
      20 B.G.C.
      21 Brigade Transport Officer.
      22 Brigade Signal Officer.
      23 Staff Captain.
      24 War Diary.
      25 File.

SECRET AND URGENT.
================

O.C. 9th Royal Scots.
     4th Seaforth Highrs.
     4th Gordon Highrs.
     7th A. & S. Highrs.
H.Q. 152nd Inf. Brigade.
     153rd Inf. Brigade.

Reference 154th Inf. Brigade O.O. No. 156 of 21st December following amendments are made to time and rendezvous for guides.

Incoming Battalion.	Guides detailed by.	To be at	Number of guides.
8th Gordon Highlanders.	7th A. & S. Highlanders.	Battalion H.Q. J.17.a.8.7. At 5 p.m.	1 guide per platoon. 1 guide per Coy. H.Q.
6th Seaforth Highrs.	9th Royal Scots.	Cross Roads J.8.c.2.1. At 4.15 p.m.	1 guide per platoon. 1 guide per Coy. H.Q. 2 for Battn. H.Q.
7th Black Watch) 5th Gordon Highrs.)	4th Seaforth Highrs.	Point where light railway crosses road at I.12.b.8.1. At 4 p.m.	1 guide per platoon. 1 guide per Coy. H.Q.
7th Black Watch) 5th Gordon Highrs.)	4th Gordon Highrs.	BEETROOT FACTORY I.17.d.5.8. At 4.30 p.m.	1 guide per platoon. 1 guide per Coy. H.Q. 1 guide for Battn. H.Q.

E. Shum
Captain,
Brigade Major,
154th Infantry Brigade.

22nd December, 1917.

28031 W3125/M2250 1000m 6/17 M.R.Co.,Ltd. (1367) Forms W3091.   Army Form W. 3091.

Cover for Documents.

Nature of Enclosures.

7th Argyll & Sutherland Highlanders.

War Diary.

January 1918.

Notes, or Letters written.

WAR DIARY or INTELLIGENCE SUMMARY

7th Arg. Highld. Regt N°2 — Army Form C.-2118.
Ref. 1/40 - 5/c. 1/40000
DEMICOURT / 4 0005

Place	Date JAN	Hour	Summary of Events and Information	Remarks and references to Appendices
J.17.a.5.9.	1		Enemy artillery very quiet. E.A. very active. Casualties 1 O.R. wounded.	JMcB
	2		Enemy artillery fairly quiet and also B.A. Casualties 1 O.R. killed.	JMcB
	3		Enemy artillery fairly active and E.A. fairly active. There was an inter-Company relief starting at 4 p.m. "C" Coy relieved "B" Coy in Right Front line and "A" Coy relieved "B" Coy in Left front line. "B" Coy went back to support and "D" Coy to reserve. The time was very quiet & the relief was complete by 6.30 p.m. Casualties Nil.	JMcB
	4		Enemy artillery was very quiet and E.A. fairly quiet. Casualties Nil.	JMcB
	5		Practically no enemy artillery activity and no general activity. Casualties Nil. 50 - O.Rs reported sick on parade of which 6 were sent to Hosp.	JMcB
	6		Enemy artillery & E.A. very quiet. Casualties Nil.	JMcB
	7		150 Seaforth Highlanders Battn Hd.Q., "B" & "D" Coys returned to 5th Seaforth Highlanders. Battn Hd.Q., "A" & "C" Coy to proceed to Vinçoop Camp, Fremicourt and "E" Coy to Camp at ARTILLERY LINES. Battn arrived back in billets by 9 p.m. Casualties Nil.	App I. JMcB
FREMICOURT	8		In camp. Day was devoted to cleaning up etc.	JMcB
	9		-Do- Battn supplied a working party of 6 Off., 12 Sergts & 320 O.Rs. Remainder of Battn employed on work on huts & trenches.	JMcB
	10		In camp. Battn supplied a working party of 4 Off., 14 Sergts & 350 O.Rs. Remainder employed on work on huts & trenches. Battn on route march at 12 km. - at 9.15 km. Battn	JMcB

C. 2118. 7th Army South Highlanders
Army Form C. 2118. Ref. Maps – 51c.
LENS 11

WAR DIARY
or
INTELLIGENCE SUMMARY
(Erase heading not required.)

Instructions regarding War Diaries and Intelligence Summaries are contained in F. S. Regs., Part II. and the Staff Manual respectively. Title pages will be prepared in manuscript.

Place	Date	Hour	Summary of Events and Information	Remarks and references to Appendices
BRUAY-EN-ARTOIS	22		In Billets – Continued Training. Capt A.S. HUNTER taken on strength.	9th
	23		Do.	9th
	24		Do.	9th
	25		Do.	9th
	26		Do.	9th
	27		Field Church Parade	9th
	28		In Billets Continued Training	9th
	29		Do.	9th
	30		Do.	9th
	31		Do.	9th

Spencer Tute Lt. Col.
Commanding
7th Arg. South Hrs.

A5834 Wt. W4973/M687 750,000 8/16 D.D.&L Ltd. Forms/C.2118/13.

War Diary 'G' App. I

SECRET.

Copy No. 4.

154th INFANTRY BRIGADE
OPERATION ORDER No. 1.

Reference Maps :-
    DEMICOURT 1/10,000.
    57.C.   1/40,000.

6th January, 1918.

1.   The 154th Infantry Brigade will be relieved in the line by the 152nd Inf Bde
on night 7th/8th January in accordance with attached table.

2.   The following will be handed over on relief :-

        (a) All trench maps, air photos, defence scheme.
        (b) All details of work in hand and proposed.

3.   Mining platoons will be relieved at work at 12 noon on 8th
January as under :-
                                                                Dugout at.
(a) Platoon of 9th R. Scots by platoon of 8th A.& S.H.   K.8.a.45.20.
(b)   "   "   "   "   "   "   "   "   "   K.8.a.15.25.
(c)   "   " 4th Seaforths "   "   " 6th Gordons. J.12.a.3.9.
(d)   "   "   "   "   "   "   "   "   "   J.6.c.6.4.
(e)   "   "   "   "   "   "   "   "   "   J.5.a.8.3.
(f)   "   " 7th A.& S.H. "   "   " 5th Seaforths. J.6.d.2.4.
(g)   "   " 4th Gordons "   "   " 6th   "   J.5.d.7.8.

        Mining platoons on relief will rejoin their Units.
        Battalion Commanders will ensure that no spoil is left to be
cleared away.

4.   On completion of relief, 154th Infantry Brigade will take
over accommodation vacated by 152nd Infantry Brigade, and will come
into Divisional Reserve. 4th Seaforth Highlanders will remain in
present camp.

5.   Completion of relief will be reported to Brigade Headquarters.
Code word - name of O.C. Unit.

6.   Units of 152nd Infantry Brigade in the line will come under
orders of B.G.C. 154th Infantry Brigade until 9 a.m. 8th January, at
which hour command will pass to B.G.C. 152nd Infantry Brigade.

7.   Headquarters 154th Infantry Brigade will close at J.20.c.6.8.
at 9 a.m. 8th January and open at LINDOP CAMP on arrival.

8.   Lists of trench stores handed over will be forwarded to
Brigade Headquarters by 6 p.m. 8th January.

9.   Battalions will take over the same Lewis gun anti-aircraft
positions at FREMICOURT as they held before. Until further orders
special Lewis gun sentries will not be mounted at Camps for A.A.
defence.

10.   ACKNOWLEDGE.

                                            E.T. Hunt
                                            Captain,
                                            Brigade Major,
                                            154th Infantry Brigade.

Issued by orderly at 7.30 a.m.

Copies to -
```
 1 to 9th Royal Scots.
 2  "  4th Seaforth Highrs.
 3  "  4th Gordon Highrs.
 4  "  7th A. & S. Highrs.
 5  "  154th M. G. Company.
 6  "  154th T. M. Battery.
 7  "  51st (H) Division "G".
 8  "  51st (H)    "     "A".
 9  "  51st Infantry Brigade.
10  "  152nd       "       "
11  "  153rd       "       "
12  "  Right Group Arty.
13  "  401st Field Coy. R.E.
14  "  404th    "     "   "
15  "  252nd Tunnelling Coy. R.E.
16  "  1/3rd (H) Field Amb.
17  "  No. 2 Coy. A.S.C.
18  "  Staff Captain.
19  "  Bde. Signalling Officer.
20  "  Bde. Transport Officer.
21  "  War Diary.
22  "  File.
```

Relief Table to accompany 154th Infantry Brigade O.O. No.1.
****

Serial No.	Unit.	Relieved by.	Guides.	Time and Place.	On relief proceeds to.	Remarks.
A.	H.Q. & 2 Coys. 9th Royal Scots holding Right Sub-Sector.	H.Q. & 2 Coys. 8th A. & S. Highrs.	1 per Coy.H.Q. 1 " platoon.	Entrance to TROUT ALLEY K.7.c.3.6. 3 p.m.	MIDDLESEX CAMP, FREMICOURT.	
B.	2 Coys. 9th Royal Scots at LEBUCQUIERE.	2 Coys. 8th A. & S. Highrs.	None.	---	-do-	To be clear of Lebucquiere by 2.30 pm
C.	7th A. & S. Highrs.	5th Seaforth Hrs.	1 per Coy.H.Q. 1 " platoon.	Battn. H.Q. J.17.a.5.7. 3 p.m.	LINDOP CAMP.	H.Q. & 2 Coys. will be accommodated at FREMICOURT. 2 Coys in ARTILLERY LINES I.27.a.
D.	4th Gordon Highrs.	6th Seaforth Hrs.	1 per Coy.H.Q. 2 " platoon.	J.3.c.95.70. 2.45 p.m.	LINDOP CAMP.	
E.	154th M.G. Company.	152nd M.G. Company.)	To be arranged between C.O's concerned. Relief not to commence before 4.30 p.m.	))))	Transport Lines, I.28.Central.	154th M.G.Coy. will arrange to leave one man per gun at each position for 24 hours after relief.
F.	154th T.M. Battery.	152nd T.M. Battery.)				

SECRET. Copy No...4..

154th INFANTRY BRIGADE
OPERATION ORDER NO. 2.

Reference Maps :-
  Sheet 57.C. 1/40,000.
  Trench Map 1/20,000, MOEUVRES.

1. The 154th Inf. Brigade will relieve the 152nd Inf. Brigade in the Right Sector of the Divisional Front on night of 15th/16th January, 1918, in accordance with relief table "A" attached.

2. Battalions will proceed to the line by half platoons at 200 yards distance.
    The times in the relief table have been arranged on the assumption that the weather will be dull. If the weather is bright and visibility good, the relief will be postponed by two hours, and this information will be communicated to all concerned.

3. The following will be taken over on relief :-

   (a) All trench maps, air photos and defence schemes.
   (b) Statement of work in hand and proposed new work.

4. Work on dugouts will be taken over at 12 noon on 16th January as shown in table "B". First shifts will report at those dugouts at 10 a.m. in order to ensure continuity of work.

5. Positions of Lewis Guns in A.A. positions will be handed over to Officers of Battalions of 152nd Inf. Brigade in charge of advanced parties, together with orders for anti-aircraft defence.

6. Completion of relief will be reported to Brigade H.Q. Code word - Name of O.C. Unit.

7. Units of 154th Inf. Brigade will come under orders of B.G.C. 152nd Inf. Brigade until 9 a.m. on 16th January, when B.G.C. 154th Inf. Brigade will assume command of the Sector.

8. Headquarters, 154th Inf. Brigade will close at LINDOP CAMP, FREMICOURT, at 8 a.m. and open at BEAUMETZ (J.20.c.3.8.) at 9 a.m. on 16th January.

9. Lists of Trench Stores will be forwarded to Brigade H.Q. by 6 p.m. 16th January.

10. Maps showing exact dispositions of Units in the line will reach Brigade Headquarters by 10 a.m. 17th January.

11. The Defence Scheme for Brigade in Divisional Reserve will be handed over to Units of 152nd Inf. Brigade.

12. ACKNOWLEDGE.

                                      C.L.Hunt.
                                      Captain,
                                      Brigade Major,
13th January, 1918.   154th Infantry Brigade.

Issued by orderly at 7 p.m.

Copy No. 1. 9th Royal Scots.
       2. 4th Seaforth Highrs.
       3. 4th Gordon Highrs.
       4. 7th A. & S. Highrs.
       5. 154th M. G. Company.
       6. 154th T. M. Battery.
       7. 51st (H) Division "G".
       8. 51st (H)   "   "A".
       9. 51st Infantry Brigade.
      10. 152nd Infantry Brigade.
      11. 153rd Infantry Brigade.
      12. Right Group Arty.
      13. 401st Field Coy. R.E.
      14. 404th   "   "   "
      15. 252nd Tunnelling Coy.
      16. 1/3rd (H) Field Ambulance.
      17. No. 2 Coy. A.S.C.
      18. Staff Captain.
      19. Bde. Signalling Officer.
      20. Bde. Transport Officer.
      21. War Diary.
      22. File.

TABLE "A" to accompany 154th Inf. Brigade O. O. No. 2.

Unit.	Relieves.	Leaves Billets at.	Guides.	Rendezvous and Time.	Remarks.
4th Seaforth Hrs.	8th A. & S. Highrs.	1.45 p.m.	1 per Batt.H.Q. 1 " Coy. H.Q. 1 " Platoon.	South end of TROUT ALLEY, K.7.c.3.6. 3 p.m.	(a) 6 platoons 4th Sea. Hrs. relieve 6 platoons 8th A.& S.Hrs. in LEBUCQUIERE. 8th A.& S.H. will be clear of billets by 2.30 p.m. (b) No guides will be provided for 2 platoons proceeding to dugouts at J.18.b.3.0.
4th Gordon Highrs.	6th Seaforth Highrs.	12.45 p.m.	1 per platoon.	J.3.c.95.70. 3 p.m.	
7th A. & S. Highrs.	5th Seaforth Highrs.	1.15 p.m.	1 per platoon.	J.17.a.5.7. 3 p.m.	
154th M. G. Coy.	152nd M. G. Coy.	To be arranged by C.O's direct. Relief to take place after dark.			154th M.G.Coy. will relieve 232nd M.G.Coy. in 4 M.G. positions in WALSH SUPPORT and INNISKILLING TRENCH. M.G. positions R.1. to R.4. inclusive will be taken over by 232nd M.G. Coy.
154th T. M. Bty.	152nd T. M. Bty.				

9th Royal Scots will be in BRIGADE RESERVE and will take over accommodation at LEBUCQUIERE from 4th Seaforth Highrs.
9th Royal Scots will leave present billets at 1.50 p.m., 15th January.
Advance parties will report to 4th Seaforth Highrs. by 11 a.m. on 15th January.

TABLE "B" to accompany 154th Inf. Brigade O. O. No. 2.
===*===*===*===*===*===*===*===*===*===*===

No.	Location of Dugout.	Platoon at work.	Relieving Platoon.	Under supervision of.
1.	K.8.a.45.20.	8th A. & S. Highrs.	4th Seaforth Highrs.	8th Royal Scots.
2.	K.8.a.15.25.	-do-	-do-	-do-
3.	J.6.d.2.4.	5th Seaforth Highrs.	7th A. & S. Highrs.	252nd Tunnelling Coy.
4.	J.5.d.7.8.	6th Seaforth Highrs.	4th Gordon Highrs.	-do-
5.	J.12.a.3.9.	6th Gordon Highrs.	9th Royal Scots.	401st Field Coy. R.E.
6.	J.6.c.6.4.	-do-	-do-	-do-
7.	J.5.a.8.3.	-do-	-do-	252nd . Tunl. Co.
8.	J.17.a.5.7.	5th Seaforth Highrs.	-do-	252nd Tunnelling Coy.

1. Mining platoons will be maintained at strength of 1 officer and 36 O.R.

2. No. 5 is accommodated at Post 20 Intermediate Line J.10.a.4.2.
   No. 6 is accommodated at LOUVERVAL.
   No. 7 is accommodated at J.16.c.6.7.

War Diary 'G'

S E C R E T.　　　　　　　　　　　　　　　　　Copy No. 4

**154th INFANTRY BRIGADE
OPERATION ORDER No. 3.**

App III

Reference Maps:-
　　Trench Map MOEUVRES 1/20,000.
　　Sheet 57.C. 1/40,000.

1.　　　The 6th Division (less Artillery) will relieve 51st Division (less Artillery) between 17th and 21st January, 1918. On completion of this relief, 51st Division will be in Corps Reserve.

2.　　　The 71st Inf. Brigade will relieve 154th Inf. Brigade in the Right Sector of Divisional front on night 18th/19th January in accordance with relief table attached.

3.　　　71st M. G. Company will relieve 154th M. G. Company on night 17th/18th January 1918. No. 1's will remain in line for 24 hours after relief, and will report to O.C. 154th T. M. Battery by 8 p.m. on 18th January. They will march to COURCELLES with 154th T. M. Battery on 19th January.

4.　　　The times in the relief table have been arranged on the assumption that the weather will be dull. If the weather is bright and visibility good, the relief will be postponed by an hour and a half and this information will be communicated to all concerned by 12 noon by means of code word "CLEAR".

5.　　　The following will be handed over on relief :-

　(a)　All trench maps, air photos and defence schemes.
　(b)　All trench stores. Lists of trench stores handed over will reach Brigade Headquarters by 6 p.m. 19th January.
　(c)　All details of work in hand and work proposed.

6.　　　Completion of relief will be reported to Brigade Headquarters - Code word "SNIPE".

7.　　　On completion of relief, 154th Inf. Brigade will take over accommodation in FREMICOURT Area vacated by 71st Inf. Brigade for night 18th/19th January.

8.　　　1 Officer per Company and 1 N.C.O. per platoon of the three Battalions of 71st Inf. Brigade proceeding to the front line will proceed to trenches on morning of 18th inst. Each Battalion in front line will detail 2 guides to report at Brigade Headquarters by 11 a.m. on 18th inst. to guide these parties to trenches.

9.　　　Instructions about Mining Platoons will be issued later.

10.　　　Battalions will take over Defence Scheme for Brigade in Reserve from Battalions of 71st Inf. Brigade, and orders for L.G. anti-aircraft defence of FREMICOURT.

11.　　　Headquarters 154th Inf. Brigade will close at BEAUMETZ J.20.c.8.8. on completion of relief and will open at LINDOP CAMP, FREMICOURT, on arrival.

** 2 **

12. (a) 154th Inf. Brigade will move to the COURCELLES-LE-COMTE Area on afternoon of 19th January. Orders for this move will be issued.

(b) First Line Transport (less cookers and water-carts) will be West of ALBERT - BAPAUME Road by 10.30 a.m. on 19th.

13. 154th M. G. Company will move by march route to COURCELLES-LE-COMTE on 18th January under orders of O.C. Company and will take over accommodation vacated by 18th M. G. Company. An Officer will be sent on ahead to take over billets.
154th M. G. Company will be West of the ALBERT - BAPAUME Road by 10.30 a.m. on 18th

ACKNOWLEDGE.

E D C Hunt.

Captain,
Brigade Major,
154th Infantry Brigade.

13th January, 1918.

Issued at 7 p.m. by Orderly.

Copy No. 1 9th Royal Scots.
2 4th Seaforth Highrs.
3 4th Gordon Highrs.
4 7th A. & S. Highrs.
5 154th M. G. Company.
6 154th T. M. Battery.
7 51st (H) Division "G".
8 51st (H)   "   "A".
9 51st Infantry Brigade.
10 71st   "   "
11 153rd   "   "
12 Right Group Artillery.
13 401st Field Coy. R.E.
14 252nd Tunnelling Coy.
15 1/3rd (H) Field Ambulance.
16 No. 2 Coy. A.S.C.
17 Staff Captain.
18 Brigade Signalling Officer.
19 Brigade Transport Officer.
20 War Diary.
21 File.

RELIEF TABLE to accompany 154th Inf. Brigade O. O. No. 3.

Serial No.	Date.	Unit and Sector.	Relieved by.	Guides.	Time & Place.	On relief proceeds to.	Remarks.
A.	Jan. 18th	4th Seaforth Highrs. Right Subsector.	9th Suffolk Regt.	1 per Batt.H.Q. 1 " Coy. H.Q. 1 " Platoon.	3 p.m. Centre Bn. H.Q. J.17.a.5.7.	MIDDLESEX CAMP, FREMICOURT.	9th Suffolk Regt. will not leave 5 platoons at LEBUCQUIERE. 5 Platoons, 4th Seaforth Highrs. will proceed to MIDDLESEX CAMP, leaving LEBUCQUIERE at 3 p.m.
B.	18th	7th A. & S. Highrs. Centre Subsector.	1st Sherwood Foresters.	1 per Coy. H.Q. 1 per platoon.	3.30 p.m. Centre Bn.H.Q. J.17.a.5.7.	LINDOP CAMP.	
C.	18th	4th Gordon Highrs. Left Subsector.	1st Leicester Regt.	As in "A".	3 p.m. J.3.c.95.70.	LINDOP CAMP.	
D.	17th	154th M. G. Company.	71st M. G. Company.	To be arranged between C.O's concerned.		Transport Lines, I.28.Central.	154th M.G.Co. will arrange to leave one man per gun at each position for 24 hours after relief.
E.	18th	154th T. M. Battery.	71st T. M. Battery.	-- do --	-- do --		

9th Norfolk Regt. will be in Reserve to 71st Inf. Brigade and will take over accommodation at LEBUCQUIERE vacated by 6th Gordon Highrs. on 17th January.
9th Royal Scots will remain in present billets for night 18th/19th January and will hand over accommodation to a Battalion 13th Inf. Brigade on morning of 19th January.

Army Form W.3091.

Cover for Documents.

Nature of Enclosures.

War Diary
February 1918
7th Argyll & Sutherland Highlanders.

Notes, or Letters written.

7th Arg & Suth Highrs.
Ref. Maps:- 5·Y·C LENS 11

Army Form C. 2118.

WAR DIARY
or
INTELLIGENCE SUMMARY
(Erase heading not required)

Place	Date February 1918	Hour	Summary of Events and Information	Remarks and references to Appendices
BAILLEULMONT	1		In Billets. Training	
	2		Battalion proceeded by march route to Camp in LOGEAST WOOD A.25.b.	9116
LOGEAST CAMP	3		In Camp - Held Church Parade	9116
	4		Do - Training	9116
	5		Do - Do	9116
	6		Do - Do	9116
	7		Do - Do	9116
	8		Do - Do	9116
	9		Do - Do	9116
	10		Do - Held Church Parade	9116
	11		Do - Training	9116
	12		Do - Do	9116
	13		Do - Do	9116
LEBUCQUIERE	14		Battalion proceeded by march route to CINEMA CAMP LEBUCQUIERE. In Camp. Battalion supplied working parties amounting in all to 8 Officers & 340 O.Rs.	9116
	15		In Camp - Battalion supplied working parties of 8 Offrs & 340 ORs.	9116
	16		Do - Performance of B atta Pierrot troupe - the "Toories". Played 3 round Divisional Football Tie V D.A.C. Result 5 gmls. to 0 in our favour.	9116
	17		In Camp - Held Church parade. Bombs dropped near Camp.	9116

7th Seaforth Highlanders
Army Form C. 2118.
Ref No:- 5/C
26 NS 11.

WAR DIARY
or
INTELLIGENCE SUMMARY.
(Erase heading not required.)

Place	Date 7.21	Hour	Summary of Events and Information	Remarks and references to Appendices
LEBOCQUIERE	18		In Camp. Battalion supplied working parties of 8 offrs. & 340 OR.	
	19		Do. Training.	
J.14.a.6.9.	20		Battalion relieved 6th Seaforth Highlanders in centre sector of Bayonet Front. "A" Coy on right holding front line from K.9.a.9.1. to J.6.d.95.25. and "B" Coy on left holding front line from J.5.d.9.0.25. to J.6.a.9.1. "D" Coy in support with platoons at J.6.d. & J.6.d. & two platoons at J.5.1.8.9. and "C" Coy in intermediate line running from about J.10.c. to J.14.a. Bn HQ at J.14.a.6.9. Relief was very quiet and relief was complete by 9 p.m.	Opp. 1
	21		Day was very quiet. Two patrols were sent out from 2 am to 4 am. To enemies met. Enemy artillery fairly active. T.A. quiet.	
	22		Nothing of importance.	
	23		Do. Do.	
	24		Enemy artillery fairly active especially on sunken road about J.1.b & J.8.9. Order to relieve "D" Coy relieved "A" in right front line. "C" Coy relieved "B" in left front line. "B" Coy going to this "C" Coy relieved "A" and "D" Coy to this. B.N. in reserve. Relief complete by 5 p.m. Support and 17 Coy in N.Q. trenches. One platoon of "B" Coy in STURGEON SUPPORT about J.6.d.2.4.	
	25		Enemy artillery very 2 mile to day out in STURGEON SUPPORT about J.6.d.2.4.	
	26		Enemy artillery very quiet. T.A. very active. 11 planes crossed over lines patrolling of behind own lines about 10 am.	

WAR DIARY
or
INTELLIGENCE SUMMARY

7th Army Auth. Higher. Army Form C. 2118.
Ref. Maps :- 5.Y.C.
Trench Map 1/10,000

(Erase heading not required.)

Instructions regarding War Diaries and Intelligence Summaries are contained in F. S. Regs., Part II. and the Staff Manual respectively. Title pages will be prepared in manuscript.

Place	Date	Hour	Summary of Events and Information	Remarks and references to Appendices
J.17.a.6.7	27		Our Artillery fairly active. BOURLON WOOD shelled between 6 pm & 7 pm. Hostile Artillery quiet, enemy shelled DONGNIES - BEAUHEFFZ Road and edge vicinity during the afternoon. Enemy aircraft very little activity	
	28		Hostile artillery shelled junction of CAMBRAI Road & front line. Our aircraft very active. Casualties during the month :- Nil	

JaDavid Lt Col.
Commanding
7th Army Auth Arto.

S E C R E T.

War Diary App I
G

Copy No. 3

154th INFANTRY BRIGADE
OPERATION ORDER No. 8.

Reference Maps :-
    MOEUVRES 1/20,000.
    SHEET 57.C. 1/40,000.

19th February 1918.

1.   The 154th Infantry Brigade will relieve 152nd Infantry Brigade in the Right Sector of the Divisional Front on night 20th/21st February, 1918, in accordance with Relief Table "A" attached.

2.   The following will be taken over on relief :-

    (a) All trench maps, air photos and defence schemes.
    (b) Statement of work in hand and proposed new work.
    (c) All trench stores: lists of trench stores will be forwarded to Brigade Headquarters by 6 p.m. 21st February.

3.   Work on dugouts will be taken over at 12 noon on 21st February, as shewn in Table "B". First shifts will report at these dugouts at 10 a.m. in order to ensure continuity of work.

4.   Positions of Lewis and Vickers Guns in A.A. positions will be handed over to Officers of Battalions of 152nd Infantry Brigade in charge of advanced parties.

5.   Completion of relief will be reported to Brigade Headquarters. Code word - name of O.C. Unit.

6.   Units of 154th Infantry Brigade will come under orders of B.G.C., 152nd Infantry Brigade, until 9 a.m. on 21st February, when B.G.C., 154th Infantry Brigade, will assume command of the Sector.

7.   Headquarters, 154th Infantry Brigade will close at LINDOP CAMP, FREMICOURT, at 8 a.m. and open at BEAUMETZ (J.20.c.6.8.) at 9 a.m. on 21st February.

8.   Maps showing dispositions of Units in the line will reach Brigade Headquarters by 6 p.m. on 21st February.

9.   The Defence Scheme (Provisional) for Brigade in Divisional Reserve will be handed over to advanced parties of Units of 152nd Infantry Brigade.

10.   6th Seaforth Highlanders, (152nd Infantry Brigade), will be in tactical reserve to 154th Infantry Brigade.

11.   ACKNOWLEDGE.

Captain,
Brigade Major,
154th Infantry Brigade.

Issued by Orderly at 2p

Copy No. 1 to 4th Seaforth Highrs.
" 2 "   4th Gordon Highrs.
" 3 "   7th A. & S. Highrs.
" 4 "   154th M. G. Company.
" 5 "   154th T. M. Battery.
" 6 "   51st (H) Division "G".
" 7 "   51st (H)   "   "A".
" 8 "   51st Infantry Brigade.
" 9 "   152nd   "   "
" 10 "   153rd   "   "
" 11 "   Right Group Arty.
" 12 "   404th Field Coy., R.E.
" 13 "   252nd Tunnelling Coy. (Adv. H.Q.)
" 14 "   2/1st (H) Field Ambulance.
" 15 "   No. 2 Coy. A.S.C.
" 16 "   Staff Captain.
" 17 "   Brigade Signalling Officer.
" 18 "   Brigade Transport Officer.
" 19 "   War Diary.
" 20 "   File.

Table "A" to accompany 154th Infantry Brigade Operation Order No. 8.
=*

Unit.	Relieves.	Guides.	Rendezvous and Time.	Remarks.
4th Seaforth Highlanders.	6th Gordon Highrs. Right Sub-Sector.	1 per Battn. H.Q. 1 " Coy. H.Q. 1 " Platoon.	Entrance to ROACH AVENUE, J.17.b.9.9. 6 p.m.	
7th A. & S. Highlanders.	5th Seaforth Highrs. Centre Sub-Sector.	1 per Platoon.	Centre Battn. H.Q. J.17.a.5.7. 6.45 p.m.	
4th Gordon Highlanders.	6th Seaforth Highrs. Left Sub-Sector.	1 per Platoon.	J.3.b.7.0. 6 p.m.	
154th M. G. Company. 154th T. M. Battery.	152nd M. G. Company. 152nd T. M. Battery.	) To be arranged by C.O's direct.) Relief not to commence before 6 p.m.		1 Section 152nd M.G. Coy. will be relieved in daylight in sufficient time for Section to reach LINDOP CAMP, FREMICOURT, by 5 p.m. on 20th Feb. This Section will be prepared to have guns in action for A.A. work on night 20th/21st February.

Table "B" to accompany 154th Infantry Brigade Operation Order No. 8.

Serial.	Location of Dugout.	Unit at present finding Platoon.	Relieving Platoon.	Unit in charge of work.	Platoon accommodated at.	Relieving Platoon to report.	
						Time.	Place.
1 a.	J.26.b.2.6.	4th Seaforth Hrs.	6th Seaforth Hrs.	252nd Tun. Coy.	Sunken Road, J.20.c.6.8.	10 a.m. 21st Feb.	J.20.c.6.8.
1 b.	J.26.b.2.6.	4th Seaforth Hrs.	6th Seaforth Hrs.	252nd Tun. Coy.	CINEMA CAMP, I.30.a.7.6.	do.	CINEMA CAMP.
2.	J.23.b.6.8.	7th A.& S. Hrs.	6th Seaforth Hrs.	252nd Tun. Coy.	Dugout J.17.a.2.6.	do.	J.17.a.2.6.
3.	J.12.b.4.9.	5th Seaforth Hrs.	7th A.& S. Hrs.	404th Field Coy.	Dugout J.6.d.1.0.	do.	J.6.d.1.0.
4.	K.7.d.5.9.	6th Gordon Hrs.	4th Seaforth Hrs.	8th Royal Scots.	K.7.c.5.5.	do.	K.7.c.5.5.
5.	Half work R.E. H.Q. J.17.a.5.6. Half work Bank K.13.b.5.8.	5th Gordon Hrs.	4th Seaforth Hrs.	404th Field Coy.	K.12.c.7.0.	do.	K.12.c.7.0.

NOTES :
1. Serial numbers 3 - 5 consist of 1 Officer and 37 O.Rs. (including batman).
2. Serials will work in three shifts, 4 a.m.-noon, noon-8 p.m., 8 p.m.-4 a.m.
3. Units are responsible for guiding first shifts of incoming Units.
4. Day spoiling party of 50 O.R. on dugouts at J.25.b.2.6. (at present found by 4th Gordon Highrs.) will be taken over by 6th Seaforth Highrs. at 12 noon on 21st February.

51st Division.
154th Infantry Brigade

1/7th BATTALION

ARGYLE & SUTHERLAND HIGHLANDERS

MARCH 1918

Appendices attached:-

Report on Operations 21st-26th March
Operation Orders.
Map.

WAR DIARY or INTELLIGENCE SUMMARY

Army Form C. 2118.

7th Bn Gordon Highlanders
Ref Maps 5/C
Trench 1/6 sqs 1/10000

Place	Date	Hour	Summary of Events and Information	Remarks and references to Appendices
J.17.a.57	1		Enemy artillery quiet. Hostile aircraft fairly active. Relief 4 near Warm. Disposition of Divisional front began about 3-30 p.m. (See appendices I) Relief completed by 1 a.m. Battn in Brigade Reserve at LEBUCQUIERE.	App I Warm
Ambrines Camp	2			Warm
	3		In Camp — Held Church Parade	Warm
	4		— do — Training	
J.16.c.4.1 (Sheet 5/C) N.E.	5		Battalion relieved 4th Gordon Highlanders in Support. Battn H.Q. J.16.c.4.1. Warm "A" Coy with Coy H.Q. & two platoons at J.18.a.9.9 (and tactical control of O.C. 4th Gordon Highrs) "B" Coy in INTERMEDIATE LINE J.17 and 18 "C" Coy in BEAUMETZ–MORCHIES LINE (SUNKEN ROAD J.21.d) "D" Coy LEBUCQUIERE in Battalion Reserve and orders to move to take on defences of 15-m line from J.21.d 8.7 Northwards in event of Enemy attack. Day light relief was carried out without casualties. Enemy was very quiet.	App II
	6		Work was carried on in accordance with Defence Scheme. Enemy still very Warm quiet. Casualties Nil.	Warm
	7		— Do —	Warm
	8		A raid was carried out on Enemy line at K.1.b.2.2 ? where lines crosses the CAMBRAI ROAD. Object of the raid — to obtain identification & to destroy Enemy Post. Lt W.F.MUIR-KAY m.c. was O.C. party which consisted of a Base at K1.6.1.3 of 1 Rifle + 2 Lewis gun sections and a Raiding Party of one Officer (2/Lt N Spence) & two rifle sections with a covering party of one officer (2/Lt T Gemmell) & one rifle section. Enemy was very quiet and party entered Enemy trench without opposition & found it unoccupied. Raiding party returned without casualty.	Warm

WAR DIARY
or
INTELLIGENCE SUMMARY

1/5 Arg: & Suth: Hrs

Army Form C. 2118.

Ref. maps 5"/C
Trench maps 1/10.000

Place	Date March	Hour	Summary of Events and Information	Remarks and references to Appendices
J.16.c.4.0.	9		Arrangements to relieve 4th "Gordon Highlanders" in FRONT LINE was cancelled and new dispositions were issued whereby we relieve the 4th G.H. left sector and continued to garrison support line with our "C" Coy. at J.17.c.9.2. and one Coy at J.16.c. Relief was carried out without casualties.	WAAN App III
J.18.a.9.9. (SUNKEN ROAD)	10		Enemy continued very quiet. A new Communication Trench was dug from J.18.a.9.9 to J.12.c.8.3. Batt HQ. J.18.a.9.9. Work on defences – wiring, construction of deep-dugouts, & maintenance work was continued with. Enemy very quiet.	WAAN
	11		Enemy aircraft very active in afternoon. Visibility was very good and care has to be taken to conceal work which was going on. Enemy shelled in the direction of HERMES from about 8.30 p.m. till early morning with gas shells. All garrison wore S.B.R. and Wire were no Casualties	WAAN WAAN
	12		Enemy quiet. Work on defences continued.	WAAN
	13		Enemy artillery fairly quiet. A little intermittent shelling took place during day. Our patrols were active during night, but nothing of importance was noted. Casualties Nil.	WAAN
	14		Visibility good. A great deal of aerial movement was noticed behind Enemy Lines. Enemy Artillery quiet. Casualties Nil.	WAAN
	15		Inter Coy relief was carried out. B Coy relieves A. Coy. C. Coy. relieved D Coy. Nothing of special importance occurred	WAAN
	16		Enemy artillery quiet. E. Aircraft fairly inactive. Work continued on defences. No Casualties.	WAAN
	17		– Do –	WAAN
	18		– Do – Enemy fairly active in vicinity of FLESQUIERES, causing us to be specially vigilant during night; but nothing of importance occurred. Casualties Nil.	WAAN

A5834 Wt. W4973/M687 750,000 8/16 D.D. & L. Ltd. Forms/C.2118/13.

Army Form C. 2118.

WAR DIARY
or
INTELLIGENCE SUMMARY.

7th Bn. Sthn. Highrs.
Ref. Maps 57g C.
Trench maps 1/10.000

(Erase heading not required.)

Instructions regarding War Diaries and Intelligence Summaries are contained in F. S. Regs., Part II. and the Staff Manual respectively. Title pages will be prepared in manuscript.

Place	Date March	Hour	Summary of Events and Information	Remarks and references to Appendices
	19		Enemy shelled in vicinity of DEMICOURT & Battn H.Q., but was else where very quiet. Casualties Nil. Reserve trench from CRUCIFIX J12.a.8.5 to ALDGATE was commenced	
	20		Work on defences continued - wiring & construction of deep dugouts. No Casualties. Arrangements for relief by 4th Seaforth Highrs were made.	
	21	4 a.m	Enemy opened an exceptionally heavy barrage on our trenches. This continued until 9 a.m. when Enemy entered our trenches North of CAMBRAI ROAD in great force and from there proceeded to work to right & left, & down the CAMBRAI ROAD. BOURSIES was entered at about 10.30 a.m. & DOIGNIES shortly afterwards. Enemy attacked our sector from STURBEON SUPPORT NORTH, bombing down the trench & using FLAMMENWERFER. Our mining platoon at J.6.C.9.2 held Enemy back for a considerable time, but in early afternoon it was forced to withdraw along STURBEON Sup.P. towards GRAYLING SUPPORT. The ½ FRONT LINE garrison was also forced to evacuate. Enemy then attacked FRONT & SUPPORT LINES EAST of ALDGATE & before evening he had driven up to TROUT ALLEY. We occupied the reserve trench from CRUCIFIX to ALDGATE, & prepared to fight to retain these. Casualties were 10 Off missing, 1 Off. wounded, ? 50 OR (approximate).	App IV
	22	1 a.m	we received orders to evacuate our positions & take up new positions as follows - Battn H.Q J.20.d 50.a. A Coy BEAUMETZ-MORCHIES LINE J.22.e., J.28.a. B Coy. J.20.d 50.a. D Coy. B.M. LINE J.21.a.8.7 (under 4th Seaforth Highrs) C Coy. J.20 a.S.D.O.	
		7.30 a.m.	C Coy was sent to position in SUNKEN ROAD J.29.a. 9 c. Enemy shelled these positions heavily throughout the day, but did not attack. A.D. & C. Coys.	
	23		Enemy attacked our positions after & heavily shelling these on against heavy odds, when owing to flanks having been turned they were forced to withdraw. The intention was to with draw to the high ground in J.32 - 33 - 34	

A.5834 Wt.W4973/M687 750,000 8/16 D.D. & L. Ltd. Forms/C.2118/13.

WAR DIARY
or
INTELLIGENCE SUMMARY.

Army Form C. 2118.

7th Argyll & Suth. Hghrs.

Ref. maps. 57C. N.W.
Trench 11. 1/10,000

Place	Date	Hour	Summary of Events and Information	Remarks and references to Appendices
	March 23	(Cont)	to which ground the 17th Divn (which had held the HERMES defences on our right) had already retired. It was found, however, that the 17th Divn had not stayed there, but had retired through the BERTINCOURT LINE. Consequently these three Coys withdrew to BERTINCOURT LINE and took up position there until they received instructions from an officer of the 63rd Divn to rejoin their own Divn. "C" Coy went to LE TRANSLOY, "A" & "D" Coys to GUEDECOURT for the night. "B" Coy fought on until their flanks were turned when they gradually withdrew from their position at Railway embankment J.20.c.9.2 (VELU WOOD) to Corps Line. From there they were ordered to YTRES and hence to LE TRANSLOY for the night. Battn HQ. personnel had been sent to thicken up "B" Coy, & Staff withdrew to WARWICKS HQ - QUARRY J.33.a. Afterwards in touch having been lost with Coys, Battn HQ. retired gradually via BERTINCOURT to ROCQUIGNY where they were directed to REINCOURT for the night.	
	24		The remnants of "A", "B", "C" & "D" Coys were ordered to GREVILLERS where they spent the day & the night. Battn H.Q. & about 60 O.R. held Reserve trenches in N.5. Central until they were ordered to form a defensive flank facing south from BEAULENCOURT to the WEST. The line of trenches was occupied, with 4th Gordons on right in N.14.c. and d. until	

WAR DIARY or INTELLIGENCE SUMMARY.

Army Form C. 2118.

1/4 Arg: 5 Suth Highrs

Ref: maps —— 57 C. N.W.
Lens 11. 1/10.000

Place	Date March	Hour	Summary of Events and Information	Remarks and references to Appendices
	24	(Cont)	until 6/5 Gordon High'rs came to relieve us & we moved to valley in N.17.a. Heavy shelling forced our withdrawal to about N.16.d. This position was maintained until the 6/5 Gordons retired from their position in front of us without fighting, & it could be seen that flanks were being forced back, although no fighting seemed to be taking place, when it was decided to withdraw to high ground N.W. of THILLOY. When withdrawal was taking place, orders were received to march to a position of assembly at N.11.B.6.4. Battalion was ordered to hold the line covering the village of WARLENCOURT with 152 Brigade on left, and 153 Brigade on their left. Remnants of A. B. C. D. Coys had been organised by Division in 6 two Coys under Capth Heys and held line of shell holes in front of main line. Battalion was organised in depth of three lines to hold this position. About 4 a.m. it was discovered that right Division had retired to ALBERT leaving our right flank in the air. As day advanced Enemy developed an attack on our front & round our right flank. Battalion made a defensive flank facing S.W. and fought on. Reinforcements were promised & expected by 1 p.m., but as afternoon advanced no sign of any reinforcements appeared	WWWII WWIII WWIII
	25			

WAR DIARY
INTELLIGENCE SUMMARY

Army Form C. 2118.

4th Army — 5th Corps — 19th Divn.
Bde. Maj. 57th N.W.
Lens 11. 1/100,000

Place	Date	Hour	Summary of Events and Information	Remarks and references to Appendices
	Mar 14 25	(Cont)	By this time Enemy had brought up field gun batteries which were firing at point blank range. The men of the Battalion were exhausted by continuous fighting for five days, lack of sleep & proper food, & with cold. As Enemy was evidently attempting to cut us off from the right, there being no troops there to stop their passage, it was decided to withdraw. The Battalion withdrew with whole Division to SERRE au BOIS.	WarW
	26		Battalion manned an outpost line covering SERRE au BOIS. at 11 a.m. when orders were received to withdraw to another outpost line covering SOUASTRE at 6 p.m. Battalion marched to PAS for the night having been relieved by an AUSTRALIAN Battn. Casualties for 6 days fighting { 2 Off. killed 8 Off. wounded 6 Off. missing 12 OR killed — 136 OR wounded 162 OR missing	WarW
	27		Battalion marched to POMMERA where the men who were exhausted remained until buses arrived to convey them to BARLY to which place remainder of Battalion marched. Here, about 20 stragglers	WarW

WAR DIARY 7th Arg. Luth. Hghrs.

or

INTELLIGENCE SUMMARY.

Army Form C. 2118.

Ref. maps: Lens 11 1/100,000
BETHUNE (continued sheet) 1/40,000

Place	Date	Hour	Summary of Events and Information	Remarks and references to Appendices
March	28		In billets at BARLY. Cleaning up & reorganisation.	Warm
	29		Battalion marched to FREVENT & entrained for LILLERS Area. Transport went by road via ST POL.	Warm
P.g.a. CANTRAINNE	30		Arrived in billets at CANTRAINNE at 1.30 a.m. After breakfast continued with cleaning up & reorganisation.	Warm
	31		Church parade in Y.M.C.A hut at ECLÈME.	Warm

J. A. Dunn Lt-Col
Comdg 7th Arg-Suth Hghrs

ACCOUNT OF THE PART PLAYED by the 7TH ARGYLL & SUTHERLAND HIGHLANDERS in the GERMAN OFFENSIVE, 21st MARCH, to 26th MARCH, 1918, inclusive.

Ref Maps :-
MOEUVRES 1/20,000.

It is very difficult to give an accurate account of the action of the Battalion because from the 21st onwards Companies, and in many cases platoons were split up fighting on their own, and also because, owing to the numerous cases of Company and Battalion H.Q. having had to withdraw rapidly, practically all the messages received and sent have been lost and most of the leaders are casualties.

21st MARCH.

Time	
4-50 a.m.	Heavy barrage of the whole Battalion sector of both H.E. and gas began.
6-30 a.m.	H.E. Barrage continued but the gas slackened off and enabled Companies to clear their dugouts and shelters. The gas precautions were very good indeed, and no casualties occurred.
9-30 a.m.	Barrage ceased.
10 a.m.	No enemy action took place in Battalion sector until this time when the enemy had driven the 6th G.H. on our left back from BOURSIES, and they were holding a flank defence along STURGEON AVENUE, and the enemy were attempting to bomb along our front and support lines with the aid of Flamenwerfer. It became obvious at this time that the enemy had broken through north of us, and that we should have to form a defensive flank facing north I, therefore, ordered up the two platoons of "D" Coy. from BRUNO MILL to ROACH AVENUE.
11-30 a.m.	Enemy had driven us out of the front line as far as ALDGATE where a block was made, and he was held there. The block at the junction of STURGEON AVENUE and STURGEON SUPPORT still held.
1 p.m.	The enemy had driven us out of the front line as far as TROUT AVENUE where a block had been established and out of the support line as far as ALDGATE where another block had been established. Enemy was seen advancing from BOURSIES towards CRUCIFIX in J.19.a. I, therefore, decided to reinforce the platoon at the CRUCIFIX by two platoons of "D" Coy. from ROACH AVENUE.
3 p.m.	The party of 6th G.H., who had been badly attacked by Flamenwerfer and were in a state of panic, rushed across GRAYLING SUPPORT and created a panic amongst the troops there who retired until they were rallied by the Coy. Commander in SUNKEN ROAD, K.7.c.
3-30 p.m.	Situation was as follows:- "B" Coy. on the right holding same positions as before. "C" Coy. on the left holding TROUT AVENUE with blocks in front line and GRAYLING SUPPORT, remainder in the SUNKEN Road, K.7.c. "D" Coy.- 3 Platoons CRUCIFIX and reserve line, J.19.a. and b. One platoon SUNKEN ROAD, K.7.c. "A" Coy - 3 Platoons in the INTERMEDIATE Line, one platoon ROACH AVENUE.
4-30 p.m.	I ordered the platoon of "D" Coy. in the SUNKEN ROAD to man the reserve line across the valley from ALDGATE and in touch with the rest of the Company at J.19.central. These dispositions were maintained up to the time of the withdrawal.
REMARKS.	Owing to the haze the anti-tank gun was of no value until about mid-day, and then after firing a few rounds broke. The machine guns at DEMICOURT Cemetery and my troops in ROACH Avenue beside DEMICOURT had to evacuate their positions, owing to one of our howitzers shelling DEMICOURT in the vicinity of the Cemetery steadily the whole afternoon.

22nd MARCH.

1.10 a.m. Received orders to withdraw to the B.M.Line. Companies withdrew without incident, and at

5 a.m. the dispositions were as follows:-
"A" Coy. in B.M.Line in J.28.a. on right of 4th Seaforths.
"D" Coy. in SUNKEN ROAD, J.21.d. in support of 4th Seaforths.
"C" and "B" Coys. and Battalion H.Q. in SUNKEN Road, J.26.b.

At dawn and onwards throughout the day the enemy kept up an intermittent and heavy barrage on the B.M.Line, but no infantry action developed as far as this Battalion was concerned.

9 a.m. "C" Coy. were ordered up to take up a position on the road in J.28.d. in order to thicken up JARGON Trench or the HERMIES defences if necessary.

8 p.m. Two platoons of "D" Coy. were sent forward into the B.M. Line to thicken up as the 4th Seaforths had suffered pretty heavily through the barrage.

Action of "A", "D" and "C" Coys. 23rd MARCH.

At dawn heavy barrage started on the B.M.Line and continued intermittently until

12 noon, when a heavy attack developed on the 4th Seaforths' front, and they were driven back to form a defensive flank facing north. "D" Coy and together with elements of the 19th Division, who had retired from east of BEAUMETZ, the left flank of this position was completely in the air.

The enemy attacked continuously from this time onwards, and at

1 p.m. had completely turned the left flank, and the line had to be withdrawn to the railway embankment. Two platoons of "D" Coy. that remained behind to cover withdrawal were all killed or taken prisoners. At this time "C" Coy., who were still holding the line of the SUNKEN Road in J.28.b., were informed by an officer of the 17th Division that the whole of his Division was going to be withdrawn from the HERMIES defences to form a defensive flank facing east on the ridges south of the Canal in P.4.and 5 etc. This left both the right and left flanks of the position in the air. However the remnants of my three Companies and of the 4th Seaforths fought on until

3-30 p.m. when they were almost completely surrounded and had to withdraw with heavy losses. The intention was to withdraw as far as high ground in J.32. - 33 and 34 and link up with the 17th Division, but on arrival it was found that the 17th Division had not stayed here, but had retired through the BERTINCOURT Line, consequently these three Coys. withdrew to the BERTINCOURT Lines, and took up a position astride BERTINCOURT-YTRES Road with the 63rd Division. They were afterwards directed to rejoin their Division by an Officer of the 63rd Division, and at

5-30 p.m. they withdrew, and "C" Coy. went to VILLERS - AU - FLOS and continued to LE TRANSLOY for the night. "A" and "D" Coys. went through to GUEUDECOURT for the night.

Action of Battalion H.Q. and "B" Coy.

The shelling had been continuous on the dugouts and very heavy on the SUNKEN Road in J.26.b., and by

7 a.m. "B" Coy. had lost fairly heavily. The enemy were reported to be massing north of BEAUMETZ, and to be moving up on the main road towards BEUGNY. "B" Coy. was ordered to man the sleeper track from J.20.c.8.9 west as far as possible, and the 19th Division was supposed to be on their right along the railway, and the 5th and 6th Seaforths who were withdrawing from BEAUMETZ were supposed to come in on their left flank in between VELU and LEBUCQUIERE. However, the Warwicks withdrew early in the day without giving "B" Coy. any warning, and the 5th and 6th Seaforths never manned this position at all, but withdrew right through beyond VELU to the Corps Line.

10-30 a.m. Enemy attack developed on the north and west, and the shelling and machine gun fire at Battalion H.Q. became so intense that it was decided to evacuate it, consequently Battalion H.Q. personnel were sent to thicken up "B" Coy.,

and Battalion H.Q. staff withdrew to the Warwicks' Headquarters in the Quarry in J.33.a.
"B" Coy. hung on and fought magnificently with both flanks completely turned until

11-45 a.m.   when they withdrew with heavy losses to the position held by some of the 154th M.G.Coy. along the FINKEN Road, J.28.central. As the enemy had already reached VELU Wood and was enfilading this position it was decided at

12-15 p.m.   to withdraw again to the line of the railway in J.33.a.and c., thus forming a defensive flank facing west in order to allow any other troops still remaining in the B.H.Line and to the east of it to withdraw without being cut off. This position was maintained until

3-30 p.m.   at which time C.C.Coy. posted a lewis gun on the high ground about P. central to keep the enemy from debouching from VELU Wood while the remnants of the Coy. withdrew to the Corps Line. From here they were ordered to YTRES and then to LE TRANSLOY for the night.
Battalion H.Q.had by this time lost all touch with the Coys., and after putting up a fight with stragglers from all different units in the Division on the outskirts of VELU Wood had withdrawn via BERTINCOURT to ROCQUIGNY where they were directed to REINCOURT for the night.

24th MARCH.

The remnants of "A","B","C" and "D" Coys. were ordered to GREVILLERS where they spent the day and the night.

10 a.m.   Battalion H.Q. and about 60 other ranks from all Coys which had been collected the night before were ordered to hold the trenches in N.8.central with 4th Gordons on the right and 4th Seaforths on the left. Unfortunately while this party was parading for the issue of ammunition a stray H.V.shell landed in the middle of the party severely wounding the Adjutant, a subaltern and about 40 other ranks. The positions above stated were occupied until

12 noon   when orders were received that the enemy had broken through south, and we were to form a defensive flank facing south from BEAULENCOURT to the west. The line of trenches were occupied with 4th Gordons on the right in N.17.c and d. These positions were maintained until

4 p.m.   when the 6th Gordons came forward to relieve us and we moved back to shell holes in the valley in N.17.a.

4-30 p.m.   These positions were heavily shelled thus necessitating withdrawal westwards to about N.16.d.

6 p.m.   Received orders to hold the ridge in N.15.c., N.16.b.as a support to the 6th Gordons, and to give them assistance if necessary. I disposed my Battalion which then numbered about 60 other ranks along the trenches on this ridge with 4th Gordons on my left, my right in the air.

6-30 p.m.   6th Gordons withdrew without firing a shot. I caught them as they were passing through me and made them man the line on my right. These positions were maintained till

8 p.m.   when the 152nd and 153rd had withdrawn from the front of us, and although no infantry action took place on our front the enemy's very lights could be seen far round both our flanks, and decided to withdraw the whole line to the high ground N.W. of THILLOY, and while this withdrawal was taking place I received orders to march to a position of assembly at M.11.b.c.d.

25th MARCH.

The Battalion was ordered to hold the line covering the village of WARLENCOURT with 152nd Brigade on our left and 153rd on their left covering LOUPART Wood. The remnants of "A","B","C" and "D" Coys. had been organised by Division into two Companies under Capt. Heys and were occupying the line of shell holes in front of the main line. The Battalion was organised in depth, one Coy. holding the line of shell holes in rear of above line, 2 Coys. holding another line in rear of this and H.Q. and one Coy. on the ridge in M.16.c.(These Coys. were only 30 strong) and were in position by

4 a.m.   when it was discovered that instead of the 2nd Division being on our right they had withdrawn to ALBERT leaving

	our right again in the air. No infantry action developed until
11 a.m.	when the enemy occupied LARBARQUE and began massing in the low ground in M.13.a.
	The enemy were easily held as far as our front was concerned, and if our right had been protected this position could have been maintained indefinitely, but although the enemy only made half hearted attacks on our front he could be seen streaming in masses along the high ground towards EAUCOURT L'ABBAYE, and moving northwards from there towards LESARS.
12 noon.	An attack had developed by this time and the enemy brought up a field gun battery to M.8.a. which was firing point blank on our line, and orders were received that another Division would come up and reinforce us at
1 p.m.	and we were to hold this line at all costs. These orders were conveyed to the troops, and they fought magnificently until
1-15 p.m.	when, as no sign of any reinforcing division appeared, and whatever British troops there had been on our right had long before been seen streaming back towards PYS, and the enemy were obviously attempting to reach PYS before us and so cut us off, I decided to withdraw, according to written orders received the night before, and confirmed verbally by the Brigade Major, to SERRE. I consequently arranged with Major Duff, 6th Gordons, who was on my left, that I would form a defensive flank facing S.W. in order to allow him and the remainder of my own Brigade to get clear of WARLENCOURT to IRLES. This withdrawal was quite successfully carried out as far as IRLES. We received orders to maintain our position there. By this time the troops were absolutely exhausted owing to lack of sleep, cold and fatigue. However, they faced about and manned positions in front of PYS till
4 p.m.	when the whole Division withdrew.
? Sully.	The remnants of the Battalion were collected at SERRE AU BOIS.

10TH MARCH.

	Battalion manned an outpost line covering SERRE AU BOIS until
11 a.m.	when orders were received to withdraw to another outpost line covering SOUASTRE.
6 p.m.	Marched back to PAS for the night.
REMARKS.	On considering these 6 days fighting it must be borne in mind that men of this Battalion had done, some of them 16 days and all of them 14 days in the line, and owing to the impending attack and the fact that a number of patrol and working parties had to be found they had had very little sleep or rest. Consequently they were "tired" men at the start.

The Artillery support throughout the whole fighting was negligible as far as this Battalion was concerned. The enemy on the contrary had batteries in action at point blank range within half an hour after his infantry had become engaged.

We were harassed by low flying enemy aircraft, and until 25th our planes were conspicuous by their absence, but from this date onwards they did magnificent work.

No anti-aircraft gun of ours was seen in action during the whole battle. It is generally agreed in my Battalion that the enemy can throw his stick bombs further than we can throw our Mills' grenades.

The use of Flamenwerfer had a very great moral effect on the troops, although the casualties inflicted by it were small.

The work of the Battalion Transport in bringing up rations and ammunition was magnificent.

The arrangements made to evacuate wounded were scandalous, and 90 per cent of my wounded had to be abandoned to the enemy. A detailed report of this has been forwarded to the A.D.M.S. by my M.O.

It is suggested that in future, once the line has been broken, the field artillery should be allotted to an infantry Brigade to work with them entirely.

In every case the enemy massing for attack could be plainly seen by infantry, and if only they had been able to call on any guns in close vicinity massing could have been broken up before any attack developed.

Lieut.Col.,
Commanding 7th Arg.& Suth.Highrs.

10th March, 1918.

Copy No. 9

7TH ARG. AND SUTHERLAND HIGHLANDERS.

Operation Order No. 32.

8TH MARCH, 1916.

Ref. Map BEAUVRES 1/10,000.

1. RELIEF.

The Battalion will relieve the 4th Gordon Highlanders (Battalion in Front line DEMICOURT SECTOR) on 8th March.
  "A" Coy 7th Arg. & Soth. Highlanders relieves "D" Coy 4th
    Gordon Highlanders. (Reserve Coy.)
  "B" Coy relieves "A" Coy (Right Coy) 4th Gordon Highlanders.
  "C" Coy relieves "B" Coy (Centre Coy) 4th " "
  "D" Coy relieves "C" Coy (Left Coy) 4th " "
  Battalion H.Q. will be at J.12.d.4.7.

2. DISPOSITIONS.

Line will be taken over as now held by 4th Gordon Highrs, and Defence Scheme issued by 4th Gordon Highlanders will be adhered to until further orders. Trench Stores, maps and Work in hand and patrol work will be taken over.

3. TRENCH STORES.

Companies will render Trench Store lists to Battalion H.Q. by 10 a.m., 10th March.

4. GUIDES.

Right Coy. Three, at entrance to BEACH AVENUE, J.17.b.9.9. at 3.15 p.m., and one at junction of ROACH AVENUE and DEMICOURT main street at 3.15 p.m. (for Mining platoon in SUNKEN ROAD). O.C. this platoon is responsible for sending a guide to dugout at J.12.b.6.8. to guide last shift to join its platoon. This last shift will take their packs when they go on duty at 8 a.m.

Left Coy "D". One per platoon for Right front and Right Support platoons will be at junction of ROACH AVENUE and main street DEMICOURT, and for Left front and Left Support platoons at entrance to BYNGER AVENUE, J.17.b.25.55. all at 3.30 p.m.

Centre Coy "C". One per post in front line, one per Support platoon will be at junction of ROACH AVENUE and main street DEMICOURT at 3.45 p.m.

Reserve Coy "A". No guides required. Coy will proceed through DEMICOURT and ROACH AVENUE, entering ROACH AVENUE where it crosses main street at 4.15 p.m.

On arrival at Road Junction, K.7.c.75.50 party will proceed by INNISKILLING TRENCH. SUNKEN ROAD must on no account be used beyond that road junction.

H.Q. Coy will proceed by DEMICOURT and ROACH AVENUE in small parties, and will leave Battalion H.Q. at 2 p.m.

Intelligence Officer will arrange relief of O.Ps.

Before relief of 4th Gordon Highrs "A" and "D" Coys will be relieved by Coys of 4th Seaforth Highrs, this relief to be completed by 3 p.m.

"C" Coy will leave an Officer to hand over to relieving Coy of 4th Seaforth Highrs.

"D" Coy will hand over before leaving LEBUCQUIERE. No guides for 4th Seaforths will be required.

5.

In all cases Os.C. Coys will obtain receipts for Trench Stores, and cleanliness of dugouts, and hand over all permanent work parties. Maps, Defence Schemes, Air photos will be handed over on relief.

Work on dugouts, etc. being carried out as shown on attached work table.

6. VISIBILITY.

If visibility is good, relief will be postponed until 6 p.m. at which time guides will rendezvous at same places.

Postponement of relief will be communicated to Coys before 12.15 p.m. by code word "WAITING".

completion of relief will be communicated to Battalion
HQ., members name and the time.
     Coys will forward to Battalion H.Q., by 11 a.m. 9th March, a return
showing strength of Coy H.Q. and platoons.

8. WORK ON HAND.
     All work on hand for night 9th/10th will be taken over from 5th Gordon Highrs, special attention being paid to wiring.

9.   Immediately on arrival in line all men will take up fire positions,
and O.C. Coys will inspect these, and make sure that every man understands his orders in case of attack.
     In all cases platoon commanders will stay with their platoons.

10. TRANSPORT.
     "B" and "D" Coys will each leave one man in charge of limber to
return to Camp with it when horses arrive.
     Immediately after dinners, Cooks of "A", "B", "C", and H.Q. Coys will
go on in advance with advance party carrying dixies and sufficient
water for teas.
     One limber will report to O.C. "D" Coy at 1.30 p.m. for Lewis
Guns, Dixies, Coy Mess Stores for trenches, etc, and will take sufficient
water in petrol tins for teas. Limber will proceed with "D" Coy as far as
6th Seaforths' Headquarters, J.17.a.6.7. Lewis Guns, Dixies, etc. will
be carried from there.
     "D" Coy's blankets and Officers' valises will be stored
at Camp at 10 a.m., and taken to Q.M.Stores.
     T.O. will arrange to collect "C" Coy's valises and "D" Coy's surplus
Mess Stores in the afternoon. "D" Coy will leave a guard with these
until they are lifted.
     Transport for rations, petrol tins with water, and also water-carts
will arrive at road junction at J.12.d.7.5. about 6.30 p.m. O.C. Coys
will send a guide to this point to guide limbers to Coy ration dump.
     Mess-cart will be at Battalion H.Q. at 5.15 p.m. to convey Mess stores
etc to new Battalion H.Q.
     25 petrol tins of water will be sent to "B" and "D" Coys, and ten
petrol tins of water to "A" and "C" Coys. Two water-carts will be
sent in addition.
     Detailed instructions regarding water-carts will be given to
Transport Officer as they pass Battalion H.Q.

ACKNOWLEDGE.

                                              2/Lt. & a/Adjutant.
                                              7th Argyll & Sutherland Highlanders.

Copy No. 1.... File.
          2.   O.C. "A" Coy.
          3.   "   "B" "
          4.   "   "C" "
          5.   "   "D" "
          6.   "   H.Q.
          7.   Transport Officer.
          8.   Quartermaster.
          9.   O.C. 5th Gordon Hrs.
         10. " "   6th Seaforth Hrs.

Reference KK.48 of 30/3/18. I have to report as follows:-

Numbers now present with Unit who fought -

(a) In the front line and support line   330.
(b) In the Reserve Line and Intermediate line 140.
(c) In the BEAUMETZ - MORCHIES Line   360.

                                    Lieut.Col.,
                                    Commanding,
                              7th Arg. & Suth. Highrs.

31st March, 1918.

S E C R E T.

O.C. 4th Seaforth Highrs.
    4th Gordon Highrs.
    7th A. & S. Highrs.
    154th M. G. Company.
    154th T. M. Battery.
H.Q. 51st (H) Division "G".
    52nd Infantry Brigade.
    152nd   "   "
    153rd   "   "
    Right Group Artillery.
    293rd (Army) Bde. R.F.A.
O.C. 401st Field Coy. R.E.

The following correction will be made to the sketch map issued with this Brigade Operation Order No.9 of to-day.

1 Coy. 4th Gordon Highrs. attached to O.C. 4th Seaforth Highlanders will be accommodated thus :-

    Coy. H.Q. and 2 Platoons between present Battalion H.Q. at J.18.d.4.8. and FACTORY at J.18.d.3.3.

    2 Platoons in dugouts at J.18.a.8.9.

NOTE. 4 Platoons on DOIGNIES - DEMICOURT Road, as shown on sketch map.

28th February, 1918.

Captain,
Brigade Major,
154th Infantry Brigade.

S E C R E T.   Copy No...... 3

154th INFANTRY BRIGADE
OPERATION ORDER NO. 9.

Reference Map :-
MOEUVRES Special Sheet 1/20,000.   27th Febry. 1918.

1.   On March 1st and night March 1st/2nd, 1918, the front of the 51st (H) Division will be reorganised and divided into three permanent Brigade Sectors.
        The Right Sector (DEMICOURT SECTOR) will be held by 154th Infantry Brigade.
        152nd Infantry Brigade will be on the left of 154th Infantry Brigade and will hold the Centre Sector (BOURSIES SECTOR).

2. (a) The relief of 154th Infantry Brigade by Units of 152nd Infantry Brigade and 153rd Infantry Brigade, and the redistribution of Units of the Brigade, will take place in accordance with Table "A" attached.

   (b) Dispositions of Units of 154th Infantry Brigade on completion of redistribution will be as follows :-

        Brigade Headquarters   ...   J.26.b.1.9.
        4th Seaforth Highrs.   Line, H.Q. J.18.d.4.8.
        4th Gordon Highrs.   Support,H.Q. J.16.c.4.0.
            1 Coy. (tactically under O.C. 4th Seaforths) H.Q. and
              2 Platoons J.18.d., 2 Platoons J.18.a.8.9.
            1 Coy. Intermediate Line.
            1 Coy. Road, J.21.d.
            1 Coy. LEBUCQUIERE.
        7th A. & S. Highrs.   Reserve, AMBULANCE CAMP, LEBUCQUIERE.
        154th M. G. Coy.   12 guns in line. 1 Section LEBUCQUIERE.
        154th T. M. Bty.   H.Q. J.22.b.8.9.
                                4 guns in line, 2 WALSH SUPPORT.
                                                2 GRAYLING POST.

                                4 guns in Reserve, LEBUCQUIERE.

3.   All maps, aeroplane photographs, details of work, trench store lists, which concern any portion of the area which is being taken over by another Unit, will be handed over by Battalion Commanders.

4.   The Vickers guns will be readjusted to conform to the new allotment of Brigade frontages on the night 2nd/3rd March, 1918. Orders will be issued by O.C., Divisional M.G. Battalion.
        The positions of M.G's after redistribution are shewn on attached map.

5.   All Units in the present Sector of 154th Infantry Brigade on the night 1st/2nd March, 1918, will come under orders of B.G.C. 154th Infantry Brigade until 9 a.m. on 2nd March, at which hour Brigadiers will take over command of their new Sectors.

6. (a) 154th Infantry Brigade will be covered by 293 (Army) Brigade R.F.A. in the DEMICOURT SECTOR.
   (b) An Artillery Liaison Officer will live at front Battalion Headquarters, J.18.d.4.8.

** 2 **

7. Anti-Aircraft Lewis Guns will be posted as follows :-

    1 gun Sunken Road, K.13.b.3.9.
    1 gun with Coy. of Support Battalion in Intermediate Line.
    1 gun with Coy. of Support Battalion in Road in J.21.d.

8. (a) Work on dugouts will be continued and spoiling parties will be provided in accordance with Table "B". No cessation of work must be caused by the relief.
    Sappers Mates of 6th Seaforths will be relieved by 9 a.m. on 2nd March.
  (b) Detail of working parties required on BEAUMETZ - MORCHIES LINE will be issued later.

9. Administrative Instructions will be issued by Staff Captain.

10. (a) The trench wardens on STURGEON AVENUE, detailed from 154th T. M. Battery, will be relieved on 2nd March, and will rejoin their Battery.
  (b) Trench wardens (3 O.R's.) will be detailed for ROACH AVENUE from the platoons accommodated in dugouts at J.18.a.8.9.

11. 2 Sections, 401st Field Coy., R.E., will work under orders of B.G.C. 154th Infantry Brigade in the DEMICOURT SECTOR.

12. Completion of each portion of relief will be reported as follows :-
    Relief of 7th A. & S. Highrs. - Code word "LUCKNOW."
    Relief of 4th Gordon Highrs. and completion of move to Support position DEMICOURT Sector, by code word "ABERDEEN."
    Completion of redistribution of 4th Seaforth Highrs. by code word "MYSORE".
    Completion of relief of 3 guns T. M. Battery, by code word "CAMPBELL".

13. STURGEON AVENUE will be common to both the Right and Centre Brigade.

14. Headquarters, 154th Infantry Brigade will close at J.20.c.6.8. at 9 a.m. on 2nd March and open at J.26.b.1.9. at same hour.

15. ACKNOWLEDGE.

                                              Captain,
                                          Brigade Major,
                                     154th Infantry Brigade.

Issued at 7am 28/2/18

Copy No. 1 4th Seaforth Highrs.
      2 4th Gordon Highrs.
      3 7th A. & S. Highrs.
      4 154th M. G. Company.
      5 154th T.M. Battery.
      6 51st (H) Division "G".
      7 51st (H) Division "A".
      8 52nd Infantry Brigade.
      9 152nd   "   "
     10 153rd   "   "

No. 11. Right Group Arty.
    12. 293 (Army) Bde. R.F.A.
    13. 401st Field Co. R.E.
    14. 2/1st (H) Fld. Amb.
    15. No. 2 Coy. A.S.C.
    16. Staff Captain.
    17. Bde. Sig. Officer.
    18. Bde. Transport Off.
    19. Brigade Major.
    20. War Diary.
    21. File.

Table "A" to accompany 154th Infantry Brigade O.O. No. 9.

Serial No.	Unit.	Relieved by.	Guides.	Time & Rendezvous.	On relief proceeds to.	Remarks.
1.	Right Coy. 7th A. & S. Highrs.	4th Seaforth Hrs	To be arranged by C.O's.	To take place in daylight and be complete by 4 p.m. 1st March.	Intermediate Line.	Coy. will proceed to Intermediate Line & remain there until relieved at night by a Coy. 4th Gordons. Coy. will use STURGEON AV. and all available covered approaches to Intermediate Line. When relieved by 4th Gordons, Coy. will move to LEBUCQUIERE.
2.	2 Platoons 7th A.& S. Highrs. at J.19.a.8.9.	2 Platoons 4th Gordon Hrs.	do.	Will be 11`36 notified. Batt H.Q.	LEBUCQUIERE.	
3.	Left Coy.,7th A.& S.H. Reserve Coy.,7th A.& S. Hrs.(less Posts 18 & 19 Intermediate Line). Battalion H.Q. Coy.H.Q. & Platoon in Support at QUARRY, J.12.a.2.8.	5th Seaforth Highrs.	1 guide per Platoon for Coy.proceeding to Front Line and for platoon proceeding to QUARRY. 1 guide per Coy.H.Q.	10 p.m. Centre Battn. H.Q., J.15.a.5.7.	LEBUCQUIERE.	
4.	Posts 18 & 19 Intermediate Line, 7th A.& S. Highrs.	6th Gordon Highrs.	1 guide per Post.	10 p.m. Post 20, Intermediate Line,J.10.a.3.3.	LEBUCQUIERE.	
5.	4th Gordon Highrs., less 2 Platoons Left Front Coy. and Posts 23-25 Intermediate Line.	6th Gordon Highrs.	1 guide per Platoon and 1 per Coy.H.Q.	10 p.m. Post 20, Intermediate Line,J.10.a.3.3.	As stated in Para.2 (b) of O.O. No.9.	

** 2 **

Serial No.	Unit.	Relieved by.	Guides.	Time & Rendezvous.	On relief proceeds to.	Remarks.
6.	2 Platoons Left Coy. 4th Gordons and Posts 23-25 Intermediate Line.	6th Black Watch.	To be arranged by C.O's direct.	To be completed by 4 p.m. 1st March.	Will be notified.	
7.	154th T.M. Battery 1 gun in PICCADILLY 2 guns in PERC. SOUTH.	153rd T.M. Bty. 152nd T.M.Bty.	) To be arranged by C.O's direct.) Relief not to commence before 5.30 p.m.		EMBUCQUIERE.	

Suggest 4 Coy 4 G.H. to have 1 guide at Batt HQ at 7am —

TABLE "B" to accompany 154th Infantry Brigade Operation Order No. 9.

Serial.	Location of Dugout.	Unit at present finding Platoon.	Relieving Platoon.	Unit in charge of work.	Platoon accommodated at	Relieving Platoon reports etc.
1.	J.23.b.6.8. Intermediate Line.	6th Seaforth Hrs.	1 Platoon 4th Gordons from Coy. in Intermediate Line.	252nd Tunnel. Co.	Intermediate Line J.23.b.6.8.	8 a.m. 2nd March.
2.	J.12.b.4.9.	7th A.& S. Hrs.	- do -	401st Field Coy.	Dugout in 152nd Bde. Area at J.6.d.2.1.	8 a.m. 2nd March.
3.	K.7.d.5.9.	4th Seaforth Hrs.	Continues work but party to be found by 1 Platoon garrisoning WALSH SUPPORT.	8th Royal Scots.		
4.	K.13.b.5.8.	4th Seaforth Highrs.	Continues work but party to be found by 1 platoon garrisoning RESERVE Line.	401st Field Coy.		
5.	J.17.d. Intermediate Line.	6th Seaforth Hrs.	1 platoon 4th Gordons from Coy. in Intermediate Line.	252nd Tunnel. Co.	Bank at J.17.c.	8 a.m. 2nd March.
6.	K.7.c.5.9.	7th A.& S. Hrs. *& SH?*	1 Platoon 4th Gordons from dugouts at J.18.a.9.9.	-do-	J.18.a.9.9.	8 a.m. 2nd March.
7 (a)	J.21.d.4.8. BEAUMETZ-MORCHIES Line.	Two parties each of 10 O.R. to be detailed by Coy. of 4th Gordon Highrs. accommodated in Sunken Road in J.21.d. and to report daily at 8 a.m. and 5.30 p.m. commencing 2nd March.				
(b)	J.28.a.5.3. BEAUMETZ-MORCHIES Line.	As above.				

Note: Instructions for Mining Platoons to come into force from 2nd March will be issued to all concerned.

War Diary app V
G

SECRET.
****

Copy No...3..

154th INFANTRY BRIGADE
OPERATION ORDER NO.10.

Reference Map :-
   MOEUVRES Special Sheet 1/20,000.   4th March 1918.

1.   On 5th March 1918 4th Gordon Highrs. will relieve 4th Seaforth Highrs. in the DEMICOURT Sector (front line) and 7th Arg. & Suth'd. Highbs. will relieve 4th Gordon Highrs. in Support.
        4th Seaforth Highrs. on relief will move to LEBUCQUIERE and become Brigade Reserve.

2.   All details of relief will be arranged between O.C's concerned.

3.   Relief of one Coy. 4th Gordon Highrs., at present in support to 4th Seaforth Highrs., and one Coy. 4th Gordon Highrs. in the Intermediate Line by two Coys. 7th A. & S. Highrs., will be completed before relief of 4th Seaforth Highrs. is commenced.

4.   The relief will be carried out in daylight (weather permitting) at times to be arranged between O.C's concerned. If the weather is clear and visibility good, the relief will not commence before 6 p.m. Postponement of relief will be communicated to all concerned by means of code word "LUX" before 12 noon on 5th March.

5.   Maps, Defence Schemes, Air Photos and Trench Stores will be handed over on relief. 4th Seaforth Highrs. will hand over brief summary of all patrol reports during their tour in the line.

6.   Lists of Trench Stores handed over will reach Brigade Headquarters by 6 p.m. on 6th March.

7.   Completion of relief of 4th Seaforth Highrs. by 4th Gordon Highrs. will be reported to Brigade Headquarters by means of code words "300 COILS". Completion of move of 7th A. & S. Highrs. to Support Area will be reported by means of code words "250 PICKETS".

8.   Permanent working parties will be continued as follows.

   (a) Party of 2 Officers and 70 O.R. to report to an R.E. Officer detailed by C.E, IVth Corps at junction of road and railway, J.20.c,9.2, at 8.30 a.m. daily.
        To be continued by 7th A. & S. Highrs. on 5th and 6th March - 4th Seaforth Highrs. take up work from 7th to 10th March inclusive.

   (b) Party of 1 Officer and 50 O.R. to report to R.E. Officer at BEAUMETZ CEMETERY at 8.30 a.m. daily. Party to take 40 shovels and 10 picks.
        To be continued by 7th A. & S. Highrs. on 5th and 6th March. - 4th Seaforth Highrs. take up work 7th to 10th March inclusive.

   (c) Party of 20 O.R. to report to R.E. Officer at Range at .I.23.c.2.8. at 9 a.m. for work on repair of range. Party to take shovels and haversack rations, and to work till 3 p.m.
        To be detailed by 7th A. & S. Highrs. on 5th and 6th March and by 4th Seaforth Highrs. from 7th to 10th March, inclusive.

** 2 **

9. Platoons of 4th Gordon Highrs. at present employed on dugout work will be relieved by platoons of 7th A. & S. Highrs. on 5th March. First shifts of 7th A. & S. Highrs. will commence work at 4 p.m. on 5th inst.

  Platoons of 4th Seaforth Highrs. employed on dugouts will be relieved at their work by platoons 4th Gordon Highrs. by 12 midnight 5th/6th March.

  Shifts will be kept at minimum strength of 10 D.R., and if necessary men will be detailed from Echelon "B" to maintain these numbers.

10. ACKNOWLEDGE.

D. M. W. Leith, Lt.
Captain,
Brigade Major,
154th Infantry Brigade.

ISSUED BY RUNNER AT 7 A.M.

Copy No. 1 to 4th Seaforth Highrs.
     2 " 4th Gordon Highrs.
     3 " 7th A. & S. Highrs.
     4 " 154th M. G. Company.
     5 " 154th T. M. Battery.
     6 " 51st (H) Division "G".
     7 " 51st (H)   "   "A".
     8 " 52nd Infantry Brigade.
     9 " 152nd   "   "
    10 " 293rd (Army) Bde. R.F.A.
    11 " 401st Field Coy. R.E.
    12 " 252nd Tunnelling Coy. (Adv. H.Q.).
    13 " 2/1st (H) Field Ambulance.
    14 " No. 2 Coy. A.S.C.
    15 " Staff Captain.
    16 " Brigade Transport Officer.
    17 " Brigade Signalling Officer.
    18 " Brigade Major.
    19 " War Diary.
    20 " File.

War Diary G app III
3

SECRET.   Copy No.....

154th INFANTRY BRIGADE
OPERATION ORDER NO. 12.

Reference Map :-
MOEUVRES Special Sheet 1/20,000.   9th March 1918.

1.   The moves ordered in 154th Infantry Brigade Operation Order No. 11 are cancelled.

2.   The relief of 4th Gordon Highlanders in the DEMICOURT Sector will take place on 9th March, the right half Sector (front) (Posts 1 - 8) being relieved by 4th Seaforth Highlanders, and the left half Sector, front line, (Posts 9 - 15) by 7th A. & S. Highlanders.
Boundaries are shown on the attached map.

3.   Disposition of Battalion on completion of relief will be as follows :-

  4th Seaforth Highlanders.

    Battn. H.Q. J.18.d.7.8.

    Right Front Company.
    Coy. H.Q. K.8.a.2.1.
    2 Platoons Front Line, Posts 1 - 5 inclusive.
    2 Platoons WALSH SUPPORT.

    Left Front Company.
    1 Platoon Front Line (Posts 6 - 8 inclusive).
    1 Platoon Support Line.
    Coy. H.Q. and 2 Platoons SCOTCH STREET.

    Support Company.
    1 Platoon SCOTCH STREET.
    Coy. H.Q. and 2 Platoons J.18.d.7.8.
    1 Platoon INTERMEDIATE LINE, QUARRY, J.24.a.6.4.

    Reserve Company and garrison for BEAUMETZ-MORCHIES Line, J.21.d.

  7th A. & S. Highlanders.

    Battn. H.Q. Dugouts, J.18.a.9.9.

    Right Front Coy.
    1 Platoon Front Line (Posts 9 - 10 inclusive).
    1 Platoon Support Line, East of TROUT ALLEY.
    Coy. H.Q. and 2 Platoons K.7.c.2.5.

    Left Front Company.
    Front Line 2 Platoons (Posts 11 - 15 inclusive).
    Coy. H.Q. and 1 Platoon GRAYLING SUPPORT, K.7.a.1.3.
    1 Platoon STURGEON SUPPORT, J.6.d.2.1.

    Support Company.
    1 Platoon Support Line, J.12.b.6.8.
    1 Platoon Sunken Road, J.12.a.6.6.
    1 Platoon at Battn. H.Q., J.18.a.9.9.
    Coy. H.Q. and 1 Platoon INTERMEDIATE Line.

    Reserve Company.
    2 Platoons INTERMEDIATE LINE.
    Coy. H.Q. and 2 Platoons BRUNO MILL.

** 2 **

4th Gordon Highlanders.

Brigade Reserve, AMBULANCE CAMP, LEBUCQUIERE.

4. Further details of relief will be arranged between Os.C. concerned.

5. Relief will take place as soon as possible. Completion of relief will be reported to Brigade Headquarters, by means of code words "270 Petrol Tins".

6. O.C. 4th Gordon Highlanders will arrange to divide air photos.

7. (a) Work on dugouts will be continued as follows :-

No.	Dugout.	Unit.	Remarks.
1.	J.12.b.6.8.	7th A. & S. Hrs.	1 platoon will live in and work on dugout.
2.	J.23.b.6.8.	7th A. & S. Hrs.)	Platoons to be provided
3.	J.17.d.	7th A. & S. Hrs.)	by garrison of Intermediate Line.
4.	K.7.d.5.9.	4th Seaforths.	One platoon will live in and work on dugout.
5.	K.13.b.5.8.	4th Seaforths.	As in 4.
6.	K.7.c.5.9.	7th A. & S. Hrs.	1 platoon will live in and work on dugout. Owing to accommodation here being limited, corr. iron shelters must be constructed temporarily

Where fresh platoons have to be detailed for dugout work, they will take over at 12 midnight (11 p.m. Winter time) Night 9th/10th March.

(b) Reserve Company 4th Seaforth Highrs. will provide shifts for dugouts under construction in BEAUMETZ - MORCHIES Line - arrangements to be made direct between 252nd Tunnelling Coy. and O.C. Coy., 4th Seaforth Highrs.

8. Working parties ordered under this office B.64 of 8th March for evening of 9th March are cancelled.

9. O.C. 293rd (Army) Brigade R.F.A. will detail an Artillery Liaison Officer for duty at new Loft Battalion Headquarters (7th A. & S. Highrs.)

10. ACKNOWLEDGE.

                                                Captain,
                                          Brigade Major,
                                  154th Infantry Brigade.

Issued at 3.15 p.m. by Orderly.

Copy No. 1 4th Seaforth Highrs.
       2 4th Gordon Highrs.
       3 7th A. & S. Highrs.
       4 C/51 Bn., M.G.C.
       5 154th T. M. Battery.
       6 51st (H) Division "G"
       7 51st (H)   "   "A"
       8 52nd Infantry Brigade.
       9 152nd   "   "
     10 293rd Army Bde. R.F.A.
     11 401st Field Coy. R.E.

Copy No.12 252nd Tun.Coy.
     13 2/1st (H) Fld. Amblce.
     14 No. 2 Coy. A.S.C.
     15 Staff Captain.
     16 Bde. Transport Off.
     17 Bde. Signal Officer.
     18 Brigade Major.
     19 War Diary.
     20 File.

SECRET.

AMENDMENT NO.1 TO
154th INFANTRY BRIGADE
OPERATION ORDER NO. 12.

Reference this Brigade Operation Order No.12 of to-day, paragraph 3.

Dispositions of 7th A. & S. Highlanders (Loft Battalion) are amended as follows :-

Battn. H.Q., Right Front Coy., Left Front Coy. as in O.O.12.

Right Support Company.

Coy. H.Q. and 3 platoons - INTERMEDIATE Line.
1 platoon with Battn. H.Q. in dugouts at J.18.a.9.9.

Loft Support Company.

Coy. H.Q. and 2 platoons - BRUNO MILL, J.16.c.4.0.
1 platoon STURGEON SUPPORT, J.12.b.6.8.
1   "   2 Sections (including L.G. Section) J.12.b.1.1.
           2 Sections J.12.a.6.6.

            Captain,
           Brigade Major,
         154th Infantry Brigade.

9th March, 1918.

All recipients of O.O. No. 12.

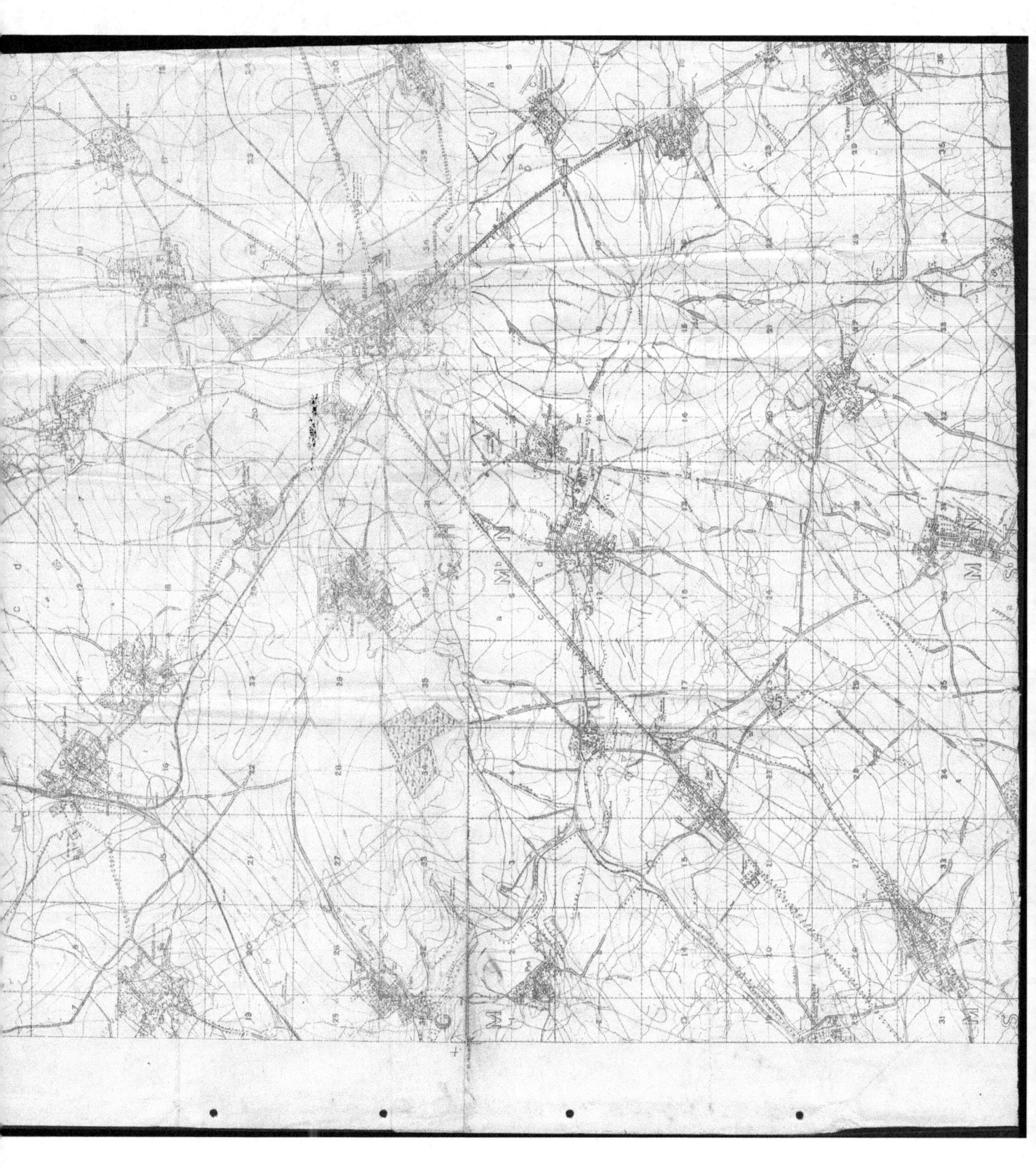

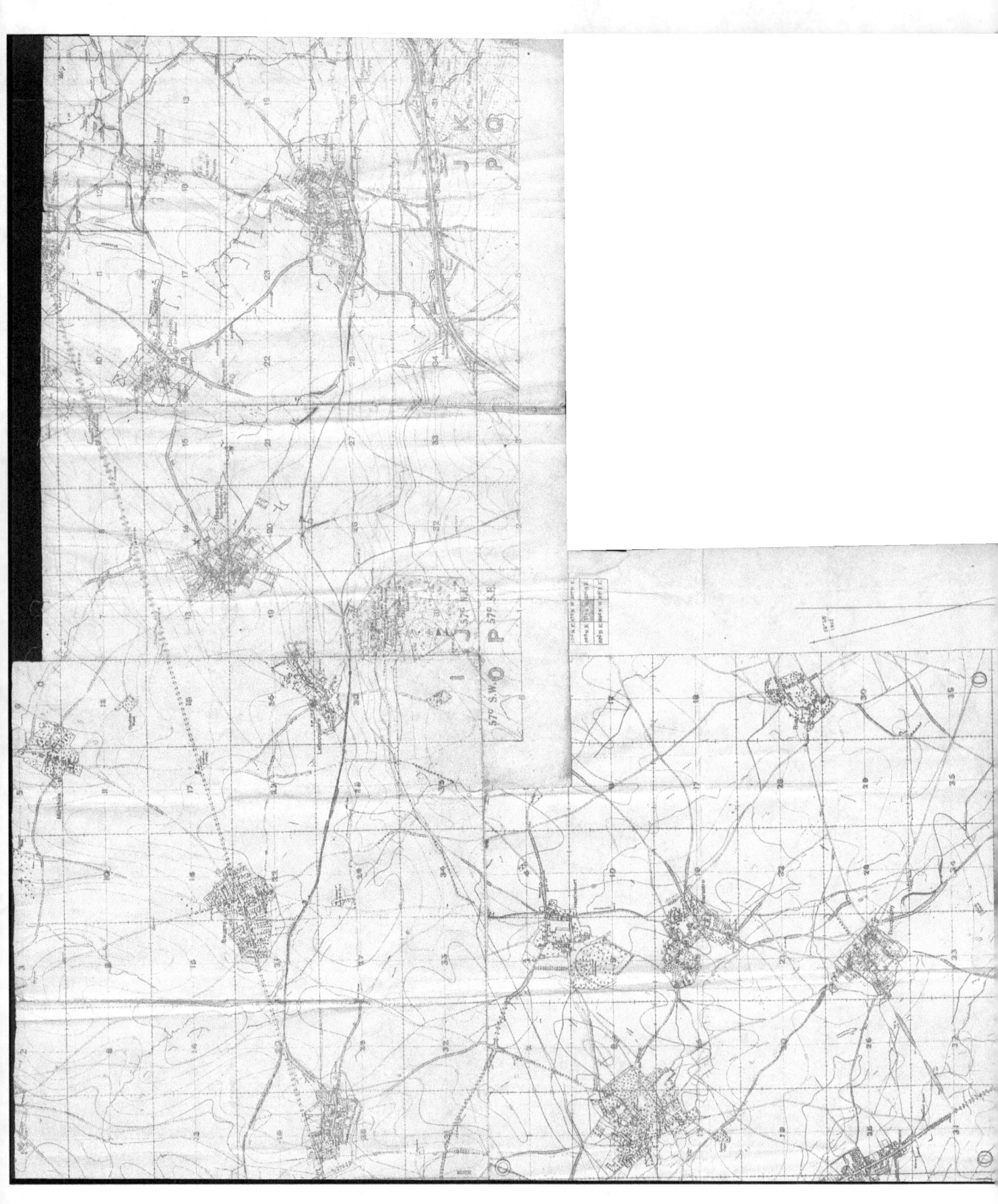

51st Division
154th Infantry Brigade.

WAR DIARY

7th BATTALION

THE ARGYLL & SUTHERLAND HIGHLANDERS

APRIL 1918

Attached :- Report on Operations

Army Form W. 3091.

Cover for Documents.

Nature of Enclosures.

7th Argyll & Sutherland Highlanders War Diary. April 1918.

Notes, or Letters written.

Army Form C. 2118.

WAR DIARY
or
INTELLIGENCE SUMMARY.
(Erase heading not required.)

Ref. MAPS 36A
HAZEBROUCK.

Place	Date	Hour	Summary of Events and Information	Remarks and references to Appendices
CANTRAINNE	1/4/18		Battalion in billets. Training and reorganization of Battn. Major D.F. Bichener rejoined 2/Lt C. Spooner posted and joined 15 Battn. from 14th A.I. Btn.	DM.
"	2/4/18		Continued training. Orders received at 11.30 a.m. that Battn. at half an hours notice to move to 1st Corps. This order cancelled at 3 p.m. Orders received at 8 p.m. that Battn. under orders of IJ Corps from noon 3rd April and in First Army Reserve.	DM.
"	3/4/18		Continued training. Major Bichener appointed in temporary command of 4" Grdn. Bn.	DM.
LOZINGHEM	4/4/18		Moved at 10 a.m. to LOZINGHEM. Battalion in billets.	DM.
"	5/4/18		Continued training	DM.
"	6/4/18		Continued training	DM.
"	7/4/18		Church parade. Draft of 10 officers & 246 O.Rs received from 14th A.I. Btn. Also draft of 146 O.Rs from Divisional Wing. Captain Casey R.A.M.C. left and Capt. Laing R.A.M.C. joined the 15 Battalion. Training Order received that Battn. moves tomorrow to Mt BERNENCHON and on completion of move will come under orders of XI th Corps.	DM.
"	8/4/18		Moved at 9 a.m. to MT BERNENCHON. In billets.	DM.
"	9/4/18			

Army Form C. 2118.

WAR DIARY
or
INTELLIGENCE SUMMARY.
(Erase heading not required.)

Instructions regarding War Diaries and Intelligence Summaries are contained in F. S. Regs., Part II. and the Staff Manual respectively. Title pages will be prepared in manuscript.

Place	Date	Hour	Summary of Events and Information	Remarks and references to Appendices
MOUNT BERNENCHON	9/4/18	9:30am	Message received from Brigade that hostile offensive now proceeding appeared to be a main attack. To retrospect, and that front line communications had been cut; that 152nd Brigade had moved to defensive localities at HUIT MAISONS and LACOUTURE.	DI.
		10:50am	Message from Brigade that 4th Gordon Highrs. & 7th A. & S. Highrs. will shortly be ready to move at short notice.	
		11:30am	Message received from Brigade that enemy attacking north of LA BASSEE Canal north Fris - Division.	
		12:30pm	Orders received to move to LOCON and LES CHOQUAUX - 2 Companies at latter place. Battalion moved as ordered, but at Bridge at W.II.a. C.o. was stopped by an Officer of the Brigade Staff and misinstructions received that the whole Battalion would proceed to W.C.a. where further instructions would be received.	
		4:30pm	Battalion arrived in W.6.d and sent one platoon by Companies to posts on the lakes in W.6.d + X.1.c. + W.12.L	
		5:6pm	Orders were received from Brigade to occupy the LOCON defences on X.2.c, X.1.a. and X.7.c. to get in touch with 153rd Brigade whose right rested about X.2.a, 5.6 next to Canal. Also to get in touch with Pioneers in 55th Division holding the MESPLAUX Group, further to form a defensive flank facing north and front of LA TOMBE, WILLOT, R.31.C and a.	
		5:30pm	"A" Coy was sent to form a defensive flank facing north in front of LA TOMBE, WILLOT, "B" Coy. was sent to occupy the defences of LOCON in X.2.a. and a. "D" Coy. was placed in support of X.1.c. and a.	

Army Form C. 2118.

WAR DIARY
or
INTELLIGENCE SUMMARY.
(Erase heading not required.)

Place	Date	Hour	Summary of Events and Information	Remarks and references to Appendices
	9/11/18	6.15 pm	Following verbal orders, "D" Coy were sent to take up a position on west of Canal north then left on track north of 152nd Brigade about the footbridge on X.3.a and their right on LE CASAN.	DM.
		10.30 pm	Dispositions were as follows — 2 Coys ("D" and "B") on right from footbridge in X.3.a. west of Canal in touch with 152nd Brigade to LE CASAN, east of Canal in touch with 55th Division. "A" Coy facing north in front of the TOMB E.W.11.C.7, "C" Coy in reserve on X.1.c. Batt. HQ. in house about W.15.K.9.8.	
		11.30 pm	Orders received to re-organise front on to a three-company front on the line of the LAWE Canal from X.14.a.0.3 to junction with 152nd Brigade at about X.2.a.3.9 and that reserve Coy on X.1.c. might be used by O.C. Battalion. Commanding Officer met OC Companies of "A", "B" & "D" Coy and instructed them to take up the following positions, each Coy with two platoons in front and two in support. "A" Coy on left in touch with 152nd Brigade about X.2.6.7.3 to about X.14.a.6.7. "D" Coy from latter point to about X.8.C.8.7. "B" Coy from latter point to X.2.a.3.0. "C" Coy on right from X.2.a.3.0. Platoons in support in rear behind their respective Companies.	
	19/11/18	4 am	Above disposition completed.	DM.
			At the same hour information was received that enemy had crossed footbridge in X.3.a. and that 152nd Brigade was going to drive them back and that the Battalion was to co-operate by fire. enemy footbridge at X.3.a.2.8	

WAR DIARY or INTELLIGENCE SUMMARY

Army Form C. 2118.

Place	Date	Hour	Summary of Events and Information	Remarks and references to Appendices
	10/4/18	5 a.m.	Verbal orders were received for "C" Coy to recce their position and to conform to those on right of "D" Coy and that any reinforcements required could be procured by Brigade.	D.M.
		6 a.m.	"C" Coy had moved to position with right at X.13.d.11. and left would 53¼. Durour and left at X.13.c.8.1 m., situated at "D.B."	
		7.50 a.m.	Information was received that support troops of 152nd Brigade were not in touch with our support, and one platoon sent to "C" Coy to gather troops.	
		11.30 a.m.	Report was received from "A" Coy of enemy concentration at footbridge and in buildings X.3.a. & b.	
		11.40 a.m.	Stokes mortars were sent to "A" Coy to endeavour to destroy footbridge.	
		1 p.m.	A report was sent to Brigade Hd.Qrs. that "B" Coy was in touch with 152nd Brigade both in front & support and that left Coy Company's depleted in the L. of LANNOY, "A" Coy having put one support platoon into the front line to effect this in X.2.B.	
		6.30 p.m.	From this time onwards enemy continued to press forward on left of Battalion and to endeavour to cross footbridge in X.3.a. Enemy brought heavy machine gun fire to bear on our front and subsequently shelled front line, and LOCON Bridge on left were gradually forced back. Lieut.Col. L.B. Durie, M.C. was wounded and Major T.M. Henderson, M.C. came on to take command.	

Army Form C. 2118.

WAR DIARY
or
INTELLIGENCE SUMMARY.
(Erase heading not required.)

Instructions regarding War Diaries and Intelligence Summaries are contained in F. S. Regs. Part II. and the Staff Manual respectively. Title pages will be prepared in manuscript.

Place	Date	Hour	Summary of Events and Information	Remarks and references to Appendices
	11/11/18	9 a.m.	During the early morning found our lost ends 152nd Brigade & never regained. In order to get touch with 152nd Brigade on left the last platoon of "A" Coy. were put out, facing from the L of LANNOI to about X.2.a.87. They failed, however, to get touch. Information was received that owing to apparent gap on our left the German Light Horse being ordered up to form a defensive flank facing north-east working on LES LOBES and turning in direction of R.26.t.5. to occupy right rear of H.M. Gordons one support platoon of "B" Coy. was sent to get forward right one support platoon of A" Coy. and left on front each into position with one sight in touch with A"Coy. and left on front each with H.M. Gordons.	DM
		9 a.m.	Orders were received for "C" Coy. to come out of Res. Gordons and to move to X.2.c. in support of A"Coy. Major T.M. HENDERSON, M.C. was killed and Bry. adv. appointed to Regiment to command.	
		10.30 a.m.	"C" Coy. was reported to be in position. In order to keep touch with H.M. Gordons who were falling back, and to prevent "A" Coy. & Platoon of "B" Coy. on left from having to swing back, the last support platoon of B. Coy. was ordered forward to keep touch with H.M. Gordons. At same time instructions were received from Brigade that a mixed company numbering 109 under an Officer of the Northumberland Fusiliers was being	

WAR DIARY
or
INTELLIGENCE SUMMARY.
(Erase heading not required.)

Army Form C. 2118.

Place	Date	Hour	Summary of Events and Information	Remarks and references to Appendices
				D.M.
		11.15 am	King sent to relieve "D" Coy. and that "D" Coy. moved in reply came back to Platoon in W.12.a. Bryans Brown.	
		11.30 am	One platoon of "C" Coy. was ordered up to support "B" Coy. in X.2.a. as others appeared to be developing from X.32.d. Another platoon & a section of "C" Coy. were sent to establish a line on the other side of the movement in X.1 based at as other had still appeared to be sharp.	
		11.45 am	Instructions were received from Brigade that owing to troops on the right falling back "D" Coy. would remain where they were.	
		2.35 pm	Orders were received from Brigade that "D" Coy. should come out of their line and dispose themselves as follows, 1 platoon in W.6.b. at disposal of H. Gordon, and 1 platoon at X.1.C. to keep up a defensive line. These dispositions were completed and 4th Gordons informed.	
		4.30 pm	Companies were shell in some positions. Heavy machine gun fire from across canal and shelling in LOC and East areas.	
		4.25 pm	Information received that 2nd Division was coming up in relief.	
		7.0 pm	Report was received that a considerable number of the enemy were in the town. It was across the canal and LE CASAN where machine guns had they had into houses and Artillery fire was asked for on these houses, also stores moving at Louisa.	

Army Form C. 2118.

WAR DIARY
or
INTELLIGENCE SUMMARY.
(Erase heading not required.)

Instructions regarding War Diaries and Intelligence Summaries are contained in F. S. Regs., Part II. and the Staff Manual respectively. Title pages will be prepared in manuscript.

Place	Date	Hour	Summary of Events and Information	Remarks and references to Appendices
	10/4/18	1 am	Warning order of relief received.	
		3.30am	Orders for relief by 2nd Royal Scots were received and all companies were instructed in relief to proceed to Assembly positions in Q.33.a.	
		5 am	Relief complete.	
			On reaching LA BASSEE Canal orders were received to line the Bank occupying to enemy, Inchebroken in Q.26. Disposition on the Bank were at once put in place. Defence of bridges in Q. in charge on PYC.	
		6 pm	On reaching movements of the enemy were seen entering the northern end of CALONNE.	
		10 pm	Orders were received that Brigade were to withdraw that night into the Divisional Reserve at BUSNES, and that officers of Canal were to be relieved over to 2nd Suffolks. On withdrawing Battalion were instructed to proceed to Brigade H.Q. at W.S.a.1.3. resting further orders marched to BUSNES.	
	11/4/18	1 am	Withdrawal complete.	
		2 am	Reported at Brigade H.R.	
		3 am	Proceeded to billets in BUSNES where Battalion remained until following day.	D.M.

Casualties during above four days:-

KILLED		MISSING		WOUNDED	
OFF.	O.R.	OFF.	O.R.	OFF.	O.R.
2	22	—	12	3	94

Army Form C. 2118.

WAR DIARY
or
INTELLIGENCE SUMMARY.
(Erase heading not required.)

Instructions regarding War Diaries and Intelligence Summaries are contained in F.S. Regs., Part II. and the Staff Manual respectively. Title pages will be prepared in manuscript.

Place	Date	Hour	Summary of Events and Information	Remarks and references to Appendices
Billet in BUSNES	14/9/18	1.30pm	Orders received that Bryans are to prepare to relieve Henry's Force east of ROBECQ today	DH.
		4pm	Orders & dispositions for above move received and that strength of the Battalion alongside men of Echelon B at present in remainder Major Shaw will join in relief. Bryans Reserve P.23.d.	
		8.30pm	Orders received to move to east trench of ROBECQ to relieve Henry's Force	
		9.30pm	Battalion moved.	DH.
	15/9/18	1am	Relief complete & Major Shaw took command. Battalion dispositions — "C" & "D" Coys in dugouts from about P.17.C.5.4. to P.30.G.5.2. posts B. Coy in Battalion Reserve in P.27.C and "A" Coy. Echelon B in Brigade Reserve at P.23.C. and 26.d. Battalion in touch with Hampshire Batt. on the right and 2nd Duke of Cornwall's Bn. on the left.	
	16/9/18	8.30pm	Instructions received that the front would be reorganised tonight and that Battalion would take the whole Brigade front from the Canal to P.24.G.5.7. taking over right as per plan issued by 5th Corps.	DH.
		10.30pm	Warning orders & relief for tomorrow received	
	17/9/18	3am	Readjustment complete. Instructions received that Brigade is attached to 61st Division.	DH.

A.5834 Wt.W4973/M687 750,000 8/16 D.D.&L.Ltd. Forms/C.2118/13.

Army Form C. 2118.

WAR DIARY
or
INTELLIGENCE SUMMARY.
(Erase heading not required.)

Instructions regarding War Diaries and Intelligence Summaries are contained in F. S. Regs., Part II. and the Staff Manual respectively. Title pages will be prepared in manuscript.

Place	Date	Hour	Summary of Events and Information	Remarks and references to Appendices
	17/4/18	2.30pm	Orders received that 4th Seaforth will relieve the Battalion to-night and that the Battalion and Echelon B will proceed back to LA MIQUELLERIE. Relief complete.	Dh.
	18/4/18	11pm	Arrived at LA MIQUELLERIE.	Dh.
	19/4/18	12.30am	Billets at LA MIQUELLERIE. Lieut. Col. J.R. Durie, M.C., rejoined from hospital.	Dn.
	20/4/18		In Billets at LA MIQUELLERIE. Companies re-organising. MAJOR I.W. WATSON taken on strength.	Dn.
	21/4/18		In Billets. Lila Church Parade. Batt⁰ moved off at 7 & 5 p.m. to relieve 4th Seaforth Highrs in ROBECQ DEFENCES.	Dn.
	22/4/18		In line holding ROBECQ Defences.	Dn.
	22/4/18		Lost attack by troops of 61ˢᵗ & 4ᵗʰ Divn lobby the line in front of Battⁿ.	
	23/4/18		In line holding ROBECQ Defences. Unsuccessful counter attack by the enemy on own Brigade Frontage on 22ⁿᵈ.	Dh.
	24/4/18		Relieved this morning by 1/4 Black watch. 153 bdy & 1 Carnells. during torn 3 hellcos S'rounded as BG HQ. was L'bardid at intrvls during relief with H.E. & Gas, especially on evening of 22ⁿᵈ & morning 23ʳᵈ.	Dh.

A 5834/1 Wt. W4973/M687 750,000 8/16 D. D. & L. Ltd. Forms/C.2118/13.

Army Form C. 2118.

WAR DIARY
or
INTELLIGENCE SUMMARY.
(Erase heading not required.)

Instructions regarding War Diaries and Intelligence Summaries are contained in F. S. Regs., Part II. and the Staff Manual respectively. Title pages will be prepared in manuscript.

Place	Date	Hour	Summary of Events and Information	Remarks and references to Appendices
	24/4/18 (cont)		What remained 11:55 a.m. and Bath marched back to billets in St HILAIRE where it was joined by Lt. B. Sudbury & draft of 5 officers & 210 O.Rs which had arrived while Bath was in the line.	O.M.
ST HILAIRE	25/4/18		In billets - cleaning Reorganizing	O.M.
	26/4/18		Do. Commenced training	O.M.
	27/4/18		Do. training	O.M.
	28/4/18		Do. Church parade	O.M.
	29/4/18		as Evening	O.M.
	30/4/18		do training	O.M.

J.R. Smith Lt. Col.
Comdg 11th E.A. Bn

7th Arg & Suth. Hrs

APRIL, 9th, 1918.

9-30 a.m.   Message received from Brigade that hostile operations now proceeding appeared to be a raid against the Portuguese and that front line communications had been cut; that 152nd Brigade had moved to defended localities at HUIT MAISONS and LACOUTURE.

10-50 a.m.   Message from Brigade that 4th Gordon Highrs. and 7th A.& S. Highrs. will stand by ready to move at short notice.

11-30 a.m.   Message received from Brigade that enemy attacking north of LA BASSEE Canal with Five Divisions.

12-30 p.m.   Orders received to move to LOCON and LES CHOQUAUX - 2 Companies at latter place.

2 p.m.   Battalion moved as ordered, but at Bridge at W.11.a.6.0 was stopped by an Officer of the Brigade Staff and instructions received that the whole Battalion would proceed to W.6.d. where further instructions would be received.

4-30 p.m.   Battalion arrived in W.6.d. and were placed by Companies in groups in the fields in W.6.d and X.1.c and W.12.b.

5-5 p.m.   Orders were received from Brigade to occupy the LOCON defences in X.2.c., X.1.d. and X.7.b. to get in touch with 152nd Brigade whose right rested about X.2.d.5.6 west of Canal, also to get in touch with Pioneers in 55th Division holding the MESPLAUX Group, further to form a defensive flank facing north in front of LA TOMBE WILLOT, R.31.c. and d.

5-30 p.m.   "A" Company were sent to form a defensive flank facing north in front of LA TOMBE WILLOT, "B" Company were sent to occupy the defences of LOCON in X.2.a. and c., "C" and "D" Companies were placed in support in X.1.c and d.

6-15 p.m.   Following verbal orders, "D" Coy. were sent to take up a position on west of Canal with their left in touch with 152nd Brigade about the Footbridge in X.3.a. and their right on LE CASAN.

10-30 p.m.   Dispositions were as follows - 2 Companies ("D" and "B") in depth from Footbridge in X.3.a. west of Canal in touch with 152nd Brigade to LE CASAN, east of Canal in touch with 55th Division, "A" Coy. facing north in front of LA TOMBE WILLOT, "C" Coy. in reserve in X.1.c., Battalion H.Q. in House about W.12.b.9.8

11-30 p.m.   Orders received to re-organise front on to a three-Company front on the line of the LAWE Canal from X.14.a.0.3 to junction with 152nd Brigade at about X.2.d.3.9 and that reserve Company in X.1.c. might be used by O.C. Battalion.

Commanding Officer met Company Commanders of "A", "B" and "D" Companies and instructed them to take up the following positions, each Company with two platoons in front and two in support, "A" Coy. on left in touch with 152nd Brigade about X.2.b.7.3 to X.2.d.3.0, "B" Coy. from latter point to about X.8.c.8.7, "D" Coy. from latter point to about X.14.a.0.7. Platoons in support in LOCON defences line behind their respective Companies.

APRIL, 10th.

4 a.m.   Above dispositions completed.
At the same hour information was received that small parties of enemy had crossed Footbridge in X.3.a. and were in Farm Buildings at X.3.a.2.8, and that 152nd Brigade were going to drive them back, and that the Battalion was to co-operate by fire.

5 a.m.   Verbal orders were received for "C" Coy. to leave their position and to come into line on right of "D" Coy., and that any reinforcements required would be provided by Brigade.

6 a.m.   "C" Coy. had moved to position with right at X.13.d.1.1 in touch with 55th Division, and left at X.13.b.8.1 in touch with "D" Coy.

7-50 a.m.	Information was received that support troops of 152nd Brigade were not in touch with our support, and instructions sent to "A" Coy. to get in touch.
11-30 a.m.	Report was received from "A" Coy. of enemy concentration at Footbridge and in Buildings X.3.a.and b.
11-40 a.m.	Instructions were sent to "A" Coy. to endeavour to destroy Footbridge.
1 p.m.	A report was sent to Brigade that left Company were in touch with 152nd Brigade both in front and support and that left Company's left rested on the L of LANNOT, "A" Coy. having put one support platoon into the front line to effect this in X.2.b.
	From this time onwards enemy continued to press forward on left of Battalion and to endeavour to cross footbridge in X.3.a. Enemy brought heavy machine gun fire to bear on our front and intermittently shelled front line and LOCON. Brigade on left were gradually forced back.
6-30 p.m.	Lieut.Col.J.A.DURIE, M.C., was wounded and Major J.M.HENDERSON, M.C., came up to take command.

APRIL, 11th.

	During the early morning touch was lost with 152nd Brigade and never regained.
8 a.m.	In order to get touch with 152nd Brigade on left the last platoon of "A" Coy. were put into position from the L of LANNOT to about X.2.a.8.7. They failed, however, to get touch.
	Information was received that owing to apparent gap on our left 4th Gordon Highrs. were being ordered up to form a defensive flank facing north-east with right resting on LES LOBES and running in direction of Q.36.b. In order to get touch with right of 4th Gordons one support platoon of "B" Coy. was put in position with its right in touch with "A" Coy., and left in touch with 4th Gordons.
9 a.m.	Orders were received for "C" Coy. to come out of their positions and to move to X.2.c. in support of "A" Coy. Major J.M.HENDERSON, M.C., was killed, and Brigadier instructed the Adjutant to command.
10-30 a.m.	"C" Coy. was reported to be in position.
	In order to keep touch with 4th Gordons who were falling back, and to prevent "A" Coy. and platoon of "B" Coy. on left from having to swing back, the last support platoon of "B" Coy. was ordered forward to keep touch with 4th Gordons.
	At same time instructions were received from Brigade that a mixed company numbering 100, under an Officer of the Northumberland Fusiliers was being sent to relieve "D" Coy. and that "D" Coy. would, on relief, come back to positions in W.12.a. in Brigade Reserve.
11-15 a.m.	One platoon of "C" Coy. was ordered up to support "B" Coy. in X.2.a. as attack appeared to be developing from X.3.d.
11-30 a.m.	Another platoon and a Lewis gun section of "C" Coy. were sent to help 4th Gordons on the other side of the main road in X.1.b.and d. as their line still appeared to be shaky.
11-45 a.m.	Instructions were received from Brigade that owing to troops on the right falling back "D" Coy. would remain where they were.
2-30 p.m.	Orders were received from Brigade that "D" Coy. should come out of their line and dispose themselves as follows- 3 platoons in W.6.b. at disposal of 4th Gordons, and one platoon at X.1.c. to help to dig a defensive line.
4-30 p.m.	These dispositions were completed and 4th Gordons informed.
7-35 p.m.	Companies were still in same position. Heavy machine gun fire from across Canal and shelling on LOCON and back areas.
7-50 p.m.	Information received that 3rd Division was coming up in relief.

10 p.m.   Report was received that a considerable number of the enemy were in the houses across the Canal in LE CASAN where machine guns had been put into position and Artillery fire was asked for on these houses, also Stokes mortars if possible.

12th APRIL.

1 a.m.   Warning order of relief was received..

3-30 a.m.   Orders for relief by 2nd Royal Scots were received and all Companies were instructed on relief to proceed to Assembly positions in Q.33.a.

8 a.m.   Relief complete.

On reaching LA BASSEE Canal orders were received to line the bank owing to enemy penetration in Q.26. Dispositions on the bank made at once with special defence of bridges as far as bridge in P.29.c.

6 p.m.   Considerable number of the enemy were seen entering the northern end of CALONNE.

10 p.m.   Orders were received that Brigade would be withdrawn that night into Divisional Reserve at BUSNES, and that defences of Canal would be handed over to 2nd Suffolks. On withdrawing Battalion were instructed to proceed to Brigade H.Q. at W.8.d.1.8, pending further withdrawal to BUSNES.

13th APRIL.

1 a.m.   Withdrawal complete.

2 a.m.   Reported at Brigade H.Q.

3 a.m.   Proceeded to Billets in BUSNES where Battalion remained until following day.

Casualties during above four days:-

	KILLED.		MISSING.		WOUNDED.
Off.	O.R.	Off.	O.R.	Off.	O.R.
2.	22.	-	12.	3.	84.

20th April, 1918.

Commanding 7th Arg. & Suth. Highrs.
Lieut. Col.,

Reference your B.M.377, para.2.

Headquarters,
154th Infantry Brigade.

LESSONS LEARNT.

No new lessons were learnt, the enemy employed exactly the same tactics here as in the SOMME, viz:- Dribbling forward to Assembly, light M.Gs.first and Infantry following, during which time a heavy barrage with 106 fuze was kept up, M.Gs. then opened destructive fire to enable infantry to get close enough for assault.

It would be very interesting to learn how the enemy maintains his supply of S.A.A. We find it hard enough to keep our 16 L.Gs.supplied, and yet he has about double the number of guns and they never show any regard for the amount of S.A.A. they are using. Some very valuable information might be obtained from prisoners of M.G.detachments on this point.

SUGGESTIONS.

That a much more offensive policy be adopted. This continual defensive action is having an extremely deleterious effect on the morale of our troops. Wherever the enemy has established himself in Farm houses etc. close to our line he ought to be raided at dusk with or without artillery. Sharp shooters should be pushed forward into Farm-houses and other cover to harass the enemy's movements. An organised offensive by about a Brigade of this Division would, I am sure, have an excellent effect on the morale of the troops.

Very vigorous steps must be taken at once to stop the policy of withdrawing as soon as the enemy have got within 200 or 300 yards of our line. This is greatly due to the fact that we have, on so many occasions, been told to hold a line "at all costs" and have been fully prepared to do so, and then orders have come to withdraw owing, generally, to flanks having been turned, consequently the men have come to think that "at all costs" means only until your flanks are threatened. I consider that the promiscuous use of the expression "at all costs" is to be deprecated.

The average type of German is a miserable creature, and is only kept going by his continuous successes, and as soon as our troops begin to show an offensive policy I am convinced that the enemy will not put up much of a fight.

20th April, 1918.

Lieut.Col.,
Commanding 7th Arg.& Suth.Highrs.

(6339) Wt. W160/M3016 1,500,000 10/17 McA & W Ltd (E 1898) Forms W3091.   Army Form W.3091.

Cover for Documents.

Nature of Enclosures.

7th Argyll & Sutherland Highlanders.

War Diary.

May 1918.

Notes, or Letters written.

Army Form C. 2118.

WAR DIARY
or
INTELLIGENCE SUMMARY.
(Erase heading not required.)

Place	Date 1918	Hour	Summary of Events and Information	Remarks and references to Appendices
ST HILAIRE	1st May		Billets Training	WD
	2nd		do do	WD
	3rd		do do Battalion Sports. Warning order received for transfer of 51st (H) DIV to XVII Corps. Orders received for Transport to proceed to ECOIVRES	
	4th		Billets Training	WD
	"	5.40 AM	Transport moved off for ECOIVRES. Movement order received for Battn. to proceed to ECOIVRES	WD
	5th	4.45 PM	Battn. marched out of Billets entrained at LILLERS detraining at MAREUIL WD	
ECOIVRES	6th		Billets VILLAGE CAMP. Warning order received to move forward to Reserve Area	WD
	7th	9.45 AM	Battn. marched from ECOIVRES to ECURIE WOOD CAMP	WD
ECURIE	8th		Battn training	WD
	9th		do	WD
	10th		do	WD
LINE	11th		Relieved 7th Bn Gordon Hrs in Left sector Brigade front, in front of OPPY WOOD. A+B Coys in front line, D in support C Coy reserve. 2 Other ranks killed 70 wounded.	WD
	12th		Holding line. Working parties, patrols. Line quiet, Harrasing fire by our artillery at night.	

WAR DIARY
or
INTELLIGENCE SUMMARY.
(Erase heading not required.)

Army Form C. 2118.

Instructions regarding War Diaries and Intelligence Summaries are contained in F. S. Regs., Part II. and the Staff Manual respectively. Title pages will be prepared in manuscript.

Place	Date	Hour	Summary of Events and Information	Remarks and references to Appendices
LBNE	13/5/15		Holding line, Working parties & Patrols. Line quiet. Harassing fire by our artillery at Night	W.R.
	14/5/15		Quiet – Company relief. D coy relieved B. C coy relieved A. 2nd Lieut Page wounded on Patrol.	W.R
	15/5/15		Lieut Cat Farquhar D.S.O wounded. Commanded Bn wh[o] relieved by Cdt Ritchie. Holding line. Working parties & patrols. Line quiet. Harassing fire by our artillery at night.	W.R
	16/5/15		Front line heavily shelled with gas from 8.00 PM. 2nd Lieuts Harkin, McKindry & Stevenson + 140 other ranks gassed.	W.R
	17/5/15		Bn relieved by 14th Bn. 70th Bn Highlanders. Took over Reserve area in BRIERLY HILL. 3 Coys in BROWN line D coy in Bn Hqrs in BRIERLY HILL. Returns owing to A.D.H.C. B.C & heavily shelled. 2 other ranks killed, 16 wounded.	W.R
	18/5/15		1.O. eng. Working parties.	W.R
	19/5/15		Working parties	W.R
	20/5/15		Working parties	W.R
	21/5/15		From 1am shelled with gas from 9PM. No casualties. Working parties.	W.R
	22/5/15		New disposition of Brigade. Motor tons our right sector of Bn. area in BAILLEUL. D 1 B. Hqrs at Railway Embankment. Working parties.	W.R

A 8534 Wt. W4973/M687. 750,000 8/16 D. D. & L. Ltd. Forms/C.2118/13.

Army Form C. 2118.

WAR DIARY
or
INTELLIGENCE SUMMARY.
(Erase heading not required.)

Instructions regarding War Diaries and Intelligence Summaries are contained in F. S. Regs., Part II. and the Staff Manual respectively. Title pages will be prepared in manuscript.

Place	Date	Hour	Summary of Events and Information	Remarks and references to Appendices
LINE	23/5/18		Batt. retired + 5th Bn Seaforth Highlanders marched to ROCLINCOURT WEST Camp.	WD
	24/5/18		Batt. training. 31 O.R. joined Battn.	WD
	25/5/18		do. 2 Officers taken on strength	WD
	26/5/18		do	WD
	27th		do	WD
	28th		do. Orders received from 154 Bde to relieve 7th Black Watch in line	WD
	29th		do. Lt Dougles Major Watson Capt Roberton + O.R. accidentally wounded during a demonstration of Bombing. Major R Ferne M.C. assumes Command. Bn relieved 7th R.H. in left Sector GAVRELLE Sector	WD
	30th		Holding line. Patrols & working parties. Line quiet.	WR
	31st		Holding line. Patrols & working parties. Line quiet. Capt Richardson & 2/Lt Morris reported for duty.	WR
	1st/6		Holding line. Patrols & working parties. Enemy quite. Word received about new disposition. The Bn held line on Bn in each. Back area Blgr 8.25 shelled with Gas shells	WR
				WR

2nd June 1918.

Alan Henry Major
Commanding 7th Bn Black Watch

S E C R E T. *War Diary "G" appt* Copy No...... 3

154th INFANTRY BRIGADE
OPERATION ORDER NO. 21.

Ref. Map :-
MARŒUIL Special Sheet: 1/20,000.

---

1. 154th Inf. Brigade will relieve 153rd Inf. Brigade in the OPPY Sector on night 11th/12th May, 1918, as under :-

   4th Seaforth Highrs. will relieve 7th Black Watch (Royal Highlanders) in Right Subsector - Battalion H.Q. B.15.c.6.1.

   7th Arg. & Suth'd. Highrs. will relieve 7th Gordon Highrs. in Left Subsector - Battalion H.Q. B.15.a.2.4.

   4th Gordon Highrs. will relieve 6th Black Watch (Royal Highlanders) in Support. Battalion H.Q. B.20.b.0.6.

   154th T.M. Battery will relieve 153rd T.M. Battery - Headquarters B.21.a.7.7.

2. Battalions proceeding to front line trenches will not pass DAYLIGHT RAILHEAD, B.19.d.4.9. before 8.30 p.m.
   4th Gordon Highrs. will not pass above point before 10 p.m.
   154th T.M. Battery will complete relief by 8 p.m.
   All movement East of GREEN LINE to be by trenches during hours of visibility.

3. Advance parties from Battalions of 154th Brigade as under will report at Battalion Headquarters in the line at 2 p.m. on 11th May.

   One Officer and one N.C.O. per Battalion H.Q.
   One Officer per Company and one N.C.O. per Platoon.
   Battalion Gas N.C.O's.
   One Officer per Battalion to act as Work's Officer.

   Above personnel will take over all Trench Stores, Gas Appliances and Reserve Rations and will make themselves thoroughly acquainted with their Sectors and will remain in the line.

4. The nucleus garrison of one platoon each to the following posts at present held as under :-

   POINT DU JOUR REDOUBT - 4th Seaforth Highrs.
   RAILWAY POST)
   RIDGE POST   )   - 4th Gordon Highrs.

will be relieved by 6th Black Watch.
   All arrangements for relief of these posts will be made direct.

5. Further details of relief will be made direct between C.O's concerned.

6. All maps, photos, schemes of work, defence schemes, trench stores, etc., will be taken over on relief. Lists of trench stores taken over will be forwarded to Brigade Headquarters by 6 p.m. on 12th May.

7/

- 2 -

7. Disposition maps showing posts and location of platoons will be forwarded to Brigade Headquarters by 5 p.m. 12th May. O.C. 154th T.M. Battery will forward map showing position of each gun.

8. (a) Echelon "B" will not proceed to trenches but will take over accommodation in BRAY WOOD, at present occupied by Echelon "B" of 153rd Infantry Brigade.

(b) Battalions of 154th Infantry Brigade will hand over their present Camps to representatives of the Battalions of 153rd Infantry Brigade which they will relieve in the line.

(c) On completion of relief all transport of 154th Infantry Brigade will concentrate in present lines at ECOIVRES.

9. Battalions will forward return to Brigade Headquarters by 8 p.m. on 11th May showing   numbers proceeding to trenches.

10. The Defence Scheme (Provisional) for Brigade in Divisional Reserve will be handed over to advanced parties of Units of 153rd Infantry Brigade.

11. Brigade Headquarters will close at A.20.d.3.2. at 11 p.m. and open at A.22.d.9.0. at 11.30 p.m. on 11th May.
B.G.C. 154th Infantry Brigade will take over command of the Sector on completion of relief.

12. Completion of relief will be reported to Brigade Headquarters by code word "MARMONT".

13. ACKNOWLEDGE.

Captain,
Brigade Major,
154th Infantry Brigade.

10th May, 1918.

Issued at 7 p.m. by Orderly.

Copies to :-
1. 4th Seaforth Highrs.
2. 4th Gordon Highrs.
3. 7th A. & S. Highrs.
4. 154th T. M. Battery.
5. 51st (H) Division "G".
6. 51st (H)   "   "A".
7. 51st Bn. M.G.C.
8. 152nd Infantry Brigade.
9. 153rd   "   "
10. 155th   "   "
11. H.Q. 15th Div. Artillery.
12. 71st Bde. R.F.A. (15th D.Arty.).
13. 401st Field Coy. R.E.
14. 1/3rd (H) Field Ambulance.
15. No. 2 Coy. A.S.C.
16. Area Commandant, ROCLINCOURT.
17.   "   "   ECURIE.
18. Brigade Major.
19. War Diary.
20. File.

S E C R E T.

War Diary 9 App II

Copy No.

154th INFANTRY BRIGADE
OPERATION ORDER NO. 22.

Reference Map :-
MAREUIL Special Sheet 1/20,000.

1. The 4th Gordon Highrs. will relieve the 7th Arg. & Suth'd. Highrs. in the Left Subsector of the Brigade Front by daylight on the 17th May, 1918.

2. All movement will be in trenches by parties not exceeding half platoons at 100 yards intervals, and relief to be completed by 8.30 p.m. All further details of relief will be arranged between C.O's concerned.

3. All Trench Stores, Aeroplane Photos and Trench Maps will be taken over and receipts forwarded to Bde. H.Q. by noon, 18th instant.

4. All work programmes will be taken over and the Brigade Working Parties detailed in B.257 will be found on 17th May as follows :-

    A, E, F, G to be found by 7th A. & S. Highrs.
    B, C, H, K   "   "   "   " 4th Gordon Highrs.
    D   "   "   "   " 4th Seaforth Highrs.

A new Brigade Working Party Table will be issued for subsequent days.

5. Completion of relief will be reported to Brigade H.Q. by the following code :-

    4th Gordon Highrs. 200422, Pte. McFAE, H.
    7th A. & S. Highrs. 213742, Cpl. FRASER, A.

6. Command of the Subsector will pass upon completion of relief.

7. Battalions to acknowledge.

Captain,
for Brigade Major,
154th Infantry Brigade.

16th May 1918.

Issued at 3.30 p.m. by Orderly.

    Copy No. 1 4th Seaforth Highrs.
           2 4th Gordon Highrs.
           3 7th A. & S. Highrs.
           4 154th T. M. Battery.
           5 51st (H) Division "G".
           6 51st   "   "A".
           7 51st BN. M. G. Corps.
           8 152nd Infantry Brigade.
           9 153rd   "   "
          10 155th   "   "
          11 H.Q. 15th Div. Arty.
          12 71st Bde. R.F.A.
          13 401st Field Coy. R.E.
          14 Brigade Major.
          15 War Diary.
          16 File.

S E C R E T.　　　　　　　　　　　　　　　　　　　Copy No. 3

154th INFANTRY BRIGADE
OPERATION ORDER No. 24.

Ref. Map :-
MAROEUIL Special Sheet 1/20,000.

1. The 154th Inf. Brigade will be relieved in the OPPY Sector by the 152nd Inf. Brigade on the 23rd May, 1918.

2. The relief will be carried out in accordance with -
   (a) Attached March Table.
   (b) Warning Order K.K.152 dated 21st May (issued to Battalions, T.M. Battery and 152nd Inf. Bde.).

3. All transport will come to point at B.19.c.5.5. Carrying parties from this point will use duckboard track and OUSE ALLEY - the Left Battalion carrying party getting from TIRED ALLEY via BRIERLEY HILL. Outgoing Units will arrange so that a long wait at those points is avoided, by transport.

4. Units of 152nd Inf. Brigade will send advance parties consisting of :-
   1 Officer and 1 N.C.O. per Battalion H.Q.
   1 Officer per Company.
   1 N.C.O. per Platoon.
   1 O.R. per gun of T.M. Battery.
   This advance party will be met by one guide from each Battalion and one guide from T.M. Battery at point where footboard track enters the trench B.19.b.55.75. at 10 a.m. and conduct them to a point to be arranged by C.O. concerned where platoon and gun teams will meet them.

5. All trench stores, air photos, and maps will be handed over to relieving Units and receipts forwarded to Brigade Headquarters.

6. All further details will be arranged between C.O's concerned.

7. Platoon in PONT DU JOUR will be relieved by 4th Gordon Highrs. by 2 p.m. 23rd May.
   Platoons in RAILWAY and RIDGE POSTS will be relieved by 4th Seaforth Highrs. by 2 p.m. 23rd May.

   Cancelled

8. Command of Subsections and Section will pass upon completion of reliefs.

9. Completion of relief will be reported by the following code telegrams :-
   4th Seaforth Highrs.　- 201742, Cpl. JOHNSON, P.
   4th Gordon Highrs.　　- 203462, Cpl. DAVIDSON, T.G.
   7th A. & S. Highrs.　 - 204873, Cpl. HUDSON, A.
   154th T.M. Battery　　- 200437, Cpl. RORIE, G.P.

10. Acknowledge,

　　　　　　　　　　　　　　　　　　　　　　　Captain,
　　　　　　　　　　　　　　　　　　　　for Brigade Major,
　　　　　　　　　　　　　　　　　　　154th Infantry Brigade.

22nd May, 1918.

Issued at 2.30p.m. by Orderly.

Copy No. 1 4th Seaforth Highrs.
2 5th Gordon Highrs.
3 7th A. & S. Highrs.
4 154th T. M. Battery.
5 No. 2 Coy. A.S.C.
6 51st (H) Division "G".
7 51st   "   "   "A".
8 152nd Infantry Brigade.
9 153rd   "   "
10 154th   "   "
11 H.Q. 15th Divl. Artillery.
12 71st Bde. R.F.A.
13 51st Bn. M. G. Corps.
14 401st Field Coy. R.E.
15 Brigade Major.
16 Area Commandant, ROCLINCOURT.
17 Town Major, ECURIE.
18 War Diary.
20 File.
19

MARCH TABLE.

Unit and present Location.	To be relieved by Unit of 152nd Bde.	Rendezvous for Guides and time.	Route for both incoming and outgoing Units.	Destinations of Units of 154th Bde.
1. 4th Seaforth Hrs. Centre Battn.	6th Seaforth Hrs.	Junction of broad gauge railway and Concrete Road, B.19.c.5.5. at 3 p.m.	See para.5 of Warning Order K.K.152.	ECURIE, A.27.c.
2. 4th Gordon Hrs. Left Battn.	6th Gordon Hrs.	Plank Road at B.13.a.7.2. at 4 p.m.	-do-	ECURIE, A.27.b.2.9.
3. 7th A. & S. Hrs. Right Battn.	5th Seaforth Hrs.	Junction of broad gauge railway and Concrete Road at 6.30 p.m.	-do-	WEST CAMP, ROCLINCOURT, A.28.a.9.5.
4. 154th T.M. Batty.	152nd T.M. Batty.	Either of above routes but not to use TIRED ALLEY before 3 p.m. or after 7 p.m.	See paras. 5 and 6 of Warning Order K.K.152.	A.20.d.3.2.
5. 154th Inf. Bde. Headquarters.	152nd Inf. Bde. Headquarters.	Junction of broad gauge railway and Concrete Road B.19.c.5.5.	OUSE ALLEY and BRIERLEY HILL. No movement will be allowed by any other route.	New Bde. Hd.Qrs. A.20.d.3.2.

S E C R E T.

App IV

Copy No. 3

154th INFANTRY BRIGADE
OPERATION ORDER NO. 25.

Reference Map :-
MARŒUIL Sheet : 1/20,000.

28th May, 1918.

1. 154th Infantry Brigade will relieve 153rd Infantry Brigade in the GAVRELLE Sector on 29th May, 1918, in accordance with relief table "A" attached.

2. Advance parties from Battalions of 154th Infantry Brigade as under will report at Battalion Headquarters in the line at 10 a.m. on 29th May.
 One Officer and one N.C.O. per Battalion H.Q.
 One Officer per Company and 2 N.C.O's per Platoon.
 Battalion Gas N.C.O's.
 (All first shifts of mining platoons (see Table "B")).
Above personnel will take over all trench stores, gas appliances and reserve rations and will make themselves thoroughly acquainted with their Sectors and will remain in the line.

3. All maps, photos, schemes of work, defence schemes and trench stores will be taken over on relief.

4. Disposition maps showing posts and location of platoons will be forwarded to Brigade Headquarters by 5 p.m. 30th May.

5. Battalions will forward returns to Brigade Headquarters by 2 p.m. 29th May showing numbers proceeding to trenches.

6. Brigade Headquarters will close at A.20.d.3.2. at 8.30 p.m. and open at B.20.b.1.4. at 9.30 p.m. on 29th May.
 B.G.C. 154th Infantry Brigade will take over command of the Sector on completion of relief.

7. Completion of relief will be reported to Brigade Headquarters by code phrase "Your B.M. 99 received".

8. (a) Echelon "B" will not proceed to trenches but will take over accommodation in BRAY WOOD, at present occupied by Echelon "B" of 153rd Infantry Brigade.

 (b) Battalions of 154th Infantry Brigade will hand over their present Camps to representatives of the Battalions of 153rd Infantry Brigade which they will relieve in the line.

9. Acknowledge.

E D C Hunt.
Captain,
Brigade Major,
154th Infantry Brigade.

Issued by Orderly at 5.30 pm

Copy No. 1 4th Seaforth Highrs.
 2 4th Gordon Highrs.
 3 7th A. & S. Highrs.
 4 154th T.M. Battery.
 5 51st (H) Division "G".
 6 51st " " "A".
 7 51st Bn. M.G.C.
 8 46th Inf. Brigade.
 9 152nd " "

No. 10 153rd Infantry Brigade.
 11 H.Q. 15th Divl. Arty.
 12 70th Bde. R.F.A.
 13 400th Field Co. R.E.
 14 1/3rd (H) Fld. Amblce.
 15 No. 2 Coy. A.S.C.
 16 Area Commdt., ECURIE.
 17 Brigade Major.
 18 War Diary.
 19 File.

TABLE "A" to accompany 154th Infantry Brigade O. O. No. 25.

Serial No.	Unit.	Relieves.	H.Q. in the line.	Route.	Guides.	Rendezvous and Time.	Remarks.
1.	4th Seaforth Hdqrs.	6th Black Watch. Right Subsector.	H.S.c.6.8.	By Arty. Route 'B' from G.5.b.7.5. - H.1.b.2.6. - TOWY TRACK - TOWY ALLEY.	1 per platoon. 1 " Coy. H.Q. 1 " Bn. H.Q. 1 for R.A.P.	H.1.b.2.6. 2.30 p.m.	Lewis guns will be carried by Lewis Gun Sections from G.5.b.2.5.
2.	4th Gordon Highrs.	7th Gordon Hrs. Centre Sub-Sector.	B.2?.c.3.?.	CONCRETE ROAD - B.19.c.5.5. - DUCK BOARD TRACK - BRIER-LY HILL - RAILWAY C.T.	As in 1.	B.20.b.1.8. 5 p.m.	Reserve Coy. will leave remainder of Battn. at entrance to RAILWAY C.T. and proceed via Railway cutting and TOWY ALLEY.
3.	7th A. & S. Highrs.	7th Black Watch. Left Subsector.	B.27.b.7.2.	CONCRETE ROAD - B.19.c.5.5. - DUCKBOARD TRACK - OUSE ALLEY - POST LINE or BROWN TRENCH.	As in 1.	B.20.b.1.8. 2.30 p.m.	Lewis Gun limbers of Left and Centre Battns. will proceed as far as B.19.c.5.5.
4.	154th T.M. Battery.	153rd T.M. Bty.	B.26.b.7.2.	To be arranged between C.O's concerned.			

NOTE:- Right Battalion will move by Left Platoons at 300 yds interval whilst on Arty Route "B" and from H.1.b.26 by platoons at 300 yds interval. Left & Centre Battalion will move by Platoons at 300 yds interval.

45th Infantry Brigade No. 227/G. – 8/5/18.

13th Royal Scots.
6th Cameron Highlanders.
11th A. & S. Highlanders.
45th T. M. Battery.

Herewith map showing enemy front line, foot bridges and artillery bridges. *on the map*

A. Ryan
Captain,
Brigade Major, 45th Infantry Brigade.

S E C R E T. — 48th Infantry Brigade No. 227/f.g. — 5/5/18.

13th Bn. The Royal Scots.
6th Cameron Highlanders.
11th A & S. Highlanders.
45th Trench Mortar Battery.

    Herewith Traces "A", "B" and "C" showing :—

"A" S. O. S. Dispositions Artillery.

"B" Trench Mortar Positions.

"C" Machine Gun Positions.

  Please acknowledge.

            Captain,
      Brigade Major, 48th Infantry Brigade.

SECRET. 45th Infantry Brigade No. 201/2 G. - 8/5/18.

13th Bn. The Royal Scots.
6th Cameron Highlanders.
11th A & S. Highlanders.
45th T. M. Battery.

Herewith trace showing S. O. S. Dispositions.

Captain,
Brigade Major, 45th Infantry Brigade

TRACE "A".

To superimpose on Sheet 51ᵇ N.W. 1/20,000.

3-18 Pds Btrs

30
GROUP 4

B
H

5   6
10-18 Pds   GROUP 3

14-18 Pds

11   12
         GROUP 2

8-18 Pds
4-18 Pds
17   18

S.O.S. DISPOSITIONS

S.O.S. DISPOSITIONS.

├──┤ 18 Pdr. Barrage.
⟷ 4·5 How. "

23

H

29
12 – 18 Pdrs.
3 – 4·5" How.

5
3 – 4·5" How.
6 – 18 Pdrs.

6 – 18 Pdrs.
11
3 – 4·5" How.

3 – 4·5" How.
14 – 18 Pdrs.
17
6 – 4·5" How.

1st C.F.A. Bde.
2nd C.F.A. Bde.
36th Bde. R.F.A.

SCALE 1: 20,000
To superimpose on Sheet 51 B N.W.

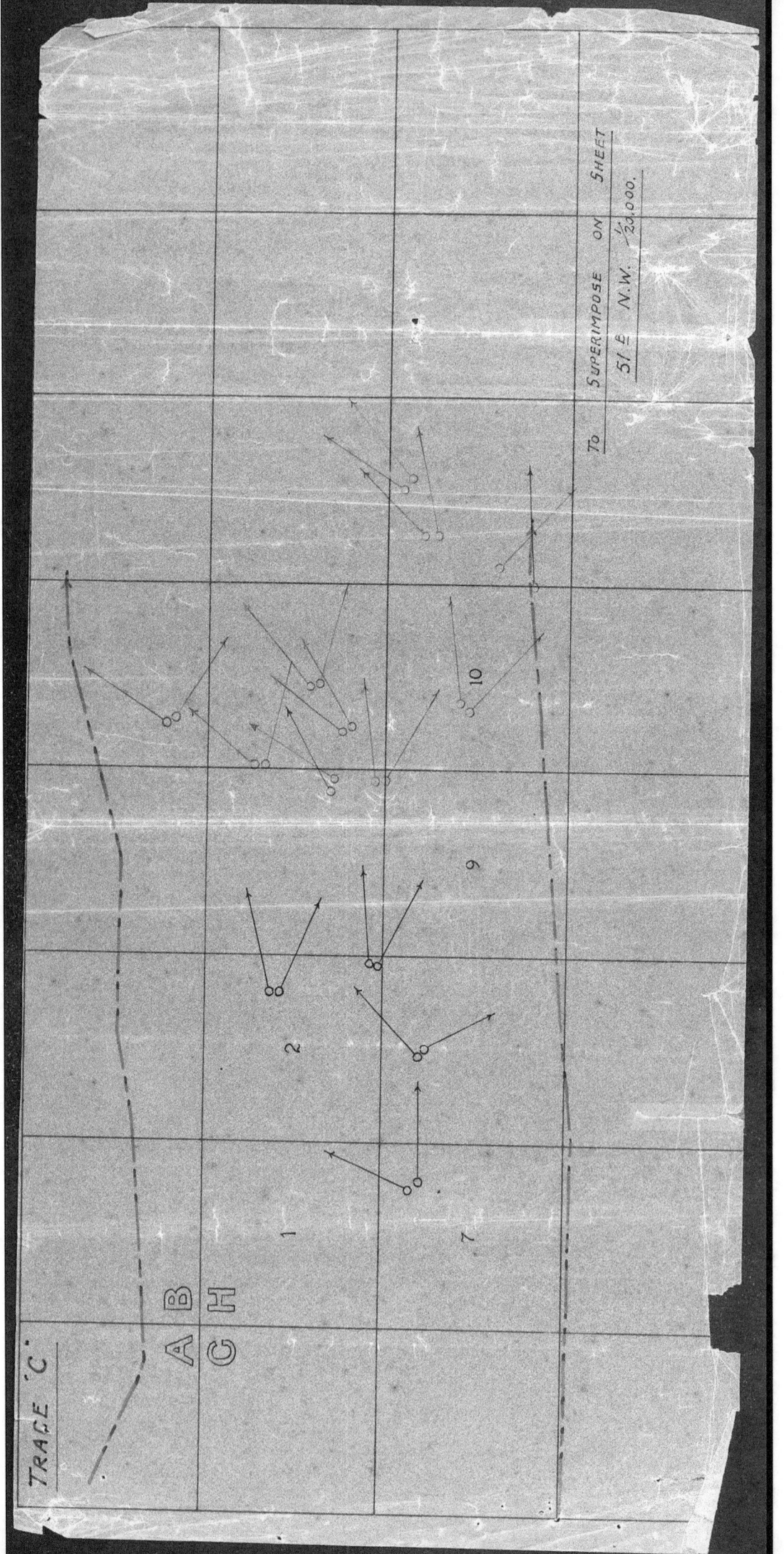

TRACE "B"

LEGEND
LIGHT TRENCH MORTARS
6" NEWTONS Ⓛ

To superimpose on sheet
51 B N.W. 1/20,000

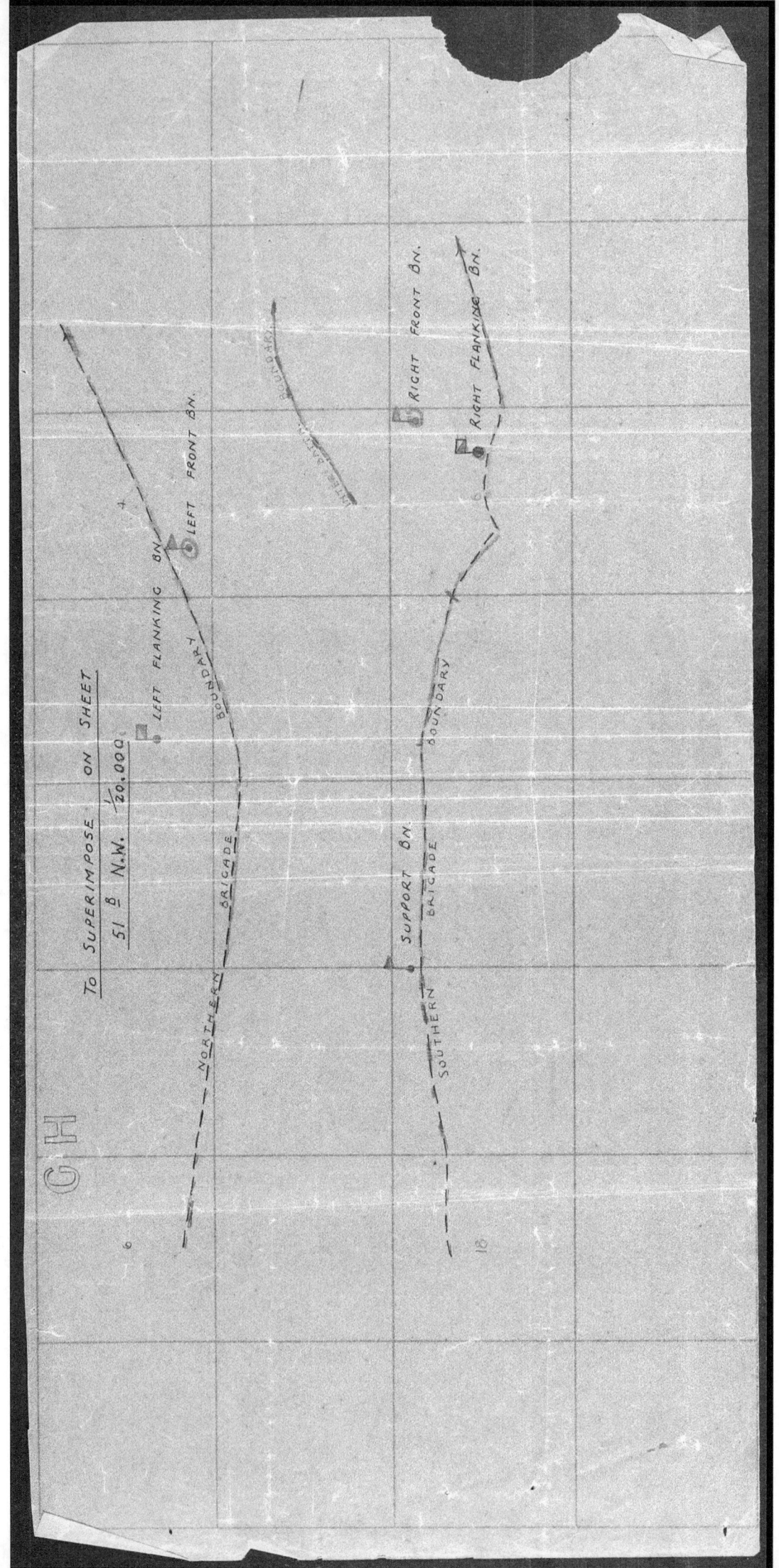

(6339) Wt. W160/M3016 1,500,000 10/17 McA & W Ltd (E1898) Forms W3091. Army Form W.3091.

Cover for Documents.

Nature of Enclosures.

War Diary
for
JUNE, 1918
of
7th Arg & Suth. H.

Notes, or Letters written.

Army Form C. 2118.

WAR DIARY
or
INTELLIGENCE SUMMARY.

(Erase heading not required.)

Instructions regarding War Diaries and Intelligence Summaries are contained in F. S. Regs., Part II. and the Staff Manual respectively. Title pages will be prepared in manuscript.

Place	Date 1918 June	Hour	Summary of Events and Information	Remarks and references to Appendices
LINE	1		Working line Patrols and working parties. Harassing fire by our artillery during evening, own received no reply. 2/Lt Murphy Evacuated	C/A
LINE	2		5/9 (H) Divisional Fld reorganised. 2 batn's heading — on eastern name. Back area B.19 & B.25 shelved with gas (mustard). Patrols & working parties.	C/A
LINE	3		Major Montier assumed command of section. Lt W. Russell M.C. 92/L. & 2/Lt Coleman evacuated. Patrols working parties.	C/A
Line	4		Duty relief. A Coy relieved D Coy, B Coy relieved C Coy. Patrols and working parties. Our artillery harassing fire all day — increasing in intensity during evening.	C/A
LINE	5		Patrols working parties. Line as usual quiet.	C/A
LINE	6		Working parties. 2/Lt T.M.B. Cunningham D.C.M. to hospital	C/A
LINE	7		Enemy artillery very quiet. Patrols working parties. Harassing fire by our artillery throughout.	C/A
LINE	8		Operation orders received from Brigade as relief by 152 Bgde. 2/Lt Orangeas wounded Lt Henderson & J.O. Mc. to hospital. 2/Lt Radcliffe with fighting patrol took a prisoner — German Sgt. Prisoner badly wounded. Information received from prisoner very useful. Patrols working parties.	C/A

Army Form C. 2118.

WAR DIARY
or
INTELLIGENCE SUMMARY.
(Erase heading not required.)

Instructions regarding War Diaries and Intelligence Summaries are contained in F. S. Regs., Part II. and the Staff Manual respectively. Title pages will be prepared in manuscript.

Place	Date June 1918	Hour	Summary of Events and Information	Remarks and references to Appendices
LINE	9		Working parties on artillery dugouts (working fine) during by Lt R.E's A/Cy employed Staff Serjeant going to 12 Coord gas Officer was examined by 2 Lts Cunning, Brooks & Stopford & Majors West & Morrow with satisfactory results. Relieved in night sector (left subsector) by Border Regt.	C.H.
LINE	10		Baton proceeded to Training Camp ROCLINCOURT (arrived 4 pm) Remainder during from & night from time 9am to 10am.	C.H.
ROCLINCOURT	11.		Training under Coy arrangements. Relieving up. Classes of Lewis gun instruction (2 o'p.m day) commenced.	C.H.
ROCLINCOURT	12.		Range practices & training of new squads in Lewis gun.	C.H.
ROCLINCOURT	13		Returned of MEDAL RIBBONS Presentation. Training of Lewis gunners continued. 8 officers & 400 men attend working parties up the line. B/Lt Bottram wounded.	C.H.
ROCLINCOURT	14		Presentation of MEDAL RIBBONS to 154 Infy Bgde by Corps Commander at ECURIE. Operation orders received from Brigade. Re rep of 153 Bgd. in left (OPPY) sector B/Lt Cunningham returned from hospital & Lt. Hil Gibbons Seconded to 154 Bgde.	C.H.
ROCLINCOURT	15		Training in Camp. Lewis gun training continued at 9.45 pm of gas projection at ECURIE.	C.H.
ROCLINCOURT LINE	16		Baton relieving 6th Black Watch in OPPY Sector. 4th Seaforth Highlanders on left & 4th Gordon Highlanders in reserve. Baton moved off from Camp at 1 pm - relief complete 5:20 pm. C & D Coys front line (2 on right & one left) A & B in reserve (A on right, B in redoubt.)	C.H.
LINE	17.		2/Lt McDonald with 6 OR. Training School training centre GRANTHAM. Patrols & working parties. 1 OR wounded.	C.H.
LINE	18.		Patrols & working parties. 10 OR wounded (1 died). Harassing fire by our artillery.	C.H.

WAR DIARY
or
INTELLIGENCE SUMMARY.
(Erase heading not required.)

Army Form C. 2118.

Instructions regarding War Diaries and Intelligence Summaries are contained in F.S. Regs., Part II. and the Staff Manual respectively. Title pages will be prepared in manuscript.

Place	Date	Hour	Summary of Events and Information	Remarks and references to Appendices
LINE	19	9.am	Bttn Cy relief. Atty relieved C.Cy. B Cy relieved D Cy. Parades inspections/Parties 2/Lt Cunningham TM.B. D.C.M. wounded by machine gun in fields in charge of wiring party. Artillery (our own) very active one night.	C.H.
LINE	20		Patrols & working parties. Artillery (our own) active at night.	C.H.
LINE	21		Patrols & working parties. 1 O.R. Killed, 1 O.R. wounded. Harassing fire by our artillery from noon to dusk & all through night. Operation orders received from Bde. re Bttn relief by 4th Bordshire.	C.H.
LINE	22	3am	Successive relief by 13th Royal Scots (15th Div) on right Cy front of Bn on out night. 2/Lts Boothman & Duncan EW rejoined from Hospital. Bttn moved back to Bde reserve 4 Cuys in aux'd aux. The railway embankment between End from HQ to left C.D.A.B1. Bttn in reserve. working parties of Protectiony where Baton arrived.	C.H.
LINE	23		Working parties. 2/Lts Radcliffe & Macqueen to this Bttn. Lt Rushbee rejoined from hospital. Enemy fired guns shelling ARLEUX & OPPY. Artillery (own) active day & night.	C.H. 2.H.
LINE	24		Working parties.	C.H.
LINE	25		Working parties. 2/Lts Walker E.G. & Duncan E.W. to Phosphate TUNNEL DUMP shelled heavily (8.30pm to 8.45pm).	C.H.
LINE	26		Working parties. Harassing fire by our artillery. 1 O.R. wounded (S.I.)	C.H.
LINE	27		Working parties. Operation orders re relief by 152 Bgde received from Bgde. Enemy anti-aircraft guns very active.	C.H.

Army Form C. 2118.

WAR DIARY
or
INTELLIGENCE SUMMARY.
(Erase heading not required.)

Instructions regarding War Diaries and Intelligence Summaries are contained in F. S. Regs., Part II. and the Staff Manual respectively. Title pages will be prepared in manuscript.

Place	Date 1918 June	Hour	Summary of Events and Information	Remarks and references to Appendices
LINE ROLINCOURT	28.		154 Bangade relieved in front OPPY section by 153 Bangade. 4th Aug Batn. in Relieved by 6th Gordon High Landers. Relief complete 6.5 pm. Batn moved back to ROLINCOURT WB camp arriving about 7 pm. 2/Lt Panton rejoined from hospital. 2/Lts Moffat W, Templeton G.A & McKean A.P joined Batn. (reinforcements)	C.H
ROLINCOURT	29		Parade in the morning. Cleaning up. R Roy by Panels Moffat (153 Bangade) at 11.10pm. no identification secured. Raid took place on left sector.	C.H
ROLINCOURT	30	9.30am	Church parade. Working Party; 6 officers & 400 O.R aip in support & reserve line.	C.H

30.6.18.

[signature] Lieut Colonel
Commanding
4th Aug 1918 Bns.

154th Brigade

51st (Highland) Division

7th Battn. ARGYLL & SUTHERLAND HIGHLANDERS

JULY, 1918.

1- Arg + Suth - Jitors

WAR DIARY

INTELLIGENCE SUMMARY
(Erase heading not required.)

Army Form C. 2118.

Place	Date 1918 June	Hour	Summary of Events and Information	Remarks and references to Appendices
ROCLINCOURT	1.		Training under Coy. arrangements in ROCLINCOURT WEST Camp.	C.H.
ROCLINCOURT	2.		Training under Coy. arrangements in ROCLINCOURT WEST Camp. Reinforcement of 153 received from Base.	C.H.
ROCLINCOURT	3.		Route of ANZIN allotted to Battn. Coy. drill. 200 x Ran Ranges (time 1 minute loader with 5 rounds application). L/T. Bantu joined. 2/Lts. Specially reported from Hospital (slip).	C.H.
ROCLINCOURT LINE	4.		Battn relieved the GAVRELLE sector by the 4th Gordon Highlanders. Battn marched from camp at 2 pm. Relief completed 6 p.m. No casualties during relief – line quiet. Patrols sent out during night.	C.H.
LINE	5.		A Coy left 13 Coy night from Coy B 13 right supports. 2/Lt ___ rejoined from hospital.	C.H.
LINE	6.		LINE quiet – on artillery action on enemy from our supports. Enemy artillery quiet. Patrols sending positive. Enemy's artillery active on myL9 – engaged target. Enemy's during. Left driving from B 11 pm. 2Lt. 9 ARLEUX and Enemy during.	C.H.
LINE	7.		Patrols sent up to see terrain on cleared -1 artillery 2/Lt ___ wounded. Our artillery very active on Patrols returning posit. On enemy lines in real- area enemy attacks quick on tracks. Casualties :- wounded 20%. (2 austr) (nex) 2/Lt Brandon 2/Lt W.E.E. men refused from hospital. Capt. S.B.M. Campbell returned on strength.	C.H.

Army Form C. 2118.

WAR DIARY
or
INTELLIGENCE SUMMARY.
(Erase heading not required.)

Instructions regarding War Diaries and Intelligence Summaries are contained in F. S. Regs., Part II. and the Staff Manual respectively. Title pages will be prepared in manuscript.

Place	Date 1916 July	Hour	Summary of Events and Information	Remarks and references to Appendices
LINE.	8.		Patrols out during night. On Artillery active – continuous harassing fire at night. Warning order from Brigade re impending relief by Canadian Division.	C.H.
LINE.	9.		Line quiet – patrols & working parties.	C.H.
LINE.	10.		Operation orders re relief received early morning from Bgde. 152 mfy. Bgde relieved by 10th Canadian Brigade. A'tey 7th Aug 7th the 46th Bn. Canadian Infantry (Tonnel?) proceeded back to TUNNELLING CAMP. ECURIE. to breakfast & ready. Relief complete. Bn. Patrols during morning patrols – line quiet – hostile artillery slightly more active. A'tey proceeded at 10.30am attacks in ANZIN. Battn. also A'tey. relieved by 87th Bn. Can. Infantry & proceeded to billets in Anzin. Enemy artillery active during relief – no casualties. Relief complete 5.10pm. Battn arrived at ANZIN at 7.10 pm, paraded 11.40 pm & marched to ARTILLERY CORNER & entrained on sidings by railway. Breaking party left for MAGNICOURT from ELOUAES at 2 pm under Lt Fraser.	C.H.
LINE. ANZIN.	11.			C.H.
ANZIN. MAGNICOURT.	12.		4.55am. Marched to MAGNICOURT arriving in breakfast. Time at 6 am. B.T.C. enfranid mfr. B.T.C. Coys to billets. Day spent resting & cleaning up.	C.H.

Army Form C. 2118.

WAR DIARY
or
INTELLIGENCE SUMMARY.
(Erase heading not required.)

Instructions regarding War Diaries and Intelligence Summaries are contained in F.S. Regs., Part II. and the Staff Manual respectively. Title pages will be prepared in manuscript.

Place	Date July 1916	Hour	Summary of Events and Information	Remarks and references to Appendices
MAGNICOURT FREVILLERS	13		A.D.M.S. coys. left MAGNICOURT. Battn. marched off at 2.30 p.m. to divisional HQ at FREVILLERS — arriving 3.30 p.m. Training areas reconnoitred by C.O. & Coy Commanders at 6 p.m. Warning order received re. long train journey at 4 p.m. — destination of Divn. unknown.	CH
FREVILLERS	14		Orders for move received 1 a.m. Church parade, Revd. E. Coy., 10 a.m. C. Coy. detailed as Regtl. entraining station BRIAS at 10.30 a.m. and marched off to entraining station. Orders received off 11.10 p.m. to move off 11.10 a.m. Trans/819 Drivers were given LT & E.C. walking wounded from hospital & aero 2/27.	CH
FREVILLERS in TRAIN.	15		CHALONS SUR MARNE area. Battn. marched off 12.15 a.m. to entraining station — arriving BRIAS 3 a.m. Entrained 5.30 a.m. Train started 6 a.m. (hour late). Route ABBEVILLE, PARIS to CHALONS SUR MARNE area.	CH
TRAIN. NOGENT.	16		Received order from division to detrain within an hour at NOGENT as enemy had attacked on wide front (50 miles) and 51st (H) Divn. was ordered up. Battn. less C. Coy detrained NOGENT at 10 a.m. and marched to nearest railway station to await arrival of C. Coy. News received Battn. Transport had 5 train left Battn. Transport had arrived at ROMILLIES and were sent by road to NOGENT in French lorries at 11.30 p.m. arrived by road. Battn. left NOGENT on road. Bn. marched during transport being thrown in road the man railway dog accident — alter two days a.d.g.	CH

A 5834 Wt. W 4973/M687 750,000 8/16 D.D. & L. Ltd. Forms/C.2118/13.

WAR DIARY
or
INTELLIGENCE SUMMARY.

(Erase heading not required.)

Army Form C. 2118.

Instructions regarding War Diaries and Intelligence Summaries are contained in F.S. Regs., Part II. and the Staff Manual respectively. Title pages will be prepared in manuscript.

Place	Date 1918	Hour	Summary of Events and Information	Remarks and references to Appendices
WOOD near CHOUILLY.	July 17.		Arrived in neighbourhood of CHOUILLY at 8 a.m.; Bivouaced in wood south of village - Batn. at 1 hour's notice. C Coy arrived during 9.30 p.m.	CH
WOOD near CHOUILLY	18		Transport arrived at 11 a.m. They had travelled about 50 miles covering a distance of 42 hours owing to station entries in support to Italian entries. Received orders to stand by.	CH
WOODS near CHOUILLY and BELLE VUE	19.		C.O. & O.C. Coys set off to reconnoitre routes at 3.45 a.m. They were turned back. C.O. OC Coys set off to reconnoitre. Batn moved off from Camp at 6 a.m. & marched to wood near BELLE VUE, arriving 12 noon. Received orders 7 p.m. to circle & commence training next morning. Left Bivouac 8.40 p.m. (H) Bn were into rations. Left for 2 hours on road position. French guides missed water and food position near MANTEUIL. Batn heel up for 2 hours on road south of MANTEUIL – no issues going up.	CH
Wood near MANTEUIL.	20		ZERO for attack 8 a.m. Batn arrived in composition at 2.45 p.m. Batn. 4th Inf. Bn the final objective of Brigade - men message of SARCY. Itales fine objective of Brigade - first objective at EVOLENE. 153 Inftry Bgde on right, 154 on left of Brigade. Division on right; 62nd Division on left of Brigade on moving forward. Boxn (C & D Coys fnp.) on attacking in left & 6 Zn In. Sheerers on leaving position 10:15 a.m. Sheerers wounded 2/Lt Musgham. Left assembly position, including 2/Lt Musgham.	

A.5834. NAV W 4973/M.687. 750,000 8/16 D.D. & L. Ltd. Forms/C.2118/13.

WAR DIARY or INTELLIGENCE SUMMARY

Army Form C. 2118.

Place	Date 1918	Hour	Summary of Events and Information	Remarks and references to Appendices
LINE.	21.		and 4th Gordon Hrs lined up, having suffered many casualties. Batn takes over line for Brigade. Brigade attacked with 4 Seaforths Hrs + 4 Gordons, 4th Gordons Hrs with a sprinkling of Batn on flanks pushing on to enemy's positions + positions of Batn were to push on flanks on enemy in mêlée. D Coy pushed forward & occupied high ground near Bois de COUTRON. C Coy pushed ahead as far as positions Forgues line base at day by 4th A.G.H. which D Coy supported. C Coy Right flg Coy on a sprinkling of 4th Seaforths at border Hrs. A Coy supported C Coy. B Coy supported D Coy. During afternoon remaining enemy were driven again to high ground held by remaining unsuccessful. D Coy — attempts Casualties for 4rd day. 2/Lt Radcliffe killed & 2/Lts. Rutherford, Monaghan, McMillan wounded. — 11 OR killed 8 2 OR wounded & 4 OR missing. Baton HQrs were in unable hutment BOULIN BOULIN Farm. — line as arranged the morning. Line improved 4th Gordons Hrs & 4th Seaforths the morning. Casualties Wounded, 2 attacked 12 OR wounded. Enemy shelling heavily + intermittently on Bayne front.	C.T. C.T.

WAR DIARY or INTELLIGENCE SUMMARY

Army Form C. 2118.

Place	Date	Hour	Summary of Events and Information	Remarks and references to Appendices
LINE	July 1916 22.		Enemy put down heavy barrage - HE gas - from 2 [hrs?] onwards on positions previously informed. Line 4th Seaforths were relieved by 5/4 Bgde reserve. Casualties 1 OR missing, 10R killed & 10 OR wounded. Enemy shelling heavy all day, & indiscriminately. Received orders at 10pm that attack resuming at 6am. 152 Bgde attached with barrage as 6pm. A. Objectives line running	Capt.
LINE	23.		between & including villages of MARFAUX and ESPILLY. 152 Bgde attack reached ESPILLY. Captured by 62 Div. 152 Bgde 154 Infantry Bgde to attack through wood and reach river & general line. Through were attained with 152 Bgde in right & 153 Bgde in left - 153 Bgde line was seen advanced The day previously no barrage was to be used for wood fighting. ZERO of attack 6am Barrage on left of 152 & of 154 Bgds. Guards Fus in reserve w/ BHQ. Gordons & Royal Scots & Royal E on right Barrage two sections of Lys Bde attached by B Coy & 9 of 8th disorganized attack. Certain day line advanced to depth of 400 yds one platoon of 5th Royal Scots on NW ridge of wood in final attempts as they were not affected by barrage. They captured 28 prisoners & 2 MGs also killed many of the enemy. In all on 9/4th Seaforths attacked. Casualties on 23rd of January 6 OR killed ≈ 250 R wounded. 0/LT McRae wounded & 2/LT Bourdon.	C.H.

WAR DIARY or INTELLIGENCE SUMMARY

Army Form C. 2118.

Place	Date	Hour	Summary of Events and Information	Remarks and references to Appendices
LINE	July 1918 24		Battn advanced into a ridge in COUTRON WOOD. Duranne Bgde disengaged. Through relief by 152 Bgde on right – 15th Bgde on left – 133 Bgde relieved by French. 154 Bgde front were by 7/AID Hrs on right and 4th Seaforth Hrs on left (see in COUTRON WOOD). A coy right front coy, B coy left (front coy), C coy left support, D coy right support – D coy still holding high ground occupied by them on first day. Battn HQrs moved on to COUTRON WOOD. Enemy shelling COUTRON WOOD accurately on paths etc. Heavy barrage put down around 10 pm on enemy front repeated area (see signals on S.O.S.). putting up red lights – on artillery reference area (see signals on S.O.S.). Casualties 4 OR killed, 14 OR wounded. Capt A S H ——— TMC & 2/Lts.	C-1.
LINE	25.		Temperate & Camp fire wounded. Fine improved in COUTRON WOOD & advanced a little. A coy inflicted losses on enemy with rifle grenades etc., knocking out 3 IMG. Casualties 2/Lt Spooner wounded, 1 OR killed, 17 OR wounded. Enemy snipers troublesome in wood, warning order re relief received.	cq.
LINE BELLEWE WOOD	26.		Enemy shelling heavier all day – increased in afternoon. Confirmation orders re relief by 152 Bgde received 11 am. Battn relieved by 7th Seaforth Highlanders. Enemy shelling heavily during night, morning casualties – Bectine Coy, 4 OR killed, 9 OR wounded – one guide having casualties. Relief complete 6.40 pm. Battn moved back via Struntonven into billets in Fnd of	

WAR DIARY
or
INTELLIGENCE SUMMARY.
(Erase heading not required.)

Army Form C. 2118.

Place	Date 1916	Hour	Summary of Events and Information	Remarks and references to Appendices
WOODS near BELLE VUE. ST DENIS.	27		BELLE VUE. Battn HQrs & Officers billeted in huts. Bgde in ST IMOGES area. Casualties 3 OR wounded. 152 & 153 Bgdes & 42 Div's a trench attacked at 7 a.m. Enemy formed the retreating. 154 Bgde ordered up. Operation orders for move off received at 12.45 p.m. Battn moved off at 2 p.m. Street ordered as before. St DENIS FARM. Battn HQrs in ST DENIS FARM. below St DENIS FARM. Casualties 1 OR (self inflicted) wounded.	C.1 C.2
ST DENIS BOIS D'AULNAY HINE	28		Battn moved off at 6 p.m. arriving at BOIS D'AULNAY at 8.45 A.M. C & D Coys lying in sunken road behind BOIS D'AULNAY. Battn H Qrs AT B Coy's in wood. Enemy shelling nearby of ARDRE. Operation orders for move up to line received at 8.45 p.m. Battn moved off 10 p.m. 154 Bgde to take over Divisional front. A/A.T.S relieving 5th S.Lts in reserve. 4th Seaforth 1Hs on 19/19. - 4th Gordon 1Hs on right. Division doing one. for a bit going up. Relief complete 5 am approx. Casualties nil.	C.4
HINE	29		Orders received for 7th AT's Bn to to up on right of Bgde front & take over line — MONTAGNE DE BLIGNY. Battn moved up at 10 pm relieving 8th R.B. and Yorks & 1 Coy 5th West Yorks (62nd Division) on Bgde frontage (8 normal) had been increased Relief complete 4.20 am on 30th. D Coy right front Coy, A Coy Centre Coy, B Coy left front Coy, C Coy in support. Casualties 8 OR wounded.	C.5

WAR DIARY or INTELLIGENCE SUMMARY

Army Form C. 2118.

Place	Date	Hour	Summary of Events and Information	Remarks and references to Appendices
LINE	14/16 July 30		Enemy shelling indiscriminately all day – roads & afterwards nearing attention. Shelling increased towards evening & intensity. S.O.S sent up by Frd line Coy about 6 p.m. Enemy tried to reach the MONTAGNE DE BLIGNY about 8 p.m. on a Cuf frd. Attack completely driven off. Barrage (ours) very good. Casualties 140 killed, 15 OR wounded 2/Lt Evans wounded, 15 OR wounded. 1/Lt Hinton wounded awaiting evac. Wounding men relief by French received. 6/nation orders received re enemy at 2.30 a.m. The Commanders & Coy Commanders of 2nd Bn 44 French Regt came up to arrange about relief. 44th French Regt relieved 152 Infy Bgde. 2nd Bn received 4th A & Bn. Relief started 10 p.m. Enemy shelling heavily during day, breaking off in evening and starting again about 9 p.m. French has casualties from gas. Coy being relieved in evening afterwards from with gas. Relief complete 11.55 p.m. Bn moved back to NANTENIL area. Casualties 11 OR wounded.	CO
	31			CH.

Total casualties from 20th to 31st July

Summary.

Officers 1 killed, 11 wounded (1 at duty). Other ranks 8 missing, 39 killed, 91 wounded (7 at duty).

WAR DIARY
or
INTELLIGENCE SUMMARY.

Army Form C. 2118.

Place	Date	Hour	Summary of Events and Information	Remarks and references to Appendices
			Summary (Continued)	

Prisoners. 1 Officer and 49 other ranks. 2 & (OR) prisoners were captured by 8th R Hy of Scots attacked.

M.G. guns. 19 captured and 9 relieved.

Other war material:- Several old trench & Division field guns 77m/m, were retaken.

During fighting in COUTRON WOOD much assistance was rendered by 40 & 76th Coy RE in clearing paths etc.

2/Lt Trempeteen Died of wounds on 27th July & 2/Lt McKean on 27th of July.

Gauche Stewart
Commanding
4th Aug Platoon Hrs

SECRET

96 46

War Diary

of

7th Battalion, Aug Fifth Do

for

August, 1918.

42.6

Army Form C. 2118.

WAR DIARY
or
INTELLIGENCE SUMMARY.
(Erase heading not required.)

Instructions regarding War Diaries and Intelligence Summaries are contained in F.S. Regs., Part II. and the Staff Manual respectively. Title pages will be prepared in manuscript.

Place	Date 1918	Hour	Summary of Events and Information	Remarks and references to Appendices
NANTEUIL. BELLE VUE.	Aug 1.		Battalion relieved by 2nd Battn, 4th French Regt. on night 31 July / 1 August, and proceeded to neighbourhood of NANTEUIL, arriving there between 12 midnight and 1 am. Battn. HdQrs in NANTEUIL village, and Battn. in wood south of it. Battalion paraded at 8-15 am, marching off 9-30am arriving BELLE VUE. marched off to wood near BELLE VUE at 11am, picking up transport and QM Stores en route - Battalion HdQrs in CHAMPILLON, Battn in wood north of village.	CA
CHAMPILLON	Aug 2.		Battalion spent day in cleaning up, etc. Coys Commanders met all Battn Commanders in Brigade at HQ. Mess at 10am, and immediately afterwards saw Company Commanders and his allotted O.R. per Company in the wood at spoke to Company Commanders and his allotted O.R. per Company in the wood near Battalion lines. Billetting party under Lieut Fraser left at 3pm to proceed in advance by 1st Brigade train from EPERNAY.	CA
CHAMPILLON EPERNAY. TRAIN.	Aug 3.		Battalion paraded 8am, less "C" Coy transport, to march to entraining station, "C" Coy detailed as Brigade entraining party, and marched off with Cooker at 12-30am for entraining station. Transport paraded and marched off to station at 6.30pm Battalion entrained 11-50am, and left EPERNAY, 12/20pm. ROUTE :- Outskirts of PARIS, ABBEVILLE, HESDIN, and BRIAS	CA
TRAIN. BRIAS SAVY-BERLETTE	Aug 4.		Detrained 5/50pm at BRIAS, waited at station for motor lorries till 9/30pm, arrived SAVY, 11 pm.	CA
SAVY.	Aug 5		Cleaning up and resting.	CA
"	Aug 6		Training under Company arrangements.	CA
"	Aug 7		Draft of 19 O.R. taken on strength. " Lewis Gun class of 18 O.R. per Coy started as before. Brigade Gas Officer	CA
"	Aug 8.		" Inspected Box Respirators. " Draft of G.C. STEWART 2/Lts. H.G.B. GUTHRIE and 109 O.R. taken on strength " A.N. FERGUSSON R.N. NISBET D. IRELAND W.F.C. RAE	CA

A5834 Wt. W4973/M687 750,000 8/16 D.D. & L. Ltd. Forms/C.2118/13.

Army Form C. 2118.

WAR DIARY
or
INTELLIGENCE SUMMARY.

(Erase heading not required.)

Instructions regarding War Diaries and Intelligence Summaries are contained in F. S. Regs., Part II. and the Staff Manual respectively. Title pages will be prepared in manuscript.

Place	Date	Hour	Summary of Events and Information	Remarks and references to Appendices
SAVY	1918 Aug 8		Parades as on 8th. Class of Scouts Signallers started	CA
"	Aug 9		" " 9th. 2 Lts. W.M.FINLAY & T.F.MORRISON & 1 O.R. taken on strength. 2/Lt. H.SPENCE rejoined from hospital.	CA
"	" 10		Church parade 10 a.m. C.O. proceeded on leave. MAJOR A.STEIN, M.C. assumed command	CA
"	" 12		Parades as on 9th. "A" & "B" Coys shooting on Miniature Range.	CA
"	" 13		" " 9th. "A" Coy allotted Range (200 yards.) "C" & "D" Coys the Miniature Range	CA
"	" 14		Parades as on 9th. One O.R. taken on strength	CA
"	" 15		Transport paraded and moved off 7.25 a.m. and proceeded by road to the vicinity of ECURIE. Battalion entrained at SAVY. STN. 3 p.m. and proceeded by light railway to ECURIE, arriving 4/10 p.m. Battalion "fell off" at 6 p.m. and proceeded via B. CONCRETE ROAD to line, relieving 4th B. NW ROYAL SCOTS. Relief complete 10/30 p.m. "C" & "D" Coys in front "C" Coy on right "A" & "B" Coys in support "B" Coy on right. Front line Companies sent out small reconnoitering patrols before dawn.	
LINE	" 15			CA
LINE	" 16		Line quiet. Patrols at night. Lt. E.R.SINCLAIR, M.C. joined Battalion.	CA
LINE	" 17		Our artillery active during day, harassing fire at night. Enemy's artillery active at intervals. Fighting patrol out at night. Lieut. A.D.MORRISON, M.C. & 2/Lt. J.MILLAR joined Battalion. & L. G.G.GIBSON rejoined from hospital	CA

WAR DIARY or INTELLIGENCE SUMMARY

Army Form C. 2118.

Place	Date	Hour	Summary of Events and Information	Remarks and references to Appendices
LINE	Aug/18		Line quiet. Daylight patrol went out and found block at TYNE ALLEY junction of TYNE & NORTH TYNE ALLEY) unoccupied — Bombs thrown at patrol from block. Gas beam projector attack on front of Division on left, consequently no patrols at night.	C.A.
LINE	Aug 19		Enemy very quiet after gas attack. Patrols Working parties at night. Fighting patrol found block in TYNE ALLEY unoccupied.	C.A.
LINE	Aug 20		Patrols & working parties at night. Enemy artillery active in afternoon and evening.	C.A.
LINE	Aug 21		Daylight patrol proceeded up TYNE ALLEY and reported block unoccupied. Lt. A N FERGUSSON admitted to hospital. Fighting patrol at night. Patrols & Working parties. 1 O.R. joined	C.A.
LINE	Aug 22		Enemy artillery active at night. Capt. C.C. JOHNSTONE Battalion, also Capt. C.C. JOHNSTONE.	C.N.
LINE	Aug 23		Line quiet. Enemy aircraft active on our lines. Fighting patrol fired on by enemy M.G. on BAILEUL–FOUREUIL ROAD. Capt. C.C. JOHNSTONE to 4 Gordon Hrs. 3 O.R. wounded.	Apps. P.
LINE	Aug 24		Enemy artillery active with H.E. and gas shells on BAILEUL. Enemy aircraft continue to patrol our line actively. Considerable movement observed in enemy lines.	Apps. P.
LINE	Aug 25		c/Capt. W.R. BLAIR, M.C. to hospital (gassed). Patrol found block in TYNE ALLEY unoccupied. Enemy artillery and aircraft active. 1 O.R. arrived (reinforcement) Bright moonlight prevented more active patrolling.	Apps. P.
LINE	Aug 26		Enemy heavy artillery active. Patrols entered MARINE TRENCH. Attack by night. Enemy aircraft. 1 O.R. Killed.	Apps. P.

Army Form C. 2118.

WAR DIARY
or
INTELLIGENCE SUMMARY.
(Erase heading not required.)

Instructions regarding War Diaries and Intelligence Summaries are contained in F. S. Regs., Part II and the Staff Manual respectively. Title pages will be prepared in manuscript.

Place	Date	Hour	Summary of Events and Information	Remarks and references to Appendices
LINE	Aug 27		Patrols pushed out and occupied MARINE TRENCH and N. TYNE ALLEY by night. No enemy resistance. Lieut. STEWART, wounded (at duty), 2nd Lt. GUTHRIE H.Q. 13 hospital. 3 O.R. Killed, 33 O.R. wounded and missing.	
LINE	Aug 28		'B' and 'C' Coys occupied and established posts in MARINE TRENCH, BELVOIR ALLEY CHICO TRENCH to VISCOUNT STREET. Enemy counter-attacked 'B' Coy who withdrew from CHICO TRENCH. Liaison established with 'C' Coy along Railway Trench. 4 O.R. wounded.	
ATHIES LINE at GREENLAND HILL	Aug 29		Battalion relieved about midnight 28/29 by 2nd Royal Berks Regt. Marched to RAILWAY EMBANKMENT behind & WEST of ATHIES. Arrived 3 a.m. C.O. rejoined Battalion after leave. 3 Coys 4th Gordons and 1 coy 6th Black Watch at 6.30 am 'D' coy attacked along with 4th Gordons and succeeded in taking GREENLAND HILL & occupied line on forward slope. Lt. IRELAND D.S.O. & Lt. T.F. MORRISON wounded. 2 O.R. Killed, 22 O.R. wounded.	
LINE	Aug 30		Patrols pushed forward and occupied line WIBBLE WAVY & WASTE 500 yds in advance. 'B', 'A', 'C' Coys in front, 'D' Coy in support. Heavy shelling on our sector. 1 O.R. wounded.	
LINE	Aug 31		Active patrols out met with resistance from enemy in FRESNES-ROUVROY LINE. 2/Lt. McLACHLAN D joined Battalion. 4 O.R. wounded.	

3/9/18

G. Baird
Lt. Col.
Commanding
4th Gordons

Army Form W.3091.

Cover for Documents.

154/51

Nature of Enclosures.

7th A. & S. H.

WAR DIARY

SEPTEMBER, 1918

Notes, or Letters written.

Headquarters,
154th Infantry Brigade.   R O 10

Herewith this Unit's
War Diary for the month
of September, 1918.

Partside
Lt-Col.
Commanding,
1-10-18.   7TH ARG. & SUTH. HRS.

Army Form C. 2118.

WAR DIARY
INTELLIGENCE SUMMARY.
(Erase heading not required.)

Instructions regarding War Diaries and Intelligence Summaries are contained in F. S. Regs., Part II and the Staff Manual respectively. Title pages will be prepared in manuscript.

Place	Date	Hour	Summary of Events and Information	Remarks and references to Appendices
LINE	Sept.1		Patrols out encountered enemy in front of FRESNES-ROUVROY LINE. Relieved by 4th SEAFORTHS in front line about midnight. (Casualties 3 O.R. wounded)	Nil
LINE	Sept 2		A Coy shelled during relief. Reached support position about 4 a.m. Battn. HQs in NORTHUMBERLAND LANE. Quiet during day. Casualties 4 O.R. killed 6 O.R. wounded. 2/Lt N. Scott joined.	Nil
LINE	Sept 3		Quiet on sector. Relief commenced with 6th Black Watch at 9 p.m.	Nil
LINE	Sept 4		Relief complete at 1.45 a.m. Battn. marched to Rly. Embankment at ATHIES.	Nil
RAILWAY EMBANKMENT ATHIES.			Billeted in huts.	
ATHIES	Sept 5		Billets cleaning up during day.	Nil
"	Sept 6		" Training by companies. Drill, shooting at ranges	Nil
"	Sept 7		" " Tactical schemes by Coys.	Nil
"	Sept 8		" " " "	Nil
"	Sept 9		" " " "	Nil
"	Sept 10		" " B.G.C's scheme for 'A' and 'B' Coys.	Nil

WAR DIARY
INTELLIGENCE SUMMARY

Army Form C. 2118.

Instructions regarding War Diaries and Intelligence Summaries are contained in F. S. Regs., Part II. and the Staff Manual respectively. Title pages will be prepared in manuscript.

(Erase heading not required.)

Place	Date	Hour	Summary of Events and Information	Remarks and references to Appendices
ATHIES and FRASER CAMP PONT ST. ELOI.	Sept 11		Drill by Coys during forenoon. At 4:30pm Battalion marched via St. Catherine – Anzin to Fraser Camp, Mont St. Eloi arriving 8pm. Relieving 7th West Yorks based near Anzin.	App P.
MONT ST ELOI	Sept 12		Billets comfortable. Heavy rain prevented active training.	App P.
MONT ST ELOI	Sept 13		Battalion ceremonial parade 9am. Open warfare tactical scheme by Coys to N.C.Os. Football in afternoon. Coy officers lecture.	App P.
MONT ST ELOI	Sept 14		Battalion tactical scheme over open country; one by defenders. Coy officers lecture to N.C.Os. Draft of 94 OR taken on strength. Football in afternoon.	App P.
MONT ST ELOI	Sept 15		Battalion paraded for Divine Service at 10:30 a.m. (B'n' side Service) at Lancaster Camp. 154 Inf. Bde. C.O.'s lecture to all Batns. Football afternoon. C.O.'s lecture at 4 p.m.	App P.
MONT ST ELOI	Sept 16		'A', 'B' & 'C' Coys. on tactical scheme 'The attack' on open country. Witnessed by G.O.C. 51st (H) Div & B.G.C. 154 Inf. Bde. 'D' Coy on tactics. Handling of Lewis Gun. Football afternoon.	App P.
MONT ST ELOI	Sept 17		C & D Coys on open warfare attack scheme. 'A' Coy. tactical scheme. 'B' Coy. inspected by G.O.C. 51st (H) Div. 'D' Coy tactics and handling of Lewis guns.	App P.

Army Form C. 2118.

WAR DIARY
or
INTELLIGENCE SUMMARY.
(Erase heading not required.)

September 1916

Instructions regarding War Diaries and Intelligence Summaries are contained in F. S. Regs., Part II. and the Staff Manual respectively. Title pages will be prepared in manuscript.

Place	Date	Hour	Summary of Events and Information	Remarks and references to Appendices
Mont St Eloi	Sept 18		A, B & C Coys. attack scheme with artillery Co-operation. D Coy at rifle range. Afternoon at Battn. Football.	
Mont St Eloi	Sept 19		A, B & D Coys. attack scheme with artillery co-operation. C Coy bombing practice. Specialists training.	
Mont St Eloi	Sept 20		Battalion Ceremonial parade 9 a.m. Coys. practice drill formations from 10 a.m. to 12-30 p.m. Demonstration of Cooperation of Tanks with Infantry at 11-30 a.m. Final of Divisional Football Cup won by 7th A. & S. H's. by 4 goals to 1 against 7th Black Watch. Presentation of medals by G.O.C. 51st D. was on. Heavy rain prevented actual training. Lectures by Coy. Officers to men. Reconnoitering parties proceed to FAMPOUX to see newly portioned of Battalion in support in GREENLAND HILL Sector. Draft of 35 O.R. arrived from U.K.	
Mont St Eloi	Sept 21		Orders to embus at 12 noon, for support lines in GREENLAND HILL Sector Postponed at 11-30 a.m. at St Gehurn trenches W.R. for W.9. 9 hrs.	
Mont St Eloi	Sept 22		Battalion parade for practice in artillery formations. Lectures to men on "Prevention of Trench Feet". 2/Lt T.F. Wensim rejoined from Hospital.	

WAR DIARY / INTELLIGENCE SUMMARY

Army Form C. 2118.

Sept. 1918

Place	Date	Hour	Summary of Events and Information	Remarks and references to Appendices
MONT ST ELOI & Support from GREENLAND HILL	Sept 24		Battalion entrained at 12 noon. Proceeded via Acq – ST. CATHERINE – ATHIES to FAMPOUX arriving 3.15 p.m. Marched to trenches and relieved 1/4th York & Lancs Regt. as Battalion in Brigade Reserve. Relief complete at 6 p.m. B, C & D Coys in CHARLIE SUPPORT, CHARLIE RESERVE & COPPER trenches, A Coy in NORTHUMBERLAND LANE. 'D' Coy Hd qurs. slightly shelled at 9 p.m. Night was quiet. About 100 gas shells in Bttn. area.	Nil.
SUPPORT LINE	Sept 25		Intermittent shelling including gun shells in Bttn area. Generally quiet. Casualties 2 O.R. Killed	Nil.
SUPPORT LINE	Sept 26		Slight intermittent shelling over area. 2 low flying enemy aircraft came over our lines. Carrying party supplied of 280 o.r. with officers to carry dummy figures for 'CHINESE ATTACK'. Returned 12 midnight to 2 a.m. 1 Platoon 'D' Coy shifted to CLYDE AVENUE. Attack by 8th Div. (left) at 6/12 midnight. Artillery retaliation on our front slight. Capt. J. Mackay joined Battalion from U.K.	Nil.
Support Line	Sept 27		'Chinese' attack on Drocourt front in conjunction with Sunday's attack by 8th Div. (left) & 4th Div. (right) at 5.30 a.m. Short light barrage on our front. Very quiet incident during day. 1 Platoon D Coy shifted from Battn. joined Battn. from U.K. CAY. to CUTE Trench. 2/Lt A.H. MacNaughton joined Battn. from U.K. Casualties 1 O.R. (gassed)	Nil.

WAR DIARY
or
INTELLIGENCE SUMMARY

Army Form C. 2118.

Sept 1918

Place	Date	Hour	Summary of Events and Information	Remarks and references to Appendices
Support Line	Sept 28		Very quiet. Occasional shelling near UPPER TRENCH including gas shell. Nil Casualties.	
Support line	Sept 29		Very quiet weather. Intermittent shelling on CUBA, UPPER trenches.	
Support line, front line, GREENLAND HILL sector. (Showery)	Sept 30		At 4.30 p.m. B & D Coys moved up to relieve two Support Coys. 4th Gordons. At 7.30 p.m. A & C Coys. moved up and relieved 2 front line Coys 4th Gordons. Relief completed about 11.45 p.m.	

Graham Lt Col.
Commanding
7th A & S Highrs.

(6392) Wt. W6192/P875 1,500,000 4/18 McA & W Ltd (E 2815) Forms W3091/4.   Army Form W.3091.

Vol 7

44.L
9S

154/51

Cover for Documents.

Nature of Enclosures.

7th Arg. & Suth. Highrs.

War Diary.

October 1918.

Notes, or Letters written.

Army Form C. 2118.

WAR DIARY
INTELLIGENCE SUMMARY
(Erase heading not required.)

Instructions regarding War Diaries and Intelligence Summaries are contained in F.S. Regs., Part II. and the Staff Manual respectively. Title pages will be prepared in manuscript.

Hour, Date, Place		Summary of Events and Information	Remarks and references to Appendices
Frontline GREENLAND HILL Sector	October 1st 1916	Line generally quiet. 'A' & 'C' Coys. had patrols out during afternoon to within 50 of FRESNES-ROUVROY line & were fired on by enemy. 2nd West Yorks Regt. 8th Division relieved Battalion at 23.59 hrs. Marched to ATHIES & embussed by Coys. arriving OTTAWA CAMP, MONT ST. ELOI about 02.30 hrs. Lieut. FERGUSON A.N. rejoined from hospital.	Nil.
MONT ST. ELOI	October 2	Battalion engaged cleaning up camp.	Nil.
MONT ST. ELOI	October 3	Battalion and Company drill parades. 2/Lt. Mackenzie to U.K. Draft of G.O.R. arrived.	Nil.
MONT ST. ELOI	October 4	Training & baths by Coys. Lecture by B.G.C. 6 all officers.	Nil.
MONT ST. ELOI	October 5	Training in attack formations by Coys. Lecture by Senior Chaplain on 'Citizenship'. Draft of J.O.R. arrived.	Nil.
MONT ST. ELOI	October 6	Battalion church parade at 10.00 h.s. 2/Lt. W. Garg to U.K.	Nil.

Army Form C. 2118.

WAR DIARY
INTELLIGENCE SUMMARY
(Erase heading not required.)

Instructions regarding War Diaries and Intelligence Summaries are contained in F. S. Regs., Part II. and the Staff Manual respectively. Title pages will be prepared in manuscript.

Hour, Date, Place	Summary of Events and Information	Remarks and references to Appendices
Mont St Eloi & Inchy. Oct 7	Battalion entrained at 18:30 hours proceed via ARRAS – MARQUION to INCHY arriving 01:00 hrs. Companies accommodated in trenches. 2/Lt. A.L. Sadler joined from U.K.	Init.
Inchy. Oct. 8.	Companies engaged improving accommodation.	Init.
Inchy. Oct. 9.	Short parades reconnaissance of area.	Init.
Inchy and St. Olle (Cambrai) Oct. 10	Battalion marched off at 08:00 hours via MOEUVRES – FONTAINE to ST. OLLE arriving 13:00 hours. In billets.	Init.
St. Olle & Escaudoeuvres to Line. Oct. 11	Battalion marched off at 13:15 hours via MARCHIENNES to field outside ESCAUDOEUVRES arriving 16:00 hrs. Enemy shelling vicinity. At 22:00 h.s. Battalion marched off by Coys. & relieved 31st Bn. Canadian Infty. in the immediate N. of INVY. Bn. HQ in INVY. B & D Coys. in front line, A & C Coys in support. Village shelled during night. Enemy casualties. Casualties NIL	Init.

WAR DIARY
INTELLIGENCE SUMMARY
(Erase heading not required.)

Army Form C. 2118.

Hour, Date, Place	Summary of Events and Information	Remarks and references to Appendices
line at INVY. 10 Mar 13	Dispositions of front Coys. altered during morning to allow 4th Seaforths to complete Brigade front. At 12 noon our barrage opened & 4th Seaforths attacked from 2000 yds in front. Position reached easily, enemy resistance weak. At 1300 hrs "B" & "D" Coys. moved forward thro' 4e Seaforths with "A" & "C" Coys. in close support. Objective – LIEU ST AMAND & ground beyond. 1500 from village attacking Coys. came under heavy MG fire & by sections rushes got within 200 of village before being held up finally where they proceeded to dig in the open. Enemy M.G.'s & artillery were very active causing many casualties in our ranks. At dusk enemy we received 6 withdraw to ridge 1500' from village which was held under fire. Night quiet & positions organized. Casualties 8 OR Killed 80 OR Wounded	LIEU ST AMAND three P.

WAR DIARY
INTELLIGENCE SUMMARY

Army Form C. 2118.

Hour, Date, Place	Summary of Events and Information	Remarks and references to Appendices
Open ground between Tilloy & LIEU ST AMAND. Oct 11/13 1918	Enemy opened counter preparation barrage between 05.15 & 06.30 hrs. At 0900 hrs. our barrage nearly 18 pounder Shrapnel opened on LIEU ST AMAND & PAVÉ WAZIENNES. "A" & "C" Coys. pushed thro' B.H.D. Coys. heads in artillery formation. Enemy put down an intense artillery m.g. barrage but line went on steadily to within 100 of village where they were held up again after suffering many casualties. Enemy artillery was firing at point blank range. & again enemy to exposed position, orders were given to withdraw which movement could not be done until dusk. [Men lay out all day under heavy M.G. fire.] Flank units were also held up. During day enemy continued heavy artillery fire. Party of 30 Reserves came out for village after dusk & were fired on by our men. Casualties Casualties. At 19.00 hrs. 4th Gordons relieved up to T [tooth] front our position. Relief completed about 21.30 hrs. Casualties :- 2/Lt SINCLAIR M.C. 2/Lt H. SEWELL Killed O.R. Killed 9, O.R. wounded 16, O.R. missing.	

Army Form C. 2118.

WAR DIARY
INTELLIGENCE SUMMARY
(Erase heading not required.)

Instructions regarding War Diaries and Intelligence Summaries are contained in F. S. Regs. Part II. and the Staff Manual respectively. Title pages will be prepared in manuscript.

Place	Date	Hour	Summary of Events and Information	Remarks and references to Appendices
Irvuy	Oct 13 (contd)		Battalion moved back into position vacated by Lt Gordon MC N.F. Irvuy & Battalion in Batt. support. Casualties Lt. E.R.Sinclair MC. 2/Lt. H.Spence, killed in action. 2/Lt. H.Russell (gassed).	Ind
Irvuy	Oct 14		Enemy shelled village during day at 16.30 hours 6th Black Watch moved up & relieved Battalion. Relief complete 19.00 hrs Battalion tps. were billeted & rested by 6th Black Watch. Details reported.	Ind
Thun St. Martin	Oct 15		Reorganisation of Companies & Casualty lists completed.	Ind
Thun St. Martin	Oct 16		Inspections &c.	Ind
Thun St. Martin	Oct 17		Battalion moved off at 17.00 hrs relieved 6th Seaforths in line N.W. of Avesnes la Sec. A + B Coys. in front C+D in Support. Battn. H.Q. in Village. The following officers reported - Lt. Drummond, Lt. Macguire T.B., 2/Lt. Cairns J., 2/Lt. Ferguson D.	Adm

Army Form C. 2118.

WAR DIARY
or
INTELLIGENCE SUMMARY.
(Erase heading not required.)

Instructions regarding War Diaries and Intelligence Summaries are contained in F. S. Regs., Part II. and the Staff Manual respectively. Title pages will be prepared in manuscript.

1918

Place	Date	Hour	Summary of Events and Information	Remarks and references to Appendices
AVESNES LE SEC	18th Oct.		Pte Bourdais allotted to allow 6th P. & L. H. to come in on left. Order then 6th A & L. H.	A.D.u.
AVESNES LE SEC	19th Oct.		TEA. & S.H. LT. GORDONS with LT. Dw on (Capt.) Canadians 1 OR wounded 4 OR wounded.	A.D.u.
			Zero fixed at 02.00 hours for 5th Div. for an advance to protect left flank 1 & 4 Bns. while they take HASPRES. MAJOR C. C. JOHNSTONE, posted to Bn. as 2nd in command	
NOYELLES	20th Oct.		Enemy retired and operation allowed accordingly. Zero was at 02.00. Bn. billeted NOYELLES without opposition. Some attempt line was advanced to near MAISON ROUGE	A.D.u.
NOYELLES	21st Oct.		Casualties 1 OR killed 10 OR wounded. Line stationary between NOYELLES and MAISON ROUGE. Casualties 2 OR wounded	A.D.u.
THIANT	22nd Oct.		At midnight on 21st patrol reached outskirts of THIANT without opposition. A Coy pushed forward to ECAILLON RIV. H.Q. moved in at 15.00 hours. M.G. Coy took 3 prisoners. Casualties 4 OR killed 6 OR wounded	A.D.u.
THIANT	23rd Oct.		At 00.00 hours LT. HETHERWICK captured a M.G. on way down and before reaching 6th B.H. at night LT. MILLAR found a bridge across the river. Relief was carried at 5 am in rain. 1 OR killed 6 OR wounded	A.D.u.
HAULCHIN	24th Oct.		Resting. Village automatic shelled at night. Some civilian casualties.	A.D.u.
HAULCHIN	25th Oct.		Cleaning up, inspection, refitment.	A.D.u.
HAULCHIN	26th Oct.		Left HAULCHIN 4 p.m. reaching MAING 8 pm. Coys left MAING for the enbushment at 11 pm on small A Coy actual forward defensive flank at ROUGE MONT facing S.E.	A.D.u.

Army Form C. 2118.

WAR DIARY
or
INTELLIGENCE SUMMARY.
(Erase heading not required.)

Instructions regarding War Diaries and Intelligence Summaries are contained in F. S. Regs., Part II. and the Staff Manual respectively. Title pages will be prepared in manuscript.

1918

Place	Date	Hour	Summary of Events and Information	Remarks and references to Appendices
MAING	27th Oct		At 6 am "C" Coy Scot was taken from Coy. & Ltd G.N. in front of FAMARS. Enemy units attacked at 12:00 hours. This reduced at 4 pm. At 10 pm C Coy came back to consolidate and other Coys moved to reinforce & LA FONTINELLE. CASUALTIES 10 OR KILLED 70R WOUNDED.	Affn.
MAING	28th Oct		At 05:15 hrs. S.H. attacked. A.B. & D Coys took over positions, M position, and consolidated the main line & reinforce. At 16:00 hrs A Coy reinforced S.H. behind MONT HOUY WOOD. LT R FERGUSON KILLED, LIEUT F MILLER	Affn.
MAING	29th Oct		At 17:00 hrs enemy attacked between from M to —————— 4 OR KILLED 27 OR WOUNDED. At 19:00 hrs relieved by 44th & 47th Bns Canadian Infantry. Bn moved back to THIONVILLE 2 OR KILLED, 5 OR WOUNDED. FORBES. Quiet.	Affn.
THIONVILLE	30th Oct		Resting.	Affn.
ST ROCH	31st Oct		Marched from THIONVILLE to ST. ROCH arriving about 14:00 hours	Affn.

Gartnell Lt Col
Commanding
4th Cdn Mtd. Bn.

NARRATIVE OF OPERATIONS

by

1/7th BATTALION ARGYLL & SUTHERLAND HIGHLANDERS.

at

LIEU ST. AMAND - October 12th - 14th, 1918.

11/12th Oct.
On the night of 11/12th October the battalion relieved the 31st Battalion of Canadians in the Sub-sector N. of IWUY between the railway and the canal de L'ESCAULT, being on the left of the Brigade Sub-sector. Relief was complete at 03.00 hours on October 12th.

12th Oct.
The following morning was occupied in taking up positions for a general attack astride the Canal de L'ESCAULT on a front of several divisions. The 5th Canadian Brigade attacking northwards with their right on the railway began to take up jumping off positions just in front of our line about 10.30 hours. By 11.00

10.30.
hours our front companies withdrew from the line and concentrated in the railway cutting between N.30.a.1.3. and N.36.a.7.5. - "B" Company on the left and "D" Company on the Right. A large number of the men lay in cubby holes dug into the cutting.

11.30.
Both companies were in position in the cutting by 11.30 hours.

About 11.45 hours the remaining companies "A" and "C" moved out of their positions now completely held by the 5th Canadian Brigade and assembled in open ground just N.E. of IWUY, with wide intervals and distances between platoons.

12.00
At noon operations commenced, the 4th Seaforth Hrs moving forward from assembly positions in N.30 a, b, and d. under a barrage to take the objective of the 154th Brigade, the spur running W. from LA MAISON BLANCHE, the 152nd Brigade attacking on their right and two Canadian Brigade on their left. The Barrage opened punctually and hostile shelling in reply was feeble until about

12.45
12.45 when 5.9 and 4.2 shells were falling hap-hazard over the entire area N. and N.E. of IWUY. The Battalion suffered no casualties however until nearly 14.00 .

The Seaforths were consolidating just in rear of their

13.50
objective at 13.50 when the barrage stopped. Our front two Coys were then just behind the barrage and in front of the Seaforths by 200 yards. The moment the Barrage lifted our men went forward, D. Coy on the right getting off first. Almost simultaneously with our rush forward the enemy guns began to play on the ground in front of us, especially in O.7. a and b., and the shelling of the ridge behind us increased in volume. The initial stages of the attack were carried out in perfect order and with a great deal of luck, very few of our men at that time having been hit. There

14.15
was no machine gun fire at all until our men were within 150 yards of the most Southern houses of LIEU ST AMAND, B. Coy being at that time about 300 yards from PAVE. A storm of machine gun fire then broke along the entire front hostile line, the cross fire from PAVE being particularly effective. About 70 men were hit at once and Lieuts. SINCLAIR and SPENCE were wounded but continued to lead their platoons. The hostile fire was very poorly aimed, many guns firing and ricocheting over the heads of the men and hitting a man here and there on the ridge and even in the RIOT de CALVIGNY where the two support Coys were now - about 14.15 - assembled.

Shell fire was now pretty general all over the area, the enemy's guns firing on the ground 50 yards S. of the villages PAVE and ST. AMAND, but the RIOT DE CALVIGNY itself was untouched, and only two or three men of the Support Coys were wounded by splinters during the whole action. - stray bullets accounting for one or two more.

/In

--2--

12.15. In spite of this sudden hail of fire platoons were seen going cautiously forward for another two or three minutes, but casualties were becoming heavy, Lieut. SINCLAIR, wounded a second time in the arm, was shortly after hit directly with a shell, and Lieut. SPENCE was shot through the head. Sections were in some

14.20 pases moving laterally to find cover, and the immediate S. of the Village which had been purposely avoided (platoons being instructed to establish themselves on the flanks) was gradually being absorbed.

14.30 About 14.30 the general forward movement had ceased altogether, and from then onwards all ground was made by individual initiative, any man standing up was shot at once. One platoon in a position about N.6.d.8.2. was still controlled by its Officer, and by crawling forward very slowly and lying in furrows of some newly ploughed ground they got within 25 yards of two machine guns in a bank at O.1.c.0.4. but before they could rush the post, several machine guns at PAVE opened a withering fire, causing so many casualties as to stop the rush, and the machine guns in front opened and prevented any further forward movement.

14.40 About 14.40 there was no movement among our troops. They were pinned to the ground and could neither move sideways or backwards. Runners got back with this information, but before any action could be taken, individual men had succeeded in working themselves to the rear, and after waiting an hour or so the enemy allowed our men to dribble back singly without sniping them.

16.00 By 16.00 nearly every man of the two attacking companies that could move, was back on the spur from which the attack commenced. A few badly wounded men were still lying out. The two support companies were organized in fire positions slightly in rear of the crest and "B" and "D" companies were organized as an outpost line running approximately from N.12.c. 2.3. to O.7.c.7.1.

17.00 It was arranged that every available gun should bombard ST.AMAND from 17.00 to 17.30 and that strong patrols should then move forward again with the object of making the village. Unfortunately about that time all the guns were moving and there was no shelling at all except for the one 18-pounder remaining to us out of the attached section. The other gun had been knocked out about 14.15 together with the ammunition wagon and most of the shells, but not before they had dealt with the particularly troublesome enemy post about O.7.b.3.8.

At 17.30 the Company Commanders on the spot decided it would be useless to attempt to move, but one platoon on the extreme right, mistaking instructions, went straight forward to within a hundred yards of the outlying houses of ST. AMAND before machine gun fire was opened on them. They then rushed forward towards the shelter of the houses and disappeared.

18.00 About 18.00 the line was slightly re-organized, "B" and "D" companies forming the outpost line, and "A" and "C" about 600 yards in rear becoming the support line, the Seaforths being the main line of resistance sandwiched in between.

12/13 Oct. Thus organised the battalion spent the night of the 12/13th October.

18.45 About 18.45 the right platoon was seen running from the Village, and what was left of them reformed behind our lines. They had spent over an hour in an exposed position being fired at from all sides at close range. In the darkness they had extricated themselves one by one. The officer was so badly gassed that he fainted on trying to walk to the aid post.

/13th Oct.

13th Oct.
08.15

The following morning about 08.15 "A" and "C" Cos. then in the main line of resistance began taking up positions just behind "B" and "D" Cos. positions preparatory to resuming the attack behind a barrage at 09.00. The enemy could see all this movement and the whole ridge was heavily shelled, hindering us considerably.

08.45

The heavies bombarded PAVE at 08.45 for 20 minutes, and appeared to blot out the whole village.

08.58

The barrage opened two minutes before ZERO about 200 yards S. of both villages and at least 450 yards in front of our men. Before the first lift our men were up with it. The hostile barrage opened at the same moment as ours, and seemed quite as heavy. A lot of 77 mm guns were firing that had not been in action the previous day. Most of this barrage fell behind our men and inflicted about 40 casualties on our companies holding the ridge.

09.10

The second lift of the barrage left the southern edge of the village untouched and hostile machine guns opened at once. A white light was fired from a position near the church and the whole line opened a withering fire.

From that time onwards the action was practically a repetition of the previous day. Sections were hunting about for cover and for concealed lines of approach but only on the right could any protection be found. There a platoon maintained itself within 50 yards of the enemy guns but could move no further. Opposite PAVE the fire was so intense as to paralyse all organized movement. Runners crawling with messages were hit. Orders could not be passed and the men nearly lay flat, trying to work themselves into the ground. Several men using their entrenching tools were hit in the arm or hand. Though they could not move our men were so close to the enemy that they could hear them shouting. Parties were seen running back to the village. A Lewis Gun managed to inflict heavy casualties on these and also to knock out a machine gun team which was shifting to another position. A lot of Germans moving N. from the near the chapel in PAVE were also brought down, but it was impossible to break up the machine gun defence, well concealed among the houses with a command of all the ground on which we lay.

10.00
10.15
18.00

After lying out for an hour and several times attempting to move forward and on every occasion suffering loss, our men gradually worked their way back. By 10.15 most of them were reforming behind our line held by "B" and "D" companies. One platoon remained out until nearly 18.00 hours having had no orders and hoping to be able to get forward. At dusk about 30 Germans came out of the village and our men had to come back.

During the afternoon attempts were made to bring in the wounded. In most cases parties succeeded in getting back without loss.

17.00

About 17.00 the line was slightly readjusted. "B" and "D" companies remained in the front with "B" on the Left in touch with the Canadians N.12.c.2.4. and "D" in touch with 4th Seaforth Highlanders at O.7.c.8.0., each company with two platoons in front and two in support. Company frontage about 800 yards with a depth of 300 yards. "A" and "C" with "C" on the Right was similiarly organized in support, South of the road running through N.18.a.

18.00
21.30

and b. The battalion was situated thus at 18.00 hours and was handed over to the 4th Gordon Highlanders at 21.30.

Battalion moved back into the support area N. of IWUY after relief.

/Total casualties

TOTAL CASUALTIES -   3 Officers and 186 Other Ranks.

Estimated Loss to Enemy by our rifle and Lewis Gun fire
              60.

Outstanding Features.

The very poor shooting of the hostile M.Gs.

The ineffective barrage of 18 pdrs on hostile posts organised among brickwork and in cellars.

The absence of hostile rifle fire.

The difficulty of fire control when under close Machine Gun fire.

The value of a few blades of grass, furrows in ploughed land etc., in gaining concealment. The average man will ignore these unless it is impressed on him during training.

The great importance of "Esprit de Section". Each man should know his Section Commander and all the men of his Section, and realise that the Section is a compact little force which will have to fight its own battle unaided.

(sgd) L. GARTSIDE.

16th October 1918.

Lieut. Col.
Commanding 7th Arg. & Suth. Highrs.

Operations of the 7th Battn. Argyll and Sutherland Highrs.
leading to the occupation of NOYELLES and THIANT between
October 17th and 22nd 1918.
※※※※※※※※※※※※※※※※※※ ※※※※※

Oct. 17th.

On Oct. 17th the Battalion relieved the 6th Seaforth Hrs in the line N.W. of AVESNES LE SEC holding positions approximately in a straight line from the village to LA MON BLANCHE. Relief was complete at 20.50. The night was quiet, the moon was nearly full but there was a thick mist. Early in the morning of the 18th the two front companies sent out two patrols to gain touch with the enemy. A M.G. post was located in the wood in O.9.c. and sniping shots came from a point about 350 yards in front of our right platoons.

The 18th was quiet except for hostile artillery activity in the early morning and just after dusk. Visibility was bad. A heavy mist lay over the ground most of the morning and cleared only a little in the afternoon.

That evening the line was re-adjusted and boundaries slightly altered in accordance with the plan of attack arranged for early morning on the 20th. The battalion side-stepped to the right, our left company being relieved by a company of the 8th Argylls and coming in on the right of the battalion line, relieving a company of the 4th Gordons. Our frontage then ran from the cross roads in AVESNES LE SEC at O.22.a.3.4. to the road junction at O.15.c.6.4. along the road, with outposts about 150 yards in front. This was held by two companies, the two in support lying about the Chateau and in the slightly Sunken road as far W. as the Min. de PIERRE.

Oct. 19th.

Most of the 19th was spent quietly. Short bursts of hostile fire were put down on our forward areas, especially in the neighbourhood of the Min. de PIERRE. During the afternoon arrangements were completed for the attack on the following morning.

About 15.45 a report was received that patrols of the 6th Argylls had failed to get touch with the enemy. Two hours previous to this one of our own patrols was fired on by snipers from about O.16.c.3.9.

Patrols were at once sent out again, but actually our front companies were on the move before they returned.

About 16.20 two companies had occupied the road from O.9.d.3.7. to O.16.b.3.7. the two rear companies assuming the dispositions of our original front line. Having ensured this line, the advance was pushed forward about 17.40, with three companies in front, the two flank companies being ordered to form deep protecting flanks, the whole moving in a sort of semi-circle on NOYELLES with flanks facing E. and W.

The remaining company with the M.G. section being ordered up from the original front line to the sunken railway in O.10.c. This company hit the railway about O.16.a.7.2. and eventually halted in O.10.b. In reconnoitring, the Company Commander with one platoon came face to face with the Boches at the banks of the river at FLEURY. The officer was within a few yards of the enemy, who seemed pacifically disposed; before he realized they were not civilians. A German officer got them to throw bombs at our men across the river. Two of our Lewis Guns opened fire and inflicted casualties. The company was eventually assembled in reserve in a square wood at O.10.c.5.4. Meanwhile the M.G. section attached had taken up a position in the woods about O.9.c. to ensure the line of the road between O.9.c. and O.16.b.

--2--

About 18.30 the three companies in front were just S. of NOYELLES, disposed in depth, the left flank resting in the railway and the right flank about I.34.d.9.1. Patrols were pushed through the village and reported it free of the enemy and also got in touch with the 6th Argylls about the Station.

At 19.00 the line moved forward and took up a position N. and E. of NOYELLES. At 19.50 it was reported that DOUCHY was unoccupied by the enemy and the 6th Argylls and ourselves moved forward across the River SELLE.

Boundaries were changed twice since 16.00 in the afternoon and accounted for a little delay in adjusting the line. The boundary between ourselves and the 6th Argylls was fixed at the forked roads I.30.c.2.7. and we were to gain touch with the 4th Seaforths at Mon ROUGE. Two companies were sent forward to take up this line just as the 6th Argylls Company moved forward to place its left on DOUCHY Cemetery.

At 21.30 the line had been taken up with two companies disposed in depth with touch on the left but not yet on the right with the Seaforths.

At 21.45 the original left front company (of the three front companies) had taken up a position in support just E. of the SELLE in I.35.a. In the meantime the remaining company and the attached M.G. section were on their way forward. This company was placed in reserve behind the right flank, in houses about I.34.d, as it was not certain how and where the troops on the right flank of the battalion were disposed.

Oct. 20th.
About 03.10 October 20th the headquarters of the 4th Seaforths arrived in NOYELLES and established themselves in the same house as the 7th Argylls. At about 03.40 the first Seaforth Company arrived at NOYELLES and went forward to take up the line South of us. About 05.00 our right flank was secured.

About 03.00 our line was withdrawn 200 yards as one of our patrols sent forward with a view to a further advance was held up by organized M.G. fire on the high ground immediately N. and E. of us and the Company Commanders on the spot decided that their position on the road was unsound.

Patrols sent out between 03.00 and 05.00 definitely located the enemy S.W. of LA MOLHE, on a track about I.30.d. and just W. of L'EPINETTE.

Before dawn the enemy pushed up two M.Gs. into Mon ROUGE and the house I.36.a.3.8.

At 08.00 a general attack was launched on the Divisional front. The two companies of 7th Argylls were met by heavy M.G. fire the moment they moved. The fire was badly aimed however and there were only six casualties. The two houses on the road in I.36.a. were charged and the enemy ran away leaving several rifles, two M.Gs. and a quantity of filled belt boxes in our hands. It was impracticable to advance beyond the road and there the line remained for the rest of the day, with the enemy posts commanding the entire ground on which we lay. There was no cover or means of approach and the men had to lie still. Lateral communication was very difficult.

At 17.00 patrols moved forward but were engaged.

At 17.25 it was reported that the 6th Argylls had made some ground just N.W. of LA MOLHE and had occupied LA CROIX STE MAIRE.

Our patrols again went forward, one towards L'EPINETTE and one to LA MOLHE and reported them clear, and about 20.00 the whole line advanced to a position flanked by LA MOLHE on the left and HILL 70 in J.26.a. on the right. The left company was occupying LA MOLHE at 21.00 but the right company did not make HILL 70 until about 03.00 on October 21st. Meanwhile a support company was working forward to fill the ground between the two hills.

At 03.00 the battalion held both hills with the

(centre

—3—

centre slightly retired, roughly in J.25.central. Sniping was going on from the direction of BOIS DE L'ENTREE during the early hours of the morning.

Before moving forward the right flank on HILL 70 was consolidated and the M.G. section attached was ordered to send there the two guns which had been assisting the LA MOLHE Company, four guns being in defensive positions in J.26.a. by about 04.30. This consolidation was very difficult owing to the inability of Unit Commanders to recognise their positions on the map.

The whole night was bright and fairly clear and this factor turned out to be essential.

about 05.00 With HILL 70 secured by one company and 4 M.Gs. one company was ordered to CHLLE LOUVIERE to cover the approaches from the River ECAILLON.

" 07.00 One company moved along the railway towards THIANT while the last company moved up in support in the railway cutting in J.19.c. Nothing was heard of the company making for THIANT until about 10.00. It had moved up in the half light unseen by the troops on HILL 70 and had disappeared in the village. Shots fired at CHLLE LOUVIERE during the morning were thought to come from the S. end of the village, but actually were fired from the enemy positions E. of the river about J.21.b.7.2.

08.00 This company ("A") entered the village at 08.00. A patrol moving down the street passed the Church was heavily engaged by M.G. fire and it was soon found that the enemy would deny us the passage of the river. The Company was then disposed along the W. edge of the stream, mostly in houses and hedgerows, with one post near the rubber factory where it got in touch with a patrol of 6th Argylls which had come across from PROUVY after gaining touch with the Canadians. At 09.45 we were in touch with a post found by the M.M.G. battery attached to the 46th Canadian Regiment at J.15.b.6.8. on the railway.

10.00 At 10.00 the company in the railway bank was sent forward to occupy the S. half of THIANT with posts organized to enfilade the river to the South, and cover the ground in J.22 and J.28.

13.00 At 13.00 battalion H.Q. moved from L'EPINETTE into THIANT. Shelling of the village began about 11.00.

15.30 At 15.30 the enemy put down a short but very fierce bombardment on our front positions in the village. A rumour spread that we had been counter attacked and driven out of the village. Actually no Infantry action took place, and the only casualties were one man wounded and six buried and our positions remained intact.

Three times during the afternoon and evening attempts were made to get across the river. About 20.00 an officer and 2 O.Rs. got across unseen and rushed a M.G. post from the flank. The crew ran away and the officer brought the gun back, but was heavily fired on from several directions in moving in front of a burning house. On attempting to get a platoon across, the enemy put down a strong M.G. barrage and shelled the water's edge with T.Ms.

Oct. 22nd. Most of the 22nd was spent in reconnoitring the river for means of crossing, and in observing the enemy's dispositions on the E. bank.

Since 11.00 on the 21st the shelling had been almost continuous, but there was no heavy barrage put down on the 22nd.

In the evening the battalion was relieved by the 7th Black Watch. After relief was complete – at 21.00 – one platoon succeeded in placing a footbridge across the river at J.16.c.45.65., before withdrawing.

The battalion was in billets at HAULCHIN at about 12.30 hours.

Casualties – 6 O.Rs. killed.
2 Offs. wounded.
55 O.Rs. " (Sgd) LIONEL GARTSIDE.LT.COL
Commdg. 1/7th Bn. A. & S. Highrs.

Narrative of Operations of 7th Bn. Argyll and
Sutherland Highlanders from October 23rd to
October 31st, 1918, in the neighbourhood of
FAMARS.

Oct. 23rd.   Battalion in HAULCHIN. Very little enemy shelling.

Oct. 24th.   The village was shelled from 11.00 to about 18.30, without intermission. Probably over 350 shells fell in and around the village, but principally on the approaches and on the Eastern edge. Several civilians wounded, but the battalion casualties were only 4 of which one was killed.

Oct. 25th.   Enemy continued to shell the village intermittently.

Oct. 26th   The battalion marched from HAULCHIN to the railway
16.30   arch at J.15.a.7.2., where it halted until the situation in the line was known more accurately.

18.00   At 18.00 the battalion moved forward to MAING and
20.00   remained in the sunken road in J.24.d. from 20.00 till close
23.00   on 23.00, when companies went forward to take up positions forming a main line of resistance to the 4th and 6th Gordon Hrs covering FAMARS, with one company ensuring the right flank at the junction of the 51st and 4th Divisions.

Oct. 27th.   At about 01.00 on the 27th, the Battalion was disposed
01.00.   with one company E. of ROUGE MONT and 3 Coys in the Railway Bank between K.13.b.7.3 and the Divisional Boundary K. 20. d. 8.1. In the event of the 4th Seaforth Hrs moving forward out of the Railway Bank at and S. of LA FONTENELLE, our left Coy. had orders to move to the N. of the road in K.13.b and strengthen the left along the railway bank.

     Battalion H.Q. remained in MAING.

04.45   During the early morning it was arranged we should relieve 4th Gordon Hrs in the line. On going forward to reconnoitre the 2 C.Os. mutually decided that a relief at that time 05.30 was impracticable owing to the visibility. The orders cancelling the relief reached one Company "C" too late and when the left of the line was visited later, it was found that this Company had moved across and taken over the front defences of FAMARS in K.9 /f a and c. Shortly after this the 6th Gordon Hrs applied for relief of their Coys holding the E. flank of FAMARS from K.9.d.1.4 to K.15.b.3.0 and under orders D. Coy was sent forward for this purpose. Arrived at the Sunken Road K.15.d , the C.O. decided it was too hazardous to attempt movement by daylight and the Company was redisposed in the railway bank in K.20.d. Thus the Companies remained until 22.00.

     About 12.00 a heavy hostile barrage fell on FAMARS and near the line of the cart road running through K.8 followed by a half hearted attack on the village from a hostile position in the Northern houses. There was a little machine gunnery and sniping, but the Boche Infantry turned and ran, and our Lewis Guns killed quite a few.

22.00   Preparatory to an attack on the following morning the battalion was redisposed during the early hours of the evening. At 22.00, the Company at ROUGE MONT was relieved by a Company of 6th Seaforths and together with the two companies in the S. end of the railway in K.14.c. and K.20, took up new positions along the railway bank from K.13.b.7.3. Northwards to about K.7.d.65.25, thence to turn in Sunken Road at K.7.d.3.8., thence along the road to K.7.a.6.2.

Oct. 28th   "C" company in FAMARS was relieved during the night
02.00   by 6th Seaforths and at 02.00 on the 28th took over the position forming a flank between the 4th Seaforths.jumping off line and the left of the 6th Seaforths. Thus disposed the battalion spent the early hours of the 28th.

05.15   At 05.15 the attack on MONT HOUY commenced.

06.00   About 06.00 the three companies in the reserve positions in K.13.b. and K.7.d. moved forward to the original jumping off line and consolidated it, "C" company on the right being prepared to extend its area Northwards to link up with the

/4th

4th and 6th Seaforths as the 4th Advanced.

The attack gained very little headway on the right flank however. To assist it "C" Company endeavoured to push forward posts along the road in K.9.a. The houses in the extreme N. end of the village were still held by the enemy and efforts to dislodge these were made during the morning and afternoon.

12.30 About 12.30 orders were sent to one company in the jumping off line to go forward through MONT HOUY WOOD to strengthen the line of the 4th Seaforths in the centre about LE CHEMIN VERT. By the time these orders reached the Company Commander, our front troops were back to the quarry and the S. edge of the wood, and the enemy who had never been mopped up from the interior of the wood successfully prevented any general move forward. This company however, together with a mixed company of 4th Seaforths, formed and consolidated a line about 200 yards to the S. of the Wood,
14.45 about 14.45

Digression Previous to this about 11.00, the company on the left,
11.00 whose original role was to exploit success Northward to E.20.central, had formed a thin line of resistance between POIRIER Station, the quarry in K.2.a and the Wood in K.2.b, in an effort to hold on to the ground taken in first move by the 4th Seaforths. This line, when the Seaforths gave way, was driven back on the right and withdrawn into K.1.b.

When the line was established S. of the wood at 14.45 this company left stray posts in POIRIER Station and in the road at K.1.b.6.1/ and placed its strength, to ensure the left flank, in the N.W. end of LA FONTENELLE. At 15.00 the line was disposed in this way but the news was slow to reach the various headquarters, and orders had been sent to the remaining company in the original jumping off line, at the request of the 4th Seaforths, to push one platoon into MONT HOUY to clear it up, and another platoon into K.1.b. to strengthen this flank. This latter platoon was
15.40 despatched, and formed posts from the bridge at K.1.b.1.4. S.E wards along the road. The platoon orderd to clear up MONT HOUY was retained as the line S. of it was held quite thickly enough.

At 16.45 the enemy put down a heavy barrage over the whole forward area. At this time about 150 civilians, mostly women and children were straggling westwards from FAMARS along the ~~main road~~ MAING Road which was shelled intermittently during the whole action. The sight of these people was most distressing. The barrage was accompanied by a counter attack very feeble on FAMARS from the North where our Lewis Guns easily dispersed the few Infantry who ventured close enough.

During the afternoon 4th Gordon Highrs. had come up to the main line of resistance along the railway bank. At 17.00 one company under Capt. GILES was pushed forward to hold LA FONTENELLE.

About 21.00 the 6th Argylls with two companies took over the front line from FAMARS exclusive to the canal. "C" Company remained in FAMARS which still held enemy posts in its Northern houses.

The three remaining companies came back to the jumping off line. This readjustment was complete at 02.45 on
Oct. 29th. Oct. 29th.

The morning of the 29th was very quiet. From houses in FAMARS some of our men killed Germans moving about in K.3.

About 16.00 the enemy attacked from MONT HOUY WOOD Southwards probably with the intention of gaining the quarry. Attack beaten off by 6th Argylls.

At 19.00 the 44th and 47th battalions of Canadians

/commenced

Oct. 30th.   commenced taking over the whole forward area.
             By 02.00 on the 30th the Battalion was
             billeted in THONVILLE.

                              (Sgd) LIONEL GARTSIDE, Lt. Col.
                         Commanding 1/7th Arg. & Suth'd. Highrs.

Army Form W.3091.

Cover for Documents.

Nature of Enclosures.

7th Argyll & Sutherland Highlanders

WAR DIARY

NOVEMBER 1918.

Notes, or Letters written.

Army Form C. 2118.

WAR DIARY
or
INTELLIGENCE SUMMARY.

(Erase heading not required.)

Instructions regarding War Diaries and Intelligence Summaries are contained in F. S. Regs., Part II. and the Staff Manual respectively. Title pages will be prepared in manuscript.

Place	Date 1918	Hour	Summary of Events and Information	Remarks and references to Appendices
St. Roch	1st Nov		Companies engaged cleaning equipment & billets	
St. Roch	2nd Nov		" " " "	
St. Roch	3rd Nov		Church Parade. Corps Commander present.	
St. Roch	4th Nov		Companies on training area practising attack formations	
St. Roch	5th Nov		do.	
St. Roch	6th Nov		do. Lecture by C.R.A.	
St. Roch	7th Nov		do. CAPT. J.N.F. MACDONALD TO 6/H 7TH GORDON HRS.	
St. Roch	8th Nov		do.	
St. Roch	9th Nov		do.	
St. Roch	10th Nov		Church Parade. US. O.S. Stewart & B. Drummond to L.R. Gordons 16. 2/L. Cumming to T.M.B's.	
St. Roch	11th Nov		Armistice. Holiday. Matches, Sports	
St. Roch	12th Nov		Companies training. Drill, Saluting &c.	
St. Roch	13th Nov		Battalion marched to Thun l'Eveque to watch a 3 country championship	
St. Roch	14th Nov		Companies training - lecture educational	
St. Roch	15th Nov		do. do.	

Army Form C. 211

WAR DIARY
INTELLIGENCE SUMMARY.
(Erase heading not required.)

Instructions regarding War Diaries and Intelligence
Summaries are contained in F. S. Regs., Part II.
and the Staff Manual respectively. Title pages
will be prepared in manuscript.

Place	Date	Hour	Summary of Events and Information	Remarks and references to Appendices
St. Roch.	18th Nov		Company Training. Drill. 2/Lt. A Pendergest, A. Lister & A.C. Muir joined (reinforcements)	
St. Roch.	19th Nov		Church Parade. Lectures (officers)	
	20th Nov		Training by Companies. Football practice	
St. Roch.	19th Nov		Battalion route march.	
St. Roch.	20th Nov		Training by Companies. Drill.	
St. Roch.	21st Nov			
St. Roch.	22nd Nov		Battalion route march. 2/Lt R.B MacDonald joined Bn.	
St. Roch.	23rd Nov		Coy training. Boxing tournament.	
St. Roch.	24th Nov		Battalion church parade.	
St. Roch.	25th Nov		Coy & Battalion drill parades, lectures and football	
St. Roch.	26th Nov			
St. Roch.	27th Nov			
St. Roch.	28th Nov			
St. Roch.	29th Nov		Divisional Sports	
St. Roch.	30th Nov			

Gausden
Lt. Col.
Commanding
7th Arg. & Suth. Highrs.

Army Form W.3091.

Cover for Documents.

Nature of Enclosures.

7th Arg & Suth. Hrs.
War Diary
December 1918.

Notes, or Letters written.

Army Form C. 2118.

WAR DIARY
December 1918.

INTELLIGENCE SUMMARY.
(Erase heading not required.)

Instructions regarding War Diaries and Intelligence Summaries are contained in F. S. Regs., Part II. and the Staff Manual respectively. Title pages will be prepared in manuscript.

Place	Date	Hour	Summary of Events and Information	Remarks and references to Appendices
ST. ROCH (CAMBRAI)	Dec.1 to Dec.31		Education classes commenced. Drill by Companies. Salving of shells, equipment &c in vicinity of training area. Church parades. Football and sports.	Appx.
	8/12/18		Lt J. McLEAN, and 2/Lt J.B. MACKAY Joined Battn	
	8/12/18		Lt E.W. DAVIDSON " "	
	18/12/18		Lt W.A. McL. ROBB " "	
	30/12/18		A/Capt. S.B.M. COUPAR. Duty at No. 56 C.C.S.	
	31/12/18		MAJOR A. STEIN, M.C. Joined Battn	

J.A. Dewn Lt. Col.
Commanding 7th Cam. Hghrs.

WAR DIARY / INTELLIGENCE SUMMARY

Army Form C. 2118.

(Erase heading not required.)

Place	Date	Hour	Summary of Events and Information	Remarks and references to Appendices
St. Roch (contd)	1st Jan		New Years Day. Holiday. Football & other sports. Lt.Col. Dunne? DSO & HQ Coy on arrival of Battn. from St Col. & Gautrecke, DSO.	
St. Roch	2nd		Demolition Classes & Sports. Advance billeting party left for La Louvière	P.P.
St. Roch	3rd		Training. Class & Battn.	P
do	4th		Holiday. Football	H
do	5th		Church Parade	P
do	6th		}	
do	7th		} Education Classes & Games etc.	P
do	8th		}	
do	9th		}	
do	10th			
St.Roch & La Louvière	11th		Battn. entrained at 0800 hrs & proceeded via Valenciennes - Mons to La Louvière arriving about 1500 hrs. Billets scattered throughout town. Battery comfortable.	P
La Louvière	12th		Church Parade.	
do	13th		Education Classes	D
do	14th		}	
do	15th		Tug-of-war against 4th Yorks. Battn. Lost.	P
do	16th			
do	17th		Parade & Education Classes daily. Football v. Durh. Champion ship	P
do	27th		1st a.c. 4 Goals 8th Royals (Scots) (Scots) old men proving too strong for young ones.	
			7th a.c.h. 5 pts. 49th C.f.f (Rough)	

Page 2
Jan. 1919
Army Form C. 2118.

WAR DIARY
INTELLIGENCE SUMMARY.
(Erase heading not required.)

7th QVRS H.

Instructions regarding War Diaries and Intelligence Summaries are contained in F. S. Regs., Part II. and the Staff Manual respectively. Title pages will be prepared in manuscript.

Place	Date	Hour	Summary of Events and Information	Remarks and references to Appendices
Blommes	28 Jan		Prince of Wales visited Battalion.	
do.	29		Classes & Schools. 50 men proceeded for Newbiggin, Football	A.
do.	30		Div. Championship. 7 QVR v 1/5 Durham D.L.I. 1 goal.	
do.	30		Battalion Parade. Ceremonial.	B.
do.	31		Funeral of late Pioneer Dick. Championship	C.
			7th QVRS Hrs. 9 grade 6th QVRS Hrs. 1 goal.	

31st January 1919.

J. B. Dunn
Lieut Col.
Commanding
7th Bng. Rifle Bde

7th Bn. South. Lan.
February 1919

WAR DIARY
or
INTELLIGENCE SUMMARY.
(Erase heading not required.)

Army Form C. 2118.

Vol 57

Place	Date	Hour	Summary of Events and Information	Remarks and references to Appendices
LA LOUVIÈRE	1		Holiday. Football in Divisional Championship. 7th S.L.R. v. 11th R.S. Scotland 2	
	2		Church parade.	
	3		Education Classes. Drill Shooting Range.	
	4		as. Salvage Parties	
	5		Baths. Training by Coys.	
	6		Education Classes. Training. Salvage. Farewell meeting of Battalion.	
	7		Kit inspection. Cleaning expect. 65 O.R. and 3 offs. proceded	
	8		for demobilization. Capt. S.V. Dottie M.C. Lt. A.D. Morrison M.C. Lt. J. Walker	
			57 O.R. and 20ffs proceded for demob. to (Lt. 96 Ebors, 2/Lt N9367)	
			party of 54 O.R. + 3 offs. proceded to 1/4 London R. of F. Timperland	
			H R13 MacDonald, 2/Lt W. Cumming, and H.L. Walker	
	9		Church parade.	
	10		Salvage. Recruiting Parties. 7th A.T.S.R. declared winners	
			of Div. Football Championship	
	11		Training by Coys.	
	12		Baths. Training by Coys.	
	13		79 O.R. + 2 offs. proceded for demobilization (Capt. Emrys Mc Stambaugh)	
			Lectures on benefits of Armies of Occupation by Ed. Commission.	
	14		Parades by Coys. 160 O.R. proceded for demobilization	

WAR DIARY
or
INTELLIGENCE SUMMARY
(Erase heading not required.)

Army Form C. 2118.

Place	Date Feby	Hour	Summary of Events and Information	Remarks and references to Appendices
La Louvière	15		Sunday Coy. Sgts. Holiday	
	16		Church Parade	
	17		Coy Parades. Handling of Arms Drill	
	18		do	
	19		do	
	20		Baths. 52 O.R. proceeds for demobilization	
	21		Reconnoitering area for Salvage	
	22		Holiday. 14 O.R. proceeds for demobilization	
	23		Church Parade.	
	24		Coy. Drill Parades. Funeral of C.Q.M.S. Greenshields, M.M. (17 yrs Service) attended by Battalion	
	25		Coy Drill Parades	
	26		do.	
	27		do.	
	28		do.	

J.D. Irvine
Lt Colonel
Commanding
7th Arg. & Suth. Hrs

1/7th Argyll & Suthd Hrs
March 1919

Army Form C. 2118.

WAR DIARY
or
INTELLIGENCE SUMMARY.
(Erase heading not required.)

Place	Date	Hour	Summary of Events and Information	Remarks and references to Appendices
LA LOUVIÈRE.	MARCH			
	1.		Company Parade. — 29 O.Rs. proceeded for demobilisation. — Surname time come into force.	
	2.		Company Parade. — do — and salvage.	
	3.		do — "A" & "B" Coys. amalgamated to form No. 1. Coy.	
	4.		do — "C" & "D" Coys. do No. 2. Coy.	
	5.		Company Parade.	
	6.		do. — 7 O.Rs. proceeded for demobilisation	
	7.		do.	
	8.		Holiday.	
	9.		Church Parade. — Kit Inspection.	
	10.		Company Parade. — Salvage.	
	11.		do.	
	12.		10 Officers and 200 O.Rs. proceeded to join 10th Arg & Suthd Cos 1st in Army of Occupation.	
	13.		Concentration of CADRE and surplus personnel.	
	14.		Cleaning and old billets and returning barrack furniture to Burgo-master.	
	15.		Do.	
	16.		CADRE and surplus personnel move to SENEFFE.	

PAGE 2.

7th Argy. & Suth'd High'rs
March 1919

WAR DIARY
or
INTELLIGENCE SUMMARY.

Army Form C. 2118.

(Erase heading not required.)

Place	Date	Hour	Summary of Events and Information	Remarks and references to Appendices
SENEFFE.	MARCH 17.		Cleaning and checking mobilisation equipment.	
	18.		Do.	
	19.		Do.	
	20.		Do.	— 5 ors. & 2 Officers proceeded for demobilisation 2/R Fraser & W.S. McLean.
	21.		Do.	
	22.		Do.	
	23.		Church Parade.	
	24.		Cleaning and checking mobilisation equipment.	
	25.		Do.	
	26.		Do.	
	27.		Do.	
	28.		Do.	— 1 or proceeded for demobilisation. Transport now without any horses.
	29.		Do.	
	30.		Church Parade — 1 or proceeded for demobilisation.	
	31.		Cleaning and checking mobilisation equipment.	

JA Dunne Lt Col.
Comg 7th Argy. & Suth'd High'rs

Daily Strength Return – 1/3/19 – 31/3/19

1919 March	Increase or Decrease	Strength Offs.	Other Ranks
		29	346
1	2 officers demobzd (leave). 1 Officer transferred 154th Inf. Bde. 1 OR demobzd. (from Corps) 29 OR demobzd	26	316
2.	1 OR to Hospital.	26	315
6.	7 OR proceeded for demobzn	26	308
7	1 OR to Hospital	26	307
8	1 OR from Hospital	26	308
9	1 OR to Hosp 1 OR from Hosp	26	308
10.	2 OR to Hosp	26	306
11	1 OR to Hosp	26	305
12	10 Offrs. 200 OR trans. 10 A.&S. Hrs.	16	105
13.	1 Offr demobzd	15	105
19.	2 Offrs. 5 OR demobzd 1 OR to Hosp	13	99
20.	1 OR returned from Hosp	13	100
24	1 OR to No. 7 Prison, Calais	13	99
27	1 OR demobzn (leave)	13	98
28	1 OR demobzn	13	97
30	1 OR demobzn 5 OR trans. School of Cookery, Etaples.	13	91
31	6 OR trans. 5th Arg & Suth Hrs. (on proceeding on leave)	13	85

Effective strength 31/3/19 – 13 offs 85 OR

www.ingramcontent.com/pod-product-compliance
Lightning Source LLC
Chambersburg PA
CBHW081426300426
44108CB00016BA/2314